Air Transport Labor Relations

Robert W. Kaps

Southern Illinois University Press

Carbondale and Edwardsville

Library of Congress Cataloging-in-Publication Data

Kaps, Robert W., 1943–
    Air transport labor relations / Robert W. Kaps.
            p.   cm. — (Southern Illinois University Press series in aviation
management)
    Includes bibliographical references and index.
    1. Airlines — Employees — Legal status, laws, etc. — United States.
2. Collective labor agreements — Aeronautics — United States.
3. Collective bargaining — Aeronautics — United States. I. Title.
II. Series.
KF3580.A8K37   1997
344.73'01890413877—dc20
[347.3041890413877]   95-10267
ISBN 0-8093-1776-1 (cloth : alk. paper)   CIP

Contents

List of Figures   *ix*

List of Tables   *x*

Preface   *xi*

Acknowledgments   *xiii*

Abbreviations   *xiv*

Part 1

1.

Labor Law and Public Policy   3

Introduction   *3*
   Transportation Policy   *3*
   Labor Regulation   *5*
The Aviation Industry   *5*
   Aviation Manufacturing   *5*
   The Air Transport Sector   *6*
   General Aviation   *8*
   Government Aviation   *9*
Federal Civil Service Labor Law   *9*
   Political Appointment   *10*
   The Merit System   *10*
   Public Labor Unions   *11*
   Public Sector Collective Bargaining   *11*

2.

*Early Collective
Bargaining Legislation*   13

Introduction   *13*
   Early Judicial Actions   *13*
   National Railroad System
      Development   *14*

Legislative Beginnings   *16*
   The Arbitration Act of 1888   *16*
   The Sherman Antitrust Act   *17*
   The Erdman Act of 1898   *18*
   The Newlands Act of 1913   *19*
   The Adamson Act of 1916   *19*
Nonrailroad Labor Activities   *20*
   The Clayton Act of 1914   *20*
   Railroad Labor Gains   *21*
   The Transportation Act of 1920   *22*
Summary   *22*

3.

*Major Collective
Bargaining Legislation*   23

Introduction   *23*
The Railway Labor Act   *23*
   Origins   *23*
   Early Judicial Challenges   *25*
   Depression Era Unionism   *25*
   Provisions of the RLA   *25*
   The National Mediation Board   *27*
   The RLA Amendment of 1934   *27*
   The RLA Amendment of 1936   *28*
   The RLA Amendments of 1940 and
      1951   *28*
The Norris-La Guardia Act of 1932   *30*
The National Labor Relations Act   *31*
   The National Industrial Recovery Act   *31*
   Origins of the NLRA: The Wagner Act   *32*
   NLRA Amendment: The Taft-Hartley
      Act   *33*

Contents

NLRA Amendment: The Landrum-Griffin Act 36

The Airline Deregulation Act of 1978 38

Other Laws Affecting Labor Relations 38

Summary 40

Additional Study Material 42

Detailed Examination of the Events Leading to Rule #83 Decision 42

Two Labor Laws Are One Too Many 55

Call to Revisit Railway Labor Act Receives Mixed Reactions from Parties 56

Part 2

4.

Elections, Certifications, and Procedures 65

Introduction 65

Interstate Commerce 65

The Process under the Railway Labor Act 65

Employees Subject to the RLA 65

Employers Subject to the RLA 67

Organizing Employees under the RLA 67

Procedures of the National Mediation Board 67

Class and Craft Determination 72

Representation Election 74

Election Rule Exceptions 75

Mergers and Acquisitions 78

The Process under the National Labor Relations Act 80

Employees Subject to the NLRA 80

Supervisory Personnel Subject to the NLRA 80

Managerial Personnel Subject to the NLRA 80

Employers Subject to the NLRA 81

Procedures of the National Labor Relations Board 81

Determining Bargaining Units 83

Craft, Departmental, or Industrial Units 85

Certification Election 85

Summary 87

Additional Study Material 88

Examination of the Events Surrounding the Strike by Trans World Airline Flight Attendants 88

5.

Contractual Negotiations 97

Introduction 97

Negotiation Procedures under the Railway Labor Act 98

Contractual Status 98

The Negotiation Time Fame 98

Mediation 100

Emergency Boards 102

Strikes 103

Negotiation Procedures under the National Labor Relations Act 104

Bargaining Topics 104

The Contract Negotiation Process 105

Self-Help 105

Mediation 107

Arbitration 108

Actions During a Strike or Lockout 108

Summary 109

6.

Grievance Procedures 111

Introduction 111

Statutory Alternatives 111

Grievance Definition 111

Contract Administration 112

Grievance Procedures 113

Grievance Arbitration 113

Grievance Arbitration under the Railway Labor Act 114

The System Board of Adjustment *115*

Overruling Arbitration Decisions *115*

Arbitration Costs *116*

Grievance Arbitration under the National
Labor Relations Act *117*

Overruling Arbitration Decisions *117*

Selecting an Arbitrator *118*

Arbitration Costs *118*

Summary *118*

Additional Study Material *119*

Grievance Procedure Contained in the
Contract Between the International
Association of Machinists and
TransWorld Airlines *119*

Grievance Procedure Between the
Communications Workers of America
and Southwestern Bell Telephone
Company *127*

7.

Unfair Labor Practices 130

Introduction *130*

The Role of the Railway Labor Act *130*

Unfair Labor Practices under the RLA *130*

Rulings of the National Mediation
Board *131*

Court Decisions *133*

Featherbedding *135*

The Provisions of the National Labor
Relations Act *136*

Rulings of the National Labor Relations
Board *136*

Unfair Labor Practices under the
NLRA *136*

Activities Prohibited under the NLRA *137*

Summary *139*

Additional Study Material *140*

National Mediation Board Rulings in
Laker, Key, and America West
Certification Elections *140*

Sample Management Guide to Permissible
Campaigning under the Railway Labor
Act *185*

Sample Materials Provided to Frontline
Managers During an Antiunion
Campaign under an NLRA
Environment *189*

Part 3

8.

The Labor Relations Environment 197

Introduction *197*

The Civil Aeronautics Board *197*

Certificates of Public Convenience *197*

Mergers *198*

Fare Provisions *198*

The Mutual Aid Pact *198*

The Transition to Deregulation *199*

Deregulation *199*

The Labor Relations Environment: 1978 to
the Present *205*

Cost Reduction *207*

New Entrants *207*

Mergers *208*

Summary *210*

9.

Annual Activity 211

Introduction *211*

1978 *212*

Contents

1979 *213*

1980 *214*

1981 *215*

    The PATCO Strike *216*

    The Braniff Bankruptcy *217*

1982 *217*

1983 *218*

    The Two-Tier Wage Plan *220*

    The Continental Bankruptcy *220*

1984 *221*

1985 *223*

1986 *224*

1987 *225*

1988 *227*

1989 *228*

1990 *229*

1991 *229*

1992 *230*

1993 *231*

1994 *231*

1995 *233*

Additional Study Material *234*

    Recent Rulings by the National Mediation
    Board and the Courts on Questions
    Arising under the Railway Labor
    Act *234*

10.
The View of the Unions 239

Introduction *239*

Unions since Deregulation *239*

Results of a Survey of Airline Unions *241*

Summary *245*

Appendix. The Railway Labor Act *251*

Notes *273*

Glossary *285*

Name Index *291*

Subject Index *293*

Figures

Figure 4-1. Railway Labor Act representation process   *68*

Figure 4-2. National Mediation Board application for investigation of representation dispute   *69*

Figure 4-3. National Mediation Board union authorization card   *70*

Figure 4-4. National Mediation Board standard ballot   *76*

Figure 4-5. National Mediation Board Laker ballot   *77*

Figure 4-6. National Mediation Board Key ballot   *79*

Figure 4-7. National Labor Relations Board representation petition   *82*

Figure 4-8. National Labor Relations Act representation process   *83*

Figure 4-9. National Labor Relations Board union authorization card and International Association of Machinists authorization card   *84*

Figure 4-10. National Labor Relations Board notice of election   *86*

Figure 4-11. National Labor Relations Board ballot   *88*

Figure 5-1. Railway Labor Act collective bargaining process   *99*

Figure 5-2. National Labor Relations Act collective bargaining process   *107*

Figure 6-1. Railway Labor Act airline grievance procedure   *115*

Figure 6-2. National Labor Relations Act grievance procedure   *117*

Tables

1-1. Aviation Industry Employment in the United States in 1983 and 1992 *6*

1-2. Sales in the Aviation Manufacturing Industry in 1983 and 1992 *6*

1-3. Major Aviation Manufacturing Companies *6*

1-4. Commercial Airlines *7*

3-1. Major Labor Relations Laws *24*

3-2. Provisions of the Railway Labor Act *29*

3-3. Major Provisions of the Wagner Act *34*

3-4. Major Provisions of the Taft-Hartley Act *37*

3-5. Legislative Differences Between the Railway Labor Act and the National Labor Relations Act *41*

4-1. Jurisdictional Standards of the National Labor Relations Board *66*

5-1. Categories of Bargaining Subjects Assigned by the National Labor Relations Board *106*

7-1. Unfair Labor Practices *137*

8-1. Impact of Deregulation on New Entrant Airlines from 1979 to 1984 *209*

8-2. Airline Bankruptcies from 1979 to 1984 *210*

9-1. Section 401 Carrier Certification Activity in 1979 *213*

9-2. Section 401 Carrier Certification Activity in 1980 *214*

9-3. Section 401 Carrier Certification Activity in 1981 *216*

9-4. Section 401 Carrier Certification Activity in 1982 *218*

9-5. Section 401 Carrier Certification Activity in 1983 *219*

9-6. Section 401 Carrier Certification Activity in 1984 *221*

9-7. Section 401 Carrier Certification Activity in 1985 *223*

9-8. Section 401 Carrier Certification Activity in 1986 *224*

9-9. Section 401 Carrier Certification Activity in 1987 *225*

9-10. Section 401 Carrier Certification Activity in 1988 *227*

9-11. Section 401 Carrier Certification Activity in 1989 *228*

9-12. Section 401 Carrier Certification Activity in 1990 *229*

9-13. Section 401 Carrier Certification Activity in 1991 *229*

9-14. Section 401 Carrier Certification Activity in 1992 *230*

9-15. Section 401 Carrier Certification Activity in 1993 *231*

9-16. Section 401 Carrier Certification Activity in 1994 *231*

9-17. Section 401 Carrier Certification Activity in 1995 *233*

10-1. Airline Industry Employment since 1978 *240*

10-2. Surveyed Airline Unions *241*

10-3. Unionized Airline Employees by Craft and Class *241*

10-4. Union Membership in 1979 and 1989 and Net Gains/Losses *242*

10-5. Reasons Reported for Changes in Union Membership *242*

10-6. Ranking of Negative Impact of Deregulation Activities on Unions *242*

10-7. Impact of Airline Consolidation According to Unions *243*

10-8. Positive Aspects of Union Membership According to Unions *244*

10-9. Three Most Important Bargaining Issues According to Unions *245*

Preface

The body of legislation governing labor relations in the private sector of the U.S. economy consists of two separate and distinct pieces of legislation: the Railway Labor Act, which governs labor relations in the railroad and airline industries, and the National Labor Relations Act, which governs labor relations in all other industrial sectors. This book examines air transport labor law in the United States and the underlying legislative and policy directives established by the federal government that define the labor relations process in this sector.

The U.S. government is confronted with several, often conflicting, goals and objectives regarding transportation policy. First, the government seeks to encourage the best, most efficient transportation service possible. This policy goal was achieved by the creation of a legislative framework that encouraged substitution of capital for labor in the production process. One example of this type of productivity improvement policy directive is a tax incentive for the purchase of advanced technology equipment, instead of a tax or other incentive for improving labor productivity levels. The U.S. transportation sector has always relied heavily on advances in technology for productivity gains, not on improvements in labor efficiency. This bias toward technological productivity improvement instead of labor productivity improvement is mainly due to federal policy initiatives. This point is of particular importance in the air transport sector because of the historically higher compensation packages that these workers have enjoyed relative to their counterparts in the remainder of the economy.

Second, the government has the goal of full employment of its citizenry. The government created a legislative framework specifically for the transportation sector that supported the efforts of organized labor in securing and stabilizing jobs. One primary function of any organized labor group is to protect as many jobs as possible. Because of the unprecedented turmoil deregulation has created in the aviation industry, job protection is the number one priority of all transport labor unions. The government has created a legislative framework that clearly supports organized labor in this respect.

Finally, the overriding public policy goal for the transportation sector is stability and continued service. The ability to provide uninterrupted transportation service is vital to national defense and economic growth. In most other industries, production can cease, at least temporarily, without causing any significant negative impact on the general economy. But when transportation stops, production stops, making continuous service a national necessity. The general public is indifferent about who wins labor-management struggles as long as efficient transportation service continues to be available. Thus, Congress enacted a statute—the Railway Labor Act—designed to ensure the stability and continuity of the nation's rail system in times of labor strife. Primarily because of the importance of airmail transportation, the act was extended to cover the air transport sector as well.

This book describes the special laws, regulations, and procedures that the federal government has imposed on both management and organized labor in the railroad and airline industries and that are embodied in the Railway Labor Act. It examines aviation labor laws and the rationale behind the establishment of these special regulations for addressing transportation labor disputes. This book also presents a discussion of the general economic, legal, and political conditions that caused these public policy decisions to be pursued.

Students and practitioners of aviation management will come in contact with both the specific transportation labor legislation, the Railway Labor Act, and the general labor legislation, the National Labor Relations Act. It is necessary, therefore, that they gain an appreciation of the similarities and differences of the underlying public policy goals of the two acts and acquire an understanding of the collective bargaining processes of each act. This book highlights both areas, placing primary emphasis on the Railway Labor Act, because the bulk of the air transport sector workforce falls under its jurisdiction.

Part 1 of this book introduces the topic of labor policy, presents a history of the labor movement in the United States, and discusses early labor legislation and the subsequent major labor statutes in effect today. Part 2 examines the election, certification, contract negotiation, dispute resolution, grievance procedures, and questionable labor practices contained in the Railway Labor Act and provides a comparison to those same or similar processes and procedures contained in the National Labor Relations Act. Part 3 examines labor relation in the airline industry as it has evolved. Particular attention is directed at the effects of deregulation on the air transport collective bargaining process and the emerging trend of transport union equity participation.

It is anticipated that this text will be used primarily in undergraduate aviation programs. Students and practitioners in the fields of aviation management, public administration, and law may also find it useful.

Acknowledgments

I would like to express my thanks for the many useful comments, suggestions, and critiques provided by colleagues, students, and friends toward the completion of this book. Originally begun as a primer of notes for labor classes, it developed into its present form due to the prodding, pushing, and encouragement of David NewMyer, Chair of the Department of Aviation Management and Flight at Southern Illinois University at Carbondale. But for his efforts, this task never would have been undertaken. His negotiating skills far exceed the scope of this labor treatise.

It is a long way from presenting "openers" at the table to finalizing a contract. So it is with writing a book. This culmination never would have been achieved without the editorializing, rewriting, reformatting, reworking, and research done by Jeffrey Hartung, the "ghostwriter" of this work. His involvement moved this work from the caucus room to the contract ratification theater. I hope that some benefit comes of this writing for students of aviation. For me, the great benefit of this book has been the friendship acquired with Hartung. He is, without a doubt, one of the most knowledgeable individuals I have met when it comes to the operation of the airline business.

I must also recognize Lawrence Truitt, who contributed substantially to the preface and to chapter 1.

I am greatly indebted to the many professionals at Southern Illinois University Press. My greatest debt is to Editorial Director Jim Simmons, who handled the tedious and lengthy process with patience and good humor. But for this latter characteristic of his, the process might never have come to fruition.

Many students and other individuals contributed by adding research and source information and by validating industry data. Special recognition goes to Manfred Stinson and Tracy Speck, both of whom are now gainfully employed in the service of U.S. military aviation. Additionally, O. V. Delle-Femine, President of the Aircraft Mechanics Fraternal Association, provided critical inputs and comments as well as a wealth of memories of all those years across the negotiating table. Finally, many thanks to Emil Fett, who in his role of as project Supply Quartermaster, elevated the naval science of "Comshaw Acquisition" to an art form.

The above listings make it evident that this book is the result of a collective process. Thus my gratitude belongs with each and every contributor, from students, to faculty, to industry labor professionals, to other interested parties, to friends who contributed their time, effort, and support. To those who know who you are, my deepest appreciation. I see no gracious means by which traditional responsibility for errors of omission or commission can be avoided.

Abbreviations

The following acronymns are commonly used in the aviation field and are used throughout this book.

AFA	Association of Flight Attendants
AFL	American Federation of Labor
AFL-CIO	American Federation of Labor and Congress of Industrial Organizations
ALPA	Air Line Pilots Association
AMFA	Aircraft Mechanics Fraternal Association
CAB	Civil Aeronautics Board
ESOP	Employee Stock Ownership Plan
FAA	Federal Aviation Administration
FMCS	Federal Mediation and Conciliation Service
IAM	International Association of Machinists
IAMAW	International Association of Machinists and Aerospace Workers
IBT	International Brotherhood of Teamsters
IFFA	Independent Federation of Flight Attendants
NIRA	National Industrial Recovery Act
NLRA	National Labor Relations Act
NLRB	National Labor Relations Board
NMB	National Mediation Board
NRAB	National Railroad Adjustment Board
RLA	Railway Labor Act
TWU	Transport Workers Union

Part 1

1

Labor Law and Public Policy

Introduction

This book is about U.S. transportation labor law and the public policy decisions that shaped it. As is true with many abstract concepts, no single, widely accepted definition of the term *public policy* exists. The term *public* has many connotations, depending on context and perspective. The term *public* is relative, and as Miles's Law states, "where you stand depends upon where you sit."[1] In the context of policy initiatives as used throughout this book, the term *public* refers to the government.

A standard dictionary definition for the term *policy* is "a definite course of action adopted for the sake of expediency, facility, etc."[2] Thomas R. Dye has defined public policy as "whatever governments choose to do or not to do."[3] Thus, since it refers to the actions of government and the goals and values that determine those actions, public policy can be considered "an intentional course of action (or inaction) followed by the government."[4]

Transportation Policy

The role of transportation is so vital to society in general and to commerce in particular that governments have always treated it as a special industry, one that is particularly affected by the public interest. In 1877, the famous court case *Munn v Illinois* (94 US 113) established the right of the state, in the absence of congressional regulation, to regulate business enterprises that provide essential public services. In writing for the majority, Chief Justice Morrison Waite cited a common property law principle that was over two hundred years old. Waite wrote: "Property does become clothed with a public interest when used in a manner to make it public consequence, and affect the community at large. When therefore, one devotes his property to a use in which the public has an interest, he, in effect, grants to the public an interest in that use, and must submit to be controlled by the public for the common good."[5]

Munn v Illinois established the constitutionality of government regulation of private enterprise. Transportation is not only important to the national economy; it is also vital for national defense. This national defense linkage caused virtually every developed country in the world (except the United States) to develop publicly owned and operated systems of railroads and airlines. Thus, employees of these nationalized transport industries are government employees and fall under their nation's civil service labor laws. Many of these nations are now seeking to privatize their transportation systems, adding complexity to the global transportation labor relations equation.

Adhering to the philosophy of capitalism and private enterprise, the United States has always had a privately owned railroad and airline industry (with the exception of Amtrak). Because of the unique relationship between transportation and the public interest, the U.S. government believed it necessary to pursue different public policy initiatives in the transportation sector than those followed in other sectors of the economy. Whenever government decides to undertake a new public policy directive or alter an existing one, it frequently does so through the legislative process, by enacting statutes designed to accomplish its goals. In general, transportation policy can be grouped into two broad categories: developmental (subsidy) policy initiatives and regulatory policy initiatives.

Developmental Policy Initiatives. The federal government has long followed a policy of subsidizing transportation activities to achieve certain national goals and objectives. Public subsidization of the private transportation sector has been justified on the grounds that an efficient rail and air transportation system is an "essential public good" and is "critical to the national defense." The essentially private transportation sector has been viewed by the federal government as being in the same class as a pure public good such that, when produced, it is available to all citizens without restriction. It is this "public good" philosophy that has also led to federal subsidization of the nation's system of airports and airways.

Transportation is also subsidized because it is essential for economic growth. There are significant direct and indirect benefits associated with efficient private transportation systems that warrant public investment. For example, the U.S. government promoted both railroad and air transportation because of their ability to carry the mail, which is closely linked to commerce. In addition, mass production is not feasible without an efficient system of distribution.

Regulatory Policy Initiatives. Laws that establish standards of conduct and affect the behavior of other governmental organizations or private organizations through legally enforceable methods are called regulation. The most widely recognized type of regulation associated with the airline industry is safety regulation. Another well-known type of government regulatory activity that was once present in the aviation industry was economic regulation via the **Civil Aeronautics Board** (CAB), which controlled entry, fares, and mergers. (See the glossary for definitions of terms in **boldface**.) This level of regulation ended with the passage of the **Airline Deregulation Act of 1978**. The government's approach to labor-management relations also involves regulation. In fact, regulation is the favored governmental policy instrument to achieve its primary transportation goal—stability.

The government finds regulation an appealing policy instrument because it can promulgate regulations at little cost to itself. Regulatory costs incurred are transferred from the government to the regulated industry. The affected industry then passes these costs on to its customers. Regulation thus generates a lumpy distribution of costs and benefits. As will be seen in later chapters, the traveling public has absorbed the brunt of the cost of regulating the air transport industry, and air transport labor has been a prime beneficiary of that same governmental regulation.

Transportation is regulated because of the positive and negative externalities often associated with it. An externality is a consequence of the activity of an individual or firm that is incidental (or "external") to but indivisible from its main activity and that affects the utility of another individual or firm favorably or unfavorably.[6] For example, an airline allows passengers to travel long distances quickly, but it also produces noise and air pollution—two typical external costs.

The U.S. government imposed comprehensive economic regulation on the airline and railroad industries until the late 1970s. Economic regulation was also deemed necessary because of negative "public good" externalities—in this case, because of the oligopolistic imperfections extant in the air and rail transport market structures. Federal economic regulation was imposed on the air transport industry in 1939 because of the belief that the industry was prone to either "destructive competition," on the one hand, or "monopoly abuse," on the other.

In 1978, after forty years of strict economic regulation, the industry was deregulated on the rationale that these fears were unwarranted. A majority of the transportation policymakers and elected officials believed that the market characteristics of the airline industry would allow it to operate in a fashion approaching pure competition without governmental economic regulation. The elimination of most economic regulations, without any adjustment to other interrelated air transport regulatory statutes, has had important and profound consequences on the **collective bargaining** process in the air transport sector, because labor represents the single largest operating cost of major carriers.

Labor Regulation

The **Railway Labor Act** (RLA) of 1926 established the regulatory framework for the labor relations process in the railroad industry. The primary purpose of the act was to define a specific process that railroad management and union labor would use to satisfactorily negotiate labor contracts and settle disputes without resorting to the ultimate **self-help** weapons, the **strike** and the **lockout**. The importance of airmail transportation coupled with a strong lobby by the Air Line Pilots Association (ALPA) led the government to amend the RLA in 1936 to encompass the airline industry. The appendix contains the full text of the amended RLA.

The provisions embodied in the RLA preceded labor legislation affecting the rest of the major industrial economy by almost ten years. Many aspects of railway labor legislation served as an example for subsequent federal legislation designed to reduce the number of labor disputes in other parts of the economy. The guarantee of the right to organize and bargain collectively came later for all workers who could be reached by Congress. Insistence on collective bargaining as the "first line of defense" also came later for other workers. Government action to mediate disputes has been favored for a long time and strongly urged in recent laws. Finally, the idea of a **cooling-off period** during which efforts are made to try to settle the issues involved came in the **Taft-Hartley Act**. The precedent of the RLA in this type of provision is clear. Railway labor legislation has therefore maintained a considerable degree of continuity of operation and has set patterns in other laws.[7]

Not until the passage of the **National Labor Relations Act** (NLRA) of 1935 (the **Wagner Act**) did the federal government enact successful nationwide federal labor legislation. The NLRA was built on the basic concepts of the RLA, and although the two acts are similar in some respects, there are substantive differences between them. These differences in rules and procedures are discussed in later chapters.

The Aviation Industry

The "aviation industry" consists of several distinct segments: aviation manufacturing; the air transport sector, which encompasses the major, national, regional, and commuter airlines; general aviation (including fixed-base operators and corporate aviation); and government aviation (including federal and state government aviation agencies, such as the Federal Aviation Administration). Each segment is subject to its own labor laws and practices. No single labor statute, organization, or agency encompasses all workers in the aviation industry. Rather, any given law may or may not apply to an aviation employee or employer. A brief discussion of each segment of the aviation industry and the labor statutes that apply to it follows.

Aviation Manufacturing

The aviation manufacturing industry is involved in three areas of production: defense, space, and commercial. As shown in table 1-1, in terms of employment, aircraft/airframe manufacturers dwarf the remainder of this segment of the industry. In 1992, aircraft/airframe manufacturers accounted for almost 64 percent, or 1,817,335, of the total 2,833,035 workers em-

Table 1-1
Avaiation Industry Employment in the
United States in 1983 and 1992

Segment of the Industry	Total Employment	
	1983	1992
Aviation Manufacturing	1,316,000	1,817,335
Major/National/ Regional Airlines	350,000	601,700
General Aviation (including fixed-base operators, corporate aviation, etc.)	250,000	273,000
Government	90,000	141,000

Source: Data from United States Bureau of
Labor Statistics.

Table 1-2

Sales in the Aviation Manufacturing Industry
in 1983 and 1992

Area of Production	1983	1992
Defense	$41.6 billion	$51.8 billion
Commercial	$19.1 billion	$50.9 billion
Space (and other)	$5.9 billion	$12.3 billion

Source: Data from Aerospace Industries Association.

ployed in aviation. Many of these manufacturers produce products for both defense and commercial uses. As indicated in table 1-2, defense ranks first in sales volume, commercial sales second, and space a distant third.

Table 1-3 lists the major companies involved in aviation manufacturing, which include such familiar names as Boeing, McDonnell Douglas, General Dynamics, General Electric, and United Technologies.

Organized labor employed by these industrial giants falls under the jurisdiction of the National Labor Relation Act. **Rank-and-file employees** of many of these firms are represented by such well-known labor organizations as the United Auto Workers, the International Brotherhood of Teamsters (IBT), and the International Association of Machinists and Aerospace Workers (IAMAW). There are also workers at several of these firms who are not represented by any union. Labor in this segment of the aviation industry falls under the jurisdiction of the NLRA, not the RLA.

The Air Transport Sector

Commercial airlines are classified on the basis of annual revenue generation. Major airlines generate more than $1 billion in annual revenue, national airlines from $75 million to $1 billion, and regional and commuter airlines up to $75 million. Table 1-4 lists the major and national

Table 1-3

Major Aviation Manufacturing Companies

Industry Component	Major Manufacturer
Defense	General Dynamics, McDonnell Douglas, United Technologies, General Electric, Boeing, Lockeed
Commercial/Civil Transport	Boeing, McDonnell Douglas, Lockheed, Helicopter, Sikorsky/United Technologies, Bell/Textron, Hughes
General Aviation	Cessna, Piper, Lear, Canadair, Beech-Raytheon
Space	Rockwell International, Martin Marietta, McDonnell Douglas, General Electric, Computer Sciences, Bendix

Source: Data from Aerospace Inductries Association.

commercial airlines, which together employed about 601,700 workers in 1992.

Major and National Airlines. Employees of major and national airlines fall under the jurisdiction of the RLA. Airline **labor unions** are **craft unions**, which means that no single union represents all the airlines employees. Pilots, flight attendants, and mechanics are usually represented by separate labor organizations. No hard and fast rule dictates which particular labor union will represent each of the employee groups or crafts, but air transport employees typically belong to one of only a handful of major labor unions. For example, most air transport pilots are represented by the ALPA, flight attendants by the Association of Flight Attendants, and mechanics by the IAMAW. Other craft-specific air transport unions represent other classifications, such as stores personnel, customer service agents, clerical employees, dispatchers, and so on.

Although the IAMAW is highly visible in these classifications, so are the IBT, the Transport Workers Union, and several of the larger carrier-specific unions, such as the Independent Federation of Flight Attendants formerly at Trans World Airlines, the Allied Pilots Association representing the pilots at American Airlines, and the Aircraft Mechanics Fraternal Association recently involved in a representation filing with Continental and United Air Lines. No matter which union organization they belong to, employees of the major and national airlines fall under the legal framework of the RLA.

Foreign flag carriers are not considered part of the U.S. aviation community. They do, however, employ a significant number of U.S. citizens in gateway cities, and with the advent of open-skies bilateral agreements, they could employ significant numbers at other U.S. locations in the near future. Although regulation of such airlines resides in their home country's air transport regulatory legislation, they must subscribe to U.S. Federal Aviation Administration (FAA) air regulations if they seek entry to U.S. airports. They are also subject to U.S. labor regulations and to other employment regulations that govern their workers based in the United States. When union representation is sought on U.S. soil by employees of these foreign carriers, the tenets of the RLA apply. For example, clerical employees of Air India, Egypt Air, Alitalia, and Mexicana are represented by the IAMAW; El Al mechanics are also represented by the IAMAW.

Regional and Commuter Airlines. The regional and commuter airline industry has a relatively

Table 1-4
Commercial Airlines

Major Airlines (more than $1 billion in annual revenue)		National Airlines ($75 million to $1 billion in annual revenue)	
American Airlines	Northwest Airlines	Air Wisconsin	Mark Airlines
American West Airlines	Southwest Airlines	Alaska Airlines	Midwest Express
Continental Air Lines	Trans World Airlines	Aloha Airlines	Southern Air
Delta Air Lines	United Air Lines	American Trans Air	Tower Airlines
Federal Express (cargo)	USAir	Emery	United Parcel Service
		Evergreen Airlines	USAir Shuttle
		Hawaiian Airlines	West Air
		Horizon Airlines	World Airlines

Source: Data from Air Transport Association.

short history of operation in the United States. Although the CAB had long exempted a class of small commercial air taxis from the requirements for **Section 401 certification**, it was not until 1969 that the board recognized the growing need to establish a class of small scheduled airlines; thus, the commuter airlines were born.[8] In that year, the CAB amended Part 298 of the Civil Aeronautics Act, to allow airlines that operated at least five scheduled round-trips per week between two or more points to receive exemptions from 401 economic regulation. To meet CAB requirements, such carriers, called Part 298 operators, could not operate aircraft exceeding 12,500 pounds maximum gross weight, which effectively limited the size of aircraft to those seating nineteen passengers. These passenger and load limitations were eased over the years, allowing aircraft seating up to thirty passengers by 1972. Passage of airline **deregulation** in 1978 established a new classification for these commuters, classifying them as regional airlines and permitting these carriers to operate aircraft having sixty seats or less.

Today, regional airlines play an increasingly important role in the national air transportation system. The vast majority of airports in North America receive scheduled service from regional airlines. Airports served by the industry totaled 811 in 1990, with 71 percent of these airports exclusively dependent on regionals to service their commercial aviation needs. By contrast, the major airlines served only 32 percent, or 275 airports.[9]

Regional airlines employed about 35,000 people in 1990, including 11,980 pilots, 4,920 mechanics, and 2,485 flight attendants.[10] Like employees of major and national air carriers, these workers fall under the jurisdiction of the RLA. It is difficult to determine in general whether these employees are represented by a labor union, both because of the diversity of the industry itself and because of the number of mergers and code-sharing arrangements that characterize the regional airline industry. In 1991, forty-two of the top fifty regional carriers, which accounted for 96 percent of the regional service for that year, had formalized code-sharing agreements and had begun to use the two-letter code of a larger airline to list their flights.[11] These relationships between regional and major or national carriers vary from outright ownership by major or national carriers (fifteen airlines) to partial ownership by major airlines (three airlines) to pure marketing alliances devoid of any ownership by major airlines (twenty-four airlines).

The regional airline industry's integration into our nation's air transportation system and its importance within that system are growing. The importance of regional airlines is expected to increase in the future, because the growth that characterized the 1980s is expected to continue throughout the 1990s. As the regionals continue to integrate with the majors and the level of industry concentration increases, it is likely that employees of the regionals will be represented by the same unions that represent employees working in the same crafts for the regionals' major partners or parents.

General Aviation

An important, yet largely overlooked, component of the aviation industry is general aviation. There is no legal definition for the term *general aviation*. Rather, it is generally used to denote a type of aircraft or aviation activities. The term often has a negative context, when it is used to make inferences concerning all segments of the aviation industry (except for air carrier and military operations).[12] It encompasses a diverse range of aviation activities, from ab initio flight training to the intercontinental jet transportation of executives and public officials. General aviation includes fixed-base operators, business and executive transport, and operations involving helicopters and light aircraft. It includes not only private pilots flying for pleasure but the emergency air ambulance and the police officer or radio newsperson observing traffic.

In number of aircraft, number of pilots, and number of airports and communities served, general aviation is the largest segment of aviation. It is important not only as a key component of the aviation system but as a contributor to national, state, and local economies. It provides aviation services that commercial airlines cannot provide. The production and sale of general aviation aircraft, avionics, and other aviation equipment, along with the provision of support services—such as flight schools, fixed-base operators, finance, and insurance—make the general aviation industry an important contributor to the nation's economy.[13]

General aviation is the dominant force in the sky, accounting for 98 percent of the civil aircraft fleet, 84 percent of civil operations (takeoff or landing) at FAA-towered airports, and almost 84 percent of the total hours flown by the U.S. civil aircraft fleet.[14] Yet it is largely unnoticed and unappreciated. Because of the wide diversity of general aviation and the absence of comprehensive reporting requirements, citing employment statistics is difficult. Most of the estimated 260,000 general aviation workers in 1989 were either pilots or mechanics employed by fixed-base operators or corporate operators.[15]

The estimated 3,500-plus fixed-base operators are the "front line" or "grass roots" of aviation.[16] They are the privately owned and operated businesses that offer a wide range of services, including aircraft sales and service, maintenance, and fuel; aircraft storage; and a variety of other support services. Of the estimated 3,500 fixed-base operators, approximately 2,500 fall in the category of small fixed-base operators, or mom-and-pop shops. There are several large, multimillion-dollar fixed-base operators, but even they are small when compared to an airline operation. Most, if not all, employees of fixed-base operators work as "employees at will" or as independent contractors, and the vast majority are not represented by any labor union.

The same is true for pilots and other personnel of corporate flight departments and other business aviation operations. The General Aviation Manufacturers Association estimated that forty-five thousand people worked in corporate flight departments in 1979.[17] Although noting "the absence of accurate information and data," a Transportation Research Board workshop of corporate aviation specialists predicts continued growth for business and executive general aviation operations.[18] These researchers expect no shortage of pilots in the near future, although they predict a continuing shortage of qualified maintenance and ground support technicians. It is unlikely that either of these groups will be pursued by organized labor in the foreseeable future.

Although general aviation plays a critical role in our nation's air transportation system, it remains largely invisible to the general public. Should any unions seek to organize the general aviation segment, any such activities would be governed by the NLRA.

Government Aviation

There are approximately eighty thousand federal employees directly involved in the transportation sector. Some of these federal transportation employees are members of public unions. Federal employees, union or otherwise, do not fall under the jurisdiction of either the RLA or the NLRA. Rather, all federal employee labor relations issues are governed by the Civil Service Reform Act of 1978. This enabling legislation established the Federal Labor Relations Authority to oversee all civil service labor relations matters. State and local civil service employees working in the transportation sector are governed by their state's or city's version of civil service regulations.

Federal Civil Service Labor Law

Although not directly related to the air transport sector, any discussion of federal labor legislation would be incomplete without an examination of federal civil service labor laws. This section provides a brief overview of the history of the enabling legislation and processes and procedures used by the government and the various public union organizations in the civil service collective bargaining environment.

There are about fifteen million people employed in all capacities by the three branches of government in the United States. Approximately one-third of these government employees are members of public unions. Government organizations in the United States use two different personnel appointment and management systems. The first is political appointment and election. The second is objective merit determination systems.

Political Appointment

Political appointment and election has a long history in the United States at the federal, state, and local levels. No other country in the world elects or appoints as many of its administrators as does the United States.[19] The political appointment system dates back to colonial times and was known as the spoils system under President Andrew Jackson. Jackson believed that to the victor go the spoils and that patronage appointments were a practical and appropriate way of rewarding loyal political supporters. The political appointment system still exists for some federal positions and for many state positions. But the patronage system caused such a serious decline in administrative ethics, efficiency, and performance during its heyday that politicians were forced to heed the calls for reform of the system.

The Merit System

The Pendleton Act. In 1883, an alternative method of recruitment, the merit system, was introduced with the passage of the Pendleton Act. This legislation established a systematic procedure for hiring and employing all categories of civil servants. The merit principle has continued to flourish and today embraces over 90 percent of all federal positions, including employees of the Department of Transportation, the FAA, the National Transportation Safety Board, the **National Mediation Board**, and the **National Labor Relations Board**. In addition, increasing numbers of state and local government employees are hired and managed under the merit system, including employees of state and local aviation agencies and local airports.[20] Today, approximately two-thirds of the states have merit systems that cover most of their employees.

The public personnel system adopted under the Pendleton Act involved the selection of public employees based on open competitive examinations (civil service exams), the establishment of tenure (job protection), and the creation of strict job classifications and procedures for advancement and promotion. The act remained in force until 1978, when reform issues were addressed.

The Civil Service Reform Act of 1978. The Civil Service Reform Act constitutes the centerpiece of present federal personnel policy. The principal achievements of the act were the separation of many of the managerial, political, and legal aspects of federal employment practices and procedures. These functions, once administered by a single organization, the Civil Service Commission, are now divided among three separate personnel organizations. The Office of Personnel Management is the agency charged with establishing the rules governing federal civilian employment procedures and practices. That office reports directly to the president of the United States.

The Merit System Protection Board. The Merit System Protection Board is charged with resolving all appellate and quasi-judicial issues arising from federal employment procedures and practices. This board deals with the legal concerns of federal personnel management. It decides most complaints and appeals, issues regulations regarding the nature and scope of its review, and establishes time limits for settlement of appeals. It also orders corrective and disciplinary action against employers or departments and agencies, if required.

The Federal Labor Relations Authority. The Federal Labor Relations Authority oversees the process of collective bargaining in the federal sector. It makes a variety of rulings concerning fair and **unfair labor practices** and those aspects of employment that are allowable for collective bargaining. It has the authority to resolve questions concerning the representation of federal employees by labor unions and can play a role in the resolution of disputes between the unions and government.

Public Labor Unions

Until the 1960s and the Great Society program of President Lyndon Johnson, collective bargaining in the public sector was considered antithetical to a constitutional democracy. It was considered absurd that organized public employees could bargain with the government as coequals or that matters of public personnel policy would be determined in any forum other than the legislative, executive, or judicial. In particular, strikes were feared because they represented a breakdown of the public order and, consequently, could lead to chaos. Many states considered collective bargaining a threat to their sovereignty, and the federal government had no general policy or practice for collective bargaining with its employees.[21]

These attitudes toward collective bargaining changed with remarkable rapidity. In large part, the rise of public collective bargaining has been related to the growth of public employment and the political pressure exerted by the unions. Many unions view the public sector as a promis-

ing recruiting ground from which they can draw new members to offset the decline in union membership in the private sector. The 1960s and 1970s were times of unprecedented growth in public sector unionism. Today, public sector collective bargaining is found throughout the federal government and in most states. It does, however, remain a patchwork of practices and procedures. There is, as yet, no comprehensive law covering all aspects and levels of government unionism. Despite these nonuniform practices, a basic bargaining pattern has emerged in the public sector, patterned after private sector procedures.

Public Sector Collective Bargaining

The basic public sector pattern for collective bargaining is as follows. Civil servants in the same occupations and classifications organize into **bargaining units** through an election or through submission of union membership cards to the appropriate government agency. Exclusive recognition of a union occurs when a majority of the employees in that bargaining unit want representation by a single union that will bargain for all employees in that unit. Precisely what can and cannot be bargained over is called the scope of bargaining. It may be relatively comprehensive and include wages, **benefits**, hours, position classification, promotion procedures, overtime assignments, and working conditions. Or it may be very restrictive and confined largely to issues of discipline and the issuance of safety equipment, coffee breaks, and parking spaces. The scope of bargaining is composed of items over which bargaining is mandatory—items that are permitted and items that are prohibited. When labor and management cannot agree on matters that are subject to mandatory bargaining, an **impasse** results. Resolution of the impasse can take many forms, including **mediation**, **fact finding**, and **arbitration**.

Several limitations placed on public sector labor relations make the collective bargaining process quite different from private sector practices. Most notable are serious restrictions on the scope of bargaining and the virtual prohibition on strikes. Many governmental agencies have enacted strong **management rights clauses** that severely limit the items over which collective bargaining can take place. These limitations often encompass the fundamental conditions of work. For example, in some agencies and jurisdictions, school teachers cannot bargain over the number of pupils in a classroom. At the federal level, most nonpostal workers are prohibited from bargaining over wages and hours. These restrictions are the legacy of constitutional sovereignty—the government remains the supreme representative of the citizenry, including those represented by a labor union.

In addition to the limitations on the scope of bargaining, there is a virtual prohibition on the right to strike in the federal government. Most individuals are familiar with the 1981 strike by the Professional Air Traffic Controllers (PATCO), where the federal air traffic controllers challenged this prohibition by striking over working conditions. President Reagan sent the PATCO controllers, and the entire public labor force, a sobering message: "There is a law that federal unions cannot strike against their employers, the people of the United States. What they did was terminate their own employment by quitting."[22]

Like the federal government, all but nine states have absolute prohibitions against the right of public workers to strike or create work stoppages of any kind. Employee bargaining units that violate these restrictions face statutory and court-ordered penalties. Although not always effective, these restrictions raise the costs of strikes and stoppages to the unions and the employees and deter such activities. Many people question what purpose and use a public union is without the right to strike. George Meany, former president of the **American Federation of Labor and Congress of Industrial Organizations**, once stated that "a free and collective bargaining system contemplates that at the end of the road there can be a strike. . . . If you don't like that idea, then take out the word free."[23] In the absence of the right to strike, other means of resolving disputes are required. Thus, arbitration, mediation, and fact finding are endemic to federal civil labor relations procedures. They are also part and parcel of the RLA and the NLRA, but to a lesser degree.

The brief examination of federal, state, and local government labor relations regulations and procedures in this chapter has provided sufficient exposure to the civil service environment. Further discussion of this complex topic is beyond the scope of this book. Therefore, we leave civil service collective bargaining at this point and concentrate exclusively on the labor relations issues in the private sector of the transport industry.

2

Early Collective Bargaining Legislation

Introduction

Most historians trace the American labor movement to the early 1800s. During the 1820s and 1830s, carpenters, masons, painters, and other skilled workers established citywide organizations to obtain better pay.[1] The object of these early organizations was to uphold the price of labor against the encroachment of the employers.[2] These associations focused on disputes involving working hours and apprenticeship programs designed to ensure the hiring of members of a particular trade. The first organizing efforts took place among groups of isolated workers in Philadelphia in the late 1820s.

In actions not unanticipated—because of the adversarial relationship between management and labor extant at this time—workers agreed to a certain wage level and pledged not to work for any employer who refused to pay this amount. Proving themselves willing to strike, although usually for only a short time, the citywide organizations were both aggressive and quite successful at achieving their goals.[3] Employers and the courts viewed early trade union attempts as common-law criminal conspiracies whose activities damaged commerce and trade.

Early Judicial Actions

Under common law, such actions as the withholding of services by employees were deemed illegal conspiracies, and workers were often prosecuted when strikes occurred. Under both English common law and statutory law, the very existence of unions was unlawful. Because English

law provided the precedent for the early American courts, such an attitude became prevalent in the U.S. system.[4] The success of employers in this area was most pronounced in the Federal Society of Cordwainers decision, in which cordwainers (shoemakers) joining in a strike in 1806 were found guilty of joining a conspiracy in restraint of trade. In the Cordwainers decision, the justice stated: "The rule in this case is pregnant with sound sense and all the authorities are clear on the subject. Hawkins, the greatest authority on criminal law, has laid it down, that a combination to maintain one another, carrying a particular object, whether true or false, is criminal."[5]

This decision established the "conspiracy doctrine" by which courts could forestall unionization activities whenever they deemed such activities illegal. Though local unions achieved minor victories despite the Cordwainers decision, the economic depression in the 1830s crushed much of the labor movement. But the fledgling labor movement was not so easily vanquished. As movement and growth continued, the unions found themselves facing another legal adversary, the state courts. The decisions of these courts often went against early unionization attempts, until 1842, when Chief Justice Lemuel Shaw of Massachusetts ruled in **Commonwealth v Hunt** that trade unions were lawful and that strikes for a **closed shop** were legal.[6] Although Justice Shaw's decision was not binding outside Massachusetts, judges in other states accorded it substantial weight as a precedent, and his decision marked an important liberalization of judicial tolerance for union activities.

National Railroad System Development

The introduction and expansion of railroads in the United States was the principal reason behind the transformation of the union movement from city organizations into nationwide labor organizations. In nineteenth-century America, railroads were the essential means of transportation. Both passenger and freight rail service played a crucial role in the transformation of the United States from a sparsely settled nation, largely composed of self-sufficient and isolated farm communities, to an industrialized, urbanized giant.[7] With the expansion of the railroad system, the groundwork was laid for the birth of bona fide national labor organizations.[8] Because railroads cast such a large shadow across our nation during the post–Civil War industrialization movement, early legislative attempts at creating public policy toward organized labor focused on the railroad workplace.[9]

Goods from newly accessible manufacturing centers, delivered ever more ubiquitously by the expanding rail transportation system, flowed into formerly stable and profitable markets. The flow of these new goods pressured employers to develop cost-cutting measures to remain competitive. The resultant labor atmosphere was like that in the post–airline deregulation era. To decrease labor costs, employers introduced women and children into the workplace, farmed out work to prison inmates, and generally reduced wages while increasing working hours.[10]

Predictably, labor reacted by escalating and institutionalizing union activities to improve their bargaining position. Early attempts at national unionization began in the 1850s and 1860s, with such organizations as the National Typographers Union (1852), the Hat Finishers (1854), the Stone Cutters (1855), the United Cigarmakers (1856), and the Iron Molders (1859). Most **na-tional unions** had humble beginnings and lasted for only a short while. In the early 1870s, there were approximately thirty national unions, and total union membership was approximately three hundred thousand.[11] Although employer opposition and the continual economic depression of the 1800s caused some of these groups to wane, they did not disappear. Over time, they stressed and pressed for negotiation with employers and for arbitration of disputes.

Though generally separate and distinct from other workers, railroad workers organized in the 1860s and 1870s to deal collectively with the problems of hazardous employment, long hours, and low wages. Between 1880 and 1893, four large brotherhoods emerged as the leading representatives of railroad labor, and they have subsequently become known as the Big Four. They are the Brotherhood of Locomotive Engineers, the Brotherhood of Locomotive Firemen and Enginemen, the Order of Railway Conductors, and the Brotherhood of Railroad Trainmen. A fifth large union, the Switchmen's Union of North America, organized in 1894. In these formative years of railroad unionism, efforts to recruit all railroad workers into an all-embracing labor organization called the Knights of Labor were unsuccessful, as was an attempt in 1894 to organize all railroad workers into a single comprehensive union known as the American Railway Union.[12]

The Knights of Labor. Despite the major railroad unions' disinterest in including themselves in an all-embracing labor organization, the first national federation to remain active for more than a few years was the Noble Order of the Knights of Labor, founded in 1869. It was established by a group of garment workers and included farmers and merchants as well as wage earners. The goals of the group included the abolition of child labor, equal pay for equal work, and an eight-hour workday. Initially, the Knights were formed as a secret society of moralists and reformers.

Their goal and main platform was to attack the ills created by an industrial society while protecting the rights of the workers.

Even though the leadership of the organization was essentially idealistic, favored social reform, and preferred arbitration over strikes, the Knights of Labor achieved national attention when the group won a strike in 1865, under the guidance of Terrence V. Powderly, against railroads owned by millionaire Jay Gould. Most conspicuous was a successful strike against the Wabash Railroad in 1885, which took place after Gould attempted to break the union by laying off its members. This strike, over wages, was not won easily, and it was characterized by violence. But the national publicity it received added impetus to the organization, so that by the middle of 1886, membership in the Knights of Labor reached seven hundred thousand.[13]

Because of other, unsuccessful strikes, however, especially those that were lost against the same railroad mogul, the group's effectiveness waned. By 1900, the organization had ceased to exist.[14] The Knights of Labor disappeared from the labor scene almost as quickly as the group had come onto it.

The American Federation of Labor. Despite the dissolution of the Knights of Labor, the impact of the national union and the strike weapon had been established, and following the example of that early organization, other national unions took its place. The most vigorous organization in pursuit of the national union concept was the **American Federation of Labor** (AFL), whose main platform insisted on the strike as the ultimate weapon to achieve its aims and goals.

Begun in 1886, the AFL, under the guidance of Samuel Gompers, later known as the father of the American labor movement, had a significant impact on the course of American unionism. Under Gompers, the AFL sought to unite all workers in singular occupations (job classifications) and to apply the principle of exclusive jurisdiction. The

goal of the organization was to organize craft, or skilled, workers only and to focus on gaining strength through the political process.

Gompers established an AFL platform that, in many respects, survives to the present day. This platform consists of

1. Establishing one union for each craft, each union having its own sphere of jurisdiction into which no other union could trespass

2. Permitting each national union to be autonomous

3. Concentrating on wage-centered gains through collective bargaining

4. Avoiding political alliances with any particular party, using instead collective union votes to defeat politicians with antiunion bias

5. Utilizing the strike as labor's ultimate weapon when collective bargaining does not produce desired results

With the establishment of the AFL platform, the labor movement had taken root, and by 1914, the AFL-represented unions had more than two million members.

Railroad Labor Disputes. As rail service grew, the goods it carried and the transportation it provided became less of a luxury and more of a necessity. Rail strikes and work disputes became commonplace, impacting strongly on the public interest by denying consumers basic goods and services that they had come to expect and demand. Opposition to union organizations increased during the late 1800s. Employers exchanged blacklists of workers suspected of union membership, preventing them from finding employment. Factory owners hired **strikebreakers** and armed guards to crush strikes. In the public interest, the state or federal government often approved the use of federal troops to quell strikes, claiming that strikes were still illegal because they restrained trade. Many states passed laws to restrict union activity.[15] The 1880s and 1890s saw a series of bitter labor disputes accompanied by violent strikes and even death.

The most notable violent activities of this era were several strikes and union-related activities that severely impeded the unions' ability to generate supportive legislation. For example, the **Haymarket Riot of 1886** increased antilabor feelings throughout the country. During a meeting of workers held in Haymarket Square in Chicago to protest police activity against strikers in a local industrial plant, an unknown person threw a bomb into the assemblage, and a riot broke out. Eight police officers and two other persons were killed, and the press and the nation blamed the labor movement for the violence.[16] The public was shocked by the affair, and the nation's press universally condemned unionists as radicals, anarchists, socialists, and aliens.[17]

Several other bitter and damaging strikes hurt the labor movement during this period. One was the Homestead Strike of 1892, which involved the Carnegie Steel Company and the Amalgamated Association of Iron, Steel, and Tin Workers. After a strike had been called, the company hired guards from the Pinkerton Detective Agency to protect the steelworkers. Violence broke out between the strikers and the Pinkerton guards, and several people were killed.

Another violent dispute, the Pullman Strike, occurred in 1894. In this instance, employees struck to protest a wage cut. In sympathy, members of the American Railway Union supported the strike by refusing to handle the company's cars. The federal government sent troops to end the strike, declaring that it interfered with mail trains. By the end of the strike, thirty-four strikers had been killed, and federal or state troops had been called out in Illinois, Indiana, Nebraska, Iowa, Oklahoma, Colorado, and California.[18]

The late nineteenth century witnessed a flurry of strike action. According to government records, 509 rail strikes involving 218,000 workers occurred between 1881 and 1905.[19] In number of strikes, railroads were fourteenth on a list of eighty-one industries; the coal industry was listed first with 3,403 strikes.[20]

Legislative Beginnings

As early as 1882, the U.S. Senate, concerned about the substantial strike activity, sought to remove the cause of strikes and prevent their reoccurrence by directing a Committee on Labor to establish a Senate commission to investigate labor issues. The result was four volumes of testimony on labor strife but no legislative action.[21] Similarly, a House of Representatives committee was also considering legislation to curtail strike activity. Although failing to provide any action, the House committee did recommend voluntary arbitration for the settlement of disputes.

The Arbitration Act of 1888

In 1886, another bloody dispute arose against the Gould Railway System, followed by similar occurrences against the Chicago, Burlington and Quincy Railroad in 1888.[22] In response, the government attempted to reduce disputes in the railroad industry by establishing the Arbitration Act of 1888. This act, although virtually unused, was the first federal statute to address labor issues in the railroad industry. The tenets of the act provided for adjustment of disputes through voluntary arbitration and investigation. To facilitate the handling of disputes, the act called for the establishment of a panel of three **arbitrators** to whom both parties to a dispute could bring the issue for resolution.

The relationship between labor and management was so strained during this period, with virtually no **good-faith bargaining** by either of the parties, that the Arbitration Act went unused. But one portion of the act—the provision that gave the president of the United States the authority to investigate the causes of any labor disputes when requested by one of the parties to the dispute or by the governor of any state affected by a rail dispute—later led to more legislation when invoked in the infamous Pullman Strike.

The Sherman Antitrust Act

While labor was vying for its place in the sun, the business industry was feeling strong public pressure to curtail its own monopolistic tendencies, having achieved tremendous economic power. In 1890, Congress passed new legislation presumably aimed at big business monopoly excesses: the Sherman Antitrust Act. The Sherman Act was designed to make monopolies and combinations that restrained trade illegal.

Initially conceived to curb monopolistic abuses of large business combinations, the act proved more successful against organized labor. Violation of the Sherman Act warranted the issuance of **injunctions**, with enforcement and fines, jail terms, and damage restitution up to triple the amount of actual damages. Sections 1 and 2 of the act stated: "Every contract, combination . . . or conspiracy, in restraint of trade or commerce . . . is . . . illegal."[23] Violators of Sections 1 and 2 were subject to fine and/or imprisonment. Section 4 provided for the use of injunctions to curtail **picketing**, **boycotts**, trespass, and the use of force.

Based on the body of this act, management found a new weapon in their arsenal for combating union activities: the injunction. These antitrust provisions were first used against organized labor, rather than business entities. Opponents of labor turned to civil actions to thwart and curtail unionism, primarily initiating suits to enjoin certain labor activities. The courts had previously recognized a general right to advance the interest of workers (*Commonwealth v Hunt*), but this right was narrowly interpreted. Any activity that, in the mind of the courts, impacted on the public welfare was a legitimate subject of injunction.

In *Plant v Wood*, decided in 1900, this attitude was clearly demonstrated when the court enjoined striking and picketing that attempted to enforce a demand that an employer could hire only union members. The court held that the demands of the union were not sufficient to justify interference with the employer's right to be "free of molestation."[24] In this same opinion, however, the elements of judicial discord were indicated in Chief Justice Holmes's dissenting opinion. Chief Justice Holmes wrote: "Unity of organization is necessary to make the contest of labor effectual, and [labor unions] lawfully may employ in their preparation the means which they might use in the final contest."[25]

Use of the injunction later made a significant appearance in the Pullman Strike, a dispute that brought a variety of legislative laws into play to quell strike activities. In that dispute, employees of the Pullman Palace Car Company, manufacturers of railroad cars, struck to protest a wage cut. Layoffs and wage reductions of 40 percent, made necessary by financial losses at Pullman's production facilities, but not accompanied by equally downward adjustment in housing rents in the company town of Pullman, Illinois, caused workers to strike on May 11, 1894.[26] Members of the American Railway Union, a group of railroad workers headed by Eugene V. Debs, declared a **sympathy strike** and refused to handle the company's cars.

Since the strike involved railroad workers, it was hoped that the enactment of the Arbitration Act of 1888 would work to resolve the differences. Unfortunately, the legislation was found to be without teeth, and it became necessary to utilize the provisions of the Sherman Act to secure injunctions against Eugene Debs, president of the American Railway Union, and against the union itself. The injunction was sought by the U.S. attorney general on grounds of interference with the delivery of the mail by train. Armed with this weapon, federal troops were called in at the first sign of a minor infraction.

Debs and other union leaders were ultimately sent to prison, and the American Railway Union was so weakened that it dissolved three years later. After the Pullman Strike, labor injunctions were commonly issued. Prior to 1931, some

1,845 injunctions were issued by state and federal courts in labor disputes.[27]

The best example of management's usage of the Sherman Act occurred in 1902, in a case called the *Danbury Hatters*, or *Loewe v Lawler*. During a strike against Loewe and Company, a hat manufacturer in Danbury, Connecticut, the union called a boycott, a secondary action by unrelated unions, against suppliers of the struck company. This action effectively stopped Loewe and Company from receiving raw goods that would have permitted the company to continue operations despite direct union action against them. Injunctions were ordered requiring the union to return to work, and, more significantly, suits were filed for losses incurred due to "restraint of trade."

In a sweeping Supreme Court decision, a judgment was given in favor of the company for over $250,000.[28] This **award** was a staggering setback for unions. In addition, the Supreme Court decision outlawed the use of **secondary boycotts**. This provision remained effective and made secondary boycotts illegal until the 1932 passage of the **Norris-La Guardia Act**. It was then reactivated by the passage of the Taft-Hartley Act in 1947 and applied to all industries except those under the RLA.

By the time of *Loewe v Lawler*, the balance of power in disputes had decidedly swung to management. In the management arsenal were the use of injunctions, strikebreakers (i.e., organizations similar to the Pinkerton Agency), federal troops, and a new antiunion agreement, the **yellow-dog contract**.

Yellow-Dog Contracts. Beset by continuous strike activity, employers set out to find ways to discourage their employees from involvement and membership in union activities. The yellow-dog contract, or union-free agreement, provided such relief. This contract, entered into between employers and workers, bound the employees to refrain from becoming members of a union or engaging in union activity while employed by a company. It became a de facto condition of employment.

Though the yellow-dog contract was believed by unions to be unconstitutional, the Supreme Court not only upheld its validity in 1917 but further permitted lower courts to issue injunctions for enforcement.[29] As a result, a company could require a yellow-dog contract as a condition of employment and could also terminate an employee if he or she refused to sign one. Beyond employee enforcement, injunctions could also be issued against any union attempting to persuade workers to violate their agreements.[30]

The Erdman Act of 1898

Although the vast majority of union activity was outside the railroad industry, the preservation of public interest remained paramount. As a result, greater legislative emphasis was applied to labor relations issues involving the operation of interstate train service.

Recognizing the inadequacies of the Arbitration Act of 1888 in the Pullman Strike, Congress set out to consider other alternatives to resolve railroad disputes. In 1898, it passed the Erdman Act, introducing for the first time the possibility of mediation between the parties. This law, with its mediation provision, was less abrasive to both parties to a dispute, allowing for a third party to help reach an accord. Should such attempts at mediation fail, the act provided that the **mediators** were to urge the parties to submit to voluntary arbitration of the dispute. The modus vivendi would be to establish a three-party panel, with one member who represented labor, one who represented management, and a third, neutral party. When convened, both parties to a dispute were to maintain the status quo, or to continue working under the old agreement, until the arbitration session culminated. Under the Arbitration Act of 1888, the parties may have been forced into an agreement.

Because of the broad use of yellow-dog contracts by railroad employers, the original Erdman Act included a section prohibiting railroad discrimination against a worker because of union membership. This section clearly ran contrary to the antiunion feeling of the majority of employers and did not go unchallenged. It was later declared unconstitutional.[31] In the view of the Supreme Court, the act violated the Fourteenth Amendment by depriving the employer of "property without due process of the law." In addition, the commerce clause of the Constitution did not empower Congress to regulate employer-employee relationships.

Despite its enactment, the Erdman Act went virtually unused for seven years and only became operational when management voluntarily chose to recognize a union. But from 1906 until the act was amended in 1913, sixty-one disputes were settled under the act's mediation provisions.

The Newlands Act of 1913

By 1913, railroad labor disputes were being considered separate and distinct from union activity in other areas of commerce. Legislative policy was evolving similarly. Recognizing the success of the latter years of the Erdman Act—that mediation rather than arbitration was leading to the resolution of labor disputes—Congress amended the Erdman Act. The Newlands Act of 1913 established a permanent board for handling railway labor disputes.

The Board of Mediation and Conciliation became responsible for all activities under the Newlands Act and for the interpretation of agreements when submitted to their authority. Like the panel stipulated in the Erdman Act, this permanent board of mediation also consisted of three members, one being a neutral party. In addition, the act created a permanent voluntary arbitration board, which was instructed to confine its decisions to the specific matters of each case. Unlike the Erdman Act, the Newlands Act permitted the mediation board to offer its services without first having been invited into the dispute by either the labor unions or the carrier.[32]

The Adamson Act of 1916

Usage of the Newlands Act by the railroads and their unions was widespread and met with a high degree of success. But in March 1916, the Big Four brotherhoods presented a uniform demand for eight-hour workdays to all American railroad companies. Their demand called for a standard day of eight hours or one hundred miles of travel, whichever came first, and time and a half for overtime. The response from the railroads was predictably negative, and the parties entered into protracted negotiations over the issue. Frustrated in their attempt to secure contractual language through direct negotiation with the railroad management, the unions refused to submit the matter to the Board of Mediation and Conciliation, settling instead on the strategy of calling for a nationwide strike.

Seeking to avert the consequences of a national rail strike, the Chamber of Commerce of the United States petitioned Congress to direct the Interstate Commerce Commission to investigate union wage and hour demands. At the same time, President Wilson appealed to the carriers and unions to find some commonality in their respective positions. He was answered by a strike call, to become effective on Labor Day 1916.

One day prior to the scheduled strike, the workers and their unions agreed to forgo their action if federal law was enacted allowing for a workday to be only eight hours in duration. In response, Congress enacted the Adamson Act, which provided for an eight-hour workday on the railroads only. On September 5, 1916, the Adamson Act was passed and signed by President Wilson.[33]

Immediately after its passage, railroads' ownership contested the Adamson Act on the grounds that it was unconstitutional. In retaliation, the railroad unions prepared for and rescheduled another nationwide strike. The Supreme Court, weighing the evidence, concluded that the law was not in conflict with constitutional or congressional rights to regulate trade.[34] The decision was handed down the very day the brotherhoods had selected for commencement of strike action. Railroad labor policy was evolving at a more rapid pace than the legislation affecting other industries.

Nonrailroad Labor Activities

Though strides in labor-management relations were being made in the railroad industry, labor in general was not faring as well in the legislative arena. The Sherman Act was a definite barrier to nonrail unions' ability to organize and bargain collectively. Later, in the early 1900s, the movement suffered a number of setbacks. In a 1905 ruling, the Supreme Court held that minimum-wage laws were unconstitutional because they restricted the right of an individual to contract for employment. The decision was based on the principle of "liberty of contract," derived from the Fourteenth Amendment of the Constitution.[35] This decision and the extensive usage of yellow-dog contracts made union activism problematic.

Despite setbacks, the movement continued to struggle and gained hard-won congressional support. In 1914, Congress enacted legislation that on the surface appeared to have prolabor qualities and that was in fact designed to side with labor concerns. Pressure from the AFL after the *Loewe v Lawler* (*Danbury Hatters*) Supreme Court decision led Congress to pass the **Clayton Act**. So sweeping were some of the act's reforms favoring the labor movement that it was hailed as "Labors' Magna Charta." According to Samuel Gompers, section 6 of the Clayton Act was "a sledge hammer blow to the wrongs and injustices so long inflicted upon the workers. The declaration is the industrial Magna Charta upon which the working people will rear their construction of industrial freedom."[36]

The Clayton Act of 1914

Specifically addressing the plight of the worker, the Clayton Act noted that "the labor of humans was not a commodity or article of commerce."[37] Accordingly, unions were not illegal per se, and injunctions against unions could not be made unless they were necessary to prevent irreparable injury to property. The right to strike for "economic gains" was also addressed. Section 6 provided that antitrust laws, such as the Sherman Act, should not be interpreted or construed to prevent labor unions "from lawfully carrying out the legitimate objects thereof." Section 20 went further, barring the use of federal injunctions in disputes involving the terms and conditions of employment.

On the surface, the passage of the Clayton Act was a striking victory for the proponents of labor. But in subsequent interpretations, the courts ruled in ways that diminished labor's favorable position. The courts limited the use of boycotts and allowed unions to be sued, even though they were not incorporated or legally recognized organizations.

In 1921, the Supreme Court all but destroyed Sections 6 and 20 of the Clayton Act. Such cases as *Duplex Printing v Deering* and *Bedford Cut Stone Co. v Journeymen Stone Cutters Association of North America* provided the death knell of the favorable position originally afforded labor under that act. In sweeping decisions, the court determined that "Unions were not exempt from the provisions of the Sherman Anti-Trust Act and injunctions could be issued against employees engaging in boycotts of employers, other than their own";[38] and "Where striking activity or boycotts involve 'interstate commerce' the provisions of the Sherman Anti-Trust Act are applicable."[39]

Despite judicial setbacks, the continuing validity of yellow-dog contracts, and negative publicity, labor organizations outside the railroad industry continued to work toward their goals and increase their membership roles. But it was almost twenty years before parity was reached with the railroad unions.

Railroad Labor Gains

During World War I, union activity took a backseat to the war effort. But a significant occurrence during this period had a profound impact on railroad labor relations. Because rail service was important to the war effort, labor disputes were viewed as an ill-afforded inconvenience. To minimize rail disputes and curtail possible loss of rail service, the federal government took control of the nation's railroads in January 1918, placing them under a general director for railroad administration. The Army Appropriation Act of 1916 provided legislation permitting the president of the United States to take possession of any transportation system in time of war.[40] The act failed to establish an expiration time for such conversion. One major responsibility of the government was to ensure that compensation rates were "fair" and "just." This placed all labor-related activity under the direct control and purview of the U.S. government.

At the beginning of the war, the brotherhoods lacked both legal protection for the right to organize and procedures for settling **grievances** arising over the interpretation of collective bargaining agreements. On February 21, 1918, the director general of railroads issued Order No. 8, which protected workers from discrimination because of union membership. The government further strengthened the brotherhoods by entering national collective bargaining agreements with railroad unions.

During the two years of government control, the right to organize became an accomplished fact. The wartime establishment of regional railway boards of adjustment to settle grievances over the interpretation of collective bargaining agreements gave collective bargaining a new recognition and permanence.[41] The government had unilaterally implemented what management had sought to avoid. Yellow-dog contracts were being systematically eliminated, and third parties were making decisions on matters of railway disputes without being asked—in the name of the war effort.[42] The Railroad Administration and its director general encouraged union membership by

1. Prohibiting discrimination of any sort against the union worker[43]

2. Increasing wages across the board to levels double those at the time of the takeover

3. Standardizing wages and working conditions on a national basis

4. Imposing restrictive **work rules** over the objections of management[44]

The resultant changes to the structure of the railroad industry were pervasive. Prior to federal controls, only 50 percent of all rail workers were unionized. But by 1920, the proportion of workers who were unionized had climbed to 85 percent.[45]

The results for organized labor were overwhelming. Never before in history had so much been received by labor in such a short period of time. A monumental public policy shift had occurred. The apparent government-union adversarial relationship embodied in previous conspiracy doctrines and restraint of trade analyses was now moving away from indifference toward outright promotion. This public policy shift ignited and fueled legislation of a prounion nature. The 1920s and 1930s witnessed this shift with the development of the RLA, the Norris-La Guardia Act, the ill-fated **National Industrial Recovery Act**, the Wagner Act, and the Fair Labor Standards Act. The railroads, their unions, and governmental action toward the parties combined to lay the track for not only rail labor legislation but its spur, the remainder of industrial America.

The Transportation Act of 1920

Upon return of the railroads to private ownership, other industrial sectors showed varying degrees of interest in the activities that had taken place during the war period. The railroad unions, content with the government handling of a nationalized workplace, sought, unsuccessfully, to officially and permanently nationalize the rail industry. Since relative stability existed in the railroads during this period, Congress was anxious to continue a harmonious labor-management relationship for the public interest. Labor was anxious to retain the gains they had made, and management was equally anxious to erode these union windfalls.

The legislation Congress enacted—the Transportation Act—was a compromise between House and Senate versions desirous to retain elements of government control. All unresolved disputes were to be referred to the U.S. Railroad Labor Board for hearing and decision. This newly created board was to carry out both mediation and arbitration of disputes. The one-sided nature of the act was totally opposed by both labor and management, because it left the decision of their fates in the hands of a disinterested third party. Further, the act required that adjustment boards, created for the purpose of resolving grievances, be established between the parties to contracts.

Title III of the Transportation Act created a tripartite Railroad Labor Board to recommend settlement in labor disputes. This provision permitted the voluntary establishment of boards of adjustment to handle grievances. The right to organize was not given statutory protection. Neither the unions nor the carriers were satisfied with the new law.[46]

When enacted, the U.S. Railroad Labor Board was immediately inundated with cases. As might have been expected, the parties contested the binding nature of the board's decisions and contended the nonvoluntary nature of the act. In several court decisions, the board's enforcement powers were struck down. The Labor Board was to act as a Board of Arbitration, and no constraint was to be placed on the parties to do what the board decided.[47] The ultimate decision of the board therefore was not compulsory, and no process was furnished to enforce it.[48] These decisions and the resultant problems eventually discredited the board, despite the fact that during the five years of its life, it handled more than thirteen thousand disputes, for the most part successfully.[49]

Summary

Title III of the Transportation Act, thoroughly discredited by the courts, joined its predecessors in the dustbin of failed labor legislation. The succession of laws enacted between the 1880s and 1920 were proven defective or inadequate when applied to the important labor issues of the day.[50] A befitting epithet for Title III was given by a union president in testimony before a Senate committee. The president of the Brotherhood of Locomotive Firemen and Enginemen told Congress that the principal defect of Title III was that it was a "compromise between compulsion and persuasion. It established a board to take the place of mediators who should be persuaders and then required them to decide disputes which made them arbitrators. As soon as they began deciding disputes they immediately lost standing as mediators. Their peace-power became dependent on force and they had no force to exert."[51] Labor, management, and government had come full circle. The framework for labor relations remained a minefield strewn with ineffective legislation, uncertainty, and adversarial attitudes.

3

Major Collective Bargaining Legislation

Introduction

Labor movement formation peaked in the mid 1920s for the railroad industry and in the mid 1930s for the remainder of the industrialized workforce. The government's segregated approach to labor relations legislation allowed the railroad industry unions to emerge and evolve at a more rapid pace than the other craft and industrial associations. Despite the plethora of legislative and judicial setbacks experienced by the unions in the early 1900s, several developments in the mid to late 1920s had a positive impact on the union movement.

For example, in 1924, a totally isolated piece of legislation called the Immigration Act was enacted. This legislation limited the number of immigrants admitted to the United States. The restriction on immigration reduced the number of new arrivals competing for jobs and significantly increased the bargaining power of the American worker.

This chapter focuses primarily on legislation from the 1920s through the 1950s that affected union development. Table 3-1 lists these acts and their functions within the labor relations environment. More detailed discussion of these acts follows.

The Railway Labor Act

Origins

Within the railroad industry, union dissatisfaction with the Transportation Act of 1920 caused the railroad brotherhoods to support the independent candidacy of Robert M. La Follette for president in 1924. The brotherhoods were disappointed by the failure of the Transportation Act to establish grievance machinery and angered by appointments to the Railroad Labor Board. The railroad unions felt the existing board constituency had management leanings. La Follette's advocacy of government ownership of the railroads raised hopes for a return to the wartime prosperity the unions had enjoyed.

After La Follette's defeat, the brotherhoods began to muster nonpartisan support for the repeal of the Transportation Act. Ironically, railroad management became their most potent political ally.[1] The dissatisfaction with the Transportation Act of 1920 came because both management and labor had concerns about forced arbitration and the Railroad Labor Board's inability to enforce its decisions. Congress agreed that the labor provisions of the Transportation Act needed revision. As a result, various bills were proposed, one of which—the Howell-Barkley Bill—received very favorable response. Interestingly, this proposal was prepared by the attorney for the railroad union's and thus had the consent of the union membership.[2] Management, also recognizing the need to preserve certain elements of the voluntary dispute resolution, submitted their own version of legislation.

In 1925, a committee of management and labor representatives convened to draft a joint approach that they hoped would satisfy both labor and management. After repeated conferences, a shared draft bill similar to the Howell-Barkley proposal, the Watson-Parker Bill, received a consensus. In January 1926, this bill was presented to Congress. Having the support of both railroad management and unions, it passed Congress with a wide

Table 3–1
Major Labor Relations Laws

Act	Function
Railway Labor Act (1926)	Established the rights of railroad employees to engage in union activities; codified the collective bargaining process; established the National Mediation Board to administer the act
Norris-La Guardia Act (1932)	Restricted the right of courts to issue injunctions against unions engaging in various activities; forbade yellow-dog contracts
Railway Labor Act amendment (1934)	Amended the act to create the National Mediation Board; mandated mediation and secured union representation privileges
National Labor Relations Act (1935)	Established the rights of workers to form unions, bargain collectively, and strike; forbade employers from engaging in unfair labor practices; established National Labor Relations Board to administer the act
Railway Labor Act amendment (1936)	Amended the act to include all interstate commercial air carriers
Fair Labor Standards Act (1938)	Established a minimum wage and maximum work week; outlawed child labor
Railway Labor Act amendment (1940)	Amended the act to clarify coverage of railroad activity in the coal industry
Taft-Hartley Act (1947)	Amended the National Labor Relations Act to prohibit unfair union practices; established provisions for right-to-work laws; established procedures for emergency dispute resolution
Railway Labor Act amendment (1951)	Amended the act to eliminate the bar against closed shops
Landrum-Griffin Act (1959)	Amended the National Labor Relations Act; required unions to hold democratic elections; required unions to make annual financial disclosure to the Department of Labor

margin of victory (the vote in the Senate was 69–13, and the margin in the House of Representatives was 381–13).[3]

The only opposition came from the National Association of Manufacturers, and President Coolidge attempted to persuade the railroads to accept amendments proposed by that association. On May 20, 1926, failing to convince the railroads to accept the amendments, President Coolidge signed the RLA. The new act repealed the Erdman and Newlands Acts and Title III of the 1920 Transportation Act. Despite a number of amendments, the RLA remains valid and operative legislation today. As such, it is the oldest federal collective bargaining legislation in the nation's history.[4]

Early Judicial Challenges

The year 1926 saw the birth of the first national labor relations statute ever formulated to sanction and codify union-management collective bargaining. It provided for cooling-off periods and mediation and **conciliation** in disputes over the terms of new agreements. Since both management and labor opposed compulsory arbitration and the final determination of wages, hours, and working conditions by government edict, the act provided for a less restrictive procedure. The law preserved the right to strike after extended negotiations and mediation. To the disappointment of the unions, the act did not provide for national adjustment boards to handle grievance disputes. This deficiency was removed by amendment in 1934.

Irrespective of joint drafting of the original act by labor and management, there remained the question of constitutionality. In 1930, the constitutionality issue was resolved when the provisions of the act were upheld by the Supreme Court. In *Texas and New Orleans Railroad v Brotherhood of Railway and Steamship Clerks*, the railroad had discharged employees because of their union membership. Contrary to the decision rendered in *Adair v United States*, which challenged the Erdman Act provisions that made it a criminal offense to discharge employees for union membership, the *Texas* decision stated "The RLA does not interfere with the normal exercise of the right of the carrier to select its employees or to discharge them. The statute is not aimed at this right of the employers but at the interference of the right of the employees to have a representative of their own choosing. As the carriers subject to the Act have no constitutional right to interfere with the freedom of the employees in making their selection, they cannot complain of the statute on constitutional grounds."[5]

The change in the philosophical reasoning of the court is more evident when the decision on the *Adair* case is placed side by side with that of the *Texas* decision. In *Adair*, the court ruled that "The right of a person to sell his labor upon such terms as he deems proper, is, in its essence, the same as the right of the purchaser to prescribe the conditions upon which he will accept such labor from the person offering to sell it."[6]

Depression Era Unionism

The Great Depression of 1929, which left millions of American workers jobless, had its own special impact on the labor movement and on subsequent legislation. The Great Depression changed the attitude of many Americans. Both workers and nonworkers came to embrace the labor movement. Before 1929, most people regarded the heads of American business to be benevolent national leaders, capable of resolving any of the nation's ills. Members of the union movement were identified as dangerous radicals. Despite such contrastive stereotypes, people began losing faith in managerial leadership when business could not revive the economy. Many Americans began to believe that the way to fight the slump was to increase the purchasing power of wage earners, a philosophy espoused by most unions. The political climate changed from one favoring management to one favoring labor.

The RLA allowed the railroad unions and workers to weather the Great Depression far better than their counterparts in other industries. Wage rates were not cut, but the unions allowed the carriers to deduct 10 percent from wages during the period from February 1, 1932, through June 10, 1934. On April 1, 1935, wages were restored to their January 1932 level. The railroad employees were also helped by the Federal Emergency Railroad Transportation Act of 1933, which forbade railroad mergers that would result in job loss.[7]

Provisions of the RLA

For many years the RLA was widely proclaimed as "ideal" labor relations legislation. It avoided compulsory arbitration and encouraged industrial peace in an essential industry. Its cooling-off period and emphasis on mediation and conciliation and its provision for **emergency boards** offered multiple pathways for managing and defusing disputes in these essential national industries.

Only recently has there been an outcry to repeal the act—in particular, its secondary boycott provision. Adding to the secondary boycott dilemma is a Supreme Court ruling favoring the use of secondary picketing as a proper means of self-help during disputes with carriers. Despite such outcries, any assessment of the RLA must be kept in proper perspective. There are over seven thousand **labor agreements** in the railroad and airline industries, and about one thousand railroad and two hundred airline agreements (mostly local) are in negotiations in any given year.[8] Any measure of the effectiveness of the act must be made with reference to its original objectives to promote free collective bargaining and to protect the public from interrupted flows of commerce.[9]

Public Policy Objectives. The RLA impacts broadly on the collective bargaining process in the rail and air transport industries. As stated by the act (@ 151a; see appendix), the five general public policy objectives are

1. To avoid any interruption to commerce or to the operation of any carrier engaged therein

2. To forbid any limitation upon freedom of association among employees or any denial as a condition of employment or otherwise, of the right of employees to join a labor organization [added by the 1934 amendment]

3. To provide for the complete independence of carriers and of employees in the matter of self-organization to carry out the purpose of this Act

4. To provide for the prompt and orderly settlement of all disputes concerning rates of pay, rules, or working conditions

5. To provide for the prompt and orderly settlement of all disputes growing out of grievances or out of the interruption or application of agreements covering rates of pay, rules, or working conditions

The act imposes duties on carriers (rail and air) and on employees and their representatives. It defines rights and provisions for their protection and prescribes methods for settling various types of disputes. The act created procedures and mechanisms for adjusting differences.[10]

Major and Minor Disputes. To facilitate implementation of the general objectives of the RLA, two distinct dispute categories were defined. These consist of defining and applying appropriate action to "major" and "minor" disputes. Major disputes deal with union **certification** elections and the development of a new agreement or a change in an existing agreement. The process and procedures for handling major disputes are examined in detail in chapters 4–5. Minor disputes deal with the resolution of grievances and the interpretation or application of the existing terms of a labor agreement. Minor dispute procedures are examined in chapter 6. Congress established the National Railroad Adjustment Board to settle minor disputes arising out of grievances or application of contracts. This board, confined to the railroad industry, has final and binding authority in resolving minor disputes. Because the board is congressionally established, the cost of its operation is borne by the government.

In the airline industry, the mechanism for minor dispute resolution is different. A board similar to that in the railroad industry was never established, although it was authorized by the 1934 amendment. Title II of the RLA requires each carrier and its employees to set up a **system board of adjustment** for the purpose of adjudicating minor disputes. Title II also gives the National Mediation Board (NMB) the authority, when it deems such action necessary, to establish a National Air Transport Adjustment Board, which would function substantially the same as the National Railroad Adjustment Board. To this date, no such board has been established.[11]

The National Mediation Board

The NMB was established by Congress to administer the RLA. Its functions have been categorized as largely ministerial, and therefore it lacks the ability to make decisions involving the interpretation of the act; these remain the sole province of Congress.[12]

The NMB, established in 1934, is composed of three members appointed by the president of the United States, with Senate confirmation. These members must be persons with no past labor or railroad affiliation. No more than two members may have the same political affiliation. Each member is appointed for a term of three years, and each acts as chairperson on an annual rotation. The board may designate one or more of its members to exercise its functions in mediation proceedings and has the power to administer oaths and affirmations. The board is authorized to appoint experts and assistants to act in any capacity essential to required transactions and can assign or refer any portion of its work or functions to individual members or employees. It also has the authority to provide for salaries and expenditures necessary to complete these actions.

The NMB provides the following services to parties of a dispute:

1. Mediation of disputes relating to the changing of existing agreements affecting rates of pay, rules, and/or working conditions

2. Determination or certification of the representatives of a class or craft of employees

3. Election monitoring

4. Interpretation of agreements made under its mediation program

The purpose of the NMB is to take measures that will avoid any interruption of interstate commerce, enforce the limitations of the freedom of choice or association by the employees of an air or rail carrier, and provide a means for the prompt and orderly settlement of disputes.

The RLA relies almost entirely on the use of collective bargaining to settle labor disputes, and unlike the NLRA, it mandates mediation by the NMB should the parties reach an impasse in the negotiation process. If mediation fails, the RLA provides for a **proffer of arbitration** by the NMB. Although either party to the dispute is free to refuse arbitration, the costs of which are borne by the board, the RLA further provides that the president of the United States may convene an emergency board to investigate the dispute and recommend procedures and terms for the agreement.

The long-term effect of this required mediation procedure is that contractual negotiations can, and often do, take an exorbitant amount of time before a settlement is reached. During the mediation process, the provisions of the existing contract remain in effect, eliminating any ability on the part of the carrier or the unions to impose financial pressure. When and if a strike occurs, the provisions of the act do not prohibit secondary boycotts, as does the NLRA. This singular provision may at some time in the future cause either a congressional revision of the act or its demise altogether.

The RLA Amendment of 1934

By 1934, with the advent of the Norris-La Guardia Act and the National Industrial Recovery Act (NIRA), Congress recognized that the RLA required modifications to keep pace with the growing labor movement. The initial passage of the act had been designed to produce peaceful settlement of contract disputes, but it failed to establish freedom of association in various labor unions that were not in existence in 1926. As late as 1933, for example, 147 of the 233 largest railroads still maintained **company unions**.[13] Interest in applying the provisions of the Norris-La Guardia Act to the RLA was so strong that Joseph B. Easton, the federal coordinator of transportation, suggested they be written directly into the act.[14]

In 1934, the first of five amendments to the RLA occurred. Major importance was centered on three particular areas. Company-sponsored unions were banned from existence, as were unions dominated by railroad companies. This elimination provided the protection of the right of employees to organize for collective bargaining purposes without interference by the employer. This proscription also permanently put an end to the concept of yellow-dog contracts in the railroad industry.

Another important provision was the establishment of the National Railroad Adjustment Board, a forum to which grievances could be submitted by either party to a dispute. This board was empowered to interpret the application of bargaining agreements in existence and settle minor disputes over working conditions and contract interpretation. Thus, the 1934 amendment made arbitration of such disputes compulsory. This requirement is one of the RLA's unusual features.

In addition, the 1934 amendment saw the formation of an oversight body to administer the act—the NMB—and procedures by which that body could determine and certify collective bargaining agents. The U.S. Board of Mediation, as defined under the original act, became the NMB, with total membership reduced from five members to three.

The RLA Amendment of 1936

In 1936, Congress, prodded by a strong lobbying effort by the fledgling Air Line Pilots Association (ALPA), decided to put the tiny airline industry (twenty-four carriers with a total of 4,200 employees and 433 aircraft) under the RLA. Ten years after the original enactment of the RLA, Congress passed the Title II amendment, which applied most of the provisions of the act to air carriers engaged in interstate commerce. In the spirit of the times, Congress decided that the traveling and shipping public had to be protected against work stoppages and interruption of airborne commerce. Thus, the RLA, already successful in the railroad industry for a decade, was extended to airlines. The history of the statute

reveals that airmail transportation was the legislative issue in the minds of the politicians.

Prior Legislative Issues. Prior to their inclusion under the RLA, the air carriers that were in existence were subject to the provisions of the Norris-La Guardia Act (1932) and the NIRA (1933). The NIRA coverage resulted in one of the major standing decisions of airline labor work rules, Decision 83 of the National Labor Board, which set maximum flying hours and incremental pay plans for mileage and speed. This fundamental work rule was issued outside the purview of the RLA but remains in force because of grandfather rights. The additional study material at the end of this chapter contains a summary of the events leading up to the National Labor Board's decision to enact Decision 83.

This National Labor Board decision, the only airline determination made outside the purview of the RLA, has historically influenced pilot labor relations and negotiations. Its formula for the establishment of hourly and mileage pay rates relative to aircraft speed has led to increased wages and related benefits whenever aircraft productivity and technology improvements were made by manufacturers.[15] The essential components of this pay formula still apply to airline pilots today.[16]

The decision to place the nation's airlines under the provisions of the RLA seemed so unimportant that, two decades later, it drew only a small footnote in a college textbook covering labor-union history.[17] In most labor textbooks today, the RLA occupies less than two pages. Table 3-2 lists a summary of the provisions of the RLA after passage of the 1934 and 1936 amendments.

The RLA Amendments of 1940 and 1951

In 1940, a minor amendment was added to the RLA to clarify coverage of the act in relation to rail operations in coal mines. In 1951, the **union shop** was made a permissible form of required union membership.

Table 3–2
Provisions of the Railway Labor Act

Category	Provisions

Purpose	1. To avoid interruption to interstate commerce
	2. To provide prompt settlement of disputes in covered industries
	    a. Provisions for major dispute resolution include
	        i. Certification of election results from organizational activities
	        ii. Mediation of disputes arising under the collective bargaining process for contract renewal
	    b. Provisions for minor dispute resolution include
	        i. Interpretation, through system boards of adjustment, of existing contracts

Extent of Coverage	1. All railroads and subsidiaries of railroads covered under the original passage in 1926 2. All U.S. airlines operating under Interstate Commerce provisions and all foreign flag airline carriers operating on U.S. soil a. Added to Railway Labor Act by 1936 amendments
Negotiation Procedures	1. Section 6 notice, as outlined by the act, requires thirty-day notice of intended change to contract, working conditions, wages, etc. 2. Conferences between the parties are to be held within ten days of the Section 6 notice. 3. Strikes are not permitted during meetings between the parties until part have been released by the National Mediation Board or for ten days after direct meetings between the parties have passed.
Mediation	1. Upon impasse in negotiations between the parties, either party may request mediation from the National Mediation Board. a. The National Mediation Board may impose mandatory mediation without a request from either party if, in the determination of the board, a labor emergency exists. 2. No time limit exists for mediation. The timing of the mediation process is at the discretion of the National Mediation Board. 3. The contract under discussion remains in effect during the mediation process and for thirty days after a proffer of arbitration has been refused by either party (status quo).
Arbitration	1. As noted above, if mediation fails, the National Mediation Board must offer (proffer) voluntary arbitration to the parties. 2. When arbitration is accepted, arbitration will provide a final and binding agreement. 3. Refusal by either party to arbitration will cause the board to withdraw from the case and the status quo provision will remain in effect for thirty days (cooling-off period).

Emergency Provisions	1. Upon recommendation and report to the president of the United States, after the parties have been released and are in a "cooling-off period," a presidential emergency board may be established.
	    a. Occurs when the National Mediation Board determines that the dispute could "threaten substantially to interrupt interstate commerce" or "deprive any section of the country of essential transportation service."
	2. Establishment of an emergency board preserves the "status quo" provision of an agreement an additional sixty days.
	    a. A maximum of thirty days is allowed for the special board to make investigation and report.
	    b. Thirty days is provided after report is made
	3. Possible outcomes of the emergency board include
	    a. Presidential suggestive intervention
	    b. Congressional enactment of special legislation to address the issue
	    c. Parties resort to self-help

Right-to-Work Laws. The 1951 amendment requiring union membership is in direct conflict with the **right-to-work laws** in twenty-one states. If a union is certified as a bargaining representative in a state that has passed right-to-work laws and no provisions have been made between the employer and the union, an airline or railroad employee will be compelled to join or financially support the union certified by the NMB. Section 2, Eleventh, of the RLA specifically preempts states from making laws favoring employee rights over those of union membership.

Questioning the constitutionality of this provision, the Supreme Court stated: ". . . we pass narrowly on paragraph 2, eleventh of the Railway Labor Act. We only hold that the requirements for financial support of the collective bargaining agency by all who receive benefits of its work is within the power of Congress under the Commerce Clause and does not violate either the First or the Fifth Amendments."[18] This means that railroad and airline employees do not enjoy the benefits of a state's right-to-work legislation, because, at the minimum, they will be required to pay dues to the union for benefits received attributable to the negotiation process.

The Norris-La Guardia Act of 1932

In 1932, Congress enacted one of the first prolabor laws outside the railroad industry. It acquired its name from the sponsors of the original bill, Senator George W. Norris of Nebraska and Representative Fiorello H. La Guardia of New York. It was the first of several statutes enacted in the 1930s, a time when both Congress and the president favored collective bargaining and union organization. The preamble of the Norris-La Guardia Act makes clear the public policy of the United States and reflects the prolabor attitude of the nation during this period: "Whereas under prevailing economic conditions, developed with the aid of governmental authority for owners of property to organize in corporate forms of ownership association, the individual unorganized worker is commonly helpless . . . wherefore . . . it is necessary to have full freedom of association . . . for the purpose of collective bargaining or other mutual aid."[19]

Passage of the act curtailed management's ability to receive federal injunctions during labor disputes. Prior to enactment of Norris-La Guardia, it was only necessary for management to apply for such injunctions to receive them. Temporary restraining orders would generally be issued and received before the unions could respond, making the injunction ex parte to the unions. This ex parte injunctive relief effectively created a unilateral right of management to deter or dampen the unions' activities.

Norris-La Guardia closed this loophole and provided unions with the opportunity to appear in court and present opposing arguments on why injunctions should not be issued. This eliminated the issuance of ex parte injunctions, which management had been adept at using, with the full knowledge and concurrence of the courts. The other provision of Norris-La Guardia was equally important because it eliminated management's ability to use the yellow-dog contract. No longer would it be a risk for union organizers to approach employees who had been forced to sign such agreements. Thus, the door was opened for union expansion.

The act placed no affirmative obligation on employers to negotiate with or recognize unions. Rather, it sought to aid union organizing and collective bargaining. Its main impact was to permit the unions to exert effective economic pressure against employers. Years earlier, Samuel Gompers had proclaimed the Clayton Act to be labor's Magna Charta, but his proclamation may have been premature. With the signing of Norris-La Guardia, a wide range of aggressive tactics were given to the unions and dramatically increased their ability to achieve their objectives.

Railroad workers received a bonus from the act when Congress refused arguments calling for the exemption of railroads from coverage. Not only were the railroad employees and their unions covered by the RLA, but under Norris-La Guardia, they were permitted the use of such economic weapons as strikes, picketing, and boycotts. In summary, the provisions of the Norris-La Guardia Act

1. Forbid federal courts to issue injunctions against the following specifically described union activities:

   a. Stopping or refusing to work

   b. Union membership

   c. Paying or withholding strike benefits, unemployment benefits, and so on to those engaging in a labor dispute

   d. Publicizing a labor dispute in a nonviolent manner

   e. Assembly to organize

   f. Aid or assistance for persons suing or being sued

   g. Agreeing to engage or not engage in any of the foregoing

2. Forbid employers to require employees to sign yellow-dog contracts

The National Labor Relations Act

The National Industrial Recovery Act

With the country in the throes of depression in 1933, Franklin D. Roosevelt assumed the position of president in January of that year and immediately set in motion the New Deal, his proposal to bring the nation back to prosperity. Included in his plan were the passage of several laws that benefited labor. One of the most important was the NIRA.

The NIRA became effective in 1933. Codes in the act set minimum wages and maximum hours of work and also implemented Section 7(a), which provided for the right of labor to organize and to engage in collective bargaining.[20] It provided for the establishment of codes for "fair competition" in the industries covered. Its most important labor feature made it mandatory that any activity emanating from the act contain the following conditions:

> . . . employees shall have the right to organize and bargain collectively through representatives of their own choosing, and shall be free from the interference, restraint, or coercion of employers of labor, or their agents, in the designation of such representatives or in self organization or in other concerted activities for the purpose of collective bargaining or other mutual aid or protection. and, That no employee and no one seeking employment shall be required as a condition of employment to join any company union or to refrain from joining, organizing or assisting a labor organization of his own choosing.[21]

To handle labor disputes, President Roosevelt created the National Labor Board, later renamed the National Labor Relations Board. The latter, commencing its operation in July 1934, functioned to investigate the facts in labor disputes arising under the NIRA. The board was given the right to conduct elections among employees to determine their bargaining representatives and to certify those desired by the majority of employees.

The program was greeted with enthusiasm at first but began to run into serious administrative difficulties and faced growing opposition. The act was to expire, unless renewed, on June 16, 1935. The government claimed its power to institute the NIRA was founded on interstate commerce jurisdiction and thus that the act was constitutionally appropriate. But in *Schechter v U.S.*, a case directly emanating from the act, the Supreme Court determined: "If the commerce clause were construed to reach all enterprises and transaction which could be said to have an indirect effect upon interstate commerce, the federal authority would embrace practically all the activities of the people and the authority of the state over its domestic concerns would exist only by sufferance of the federal government."[22]

The code structure of the NIRA—which had

only three weeks to go unless renewed—collapsed with the *Schechter* decision. It had proved too cumbersome and unworkable.[23] The NIRA had, however, with its codes of fair competition, encouraged voluntary collective bargaining by employers and, like the RLA, indicated the need for federal intervention in labor disputes. The movement toward government involvement was incontrovertible, and the NIRA had laid the groundwork for the enactment of future regulation.

Origins of the NLRA: The Wagner Act

Immediately following the collapse of the NIRA, Senator Robert F. Wagner of New York set in motion replacement language contained in the Wagner Bill, which later became the Wagner Act, the foundation of the NLRA. The NLRA was enacted on July 5, 1935. It applied to all workers in interstate commerce and created the National Labor Relations Board. This act set forth the right of employees to self-organization and collective bargaining, defined "unfair labor practices," and laid down rules about the representation of employees for the purpose of collective bargaining. The act also empowered the National Labor Relations Board to prevent those described unfair labor practices that affected commerce.[24] The board was given legislative power to punish unfair labor practices and to determine which union should represent workers at various companies falling under its provisions.

The intent of the NLRA was to equalize the bargaining power of the employee. Its regulatory aspects are contained in the following statement of policy:

Experience has proved that protection by law of the right of employees to organize and bargain collectively safeguards commerce from injury, impairment, or interruption, and promotes the flow of commerce by removing certain recognized sources of industrial strife and unrest, by encouraging practices fundamental to the friendly adjustment of industrial disputes arising out of differences as to wages,

hours, or other working condition, and by restoring equality of bargaining power between employers and employees. . . .

It is hereby declared to be the policy of the United States to eliminate the causes of certain substantial obstructions to the free flow of commerce and to mitigate and eliminate these obstructions when they have occurred by encouraging the practice and procedure of collective bargaining and by protecting the exercise by workers of full freedom of association, self-organization, and designation of representatives of their own choosing, for the purpose of negotiation the terms and conditions of their employment or other mutual aid or protection.[25]

The primary objectives of the NLRA were twofold. Section 7 guaranteed employees

1. Freedom to form, join, and/or assist labor organizations

2. Freedom to bargain collectively with employers

3. Freedom to engage in concerted activity to enhance collective bargaining

Section 8 sought to keep the rights of the employees inviolate by imposing affirmative duties on the employer to deal in good faith with unions. In this area, the act listed five employer labor practices that were to be considered unfair:

1. Interference with employees' rights to self-organization

2. Discrimination against employees because of their affiliation with a labor union

3. Refusal to bargain with a labor organization of the employees' choice

4. Attempts to dominate or contribute to the support of a labor organization or to form company unions to deter the legitimate attempt by employees to select a representative of their choice

5. Retaliation against any employee for filing a complaint against a company or giving testimony against an employer

In view of the failure of the NIRA and the history of union representation movements, many employers took umbrage with the NLRA's passage and refused to comply with its procedures. Once again, the constitutionality issue was raised.

Judicial Challenge. Opponents argued that the NLRA went beyond the commerce clause and invaded the Tenth Amendment rights of the sovereign states. A second constitutional issue presented was that the employers due process of law was denied by imposing restriction on their freedom of contract. In a 1937 landmark decision, *NLRB v Jones & Laughlin Steel Corporation*, the Supreme Court upheld constitutionality by enforcing a National Labor Relations Board **cease and desist order** against a company for unfair labor practices of interfering with employees' rights to organize and bargain collectively.[26] This decision held that the law was proper extension of the commerce clause to manufacturing workers and that it was not in violation of the constitutional due process clause. The rationale for the extension of the commerce clause was that a reduction in labor strife would promote commerce between the states.

No previous period in the history of American trade unionism, other than the Great Upheaval of 1886, matched the epochal importance of the 1930s in the development of collective bargaining and industrial government for the worker. With the passage of the NIRA in 1933 and the NLRA in 1935, collective bargaining received a degree of public respectability that a century and a half of private efforts had been unable to achieve. The impact on the organizing and collective bargaining activities of the trade union movement was nothing short of phenomenal.[27]

The Wagner Act, in its desire to provide for union parity with management's rights, created a significant number of requirements for the employer. In the exuberance to pass Wagner, Congress placed restrictions on the employer and did not address similar issues relating to union activities. Only the employers were prohibited from engaging in unfair practices. This failure to incorporate the duties and responsibilities of unions went unchecked for twelve years, and it was not until the passage of the Taft-Hartley amendment in 1947 that unions were placed under similar restraints. Table 3-3 summarizes the provisions of the Wagner Act.

NLRA Amendment: The Taft-Hartley Act

The **Labor-Management Relations Act** of 1947, better know as the Taft-Hartley Act, was intended to limit some of the activities of labor unions in the United States. It amended the NLRA of 1935, which had defined unions' rights to organize and to bargain with employers.

Initially, the NLRA was the Wagner Act. But it has been amended and supplemented by additional legislation: the Labor-Management Relations Act of 1947 (Taft-Hartley); the **Labor-Management Reporting and Disclosure Act** of 1959 (Landrum-Griffin); and, more recently, Public Law 93-36 (Health Care Industry) in 1974.[28] Today, all these amendments combined make up the NLRA.

Subsequent to World War II, during which all wage increases were prohibited by the government, the United States entered its greatest period of economic growth. Unions, with their newfound freedoms, attempted to secure a large portion of this new wealth for their membership. Waves of strikes began, and in 1946, the number of work stoppages reached an all-time high. From 1945 to 1947, the country experienced nationwide strikes in the automobile, coal, oil, lumber, textiles, maritime, and rail transportation industries.

Although unions scored some of their most impressive victories during this time, many members of Congress felt that the balance of the labor-management relations equation had become too heavily weighted in favor of the unions. They believed that employers and employees needed protection against unfair labor practices of unions and that the public needed protection

Table 3–3

Major Provisions of the Wagner Act

Category	Provisions
Policy	1. To protect the right of employees to organize and bargain collectively 2. To make a policy of the United States to encourage the practice and procedure of collective bargaining and the exercise by employees of their right to organize and negotiate
Rights of Employees	1. To organize into unions of the employees' choice 2. To bargain collectively with their employer through representatives of their own choosing 3. To strike or take similar concerted action 4. To assist labor unions in the encouragement of membership
Establishment of the National Labor Relations Board	1. The board members (5) are appointed by the president of the United States. 2. The board conducts elections to determine employee representatives. 3. The board has exclusive power to prevent employer unfair labor practices.
Employer Unfair Labor Practices	1. Interfering with employee rights guaranteed under the act 2. Discrimination against employees or labor unions pursuing their rights guaranteed under the act 3. Refusal to bargain in good faith with the representatives of the employees' choice 4. Any attempt to interfere with the employees' choice to join a union
Elections	1. The National Labor Relations Board (NLRB) conducts secret ballot elections to determine employee representatives. 2. The National Labor Relations Board determines the appropriate unit (collective bargaining group) for purpose of representation and elections. a. Employee representatives shall be the exclusive representatives of the defined unit.
Limitations	1. The act was primarily concerned with the organizing phase of labor relations. 2. The act dealt exclusively with employer tactics (unfair labor practices) and did not address union activities.

against labor disputes that threatened the national health and security. The 1946 Congress was the first since 1930 with a Republican majority, and in 1947, it passed a law that amended the NLRA by placing greater restrictions on unions' behavior.[29] The Taft-Hartley Act was adopted to provide this protection. It was built on the framework of the Wagner Act and retained the provisions for exclusive representation of

employees. A new code of conduct was established for unions and their agents.

Sections 8(a) and 8(b) redefined "unfair labor practices," recognizing that both parties to collective bargaining needed protection from wrongful interference from each other. Though the unfair labor practices on the part of management remained similar to those outlined in the Wagner Act, the Taft-Hartley amendments provided greater power to combat unfair labor practices. Some unfair labor practices added were

1. Restraining or coercing employees in their selection of a bargaining or grievance representative

2. Causing or attempting to cause an employer to discriminate against an employee because of the employee's membership or nonmembership in a labor organization

3. Refusing to bargain in good faith with an employer

4. Inducing or encouraging employees to stop work to force an employee to join a union

Right-to-Work Laws. Among other provisions added, Taft-Hartley permitted right-to-work laws that allowed the states to determine whether their citizens must join a union when that union is certified by the employees of a company. The right to work without requiring union membership was nationwide until restricted by the NLRA of 1935. It was recognized again by Taft-Hartley, which made the closed shop illegal and, in Section 14(b), allowed state laws against union security measures to supersede the federal law: "Nothing in this Act shall be construed as authorizing the executive or application of agreements requiring membership in a labor organization as a condition of employment in any State or Territory in which such execution or application is prohibited by State or Territorial law."

The states then had a free choice to make union security agreements illegal. Within two years after the passage of the act, fourteen states enacted laws providing that the right of a person to work could not be denied or abridged on account of membership or nonmembership in a labor union. Organized labor denounced these right-to-work laws as management efforts to put a stop to the growth of union membership and undertook campaigns to repeal both Section 14(b) and state legislation based on it. Labor's success was minute until 1958, when the American Federation of Labor and Congress of Industrial Organizations (AFL-CIO) faced the National Right to Work

Committee in a campaign to extend the law to six more states. The AFL-CIO won all but one of the encounters. Since then, the campaigns to repeal or extend have declined in number and intensity, and the lineup of states with right-to-work laws has reached twenty-one.

Unions have sought to curb the effect of these laws by developing the **agency shop**, which requires employees, whether members or not, to pay fees to the union, particularly where such employees are receiving the negotiated benefits of union workers. Such shops are generally determined by the negotiating process between union and management. But in 1963, the Supreme Court ruled that states have the authority to make such practices illegal.[30]

Small businesses are the strongest supporters of right-to-work laws. In 1966, the states that supported the right to work were primarily located in the South and West. No major industrial states were or are included. The right-to-work states are Alabama, Arizona, Arkansas, Florida, Georgia, Idaho, Iowa, Kansas, Louisiana, Mississippi, Nebraska, Nevada, North Carolina, North Dakota, South Carolina, South Dakota, Tennessee, Texas, Utah, Virginia, and Wyoming.

Other Provisions. Other major provisions of Taft-Hartley were the elimination of **featherbedding**, or the creation of nonexistent jobs; the right of unions to insist on closed shops; permission for federal intervention in "national emergencies"; and the exemption of supervisory personnel from coverage. Taft-Hartley also limited the authority of the National Labor Relations Board.

While the act upheld collective bargaining as the preferred method of settling labor disputes, it also recognized that these procedures could often break down. Since failure to reach agreement could seriously damage the economy when national issues are concerned, alternate processes were established. In this regard, Taft-Hartley created the Federal Mediation and Conciliation Service to assist in any dispute affecting interstate commerce. To maintain control of contracts being negotiated, the act also required that labor or management notify the Federal Mediation and Conciliation Service when any changes in the terms or conditions of employment are desired by the parties.

Emergency Boards. Following the lead of the RLA, Taft-Hartley also provided for National Emergency Boards. When the president of the United States believes that an industrywide dispute could have an impact on the national health or safety, a board of inquiry may be convened to investigate and report on the facts of the dispute. The board is precluded from making recommendations, but if it believes the national health or safety is in jeopardy, the president of the United States could seek a federal injunction, effectively stopping a strike or lockout for a period of eighty days.

Subsequent to the first sixty days of the injunction, a report on the status of the dispute would be provided to the president, and within the next fifteen days, the employees of the union would be provided the opportunity to vote on management's final offer. Failing to reach any accord, the union would then be free to strike after the eighty-day expiration. At this point, the only possible action to prevent a major work stoppage would require special emergency legislation on the part of Congress.

In summary, the Taft-Hartley Act forbade unions to force employees to become members. It also banned both secondary boycotts and closed shops that required union membership as a condition of being hired. It authorized the president of the United States to impose an eighty-day delay on any strike found to imperil the national health or safety. The act allowed employers to replace striking workers, and it imposed a ban on union contributions to political campaigns. This ban was nullified later by a court ruling that held that it infringed on the constitutional right of citizens to free expression. The act retained the provisions of the Wagner Act for voting by employees on whether they wish to be represented by a union, but it restricted **representation elections** for craftworkers, professionals, **supervisors,** and custodial employees.[31] Table 3-4 summarizes the provisions of the Taft-Hartley Act.

NLRA Amendment:
The Landrum-Griffin Act

Senate investigations by the McClellan Committee during the 1950s uncovered corruption in some unions and a lack of democratic procedures in others. As happened in response to events preceding the passage of the Taft-Hartley Act, public sentiment was aroused, and legislation was demanded to protect individual workers and the public from union activities. This corruption included embezzlement from union treasuries, violence toward union members, undemocratic practices, and conversion of union resources to the personal interests of union officials.[32]

As a direct result, the Labor-Management Reporting and Disclosure Act (Landrum-Griffin Act) was passed in 1959 under the commerce clause. In its preamble, the position of Congress was clearly enunciated:

> Congress . . . finds, from recent investigations in the labor and management fields, that there have been a number of instances of breach of trust, corruption, disregard of the rights of individual employees, and other failures to observe high standards of responsibility and ethical conduct which require further and supplementary legislation that will afford necessary protection of the rights and interests of employees and the public generally as they relate to the activities of labor organizations, employers, labor relations consultants, and their officers and representatives.[33]

The act sought to impose regulation of the internal affairs of unions and to establish rights for union members. Title I of the act has been called the "Bill of Rights" of union members. It gives union members the following rights:

1. To nominate candidates, to vote in elections, to attend union meetings, and to have a voice in business transactions

Table 3-4

Major Provisions of the Taft-Hartley Act

Category	Provisions

Policy	1. To determine certain practices of labor organizations that obstruct the free flow of commerce
	2. To eliminate union practices necessary to guarantee free flow of commerce
	3. To create the Federal Mediation and Conciliation Service, which
	   a. Assists in any dispute affecting interstate commerce
	   b. Requires parties to notify the service when any change in the terms and conditions of employment is desired

Rights of Employees	1. Right to refrain from union activities, except provisions contained in union shop collective bargaining agreements.
Right to Work	1. Established state rights to outlaw union shop requirements in collective bargaining agreements a. Employees in right-to-work states can refrain from joining the union representing their bargaining unit.
Union Unfair Labor Practices	1. Refusal to bargain in good faith with the employer 2. Discriminating against employee for not engaging in union activities 3. Restraint or coercion of employees in their rights 4. Prohibition on closed shops
Restriction on Certain Activities	1. Elimination of secondary boycotts and secondary strikes 2. Prohibition of strikes during the term of a valid collective bargaining agreement 3. Elimination of strikes to force employer to make work for union members a. Outlawed featherbedding 4. Prohibition of strikes to force dislocation of one union in favor of another

Provides for Presidential Intervention	1. The president intervenes where an industry wide dispute could "imperil the national health or safety."
	2. The president appoints a board of inquiry to
	   a. Investigate and report on the facts of the dispute and the parties' positions
	   b. Make recommendations and issue injunction for eighty days if "national health or safety" is in jeopardy
	   c. After the first sixty days, give a report on the status of the dispute to the president
	3. Within the next fifteen days, a poll is taken by employees on management's final offer.
	4. After eighty days, the injunction expires, and the parties are free to exercise self-help.
	5. The president considers the possibility of congressional legislation to halt the dispute.

2. To have free expression in union meetings and business discussions

3. To vote on an increase of dues or fees

4. To sue and testify against the union and to receive all rights by law prior to any disciplinary action against them by the union

5. To be given a copy of the collective bargaining agreement under which they work

These rights and remedies granted to union members are in addition to any other rights that the members may have under other laws or under union bylaws and constitutions. If a member's rights are violated, this act allows the member to bring civil action for relief in the U.S. district courts where the violation occurred or where the main offices of the union is located.

The provisions of the Landrum-Griffin Act apply to the carriers and unions covered under the RLA. In summary, the Landrum-Griffin Act

1. Establishes a Bill of Rights for members of union organizations, which

a. Includes freedom of speech and assembly

b. Protects from an increase in dues without a vote

c. Protects against the taking of inappropriate disciplinary action by union officials against rank-and-file members

2. Requires reporting by labor organizations to the secretary of labor about union financial dealings, and thus

a. regulates union finances and administration

The Airline Deregulation Act of 1978

Much has been written concerning the positive and negative aspects of the Airline Deregulation Act of 1978. The full implications and affects are still unfolding and remain a subject of personal and congressional debate. Several congressmen have recently sought to repeal the act, particularly as it relates to airlines operating within the borders of a state. The act ended years of government control of the airline industry, particularly economic control of fares and route structures.

Airline deregulation prompted the introduction of 128 nonunion carriers; by 1987, only 34 had survived. These introductions sparked a wave of mergers by major airlines, ticketing agreements between major carriers and regional and commuter airlines, hub-and-spoke airport operations, and frequent-flier programs to promote airline allegiance.[34] In addition, price benefits to the consumer have resulted from increased competition. The downside has been increased congestion at airports and in the airways, delays in departures and arrivals, threats to safety, and a general decline in the quality of air service.[35]

Although the Airline Deregulation Act cannot be considered a labor law per se, its pervasive impact on the industry has created new frontiers in labor-management relations. The relatively stable labor relations environment of the airline industry has become an arena where the forces of economic pressure have created untold labor problems. Some might argue that without the established norms of the RLA, total chaos might have already ensued. But others, like Frank Lorenzo, former chairman of Texas Air Corporation, argue that without the RLA, the pressures of deregulation would be visited on the labor unions, and a more meaningful dialogue between the parties would ensue in negotiations.

Other Laws Affecting Labor Relations

Besides the RLA and the NLRA, other statutes and executive orders influence the labor relations process either directly or indirectly. A brief discussion of legislation applicable to all industries follows. This discussion highlights major provisions only; labor relations specialists find that a detailed knowledge of the legislation is essential.

The Interstate Transportation of Strikebreakers Act (or Byrnes Act, 1936) makes it illegal to transport or travel in interstate commerce for the purpose of interfering by force or threats with peaceful picketing by employees or with other employment rights and guarantees.

The Fair Labor Standards Act (1938) established a minimum wage and a maximum workweek and outlawed child labor. All private employers employing more than a certain number of employees and conducting business in interstate commerce are required to compensate employees with time-and-a-half pay for work beyond forty hours in a workweek.

The Bankruptcy Act of 1984 includes standards for the rejection of collective bargaining agreements when companies file for bankruptcy under a Chapter 11 reorganization plan. In cases where no agreement can be reached between the parties, the act specifies the requirements for terminating or altering provision of a collective bargaining agreement. The U.S. Supreme Court ruled in *NLRB v Bildisco and Bildisco* that it was legal for a company to petition for bankruptcy and immediately reject the terms and conditions of an existing labor agreement without waiting for approval of its petition by the bankruptcy court.[36] A similar case occurring in the airline industry centered around the abrogation of contracts in a bankruptcy proceeding by Continental Air Lines under the leadership of Frank Lorenzo.

Disagreeing with the court's decision, Congress amended the Bankruptcy Reform Act of 1978. At present, and indicative in the Eastern Airlines bankruptcy filing, a company may not reject the terms of a valid labor agreement until the bankruptcy judge has approved the firm's bankruptcy petition. To obtain such approval, the company seeking to obtain "debtor-in-possession" status must demonstrate to the court that the following conditions have been met:

1. The company must make a proposal to the union to modify the existing labor agreement based on the most complete and reliable information available at the time.

2. The company's proposed contract modifications must represent only those changes necessary to permit the successful reorganization of the firm and avoidance of bankruptcy risk.

3. The proposed contract modifications must treat all creditors, the debtor firm, and other affected parties fairly and equitably.

4. Between the time when the proposed modifications are presented to the union and the court hearing on the firm's bankruptcy petition is held, the company must bargain in good faith with the union concerning the proposed contract modifications.

5. The company must provide the union with all relevant information necessary for the union to evaluate the firm's proposed contract modification.

6. The union must have rejected the company's proposed contract modification without good cause. The burden of proof is on the union to show why the company's proposal is unreasonable or unnecessary, thereby giving the union good cause for rejecting the company's proposal.

7. In the court's judgment, a review of all the factors must demonstrate that the balance of equities clearly favors approval of the company's rejection of the existing labor agreement.

The Equal Pay Act (1963) provides that employers cannot pay different rates of pay for the same job on the basis of gender or race.

The Civil Rights Act of 1964, amended by the Equal Employment Opportunity Act of 1972, prohibits employment decisions that discriminate on the basis of race, sex, religion, color, or national origin.

The Age Discrimination in Employment Act (1967, 1984, 1986) prohibits employment discrimination against those over the age of forty and prohibits mandatory retirement except for specified occupations. At present, pilot mandatory retirement at age sixty is excluded from the act.

The Vocational Rehabilitation Act (1973) and the Disabilities Act of 1991 require holders of federal government contracts in excess of $2,500 to develop **affirmative action programs** to employ and advance qualified physically and mentally handicapped individuals.

Executive Order 11246 (1965) requires contractors underutilizing minorities and women to specify goals and develop timetables for affirmatively recruiting, selecting, training, and promoting individuals from underutilized groups.

The Occupational Safety and Health Act (1970) requires an affirmative duty on the part of employers to provide working conditions that will not harm their employees. Regulations are published by the Department of Labor and include procedures for the issuance of citations for corrections or fines where adherence to regulations are lacking.

The Worker Adjustment and Retraining Notification (WARN, 1988) requires employers with one hundred or more employees to give advance notice of sixty days to employees who will be affected by a plant closing or major layoff.

The Racketeering Influenced and Corrupt Organizations Act (RICO, 1970) forbids anyone involved in racketeering from investing in or controlling through racketeering activities any enterprise (business or labor unions) engaged in interstate commerce. Any person who suffers damages from the prohibited activities is entitled to threefold recovery of damages.

The Military Selection Act (1967) requires employers to reemploy veterans to the position they held before entering the armed services. Such restoration must be to positions of like **seniority**, status, and pay.

The Vietnam Era Veteran Readjustment Assistance Act (1974) requires employers with government contracts of $10,000 or more to take affirmative action to employ and promote qualified and disabled veterans from the Vietnam War.

The Americans with Disabilities Act (1990) provides for access to and protection in the workplace for those with physical impairments. This law prohibits discrimination in employment opportunities against disabled people; requires equal accessibility to all services provided by state and local government, including transportation; and prohibits discrimination in public accommodations.

Other laws important to labor relations include state and local ordinances, such as wage and hour regulations; the **Employee Retirement Income and Security Act** of 1974; and the Social Security Act of 1935 and its amendments.

Summary

Three principal pieces of labor legislation and their respective amendments affect employees and employers in the air transport sector: the RLA, the NLRA, and the Norris-La Guardia Act. There are many similarities and many fundamental differences between the RLA and the NLRA. Table 3-5 offers a side-by-side comparison of the major provisions of each act and the applicable influences of Norris-La Guardia on each.

One fundamental overriding question remains in our examination of the two major labor acts. Is it necessary to have two distinct sets of labor legislation, one of which, the RLA, governs only two industrial sectors employing less than a million workers total? Poignant and adroit arguments can be offered in support of either side of this issue. Any legislative attempts to combine the existing bifurcated system, by elimination of the RLA and the transference of the railroad and air transport sectors into the NLRA, must be filtered through the lens of operational history.

There have been several crippling unified national strikes under the NLRA, notably in the steel and coal industries. To date, there have been no unified national strikes under the RLA. The public policy goals and objectives of the RLA, to avoid interruption of interstate commerce and to promote collective bargaining, seem to have been achieved. Despite the relatively small number of employees covered under the RLA, there are over seven thousand labor agreements in place in the rail and air transport sector, with approximately one thousand rail and two hundred airline agreements in negotiation in any given year. Transferring these agreements to the NLRA would be a truly complex, difficult, and expensive task that might not be worth the cost and effort.

Some of the provisions of the RLA, notably the proscription of right to work and the inclusion of secondary boycott provisions, need to be revised to ensure worker rights are consistent between the two acts. This can certainly be achieved more cost effectively by congressional amendment than by repeal. But unless and until unions, management, and the American people generate sufficient political pressure on our elected representatives, these issues will remain unresolved, and the question of the necessity for bifurcated labor legislation will remain unanswered. The additional study material at the end of this chapter contains two articles that discuss this dualistic labor environment.

Table 3-5

Legislative Differences Between the Railway Labor Act and the National Labor Relations Act

Category	Provisions	
	RLA	NLRA
Contracts	Amendable; continue in perpetuity unless modified by parties	Terminable expiration date acts as "drop dead provision" unless modified
Secondary Boycotts	No provision for restriction	Outlawed by Taft-Hartley
Mediation	Mandatory	On request to the Federal Mediation and Conciliation Service
Grievance Arbitration	Mandatory	Subject to agreement between the parties
Unfair Labor Practices	None listed in the act	Enumerated and proscribed by Taft-Hartley
Right to Work	None	Provided and applicable in twenty-one states
Requirement for Representation Election	No particular citation; subject to discretion of the National Mediation Board	30 percent signatory cards from covered employees
Decertification Procedure	None listed; one union may be replaced by another	Specific procedure allowing for change of union or return to nonunion status
Featherbedding	No proscription, but distinct possibility	Made unlawful by Taft-Hartley
Judicial Review of Board Decision	No	Yes
Injunctive Relief under Norris-La Guardia	Applicable to date of airline incorporation	Yes

Additional Study Material

Detailed Examination of the Events Leading to Rule #83 Decision*

The vagaries of Washington politics caused considerable turmoil in the air transportation industry during the early New Deal. The Century strike generated wide public awareness of the role subsidies played in airline operations, but the drama of the pilots' strike temporarily overshadowed the issue of government paternalism. Even though E. L. Cord temporarily got out of the air transportation business after losing his dispute with the pilots, he left a residual legacy of mistrust and suspicion hanging over the non-mail operators. However, the independent operators found many willing listeners among New Deal Democrats for their tales of fraud and malfeasance, and just prior to the end of the Hoover Administration the Senate created a special committee, chaired by Alabama's Hugo L. Black, to investigate Walter Folger Brown's airmail policies. But even before the Black Committee began its work, the aviation trade journals were predicting severe cuts in the subsidy, since the "balanced-budget" campaign rhetoric of the early New Deal had forced Hoover to promise publicly new economies in government spending in the last days of his term. When the Post Office Department reduced the subsidies late in 1932, the temporary alliance between the major operators and ALPA, which was predicated only on their mutual fear of E. L. Cord, collapsed.[1] Indicating the irritation of airline executives over high pilot salaries, *Aviation* magazine expressed dismay over the disparity between the high pay of pilots and the low pay of ground personnel. The implication was clearly, however, that pilot salaries should be lower, not that ground personnel salaries should be higher.[2]

Shortly after the lower subsidies became effective in December 1932, the operators announced their intention to decrease pilot salaries an amount compatible with the percentage of subsidy reduction. Eastern began with a 16 percent reduction, Northwest announced a flat 10 percent cut, and all the other airlines indicated that they too would reduce salaries in the near future. One of Behncke's most insistent rationales for the creation of ALPA was that a union would prevent pay reductions. Early in the depression it was the threat rather than the fact of pay cuts which alarmed pilots, and even on lines where the hourly system of pay prevailed, such as T&WA, pilot salaries remained fairly high. But late in 1932 reality stared the pilots in the face—the rhetoric and scares were over, the operators fully intended to cut pay, and ALPA would have to produce positive results in order to justify its existence.

At the same time, there were serious problems of technological unemployment facing the profession, since the airlines were rapidly introducing more modern aircraft, such as the Boeing 247, which, because they were larger and faster, vastly increased pilot productivity and resulted in some pilot layoffs. The Century strike proved there was no shortage of pilots, and Lyman D. Lauren, the aviation writer for the *New York Times* estimated that there were over 7,000 licensed transport pilots in 1933, but he placed the total number of jobs for them at only 1,500.[3] Faced with these dismal statistics, and the obvious financial difficulties of their respective airlines, a surprising number of pilots were willing to acquiesce in the pay reduction.

Behncke, however, had to deal with a credibility crisis among the remainder of his membership, and he desperately petitioned his newfound friends in Washington for help.[4] At his request, Congressman James M. Mead of Minnesota intervened directly on ALPA's behalf. He asked Northwestern's General Manager, Colonel L. H. Brittin, to withhold action on the pay cuts until Congress and the Post Office Department had time to study the whole situation.[5] Mead also intervened with Captain Thomas Doe, the President of Eastern Air Transport. Many Congressmen were becoming increasingly suspicious of the air-mail subsidies, and the situation at the time was very tense. As an indication of the antagonism the subsidy issue aroused in Congress, the Senate deleted the entire air-mail section in the Post Office appropriation, and a conference committee only barely succeeded in restoring it. The times were uncertain as the country awaited Roosevelt's inauguration, and nobody could be sure of the direction of aviation policy in the forthcoming New Deal. While expecting and preparing for the worst, most operators saw no advantage in prematurely alienating an important member of the House Post Office Committee. Brittin and Doe, therefore, reluctantly acceded to Mead's request.[6]

"Welfare Capitalism" and the anti-union activities of American businessmen during the prosperity decade of the 1920s had decreased the strength of the American labor movement, and the downward trend in union membership accelerated with the depression. But the confidence and enthusiasm which the early New Deal generated proved very helpful to union organizers, and the thrust of its policies seemed to offer organized labor a golden opportunity to write guarantees of maximum hours and minimum wages into federal law. The prestige of the entrepreneur in American society had sagged along with the index of industrial production, and many aggrieved and embittered people who formerly looked suspiciously upon unions were now willing to countenance them. While ALPA was already an organized union, it still had need of federal guarantees of the right to bargain collectively, and the new prestige of organized labor, particularly among influential legislators, gave Behncke cause for optimism.[7]

In the interim, however, before anybody could be sure of the shape of the New Deal air transportation and labor policies, Behncke and the operators warily sparred over the pay issue. During the 1932 convention, Behncke told the dele-

gates that the House Post Office Committee had promised to await ALPA's recommendations before passing any new air-mail legislation, and early in 1933 Congressman Mead asked the pilots for their views on a variety of aviation issues, including pay, hours, and air safety. Behncke undercut the stereotype of the individualistic aviator when he triumphantly informed the delegates that the pilots could "look forward to being adequately protected by some regulation or legislation during the coming session of Congress."[8] He wanted a firm commitment from his membership as to what they wanted, and, prior to the convention, he had polled all twenty-nine of ALPA's locals asking for their ideas on such things as salaries, hours, hazard pay, foreign-duty pay, vacations, and sick leave.[9] From the composite questionnaires he determined that the pilots preferred a base pay, plus mileage pay, with increased factors for the size, speed, and weight of the aircraft, and, of course, hazard pay for night, overwater, and mountainous terrain flying. At Behncke's insistence the convention established a National Basis of Pay Committee to aid him in the effort to have Congress write federal guarantees which would apply to all airline pilots, but especially to pilots working for airlines which had air-mail contracts.[10]

The matter of a federal limitation of flying hours per month provoked some of the hottest exchanges of the 1932 convention. There was already a good deal of talk about limiting the hours of all workers to thirty hours per week, and William Green had endorsed the idea as early as 1930. The month following ALPA's convention, the AFofL formally endorsed the thirty-hour week on the theory that it would spread the available work.[11] Pilot interest in reduced hours of flying preceded such economic theorizing, deriving mainly from the fact that too many pilots spent three nights out of four away from their homes. While some pilots preferred the hefty paychecks they received for flying long hours, most pilots opted for a more relaxed routine even at the risk of lessened pay. The Department of Commerce set a maximum limit of 110 hours per month, but during busy seasons the airlines habitually exceeded this total on the theory, which the department never tested, that the maximum was meant to be an annual average rather than an arbitrary total for any one month. But to complicate matters for the pilots, many of the smaller airlines declared that they could not continue to operate if pilot hours per month were too low, and the pilots were genuinely worried about it. There was fundamental agreement, however, that the operators should not be allowed to exploit pilot labor, and John Huber spoke for the majority when he declared that "the idea behind all this is to set a regular scale . . . so there will not be any competition between the lines." The general discussion slowly yielded an understanding, for most of the delegates, that unless they stuck together and refused to fly more than other pilots, there would be anarchy within their ranks which would eventually destroy the union.

Many pilots evidenced a managerial mentality, and at times they seemed more concerned with their line's profit margin than with their own salaries. While there was some merit in this view, Behncke worried lest it dominate ALPA policy, and he insisted that ALPA must necessarily adopt a hard posture in favor of a uniform national scale. Despite this disagreement, it was apparent to almost all of the pilots that seniority should be the only factor in promotion. They openly derided the merit system, declaring that it was almost always used to favor management's cronies. They knew that they would eventually have to secure contractual agreements with the operators to use the seniority system exclusively, but Behncke persuaded them that it was better to seek federal protection before entering direct negotiations with the employers. The tricky problem of job security would necessarily involve a combination of federal guarantees and direct union-employer collective bargaining agreements. Still, until they got these agreements, federal rules governing their hours and wages would do them little good if, as one delegate put it, management could "fire an old man with a high base and start in a young fellow with a low base."[12] The times seemed propitious for a concerted effort in Washington, however, and Behncke persuaded a majority of the delegates that ALPA should delay action on direct collective bargaining.

At one point in the discussion the delegates seemed to be on the verge of adopting a variable scale on maximum hours and minimum pay which would allow for regional variations, the size of the airline, and the type of aircraft. Behncke adamantly opposed this idea, insisting on a single standard that would apply to all airline pilots everywhere. After a delegate offered a formal resolution that the hourly limit be subject to a "plus or minus fifteen hours" variation, Behncke blurted: "No! No! That is all wrong, that fifteen hour business. That leaves the sky for the limit." Since Behncke would not countenance a variable hourly limit, the convention seemed willing to adopt the Commerce Department's limit of 110 hours per month, until a delegate moaned that such a high hourly total would "just about drive us crazy on our line. With the run I'm on we would have to fly, well about damn near every day. And on account of the cancellations for weather we would just have a merry time." Behncke favored an 80-hour-per-month maximum, which was about what most pilots were then flying, and he stressed the fact that the Aeromedical Association, a private group of physicians interested in aviation medicine, endorsed his view. He had written to Frederick C. Warnshuis, the Chairman of the association, asking for a "scientific" determination of the maximum number of hours which would be compatible with safety. Warnshuis replied that, in his opinion, the Department of Commerce limit of 110 hours per month was too high, and he recommended 90 to 100 hours for day flying, 60 to 70 for night flying, with a standard figure of 80 hours per month for a combination of both types.[13] Behncke had a telling and effective point in the doctor's opinion, and the convention finally agreed to support him in his effort to make 80 hours per month the federal maximum.[14]

Behncke intended to make the Pay Committee his vehicle for Washington lobbying activities. The committee met for the first time on December 22, 1932, and promptly endorsed a pamphlet which Behncke had previously written entitled "The Truth About Pilot Pay." He subsequently circulated the pamphlet among all members of Congress and he sent dozens of copies to newspaper editors.[15] Behncke knew the operators would not delay their pay cuts much longer and he wanted to publicize the pilots' views as widely as possible. At this time he abandoned all idea of a strike, if and when the pay cuts became effective, partly because he felt that ALPA's structure was too weak to survive a major strike, but mainly because he wanted to pursue the issue in Washington.[16]

The uneasy truce which had existed between ALPA and the operators since Congressman Mead intervened to win a delay in the pay cuts ended abruptly on February 25, 1933, when a committee of executives from the nation's five largest airlines announced in New York that they were instituting a new, uniform system of hourly pay. All five lines declared that their decision to terminate mileage pay was irrevocable, and they set co-pilot pay at a flat $225 per month, regardless of the number of hours they flew. Three of the "Big Five" were already using the hourly system, but American and United, the two largest, were still paying their pilots on the old mileage basis. The new pay system raised pay very slightly on T&WA, Eastern, and Western Air Express, which were already paying on the hourly scale, but the impact of the new pay policy on United and American was to reduce salaries. United, which always treated its pilots gingerly, announced that there would be no lost pay the first year as a result of the new system of pay computation, be-

cause it would pay the pilots a "bonus" equal to the amount they would have made on the old mileage system. But United's management adamantly insisted that the new hourly method of computing pay was in effect and permanent.[17]

Behncke promptly objected to the new pay method, and he condemned the operators for deceptively calling it a "pay raise" when in fact it was a pay cut. He took a few days off to go to Washington in the hope of enlisting the aid of his friends on the House Post Office Committee, and William Green issued a statement from AFofL headquarters condemning the operators. Green insisted that it was folly for the government to cut the pay of its own employees, thus reflecting Behncke's notion that the airline pilots were "quasi-governmental" employees.[18] The operators had lent credence to this idea by citing cuts in the mail subsidy as their reason for reducing pilot pay. The President of the AFofL seemed genuinely to like Behncke, and the two were on very friendly terms. Green went out of his way to be helpful to ALPA from the very beginning of its connection with the Federation, perhaps because ALPA was one of the few unions to affiliate with it in the bleak years between 1929 and 1933. Green and Behncke shared a common Horatio Alger story background, since both had risen in the world from rural, working-class backgrounds, despite their lack of formal education.[19] But there was little the House Post Office Committee, William Green, or anybody else could do to prevent the operators from changing the basis of pay in the uncertain period before Roosevelt's inauguration. Green promised Behncke that he would use whatever influence he had with the new President,[20] and owing to his efforts Behncke received an invitation to attend a presidential "Industrial and Labor Conference" in Washington on March 31.[21] In the frantic atmosphere of Washington, however, where ardent New Dealers were already busily planning their assault on the depression, there was no place for the leader of a small union to present his case. Other far larger issues were on the minds of official-dom, and Behncke realized that he would have to swim with the tide of events for the time being.

The labor provisions of the National Indus-trial Recovery Act (N.I.R.A.), which the Presi-dent signed on June 16, 1933, were enormously important for organized labor, but for ALPA the vital aspect of the measure lay in its basic as-sumption that cooperation between labor, cap-ital, and the government offered the best solu-tion to the problem of economic collapse. The heart of the Blue Eagle crusade was its insistence that agreements between the various participants in an industry, as stated in an industry-wide "code," could restore prosperity.[22] The Air Trans-portation Code, which became effective on No-vember 27, 1933,[23] had no effect on pilot labor-ers because they were not in it—they wanted no part of it and they fought furiously to avoid any definition of their maximum hours and min-imum wages under the code. Ordinarily it might seem that the code offered an ideal vehicle for ALPA to achieve its goals. But Behncke distrusted airline management more, perhaps, than any other pilot in America. He never evidenced any sign of the managerial mentality which charac-terized so many pilots, and he stubbornly insisted that ALPA adhere to its original objective of spe-cific federal laws covering wages and working conditions of airline pilots. He refused to depend on the good will of airline managers for the sim-ple reason that he did not expect to have their good will very long.[24]

Initially, however, Behncke had to go through the motions of cooperating in the effort of the National Recovery Administration (N.R.A.) to draft a code for the air transportation industry. While many people in the N.R.A. regarded it as a straightforward method for introducing gov-ernment planning into the economy, another faction worried that the charge of "czarism" might discredit their work. General Hugh John-son, the head of the N.R.A., was in a difficult po-sition when it came to the harsh realities of ac-tually hammering out workable codes for each industry. He had grave doubts about the con-stitutionality of the N.I.R.A., and quite early he decided that, in order to avoid court tests, labor and capital would have to voluntarily assent to a code before the N.R.A. could approve it. The N.R.A., then, simply provided a forum at which the bargaining between labor and management could take place.[25]

Prior to coming to Washington for the final approval of a code, both labor and management were supposed to engage in preliminary discus-sions with the assistance of an N.R.A. functionary. General Johnson began the codification process almost as soon as the basic framework of the N.R.A. was operable in June 1933.[26] The June 15, 1933, meeting of ALPA's Central Executive Council was devoted exclusively to discussing the kind of labor provisions the pilots wanted in the Air Transportation Code. Many of the members believed the code could guarantee the kind of wages and working conditions they wanted. Beh-ncke, while not overly critical of the idea, was skeptical and he tried to tone down the enthu-siasm of the council members. He warned that ALPA must exercise extreme caution before com-mitting itself to support of the code.[27] In order to present a united front of all airline labor, Beh-ncke suggested to the July 6 meeting of the Cen-tral Executive Council that ALPA take the lead in forming a "Directorate" of all airline labor groups. Only a few airline workers were fully organized at the time, but Section 7(a) of the N.I.R.A was stimulating the growth of unionization among several groups of unorganized air workers, and Behncke wanted ALPA, as the senior air trans-port union, to occupy a dominant position. After an exceedingly lengthy meeting, however, the Central Executive Council for once failed to act as a rubber stamp for Behncke, and ordered him to concentrate strictly on the part of the code af-fecting pilots. The council decided that if the re-sults of the code discussions with the various op-erating companies were satisfactory, Behncke could then pursue his rather visionary idea of creating an Air Line Labor Executives Association similar to the organization of executives of railroad labor groups.[28]

The code conference which United held with its pilots on July 25 at the Edgewater Beach Hotel in Chicago produced an unexpectedly satisfactory result. United's management was always inclined to be lenient in its dealings with ALPA. The President of United, William A. Patterson, personally represented his company, while J. L. Brandon headed the United pilots' committee, although Behncke was a member. United's various division managers had previously held a series of meetings with their pilots in which they pointed out that changes in working conditions would be necessary with the introduction of the new Boeing 247. While there would be pilot layoffs in the future owing to the greater speed and consequent decrease in the need for pilot crews to fly the new aircraft, Patterson agreed to reemploy his old pilots as soon as possible and to abide by the rule of seniority in doing so. The old basic conflict between pilots and management over who should gain the benefits from improved technology underlay these meetings, however, and Patterson could not agree with the pilots' notion that only by retention of the mileage pay factor could they be fairly recompensed for their increased labor productivity. Patterson necessarily insisted that since the companies took the risk by investing in new aircraft, they, and not labor should reap the rewards. The conference was tense and at times strained, but Patterson's genuine desire to retain good relations with his pilots eased the situation. To prove his good will, Patterson overrode his lower-echelon managers and partially gave in to the pilots on the mileage pay question by agreeing to support some kind of mileage pay increment in the final code.[29]

Although ALPA's victory on United was significant, it was isolated. The Eastern pilots got no satisfaction from their employer, and the Chairman of the Eastern pilots' committee, Wallace S. Dawson, informed Behncke that the company had openly irritated ALPA members by hiring two Century scabs the week before the conference.[30] A few Eastern pilots favored a **wildcat strike** of short duration to protest the hiring of the two **scabs**, but Behncke counseled against it because he thought it would make ALPA appear irresponsible just when N.R.A. officials were studying the industry as a whole.[31] The Eastern pilots accomplished very little in the way of influencing the labor provisions of the code during the conference, which was held from July 28 to August 2, despite the presence of an N.R.A. official to smooth the proceedings. All the other "Big Five," with the exception of United, copied Eastern in refusing to retreat on the hourly pay issue.[32]

Shortly after the code conferences with United and Eastern were completed, Behncke formally requested similar conferences with the remaining airlines. Most of the operators proved reluctant to meet with ALPA, and they suggested that Behncke take his request to their agent, the Aeronautical Chamber of Commerce. The N.R.A.'s policy of dealing mainly with the employers and slighting labor in the initial codification process alarmed Behncke, and he grew increasingly uneasy about the kind of labor provisions the code would eventually contain. Furthermore, he realized that management would undoubtedly dominate the Code Authority which would administer the code. Fearing disaster, Behncke dropped all idea of further negotiations with the individual airlines and instead resorted to the approach he originally favored of taking his case directly to Washington.[33]

In the intervening period, Behncke concentrated on lining up a battery of supporters to testify at the code hearings. He wanted William Green to appear in ALPA's behalf, but the AFofL President was too busy, and as a substitute he arranged for Victor Olander of the Illinois State Federation of Labor to be present.[34] Olander was a lawyer, and Behncke hoped that by having him there ALPA's depleted treasury could be spared the expense of hiring legal help.[35] At Behncke's request, the August 15 meeting of the Central Executive Council named a committee of prominent airline pilots to attend the hearings, among them E. Hamilton Lee, the veteran United pilot who had been one of the principals in the airmail pilots' strike of 1919, and Mal B. Freeburg of Northwest, who had won the first "Air Mail Pilot Medal Of Honor" by saving his aircraft and passengers after a spectacular in-flight explosion and fire.[36] In addition, Dr. Ralph Green, former Chief Medical Examiner for the Department of Commerce and current head of the Aeromedical Association, agreed to testify on behalf of the 80-hour-per-month maximum.[37] A covey of congressmen would speak for ALPA, but Behncke's star witness was to be the nimble and vibrant Fiorello La Guardia, who, despite his liberalism, had been defeated in the Republican debacle of 1932 and was then running for Mayor of New York on a fusion ticket. The hearings promised La Guardia some badly needed public exposure, and he eagerly honored Behncke's plea for help. Behncke secured yet another leave of absence from United, and he was on hand at Washington's National Airport, along with a committee of pilots, to meet La Guardia when he took time out from the mayoralty campaign to fly down. They went into an immediate conference with William Green at AFofL headquarters to plan their strategy during the hearings, which would begin the following day.[38]

When the code hearings convened in the ballroom of the Hotel Mayflower under the supervision of Deputy N.R.A. Administrator Malcolm Muir, Behncke's urgency in assembling his all-star cast of witnesses received immediate justification. The rumors which had been circulating in the aviation trade journals that the operators intended to impose ridiculously high hour and low minimum-wage provisions proved to be true, thus confirming Behncke's worst fears.[39] La Guardia responded with his usual pugnacity

when he discovered that Title III of the operators' proposed code established 140 hours per month as the maximum, and $250 per month as the minimum pay. The industry's spokesman was Frederick W. Coburn, a former President of American Airways, but there were four current airline chiefs in attendance as well. Lester D. Seymour of American denied that management intended to decrease the status or wages of pilots, and he cited Title V of the code, which guaranteed the right of collective bargaining, as proof. The hour and wage provisions, he insisted, were simply minimums and maximums, and he ridiculed the idea that the major operators would ever pay their pilots so little or work them so hard. The particular figures, Seymour maintained, were "fixed with consideration for the smaller operators, at least one of whom now pays his pilots as low as $100 per month." La Guardia displayed his usual histrionics when he attacked Seymour's contentions, and he had a telling argument when he pointed out that, in the codes so far adopted, the working conditions and wages specified usually corresponded very closely to actual conditions.[40] La Guardia's argument struck a responsive chord with most air travelers. There was a rather general uneasiness among airline patrons that the operators might unduly reduce pilot salaries, and the *New York Times* expressed this fear when it pointed out that in the first six months of 1933 the airlines had flown over 25,000,000 passenger miles with only two fatalities. The newspaper attributed this safety record to pilot skill, and it believed that the industry's profit level was secondary in importance to preserving "the highest type of pilot morale."[41] Indicative of the public's support for high pilot salaries, even during the depression, the following day the *New York Times* printed a letter which declared: "If the captain of an ocean greyhound can be called a 'glorified ferryboat skipper,' . . . if an eagle can be called a 'glorified sparrow,' then a scheduled air transport pilot can be called a 'glorified chauffeur.'"[42]

Deputy Administrator Muir, harried and tired and with more important industry codes demanding his immediate attention, was inclined to approve the code despite the various objections to it. As this fact became increasingly clear to Behncke and La Guardia, they decided to press for total exemption of the pilots from the code, rather than take a chance on the hour and wage provisions becoming industry-wide standards. The thrust of their argument was that the pilots were professional workers whose wages and hours were subject to the regulation of the Department of Commerce, and hence they did not belong in the code. In his testimony, Behncke suggested that rather than writing arbitrary standards, the code should instead provide for a "planning, coordinating, and conciliating" committee to study the question of pilot labor. He believed that the committee should have one member each from the N.R.A., the Aeronautical Chamber of Commerce, and the AFofL. He preferred that the committee's recommendations be the subject of direct negotiations between the operators and the pilots. Clearly, Behncke's motive in suggesting this cumbersome arrangement was to obfuscate the issue, to use some last desperate ploy to delay approval of the Code's provisions for pilot labor.[43]

N.R.A. head Johnson, in the meantime, was in a quandary over the Air Transportation Code. It presented curious problems to begin with, because of the close association of business and government, and the pilot labor sections were even more obtuse since the Department of Commerce actually had the statutory power to regulate such things, regardless of what the code said. Malcolm Muir recommended that he accept the code despite the pilots' objections, but Johnson, with his deep fear of court challenges of the N.I.R.A.'s constitutionality, insisted that both sides agree to the code before it received final N.R.A. approval. Since the pilots adamantly refused to accept the code as it was, Muir had no alternative but to accede to their demands and

exempt them from the code altogether.[44] Behncke had demonstrated once again that his appeals to government agencies and officials could be very effective, and the decision to omit the pilots from the code was one of the stepping stones which led to complete victory for the pilots later on.

One of the factors which aided the pilots in this victory was the editorial support of the Hearst newspapers. Hearst was generally antilabor, but aviation fascinated him and for some reason he liked the pilots.[45] Before the code hearings in Washington began, Behncke wrote to the sage of San Simeon to ask for his help. Although Hearst never answered the letter, the Hearst newspapers responded with a series of editorials favorable to the idea of exempting the pilots from the code, notably in the *Washington Daily News*. Behncke always believed that Hearst had personally intervened with Hugh Johnson to help ALPA, and he later told the 1942 convention: "I got in touch with Mr. Hearst, and I don't know to this day what happened, but the next day the air carriers' code . . . was withdrawn and General Johnson announced that the airline pilots were taken out of the Code because theirs was a profession and not just a job."[46]

With ALPA out of the code and the situation highly nebulous, there was no reason for the operators to delay the institution of a national, uniform basis for computing pilot pay on the hourly system. Early in September they formally announced that the new system was in effect and permanent. Behncke had about exhausted his resources of appeal among government officialdom, he had been in Washington continuously for almost two weeks, and he knew his job with United was in jeopardy owing to his absenteeism. The last thing he wanted was another strike, since he knew that it would, in all probability, fail and discredit ALPA in the process. Behncke reassessed his position, frantically telephoned local chairmen around the country, and concluded that while some locals could endure a strike, the majority would collapse. He told the 1934 convention: "I believe that American Airways was the best balanced of all operating companies . . . They were pretty much together and I believe that [they] . . . would have walked out to a man. T&WA would have collapsed completely and I know that on United everything south and east of Chicago would have gone out, and west of Chicago it would have been just a little bit better than half."[47] Still, he could see no alternative to an old-fashioned strike confrontation with the operators over the new pay scale. While hoping that the operators would not call his bluff, he decided to threaten a strike. Behncke set October 1 as the deadline for the operators to restore the mileage system, and in order to dramatize his contention that the strike would be nationwide, he prepared a set of color charts and graphs for use in his news conference showing the geographic extent of the national airline network.[48]

At this point, the kid gloves were off and the bare-knuckles battle between ALPA and the operators was in earnest. A national strike of airline pilots was heady stuff to the press, and it faithfully reported the charges and countercharges which Behncke and the operators traded. Each side declared that the other was trying to force a national strike, and the operators even went so far as to take out full-page advertisements in several newspapers accusing ALPA of trying to wring the neck of the Blue Eagle. Behncke was rapidly developing into a major league polemicist, and he gave as good as he got in the exchanges with airline public relations men. But in one area Behncke was highly vulnerable, he was still only an employee of United, and there were limits to the patience of W. A. Patterson. Disquieting rumors began to reach Behncke that his future with United was in deep jeopardy, and at this time he began to seriously think about devoting full time to ALPA.[49]

Behncke's threat of a national strike moved Secretary of Labor Frances Perkins to arrange a thirty-day truce, which was a godsend for ALPA since it allowed time for maneuver. In the meantime, Behncke tried desperately to get ALPA's

case before the National Labor Board (N.L.B.) of the N.R.A. He believed the board would take the case because a clause in the N.I.R.A stipulated that no industry operating under a code could reduce pay levels below the pre-code level, and he argued that the operators had done precisely this. In formally requesting that the N.L.B. take jurisdiction, Behncke told the board's Secretary, W. M. Leiserson, that the operators were "gradually cutting down on salaries. Now they want us to accept starvation pay."[50]

The function of the N.L.B., composed of three members each from labor and industry, was to iron out disputes which arose over the interpretation of the codes. But as Arthur M. Schlesinger, Jr., said of the N.L.B.: "Its mandate was vague, its procedures were undefined, and its direct power of enforcement, beyond the appeal to public opinion, was nonexistent."[51] On this curious body, however, Behncke staked the entire future of his organization. Fortunately, only he knew that the threat of a strike was a hollow bluff. During the 1934 convention Behncke told the delegates: "The only way you can keep a striking element in line is to keep them informed . . . I figured it would cost $1,000 a day to conduct the strike . . . and our treasury had $5,000 and we would have lasted about five days. After that our communications would have been cut, we would have been completely broke." Furthermore, he admitted that the strike would have caused "a perfect split in our organization that would probably have never been able to mend back together."[52]

In fact, the mere threat of a strike was enough to unravel some of ALPA's locals on T&WA. ALPA's strength on T&WA was always weak, and management had considerable success when it embarked on yet another of its efforts to wreck the union. This time, the company persuaded the Master Executive Council to declare itself independent of the National on the strike issue, and former Master Executive Council Chairman W. A. Golien led the move. While a few ALPA members held out against the company union idea, most of them went along, and ALPA's strength on the line collapsed. There was also considerable restiveness among Eastern pilots because of the proposed strike, and although a company union drive there failed, Behncke had to resist pressure to withdraw the strike decree.[53] But nothing would sway Behncke at this point—the whole ALPA idea was a long desperate shot, he was determined to play the game out, and he exhibited the fanaticism of the confirmed gambler who had nothing to lose. One favorable omen for him was that the major airlines were again making a profit by late 1933, general revenues were up an average 20 percent despite the mail pay cuts, and the operators were, consequently, very reluctant to engage in a ruinous shutdown.[54] Still, they were in a better position to weather the strike than ALPA. Behncke's only real hope, then, was to get the shaky N.L.B. to accept jurisdiction so he could call off the strike before the October 1 deadline revealed ALPA's weakness.

But persuading the N.L.B. to take ALPA's case proved a difficult task, for it was inundated with code disputes and strikes in industries that were far more important than air transportation. During late September, the N.L.B. held all its meetings behind closed doors in order to keep the swarm of persistent leaders of small unions from interfering with its deliberations. William Green was on the N.L.B., but he was ill at the time, and the remaining labor members were either too busy or too tired to bother with ALPA. As the strike deadline neared, and Behncke still had not established contact with the board through conventional methods, he decided to adopt a direct approach and personally seek out one of the members he vaguely knew. Professor Leo Wolman of Columbia University was a member of the N.L.B. whom La Guardia had once introduced to Behncke, and he seemed the likely candidate for a personal contact.[55] Because of the pressure on board members, most of whom had other jobs, their home addresses were kept secret. By following the Professor home after he emerged from a twenty-four-hour N.L.B. session, however, Behncke learned his address. Wol-

man as well as other pro-labor board members had been dodging Behncke for two weeks, and needless to say he was unhappy to see the dogged aviator burst into his living room at ten o'clock at night with a wide-eyed tale of a national pilot strike. But he sat down with Behncke and, after listening to his side of the dispute, agreed to use his influence to get the case before the board. In exchange, Behncke promised to cancel the strike. The exhausted academic then retired, but Behncke spent most of the remainder of the night calling ALPA's local chairmen on his living room telephone.[56] Professor Wolman subsequently persuaded Senator Wagner to contact the "Big Five" with a request that they voluntarily withhold the pay cuts until the N.L.B. could study the situation.[57] Once again, under what had seemed impossible odds, Behncke had staved off defeat.

The N.L.B. began its hearings on the airline pay dispute on October 4, 1933. Behncke, Hamilton, and American's Master Executive Council Chairman Clyde Holbrook represented ALPA, with Victor Olander present to give them legal advice. The presidents of all the "Big Five" plus several executives from smaller lines attended the hearing, bringing with them complete batteries of corporation lawyers. The disparity between the overblown management group and the spare ALPA delegation gave the pilots an underdog's psychological advantage which outweighed the merits of the miles versus hours argument. Hamilton gave most of the oral presentation for ALPA, trying to build a case that the pilots were quasi-governmental employees and, hence, deserving of government protection. With a bow to the ghosts of Grover Cleveland and Richard Olney, Hamilton declared that even should the pilots strike they would "not be a party to retarding the U.S. Mail" but would only refuse to carry passengers and freight. He also used the rhetoric of class warfare in a tub-thumping anticapitalist harangue against the "powerful financial interests that are behind these . . . big operating companies" who were trying to crush "this splendid corps of airline pilots who are . . . going through all kinds of dangers losing one of their number . . . every twenty-nine days, and who incidentally are the first line of defense material in time of war." While he conceded that pilots frequently made more money than airline executives, he maintained that they were nevertheless a group of "mass wage earners" and that they needed special protection in order to retain the high state of morale which was essential to air safety.[58]

Things went poorly for the operators from the beginning, when Senator Wagner and Victor Olander, who were old friends, exchanged just enough banter to make them feel like they were sitting before a hanging judge. In fact, Wagner's predisposition to favor the underdog pilots and his sharp criticism of the airline executives for bringing lawyers to the hearing meant that the pilots were almost certain to receive a favorable verdict from the N.L.B. To make matters worse, the operators allowed their lawyers to begin with the legalistic argument that since the pilots were not in the Air Transport Code, the N.L.B. had no jurisdiction. Wagner replied that the labor policy of the New Deal was to play fair with unions and he rather pointedly hinted: "You are doing government work and I thought you would be first in line." Sensing Wagner's rising irritation at the operators' lawyers, Olander interjected: "If we find ourselves in a position . . . where the opposition presents its case through some distinguished lawyers who are trained in the technique of merely defending their clients, we will not get very far." The Senator agreed and promptly condemned any further "legalistic quibbling." "I am a member of the law profession myself," he said, "but we are always looking for technicalities and we can do better when these technical gentlemen are not around at all." A lawyer representing American quickly succeeded in antagonizing Wagner further by beginning his presentation with the courtroom pleasantry that he regretted "bothering gentlemen like you and asking for your intervention in a matter like this when there are so many other affairs . . . which should be

taken care of." Wagner virtually exploded: "Nobody's rights are too small to be taken care of. I do not know whether you understand that!" "Nothing is greater than the individual's rights and the smaller he is . . . the more he needs our help."[59]

The nervous airline executives squirmed as their lawyers, who were supposed to keep them out of trouble, only succeeded in getting them in deeper. In an effort to discredit ALPA, T&WA's lawyers declared that most of their pilots had resigned from the union and that it could not, therefore, speak for them. Behncke was prepared for this argument, and he called attention to a petition which a majority of T&WA pilots had previously signed designating ALPA as their bargaining agent. He denounced T&WA's labor policies and declared that the line's executives were intimidating pilots and pressuring them to resign from ALPA. He asked Senator Wagner to consider the case of T&WA pilot Wayne Williams, who was present in the room, who had been fired when he refused to cease his organizational work on behalf of ALPA. Senator Wagner was immediately interested in Williams's case because it personalized the issue, and he asked the T&WA lawyer, whose name was Henry M. Hogan, to explain his position in the light of Behncke's signed petition. Hogan declared that many of the T&WA pilots had resigned from ALPA since signing the petition, and the subsequent exchange between Senator Wagner and the lawyer ruined the operators:

WAGNER: How did you happen to see them?

HOGAN: Because I have seen copies of some letters of resignation.

WAGNER: How did you happen to see them?

HOGAN: Because I represent the company . . . and the letters were sent to us . . .

WAGNER: You are not an officer of the Association. Why should they send letters to you? How did they know the company was interested in them . . . ?

HOGAN: I imagine if you were a pilot you could answer that.

WAGNER: What? No. It might indicate that the company was evidencing a little interest in their resigning.

THOMAS B. DOE: [President of North American Aviation]: We are interested in everything they do, Senator.

WAGNER: That is something you ought not to be interested in because it is none of your business. When a man working for a concern is a member of a union and he resigns from that union and then hurries to tell his employer—well now, I am not a child . . . Wayne Williams was discharged for no other reason than his activity in organizing the pilots . . . That sort of thing must stop . . . If certain rights are given to them under the law, to organize, the government should not permit employers to discriminate against them . . . You must understand that this is a new era. There is an equality of rights that we must take into consideration. We are not living in an old century.[60]

The operators were beaten at this point, and all they could do was try to minimize their losses. Almost in chorus the airline representatives began to sing the praises of their pilots. Ernest R. Breech, a lawyer for Eastern, declared: "I for one will never subscribe to paying these fellows chauffeurs's wages because they are the greatest salesmen we have." J. Bruce Kremer, a managerial spokesman for United, added: "Candidly, knowing their fearless spirit, I think a man shows a great deal of temerity who tries to intimidate any one of them." Unimpressed, Wagner replied that it did not take much courage to fire a man, and he insisted that the pilots must receive fair treatment or he would see to it that the airlines received no more "liberal mail subsidies." He ordered T&WA to reinstate Wayne Williams immediately, and he appointed a special fact-finding board, to be composed of Behncke, Lester D. Seymour of American, and Judge Bernard L. Shientag of the New York Supreme Court, to study the pay question. He required that the committee report its findings to the N.L.B. within three weeks, and he asked the airlines to voluntarily retain the mileage

pay system until then. Considering the Senator's irate mood, the airline executives would probably have agreed to anything just to get out of the disastrous hearing.[61]

The fact-finding committee was essentially a device whereby Behncke and Seymour could present their views to a neutral, Judge Shientag, who would then make a decision. Each side could call witnesses, and the operators scored an initial victory when Eugene Vidal, Director of the Bureau of Air Commerce, agreed to testify in behalf of the hourly pay system.[62] There were a number of complex factors in the hearing, which was held on October 27 and 28 in New York City, but the essential conflict came over ALPA's contention that increased speed meant increased hazard, and that accidents were a function of the number of miles flown, rather than the number of hours flown. From this notion, Behncke could argue that the pilots should be paid on the mileage system because of the risks involved.[63] Vidal demolished this argument in his testimony, correctly pointing out that most accidents occurred on takeoff or landing and that the new aircraft, while they flew faster when cruising at altitude, actually had lower landing and takeoff speeds than the old trimotored aircraft. Before Judge Shientag, the operators were at last able to take advantage of their expensive legal talent. They presented an exhaustive series of charts and legal briefs showing that airline stockholders were sacrificing current profits in order to invest in the new aircraft, and that the stockholders, rather than the pilots, deserved the productivity gains which accrued from investing the risk capital. The presidents of all five major airlines assured Judge Shientag that they "considered their pilots in a class at least semi-professional and out of self interest wished to maintain their morale at a high level." They argued that pilot pay would average $6,000 per year under the hourly system and might go as high as $9,000 per year in some cases. To bolster their contention that this amount was satisfactory, they produced the startling information that the master of the largest ocean liner in America's merchant fleet, the 2,600 pssenger Leviathan, earned only $6,000 per year. To refute ALPA's contention that the new aircraft were more difficult to fly, the operators submitted letters from famous aviators Wiley Post and Captain Frank M. Hawks, declaring that the new aircraft were easier to fly. Post said that he accomplished a ten-hour flight in a Boeing 247 "without noticeable mental or physical fatigue."[64] The pilots looked bad in the exchange, and Behncke later ruefully admitted: "they really ganged up on us that time."[65]

Fearing that Seymour was winning the argument, Behncke asked that a "scientific study" be made of the safety factor by the Department of Labor. He had a naive faith in "statistics," and he believed that the Department of Labor would render a "good report because they would only deal with the facts, there would be no politics . . . it would be submitted to their statisticians . . . and they would make a report."[66] Judge Shientag leaned to the operators' side, but he decided he could not make a final decision on the available facts, so he returned the controversy to the N.L.B. suggesting that "the rates proposed by the operators should continue without prejudice to the contentions of the respective parties, pending a prompt, thorough, and scientific investigation . . . to be made by a government agency to be designated by the N.L.B."[67]

The Shientag decision was a blow to Behncke, but Senator Wagner reprieved him by rejecting the report. The Senator wanted a clear-cut decision, once and for all. He was tired of studies and investigations and inconclusive disputation. He allowed the operators to begin paying on the "new standardized scale," retroactive to October 1, but he warned them that the final decision, regardless of the fact-finding committee's views, would rest with the N.L.B. itself.[68]

Thinking they had won, the operators did not mount a second major offensive to influence Judge Shientag. Only Lester D. Seymour of Amer-ican came to the second meeting, held in mid-November, and he left the floor largely to Behncke. Behncke later remarked that he felt ALPA had scored well in the second hearing because "I could argue and Eddie [Hamilton] could figure." But Behncke's forensic talents were a dubious advantage, and Judge Shientag was less impressed with the substance of the debate than with the obvious fact that he would have to arrive at some kind of compromise in order to satisfy the N.L.B. He was in poor health, suffering from heart disease, and he wished to rid himself of the troublesome case. In order to resolve the question he simply combined the basic hourly pay (which would increase with the speed of the aircraft), with a very small mileage increment, and called it a compromise. In similar fashion, the Judge resolved the hours per month question by splitting the difference between the operators' preference for a ninety-hour limit and ALPA's preference for an eighty-hour limit. Needless to say, Seymour, representing all the operators, was horrified at this turn of events. What had originally shaped up as a sparkling victory for the operators had inexplicably turned into something quite different. Shientag's report represented a clear retreat from his first position in favor of straight hourly pay, and Seymour refused to sign it. Although the report established an hourly component, Behncke was willing to accept it because it was geared to the speed of the aircraft and therefore gave pilots a share of the increased productivity. Principles aside, Behncke later admitted that he liked the report because "the amount [of money] was not so bad and that is the controlling factor in a thing like that."[69]

The N.L.B. subsequently spent about two weeks converting Judge Shientag's report into a definite wage formula, and when Senator Wagner summoned all interested parties to Washington for a conference on December 14, the reluctant operators had no alternative but to attend. Wagner, however, still operating under the Johnsonian policy that labor and management must, if at all possible, voluntarily assent to all N.R.A. decisions, insisted that the pilots and the operators meet one last time to iron out their difficulties. The meeting which took place on December 15 in the Mayflower Hotel produced no general agreement, except that both sides acknowledged that there had to be *some* limit on the number of miles a pilot could fly each month, regardless of whether an hourly or mileage system of pay prevailed. The operators were well aware of the problems involved in Judge Shientag's complicated system of pay computation, but there was little they could do about it. After the meeting broke down, Behncke formally requested binding arbitration by the N.L.B. because he believed that it would favor ALPA.[70]

Behncke had been in either New York or Washington almost continuously since August, and he had not flown enough for United to remain "current," according to Department of Commerce regulations. When he returned to Chicago for the Christmas holidays, United fired him, claiming that his repeated absences had made it necessary to fill his position. Whatever good will once existed between Behncke and Patterson had long since disappeared in the heat of repeated confrontations. While Patterson probably expected to face Behncke across the bargaining table for years to come, he was not particularly anxious to continue to paying his salary while doing so. Behncke did not intend to lose his job without a fight, and he lined up support from Green, Olander, and several Congressmen in an effort to have the N.L.B. reinstate him. Mayor Edward J. Kelly of Chicago, who owed the Chicago Federation of Labor a great deal, also offered to come to Washington to testify in his behalf. Simultaneously with United's dismissal of Behncke, T&WA raised the absurd claim that ALPA was connected with the Chicago underworld. As proof, T&WA complained to the N.L.B. that pro-ALPA "elements" had assaulted one of its anti-ALPA pilots in the parking lot of the Newark Airport. Despite this climate of recrimination,

however, Behncke successfully presented his case to the N.L.B., and, on January 18, Senator Wagner ordered his reinstatement.[71]

Judge Shientag's compromise report eventually emerged as Decision 83 of the N.L.B. and it was, as a leading expert on airline labor relations has said, "without doubt . . . the most far-reaching ruling ever issued in the air line labor field."[72] Because it embodied both mileage pay and an hourly pay rate which increased as the speed of the aircraft increased, it guaranteed the pilots a huge share of the productivity gains associated with improved aircraft technology. The essentials of this pay formula still apply to airline pilots today.[73] But perhaps even more importantly, for the first time the airline pilots had persuaded an agency of the federal government to grant them special protection. In a sense, Behncke won his argument that the pilots were "quasi-governmental employees." Although Behncke would later score a stunning victory in keeping Decision 83 in the Air Mail Act of 1934, the fight over pay scale would always remain the classic example of his effectiveness in obtaining his goals through appeals to Washington.

Two Labor Laws Are One Too Many[*]

The Machinist strike at Eastern Airlines may touch off a big labor battle in Congress—but over an issue that is much narrower than the real problem. If the International Association of Machinists (IAM) sets up picket lines at railroads and other airlines, President Bush will demand that Congress amend the Railway Labor Act—which covers airline and railroad employees—to outlaw secondary picketing. The government's concern about widespread travel disruptions is understandable. But a better solution would be to dismantle the RLA, along with its obsolete strike-avoidance procedures, and transfer airline and railroad employees to the National Labor Relations Act, which covers all other private-industry employees.

*Reprinted from March 20, 1989 issue of *Business Week* by special permission, copyright © 1989 by McGraw-Hill, Inc.

The fact is that this dualism in federal labor law creates two classes of workers and employees, with different rights and duties. Under the NLRA, workers are prohibited from engaging in secondary picketing, while the RLA allows it. But an equally significant difference arises out of the provisions governing collective bargaining. The 1935 NLRA encourages "good faith" bargaining but for the most part stands aside and lets the two sides fight it out. The government intervenes only in cases of national emergency.

The purpose of the RLA, on the contrary, was to use the powers of the government to prevent strikes by union members. Back in 1926, when the Act was passed, big rail strikes could disrupt the national economy. But the RLA's cumbersome provisions, including conciliation by the National Mediation Board and numerous meaningless deadlines, permitted endless stalling. These procedures are largely responsible for the mess at Eastern and actually impede collective bargaining. Thirteen months lapsed before the NMB declared an impasse in the IAM-Eastern talks, and some bargaining rounds have lasted much longer.

The protracted negotiations at Eastern allowed by the NMB also have been criticized by Frank Lorenzo, chairman of Eastern's owner, Texas Air, but his confrontational tactics in dealing with unions only serve to damage the process. Even after the NMB's procedures have been exhausted, the President may delay a strike for 60 days by appointing an emergency board to recommend a settlement, which either side may reject. At that point, Congress normally steps in and mandates the settlement terms. The undesirable result then becomes collective bargaining by edict.

Call to Revisit Railway Labor Act Receives Mixed Reactions from Parties[*]

National Mediation Board member Patrick Cleary's recommendation that a panel be created to consider possible changes in the Railway Labor Act has drawn mixed reactions, but most observers agree that labor and management are far from a consensus on changes in the law that they might support.

Major interest in revisiting the law appears to be confined to the railroad industry, although the statute governs collective bargaining in the airline industry as well. Discontent with the prolonged process for settling contract disputes under the RLA has come to the fore as Congress has been forced to intervene to end railroad shutdowns twice in the last year. In both instances, the disputes involved efforts to resolve contracts that had been open for renegotiation since 1988.

Noting that the RLA came into being in 1926 only after representatives of both labor and management agreed on its framework, several practitioners said that it may require a similar consensus before any proposed changes are given serious consideration.

Even though congressional leaders grumble about the RLA when faced with a rail strike and calls for intervention on Capital Hill, they are not considered likely to propose changes in the system unless labor or management representatives themselves put forward some recommendations.

In a July 12 speech to railroad industry officials, Cleary, who served as NMB chairman until July 1 and remains a board member, urged formation of a panel to consider whether changes should be recommended. That panel, said Cleary, should include representatives of labor and management, as well as academics and lawmakers (135 DLRA-11, 7/14/92). He said that such a group would ideally be formed on the initiative of labor and management and urged Congress to consider only those changes on which both parties have agreed.

Cleary's recommendations were expressions of his personal viewpoint, and other members of the three-member board have not taken a position on his suggestions.

Representatives of railroad associations called

Cleary's recommendation premature since railroad negotiations that were the subject of back-to-work legislation adopted by Congress in June are still underway. That process will be concluded by early August with either voluntary agreements or an arbitrator's selection of final proposals for settlement.

Several railroad union representatives, meanwhile, viewed the recommendations with skepticism. Although rail union leaders would like to see changes in the law to clearly define the right to strike and provide a means for bringing negotiations and mediation to a speedier conclusion, they see little prospect for agreement with the carriers over how to change the law.

The Air Line Pilots Association (ALPA), on the other hand, sees nothing wrong with the RLA and maintains the view that "if it ain't broke, don't fix it." Even convening a group such as Cleary suggested would be considered a "waste of time" by ALPA, a spokesman for the union said.

Railroad Union's Priorities

Although rail union leaders appeared willing to participate on a panel to review the law, they considered the veto power over proposed changes a vital condition for union participation.

Thomas DuBose, president of the United Transportation Union, remarked that if someone "can't recognize [the RLA] is broke, than their eyesight is bad."

He said that the UTU, which claims to represent 90 percent of the operating employees in the railroad industry, would favor re-examination of the law provided that such a review is not aimed at "providing relief for the industry" or at forcing the parties to begin paying arbitration costs and eliminating the government-financed system of grievance adjustment provided under the RLA.

"If it's in the public interest to prevent railroad strikes, it is also in the public interest to pay arbitration costs" to resolve disputes, DuBose said.

He said the UTU would not dismiss recommendations for compulsory arbitration as a means for reaching contract agreements since "Congress is never going to let railroad unions exercise Self-Help." DuBose added, however, that the UTU would agree to such a system only if several other issues were addressed as well, such as adequate funding for arbitration of major and minor disputes, creation of a neutral, non-political body to encourage agreements, and protection for workers whose jobs are eliminated in railroad line sales.

Robert J. Irvin, president of the American Train Dispatchers Association and secretary-treasurer of the Railway Labor Executives' Association, said that compulsory arbitration is among the changes that he would oppose. Irvin said he would also oppose amending the RLA to prohibit secondary boycotts or revise the current union-shop rule.

Although Irvin said he would favor revisions in the law to prevent the president and Congress from intervening in rail labor disputes, he said he thinks that "the gains labor might get would not be worth the price of the trade-offs" management would demand in exchange.

Jedd Dodd, general chairman of the Pennsylvania Federation of the Brotherhood of Maintenance of Way Employees and a frequent critic of the current bargaining structure, suggested that the right to call a secondary boycott under RLA could be exchanged by the unions for protection against permanent replacement of strikers. That change should be coupled with defining the strike "as an absolute right," putting a cap on the duration of mediation, and providing full cost-of-living adjustments for the period in mediation, Dodd said.

Dodd said the law "definitely needs to be re-examined." He added, however, that he is doubtful that his concept of how it should be changed would be shared by the carriers or others outside of the labor movement.

"It is difficult to envision" how labor and management could reach agreement on revising the law, Irvin said, observing that "they can't agree on anything else."

Railroad Association Views

"I think everyone is asking is there a better way," said Edwin Harper, president of the American Association of Railroads, who agreed with chief railroad industry negotiator Charles Hopkins that it is premature to seek formation of a group to examine the law. "Our first priority is to complete the 1988 round of negotiations," he said.

Harper suggested that informal discussions between labor and management would be a better approach to examining the law than appointment of a formal commission. Cleary's proposal, he noted, recognizes that "if labor and management don't both subscribe" to any potential revisions, "it probably is not worth pursuing."

Officials of CSX Corp. think that the process could be re-examined, said a spokesman for the carrier, where a strike by the International Association of Machinists touched off a two-day nationwide rail shutdown in June when other carriers locked out workers.

"If you measure the RLA's success in preventing strikes, it has been pretty effective," said spokesman Lynn Johnson, who said that CSX has experienced just three days of strikes in the last ten years. When viewed from the perspective of how quickly the process works, however, CSX officials believe the process needs some changes. "The process takes too long," Johnson said. "negotiations can't be very productive after four or five years of posturing for a fight." He said that CSX officials who have considered the issue are less certain about how they would change the law, but added that binding arbitration is not an approach they prefer.

Officials of Burlington Northern Railroad have also said that re-examination of the law may be warranted.

Many other carriers are believed to share the sentiments expressed by Robert Schmiege, chief executive officer of the Chicago and North Western Transportation Company, in a letter following a one-day rail strike in 1991. In the letter to then-AAR President Michael Walsh, Schmiege disputed the notion that "more economically advantageous settlements" could be achieved if the RLA were revised and the unions right to strike made easier.

The RLA, Schmiege wrote, "is remarkably effective at preventing unions from achieving the legal right to strike." He argued that the current law "remains the best alternative as a legal framework to govern railroad labor relations."

No Push from Air Carriers

Robert DeLucia, vice-president of the Air Conference, sees "no push to change the act" coming from the airline industry. He added, however, "If they start the ball rolling we may get swept up in it." It would be premature to speculate about whether the airline industry would want changes in the law, he said, but the industry "will want to be a player" if a re-examination of the law gets under way. In any event, no group such as the one envisioned by Cleary is likely to be convened until after the November election, DeLucia said.

Cleary suggested that any panel convened to examine the law might consider whether railroads and airlines should continue to be covered under the same labor law given the "vast differences in the operations of these two modes of transportation."

DeLucia and several others who commented on Cleary's recommendation, however, said negotiations in the airline and railroad industries currently are treated differently under the law. There has been no presidential emergency board appointed to resolve a contract dispute in the airline industry since 1966, DeLucia said. He explained that different structures for bargaining in the industries are responsible for their different experiences under the law. In the airline industry, said DeLucia, unions and carriers bargain individually, while industry-wide negotiations involving multiple carriers and multiple unions are common in the railroad industry.

The appointment of presidential emergency boards to recommend settlement of disputes has been common in the railroad industry, and that opens the door to congressional intervention after cooling-off periods expire and the unions become free to strike. Under the RLA, the NMB can recommend appointment of an emergency board when a bargaining impasse threatens "substantially to interrupt interstate commerce to a degree such as to deprive any section of the country of essential transportation service."

Congress' Role In Rail Bargaining

Herbert R. Northrup, professor emeritus of management at the University of Pennsylvania's Wharton School, and a longtime critic of the RLA, said that "getting Congress to intervene has become part of the system" of railroad negotiations under the law.

The procedures established under the act, including the requirement that the parties maintain the status quo, the NMB's power to indefinitely hold the parties in mediation, and the potential for further government intervention through presidential emergency boards and congressional action, prevent real bargaining, Northrup said.

"To prepare for bargaining and to prepare for intervention require quite different approaches. If one expects intervention . . . it is often wiser to ask for more than expected and to yield nothing," Northrup wrote in the *Harvard Journal of Law and Public Policy* in the spring of 1990.

Northrup, who said he has been pointing out the flaws in the RLA for 50 years, held out little hope that they will be remedied by agreement of the parties, as Cleary suggested. "It is always going to be premature" to re-examine the law in view of the leaders of rail unions and carrier associa-

tions, Northrup said. They have a "vested interest in the status quo." "Something should be done" to change the system, according to Northrup, who contends that there is no justification for a separate law to cover labor relations in the two transportation industries. It is "special privilege" legislation, he added.

Robert O. Harris, a former NMB member appointed during the Carter administration said that in the airline industry, the RLA functions much as the NLRA does in other industries. One major distinction between the two statutes, he said, is the NMB's power to hold airline negotiations in mediation for an indefinite period beyond the reopening of the contract. That difference, however, benefits the airline industry because a finite date for a strike would bring a significant drop in advance bookings with each contract expiration date, Harris said.

Re-examination Requires Nudge

"There is a historical basis for hoping" that leaders of labor and management "would be able to step forward" and agree on a re-examination of the law, said Robert B. McKersie of the Sloan School at Massachusetts Institute of Technology, but he added it is doubtful that we will see that right away.

"I think it will have to be nudged" if a coalition is to be formed to consider changes in the law, McKersie said. Initiatives by government agencies, such as a staff-level examination underway at the Department of Transportation, will be "needed to stir the pot," he said. "If somebody else gets things going," McKersie said he would not rule out rail labor and management coming to an agreement on changes they would like to see made.

Harris said that Cleary's initiative fails to consider the possibility that a Democratic president could be elected this year. Union dissatisfaction is the product of "who is president, not the workings of the law," said Harris. A Democratic president, he said, would be more likely to apply pressure for a settlement before a dispute reaches the point of impasse. "If there was somebody in there pushing for settlement, things would have been different" in the recent rail disputes, said Harris, who chaired the presidential emergency board convened last year to recommend settlement of union contract disputes with major freight carriers. He also headed the special panel that ultimately imposed those recommendations as new contract terms after a one-day strike in 1991 that ended with congressional intervention.

With the exception of the Carter administration, no Democrat has reached the White House for more than 20 years, Harris said. He likened the current situation facing rail labor and management to a "boil growing for more than 20 years and finally lanced." "After the wound heals" is time enough to examine the issue, he said, suggesting that the parties should take a look at it in 1993. If they still feel the "system is no longer functioning," then a re-examination of the RLA might be warranted, he said. Making recommendations that the law be re-examined "before the dust has settled" from the current railroad disputes was not "terribly wise," Harris said.

Emergency Board Agreement

He noted that creation of the emergency board appointed last year to recommend settlement of the unions' contract dispute with major freight carriers was unprecedented because rail labor and management representatives agreed in advance to send the unresolved issues to an emergency board. In addition, the parties agreed on an extended period for the panel to consider the issues and even on who would serve on the board, Harris said.

The International Association of Machinists refused to join in the agreement, leaving that union's negotiations for a new contract with the major freight carriers still to be resolved this year and setting the stage for the recent strike by IAM against CSX.

Combining the unresolved issues in talks with all the rail unions and sending them to a single presidential emergency board in 1991 "was a terrible mistake," Harris said. He said that the initial agreement on forming the board was reached with the understanding that only the common health and welfare issues would be considered, but later all unresolved contract issues were put to the three member board. The agreement to let the board make the decisions on those issues, he said, "was abrogation of responsibility by the unions and the carriers."

Walter Wallace, a Reagan administration NMB appointee who left the board in 1990, made a similar assessment, calling the agreement on sending the open issues to the Board premature: "They agreed too quickly to go to an emergency board, and they shouldn't have done that," said Wallace, who defended the RLA as a process that promotes collective bargaining. About 98 percent of all contracts coming open under RLA are settled, Wallace said, but it's the exceptions to that rule that "get all the headlines."

Wallace said he was appalled that Cleary would make recommendations calling for review of the RLA because NMB members traditionally have maintained a low profile on the principle that you cannot be an effective mediator while also taking positions on legislative issues. Suggesting that the underpinnings of the RLA need to be examined destabilizes the bargaining process, said Wallace. "Any thought about such changes," Wallace said, is particularly inappropriate when Congress has just adopted a process to resolve the final railroad disputes.

Harris agreed that an NMB member should refrain from making recommendations about labor policy, but several members of the academic community found Cleary's recommendations appropriate. DeLucia, of the Air Conference, said the suggestions are consistent with Cleary's actions as NMB chairman calling for studies of various board procedures. "I don't see any reason he shouldn't at least raise the issue," DeLucia said.

Review of Rail Industry Suggested

Examining the railroad industry and the structure of the unions that represent its employees may be more important than revisiting the RLA, McKersie said. Too many unions are competing with one another in the industry, he said, and employee morale is so poor that it's difficult to introduce new cooperative programs that could improve labor-management relations. "Perhaps a commission to examine the bedrock of the industry" should be convened, he said. Such a group could also look at basic public policy concerns under the RLA, including the threat of secondary boycotts and the "very important Self-Help issues," he said.

Suggesting that "we have passed the phase where the unions' right to strike can be allowed" on the nation's freight railroads, McKersie said that "if we can't tolerate strikes" perhaps we should build a procedure into the law so Congress doesn't have to fashion a remedy each time there is a strike.

Morgan Reynolds, a professor at Texas A&M University, greeted Cleary's recommendation enthusiastically. The RLA "has outlived its usefulness if it ever had any," Reynolds said. He recommended that it be scrapped with the industries it covered brought under the National Labor Relations Act. "It is absurd to call the RLA structure free collective bargaining," Reynolds said. Railroad management does not know how to win a strike and the rail labor unions are frustrated by their inability to strike under the current system.

Short of repealing the law, he said, secondary picketing should be "explicitly banned" and a statement of "government neutrality" should be added to the RLA with a prohibition against the president or Congress intervening in labor disputes. Reynolds also said that parties to the collective bargaining agreements in the railroad industry should be required to pay for the administrative services they receive.

While Reynolds and Northrup called for repeal of the RLA and placing the railroad and airline industries under the NLRA, Wallace warned that such a move would "create a period of instability" that could be especially damaging to the airline industry. Dodd of the BMWE remarked that switching to the NLRA "would be preferable to the situation unions face under RLA. Under the NLRA, the parties would have to bargain in good-faith!

Part 2

4

Elections, Certifications, and Procedures

Introduction

The election and certification process under the RLA and the NLRA require an understanding of the bargaining unit from an employees' point of view. The two acts are broad in nature and are federally mandated, but their coverage does not necessarily extend to all employers or employees. This chapter specifies the jurisdiction of the various statutes of both acts. Whether workers, unions, and employers are covered by the provisions of the acts depends on the statutory definitions of the terms *interstate commerce*, *employer*, and *employee*.

Interstate Commerce

The Supreme Court has defined commerce in a series of cases in which the federal government has the ability to apply legislation affecting industries that are engaged in interstate commerce. The interpretation of Article I, Section 8, of the Constitution, was challenged in the case of *Gibbons v Ogden*. The interpretation of "Congress shall have the power to regulate commerce with foreign nations, and among the several States, and with Indian Tribes" was clarified by Chief Justice Marshall's court opinion: "It is the power to regulate; that is, to prescribe the rule by which commerce is to be governed. This power, like all others vested in Congress, is complete in itself, may be exercised to its utmost extent and acknowledge no limitation, other than in the Constitution."[1] The cases that followed established the authority and constitutionality of Congress to enact the RLA and the NLRA.[2]

In enacting these two sets of labor legislation, Congress applied the rulings of commerce and extended the definition to mean interstate commerce. The reach of the acts was based on the Supreme Court rulings of what affected commerce. This extended definition of commerce, when applied to the two labor acts, implied and established that business must be conducted across state lines. Products do not have to be physically shipped across state lines. It is sufficient that raw materials, power, or communications are used between states. The operating agencies of the two acts, the National Mediation Board (NMB) and the National Labor Relations Board (NLRB), were therefore given authority to exercise their jurisdiction over all but the smallest of businesses or airlines, particularly those airlines operating as interstate carriers only. So pervasive is the coverage under the interstate commerce definition that the NLRB has found it necessary to limit its jurisdiction. Table 4-1 lists the jurisdictional limitations imposed by the NLRB.

The Process under the Railway Labor Act

Employees Subject to the RLA

The RLA expressly includes in its definition of *employee* every person in the service of a carrier who performs the work of a "subordinate official." This definition is in direct contradiction with that of the NLRA, which excludes "any in-

Table 4-1

Jurisdictional Standards of the National Labor Relations Board

Jurisdiction	Standard
Nonretail business	Direct sales of goods to consumers in other states or indirect sales through others (called outflow) of at least $50,000 annually; or direct purchases of goods from suppliers in other states or indirect purchases through others (called inflow) of at least $50,000 annually
Retail firms, hotels, motels, residential apartment houses, and taxicab companies	At least $50,000 total annual volume of business. Where the employer may own more than one facility in one or more states, the dollar volume from all plants or locations is totaled to determine the annual dollar volumes of business
Office buildings	Total annual revenue of $100,000, of which $25,000 or more is derived from organizations that meet any of the standards except the indirect outflow and inflow standards established for nonretail enterprises
Public utilities	At least $250,000 total annual volume of business, or $50,000 direct or indirect outflow or inflow
Newspapers	At least $200,000 total annual volume of business
Radio, telegraph, television, and telephone enterprises	At least $100,000 total annual volume of business
Transit systems, law firms, and day care centers	At least $250,000 total annual volume of business
Transportation enterprises, links and channels of interstate commerce	At least $50,000 total annual income from furnishing interstate passenger and freight transportation services; also performing services valued at $50,000 or more for businesses that meet any of the jurisdictional standards except the indirect outflow and inflow standards established for nonretail enterprises
Privately operated health care institutions	At least $250,000 total annual volume of business for hospitals, at least $100,000 for nursing homes, visiting nurses associations, and related facilities; at least $250,000 for all other types of private health care institutions defined in the 1974 amendments to the act. The statutory definition includes "any hospital, convalescent hospital, health maintenance organization, health clinic, nursing home, extended care facility, or other institution devoted to the care of the sick, infirm, or aged person." Public sector hospitals are excluded from the jurisdiction of the National Labor Relations Board.
Associations	The annual business of all association members is totaled to determine if the association itself in its role as employer meets the appropriate dollar standard (e.g., retail association, health care association, hotel association, etc.).
National defense	The act covers all enterprises affecting commerce when their operations have a substantial impact on national defense, regardless of whether the enterprise meets any other dollar jurisdictional standard.
Private universities and colleges	At least $1 million gross annual revenue from all sources (excluding contributions not available for operating expenses because of limitations imposed by the donor)

Source: Data from *A Guide to Basic Law and Procedures under the National Labor Relations Act* (Washington, D.C.: U.S. Government Printing Office, 1976).

dividual employed as a supervisor." Consequently, under the RLA, foremen and other members of the supervisory staff are considered employees and have the attendant rights of self-organization, representation, and freedom from interference and coercion by employers.

The term *subordinate official* was applicable to the railroad industry when the RLA was enacted. It was never a part of airline labor terminology. Consequently, the majority of cases questioning the definition and duties of a subordinate official come from the airline industry. As a result, the NMB adjudicates these particular questions.[3]

Unfortunately, the NMB has a history of deciding these questions on an ad hoc basis that tends to reflect the attitudes and political leanings of the board members then serving. The board has never developed a specific and consistent definition for *subordinate official*. The board does, however, tend to follow the argument that the union attempting to organize a particular segment carries the burden of proof if and when the employer puts the status of individuals in question by asserting that they are managers who do not "perform work as an employee or subordinate official."[4] The board's present position is that "the burden of proof required to persuade the Board to overrule the mediator's preliminary determination rests with the carrier or organization appealing the determination."[5]

Employers Subject to the RLA

Title I of the RLA defines railroad carriers by reference to the Interstate Commerce Act, and Title II extends the RLA to "every common carrier by air engaged in interstate or foreign commerce, and every carrier by air transporting mail for or under contract with the United States Government." Where no U.S. mail is transported, purely intrastate operations are not subject to the NMB's jurisdiction. Likewise, the board's authority over international carriers does not transcend the territorial boundaries of the United States, and only employees and carriers actually working and operating in the United States or its territories may be covered.

Organizing Employees under the RLA

Under the RLA, the NMB is charged with the responsibility of certifying the representatives of the employees' choice. This responsibility of action is exclusive and nonrenewable.[6] The decision of the board in certification determinations is authoritative.

In determining who is eligible to represent employees, the RLA defines *representative* as "any person or persons, labor union, organization, or corporation designated either by a carrier or group of carriers or by its or their employees, to act for it or them."[7] The duties of the board with respect to the selection of employee representatives are defined as follows:

If any dispute shall arise among a carrier's employees as to who are the representatives of such employees . . . it shall be the duty of the Mediation Board, upon request of either party to the dispute, to investigate such a dispute and to certify to both parties, in writing, the name or names of the individuals or organizations that have been designated and authorized to represent the employees involved in the dispute, and certify the same to the carrier. . . . In such an investigation, the Mediation Board shall be authorized to take a secret ballot of the employees involved, or to utilize any other appropriate method of ascertaining the names of their duly designated and authorized representatives in such a manner as shall insure the choice of representatives by the employees without interference, influence, or coercion exercised by the carrier.[8]

Procedures of the National Mediation Board

The duties outlined in the preceding quote from Section 2, Ninth, of the NMB rules set forth the activities and procedures to be followed by the board in certification proceedings. Figure 4-1 shows the steps required for certification under the RLA. A list and discussion of each pro-

Figure 4-1. Railway Labor Act representation process

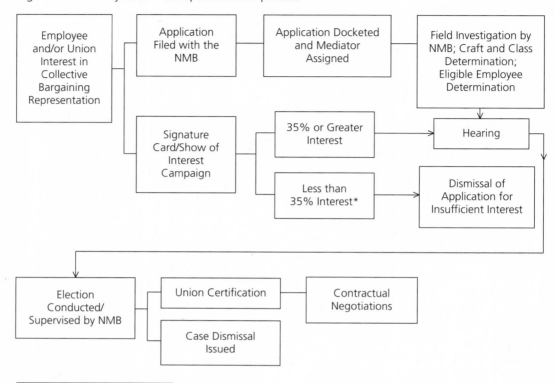

*At least a majority of the craft or class is required if the employees are represented by another union.

cedure follows, in the order in which the procedures are implemented by the board.

Disputes. The NMB is only responsible for disputes concerning representation. In such disputes, only the employees or employee groups are party to any question of representation. The employer has no statutory rights as a party, and the Supreme Court has explicitly held that the employer is not entitled to be heard at any proceedings convened to resolve the dispute.[9] Consequently, the employer has no role or voice in determining the existence of a dispute. In contrast, an employer is an "interested party" under the NLRA and may, under certain circumstances, initiate an investigation by petitioning the NLRB.[10]

Section 2, Ninth, of the RLA states that the employer's involvement may consist of only providing information necessary to determine eli-

gibility of employees or, in the worst case scenario, to commit a practice determined to be interference with an employee's right of selection.

Application. Figure 4-2 is the NMB application for representation, and figure 4-3 is a sample NMB **authorization card**.

Application procedures are specified at Section 1203.2 of the RLA and provide that application cards must be received from interested parties along with a formal application from the party interested in representing the employees. Contained in the application must be the name or description of the craft or class of employees involved, the name of the invoking organization, the name of the organization currently representing the employees, if any, the estimated number of employees in each craft or class involved, and the number of signed authorizations sub-

Figure 4-2. National Mediation Board application for investigation of representation dispute

Form N. M. B.-3
(Revised 5-11-78)

NATIONAL MEDIATION BOARD

Form NMB3 approved.
OMB No. 3140-0002
(Exp. 11/30/89)

APPLICATION FOR INVESTIGATION OF REPRESENTATION DISPUTE

TO THE NATIONAL MEDIATION BOARD,
Washington, D.C. 20572

A dispute has arisen among the employees of ....
(Name of carrier)

as to who are the representatives of these employees designated and authorized in accordance with the requirements of the Railway Labor Act. The undersigned, one of the parties to the dispute, hereby requests the National Mediation Board to investigate this dispute, and to certify the name or names of the individuals or organizations authorized to represent the employees involved in accordance with Section 2, Ninth, of the Act.

Parties to dispute

....
(Petitioning organization or representative)

.... Date ....
(Organization holding existing agreement, if any, and date thereof)

....
(Other organizations or representatives involved in dispute)

If more than one craft or class, list separately	Estimated Number of Employees
Craft or class of employees involved	
1.	....
2.	....
3.	....
4.	....
5.	....
6.	....
.... (Use separate line for each craft or class)	....

Evidence of representation

This application is supported by (check applicable box):
☐ At least a majority, if the employees are represented.
☐ At least 35%, if the employees are unrepresented.

Signed at .... this .... day of ...., 19....

Name ....
(Signature of applicant)

Title ....

(File this application in duplicate)
(If necessary, use and attach additional sheet)

GPA: 980-328-887

mitted from employees in each craft or class. The RLA stipulates that "the applications should be signed by the chief executive of the invoking organization, or other authorized officer of the organization. These disputes are given docket numbers in series 'R.'"[11]

If the employees are not represented by an individual or labor organization, "a showing of proved authorizations from at least thirty-five (35) percent of the employees in the craft or class" must be made before the NMB will take any further action.[12] Employees who are represented by a valid contract must have a showing of cards from at least a majority of the craft or class.[13]

The NMB procedures, particularly in the percentage required to obtain board intervention,

Figure 4-3. National Mediation Board union authorization card

```
┌────────────────────────────────────────────────────────────────────┐
│              _____ UNION AFL-CIO                                │
│                                                                      │
│  I accept membership in _____ Union, AFL-CIO of my own free will │
│  and authorize this union to represent me in negotiations with my    │
│  Employer about wages and all other conditions of employment.        │
│                                                                      │
│  _____   │
│  NAME                               DATE                             │
│  _____   │
│  SIGNATURE OF EMPLOYEE                                               │
│  _____   │
│  ADDRESS                                                            │
│  _____   │
│  EMPLOYER                           DEPARTMENT                       │
│                                     (____)                           │
│  _____   │
│  SHIFT        JOB        RATE       WORKERS HOME TELEPHONE #         │
│  _____   │
│  WITNESS                                                            │
└────────────────────────────────────────────────────────────────────┘
```

are much different from the NLRB's requirements of 30 percent for either a representation or **decertification election**. The RLA implies that 35 percent is required to obtain a certification election and at least 50 percent to change present representation. There is no language in the RLA that allows employees to decertify a union or representative and return to a nonrepresented state: "The only effect of certification by the Board of a new representative is that the employees have chosen other agents to represent them in dealing with the management under the existing agreement."[14]

This rationale clearly shows that contracts under the RLA are amendable, whereas contracts under the NLRA are terminable. The additional study material at the end of this chapter contains a salient example of this statutory contractual difference between the RLA and the NLRA. Trans World Airlines and its owner, Carl Icahn, attempted to replace striking union flight attendants by hiring replacements and offering the replacements a different, nonunion employment contract. The union filed a dispute with the NMB. The board intervened and ruled that TWA must recognize the existing union as the "duly autho-

rized and elected representative for all flight attendants at TWA." This case clearly established that both elections and contracts under RLA can only be amended, not eliminated.

Investigation. The NMB makes a review of all applications it receives to confirm that the **craft and class determinations** are correct. The board also determines whether bar rules (see the following section) are applicable and whether there is sufficient employee interest. Unless the application is improper, it is given an "R" docket number and assigned to a mediator for field investigation. The investigating mediator will accept authorization cards from employees up until the time he or she reports back to the board.[15]

Bar Rules. The NMB will refuse to accept an application under certain circumstances:

1. Where an application has previously been made and a representative certified, a two year moratorium will exist for the same craft or class of employees on the same carrier.

2. Where an election was held on a carrier and where less than a majority of eligible voters participated in the election, the Board will require a one year moratorium.

3. Where dismissal of a prior docketed application lacked a sufficient showing of interest, the moratorium will last one year.[16]

The NMB is not required to hold an election to determine representatives. The act specifically provides that the board "shall be authorized to take a secret ballot or to utilize any other appropriate method."[17] The board holds sole discretion in deciding to hold an election or certify on the basis of authorization cards. The board cannot be compelled or required to divulge the names of the employees signing cards. The board is obligated to reveal only the number of proved authorizations.[18] If there are allegations of fraud, the board has the sole authority to make a determination, provided the board does not abuse that discretion.

A relatively recent U.S. Court of Appeals decision demonstrates the problems inherent when the NMB certifies a representative without an election. The Teamsters Union, which was attempting to organize employees of the International In-Flight Catering Company, a Hawaiian-based subsidiary of Japan Airlines, produced and distributed an employee signature card that read: "I authorize the Airline Division of the International Brotherhood of Teamsters to request the National Mediation Board to conduct an investigation and a representation election, also to represent me in all negotiations of wages, hours and working conditions in accordance with the Railway Labor Act."[19] The NMB compared signatures on the signed cards against signatures found in the employer's records and certified the Teamsters as representative without an election.

The district court set aside the certification and was highly critical of the NMB's process. The NMB merely checked signatures and refused to explain to the court what further investigation it conducted. The court held that cards asking for an election were incompetent evidence that the employees had chosen the Teamsters as their sole bargaining agent. The court stated:

> It is not a usual practice of the NMB to resolve representation disputes without an election. Plaintiff's uncontradicted evidence . . . estab-

lishes that the NMB used a check of authorizations as a means of resolving representation disputes in 12 out of 462 representation cases in the airline industry, involving less that 1/2 of 1% of eligible employees. On the facts before the court, Defendant NMB issued the certification to Plaintiff IICC and Defendant Teamsters in case R 4476 without conducting the investigation of choice of representative required by the statute, and without any competent evidence that a majority of IICC's employees had designated or selected Defendant Teamsters as their bargaining representative. The NMB's certification in this case failed to comply with the requirements of Section 2, Ninth of the Act and constituted an act contrary to the statute and in excess of its authority thereunder, and is therefore null, void and of no effect. We do fault the NMB for its pertinacious adherence to a position that flatly contradicts the intended meaning of the employees who had signed the Request for Election card, the plain language on the card itself, and the spirit of the RLA. It is a perversion of the search for truth and the policy of the RLA for the NMB to continue to insist, in these circumstances, that it conducted an investigation and discharged its duty under the RLA.[20]

Unfortunately for management, this case does not stand for the proposition that certification without an election is legally prohibited. As noted earlier, the board is free to make its determinations at will. Furthermore, it does so in its own time. Although the act requires the investigation and the identity of the representative thirty days after the application is received, the actual practice of the board has been to exceed that requirement whenever the facts of the case or the board's workload require.

The Supreme Court has stated that the board's duty to investigate requires the finding of certain facts to support the ultimate finding of fact that a certain group is the employee representative. These facts are

1. The number of eligible voters
2. The number participating in the election
3. The choice of the majority of those who participate[21]

Although these basic facts would appear to require an election, one is not required. If an election is not held, similar, analogous findings must be ascertained by the method actually used by the NMB.

A showing of interest must be present to fulfill the board's basic requirements for certification. No specific format is required for such a showing, but the universal approach generally rests with authorization cards. Interestingly, there is no standard format for authorization cards. Excluding those made by a representative for this specific purpose, cards may be accepted in any form as long as they can be proved valid. The cards, to be acceptable, must be dated and signed by the employee, and the date on the cards must be no more than one year before the date of the application.

After reviewing the report of the mediator's field investigation, the NMB either dismisses an application or finds that a dispute does exist and orders a determination of the choice of a majority of the employees.

Participation. The RLA provides that if an election is to be held, the designation of the eligible employees shall be made by the NMB. Two relevant board rules govern the designation of eligible employees: (1) "In the conduct of a representation election, the Board shall designate who may participate in the election, which may include a public hearing on craft or class, and establish the rules to govern the election";[22] (2) "When disputes arise between parties to a representation dispute, the National Mediation Board is authorized by the Act to determine who may participate in the selection of employees representatives."[23]

Class and Craft Determination

The concept that dominates employees' choice of a representative under the RLA is embodied in the class or craft determination. This single decision is paramount to determining which employees will be allowed to vote in a representation election, because it determines the bounds and/or positions for which the representing party may seek coverage. The NMB must first define the area covered by the interested parties: "In the conduct of any election for the purposes herein indicated the Board shall designate who may participate in the election and establish the rules to govern the election, or may appoint a committee of three neutral persons who after hearing shall within ten days designate the employees who may participate in the election."[24]

The act provides that if an election is to be held, a designation of eligible employees must be made. This determination establishes the class of employees or the particular craft to be represented. The policy of the board is based on the language of the act: "The majority of any craft or class of employees shall have the right to determine who shall be the representative of the craft or class."[25] This language has consistently been interpreted to mean that all employees of any single carrier who belong to the same craft or class must comprise a single unit for the purpose of selecting one representative. For example, all the airframe and power plant certified mechanics employed by a single carrier throughout its system comprise a unit for selection of a representative.

The board has taken the position that a class or craft must be carrier-wide in its scope, but the board still has to determine the makeup of the appropriate unit. In making these determinations, history indicates a heavy reliance on customary and established practices indigenous to that group. In a 1940 decision regarding the Seaboard Air Line Railroad, guidelines were established that have remained the hallmark for decisions to this day. From that decision, the following five elements are present in the determination:

1. Composition and relative permanency of the groupings along craft or class lines for representation purposes which the employees have voluntarily developed in the past among themselves. . . .

2. The extent, nature, and effectiveness of

the collective bargaining arrangements and labor agreements developed by the employees interested in the dispute with the carriers employing them.

3. Duties, responsibilities, skill, training, and experience of the employees involved and the nature of their work.

4. Usual practices of promotion, demotion, and seniority observed or developed for the employees concerned.

5. Nature and extent of the communities of interest existing among the employees.[26]

The class or craft terminology was added to the RLA when the act was amended in 1934. The act implies that the two terms are synonymous. But the terms were identified thus: "While 'craft' and 'class' may not be synonymous as used in the Act, this could only be because 'class' may be more comprehensive."[27]

The term *craft* has been defined as "those engaged in any trade, taken collectively." The term *class* has been defined as "a group of individuals ranked together as possessing common characteristics or as having the same status." The author of the bill, Mr. Eastman, explained the term *craft or class*, as he had used it before a Congressional Committee, as "all of the employees of the carrier, no matter in what shop they were located, who did that particular kind of work."[28]

The determination of crafts and classes has always been the exclusive prerogative of the NMB. This has been demonstrated by the hearings the board has convened to determine jurisdiction: "At the conclusion of such hearings the Board customarily invites all interested parties to submit briefs supporting their views, and after considering the evidence and briefs, the Board makes a determination or finding, specifying the craft or class of employees eligible to participate in the designation of representatives."[29] This statement indicates that the determination of eligible employees is equivalent to the determination of the craft or class to be represented. A hearing on this matter is only required if the interested parties to the dispute request one, and then only if the board itself does not intend to designate the class

or craft. The implications are that a hearing will not be held if the contesting parties agree on the employees eligible to participate.

If the board decides to hold a hearing and appoints a committee of three neutral persons, they will usually invite the employer to present factual information. However, because the employer is not an interested party under the RLA, "whether, and to what extent, carriers will be permitted to present their views on craft or class questions is a matter that the Act leaves solely to the discretion of the Board."[30]

This ambiguity and vagueness of terminology has proved frustrating to the carriers. Determining the divisions within their workforce, who may represent that workforce, and which positions may or may not be included have been problematic for carriers. To the boards credit, attempts have been made to define the terminology more precisely. The board's attempt for the airline industry follows:

> . . . a 'craft or class' in the air transport industry means a well-knit and cohesive occupational group which has been developed over a period of years in the course of general voluntary association of the employees into collective bargaining units. The fact that a number of rather well defined occupational groups may now be covered in one working agreement is not conclusive evidence that such coverage determines the 'Craft or Class' in that particular instance. Accordingly, it becomes necessary to examine the occupational groupings as they have emerged over a period of years in the airline industry, and to determine whether such groupings are uniform to the extent that they might now be termed 'crafts or classes' under the provisions of the Railway Labor Act.[31]

The generally recognized "crafts and classes" referred to in the board's definition were in existence in the railroad industry when the act was passed in 1926, and the determinations were basic to the act itself. But a long-standing history was not evident in the air industry in 1936, when the RLA was amended to cover air carriers. Consequently, the majority of representation activity in the years prior to deregulation of the air transport industry were from the airlines. A relatively recent ruling indicates the continuing dilemma: "Two issues affecting the Carrier's employees have been addressed by this proceeding: 1) whether personnel of United Air Lines, described as Passenger Service Employees, are properly an independent craft or class for the purposes of Section 2, Ninth, of the Railway Labor Act; and 2) which classifications are appropriately incorporated within such craft or class should it be identified as a separate and distinct grouping for collective bargaining purposes."[32]

Present Determinations. The NMB, in making determinations for the airline industry, has taken two steps forward and one backward in its attempts to apply the origins of the class or craft determinations from the railroad industry to the airlines. The industries differ significantly, but short of new issues arising, a fair separation has been made.

The flight personnel class has been easily defined by its own nature to include flight deck personnel in the pilot category. Although this category appears today to be homogeneous, in one NMB determination, the board held that flight engineers were essentially flying mechanics and were to be listed under the craft of the airline mechanic.[33] In a separate NMB determination, however, flight engineers were listed neither separately nor with the mechanics but instead with the pilot craft or class.[34]

The flight attendants class (stewards, stewardesses, and pursers) seems to be well understood as a class and craft encompassed by flight personnel.

The majority of class and craft determination controversy stems from the area of ground personnel. The controversy has stemmed from the commingling of a variety of different groups. Included in these have been mechanics, clerical workers, office employees, stores workers, fleet and passenger service workers, and stock and stores employees. Despite the controversy, recent cases have shown that a basic degree of uniformity exists.[35]

The class of airline mechanics and related personnel includes aircraft mechanics, aircraft cleaners, parts washers, plant maintenance mechanics, and the service group known variously as "ground service personnel," "fleet service personnel," and "utility personnel."[36] The latter can include fuelers, internal and external aircraft cleaners, and janitorial workers in airport hangars and buildings.

In a decision rendered in 1934 pertaining solely to the railroad industry, the craft or class of clerical, office, station, and storehouse employees (including office janitors, ticket agents, and freight and baggage handlers) was recognized. With the exception of the following classification, this definition holds today.

The final class is that of stocks and stores employees. Originally, employees whose chief functions are to receive, issue, check, store, and inventory supplies were placed in the clerical class or craft. In 1953, two unpublished NMB cases changed this to include stocks and stores employees in a separate craft or class.[37]

Many unions, principally the International Association of Mechanics and Aerospace Workers, have been the beneficiaries of such a huge classification of employees, particularly the category of mechanics and related employees. Still, despite the broad coverage, other unions—namely, the Aircraft Mechanic Fraternal Association (AMFA)—believe that mechanics in the industry are and should be a distinct class. Historically, the AMFA has lobbied for this change, albeit unsuccessfully to this point. Recently, AMFA petitioned for separation of the mechanics at Continental and United Air Lines. In late 1994, the board refused to separate the mechanic classification from the airline mechanics and related class and craft.

Representation Election

The RLA provides that when an election is called, "The majority of any craft or class of employees shall have the right to determine who shall be the representative of the craft or class for the purposes of this chapter."[38] Although a majority of eligible voters must participate, a union does not have to receive the vote of a majority of the number of eligible members to be certified. The union only needs to receive a majority of the votes actually cast in the election, as long as a majority of eligible voters participated. Thus, it is possible that a union may be certified if it receives the votes of only 26 percent of the number of eligible voters. It would appear that if a craft or class contained 1,000 employees, it would be necessary for at least 501 to vote in favor of a union for it to become certified representation. But this is not the case.

In *Virginia Railroad Company v System Federation No. 40*, the policy was established that although a majority of eligible voters must participate, a requirement fulfilled by the mere fact that the craft or class is under an organizational attempt, the board will consider an election valid if a majority of the craft class participated in the election.[39] If 501 of 1,000 employees cast a vote during the election, and if 251 vote for a particular representative, that representative could be certified as the official bargaining representative of all the craft or class, with as little as 25–26 percent of the employees actually casting a vote in favor of that particular representative.

Moreover, when the votes are cast, for whom they are cast also has its own special implications. If votes are supposed to be cast concerning only one union, votes for "No Union" and write-in votes for any other organization or individual will be considered a vote for unionism. Figure 4-4 shows the NMB standard ballot used in most elections.

In a March 1991 election at Command Airways, a feeder carrier for American Airlines, the Transport Workers Union (TWU) won an election where they did not receive an actual majority of votes cast. Seven write-in votes were made in favor of the Association of Professional Flight Attendants, making the actual final outcome 32 in favor of representation, 25 against, and 7 for another union. The TWU had received exactly 50 percent of the eligible votes cast. The NMB ruled that the 7 votes for the other union were, in fact, votes for unionism and held that the final election outcome was therefore 39 for and 25 against. The NMB then certified the TWU as representatives of the flight attendants. A true majority in favor of the particular union on the ballot is not the only criteria for certification.

The Supreme Court, in hearing the 1965 *Brotherhood of Railway and Steamship Clerks* case, established the rules concerning the board's conduct in elections:

1. The details of an election are to be left to the final determination of the board.

2. Board election rules are not subject to judicial review unless there is a showing that it has acted in excess of its statutory authority.

3. The election ballot does not have to contain a box allowing employees to vote for "no union."

4. Employees do have the option of rejecting collective representation, and this option is sufficiently satisfied by the board policy of effectively treating nonvoters as having voted for no representation.

In this same Supreme Court finding, a specific ballot provision was approved that implies that a minority can certify a representative: "No employee is required to vote. If less than a majority of employees cast valid ballots, no representative will be certified."[40] Although the board has in its history conformed to the proposition that a nonvote will be considered a vote against representation, it is apparent that the precedent can be changed at the board's discretion.

Election Rule Exceptions

Since the establishment of the NMB in 1934, only two cases have surfaced where it was not necessary for the majority of employees to cast ballots for the election to be declared valid and where the majority of valid ballots actually cast determined the outcome. In both cases, commonly referred to as the Laker and Key ballot cases, the board's position was predicated on the belief that management had interfered with the

Figure 4-4. National Mediation Board standard ballot

Form NMB-R-2(a)
Rev. 7/89

UNITED STATES OF AMERICA

OFFICIAL BALLOT OF NATIONAL MEDIATION BOARD

Involving   CASE NO. _____

Employees of

_____

A dispute exists among the above named craft or class of employees as to who are the representatives of such employees designated and authorized in accordance with the requirements of the Railway Labor Act. The National Mediation Board is taking a SECRET BALLOT in order to ascertain and to certify the name or names of organizations or individuals designated and authorized for purposes of the Railway Labor Act.

INSTRUCTIONS FOR VOTING

No employee is required to vote. If less than a majority of the employees cast valid ballots, no representative will be certified. Should a majority vote to be represented, the representative which receives a majority of the votes cast will be certified.

If you desire to be represented by:

Mark an "X" in this square. . . . . [ ]

If you desire to be represented by:
ANY OTHER ORGANIZATION OR INDIVIDUAL
Write name of such organization or individual on the line below:
_____ , AND

Mark an "X" in this square. [ ]

NOTICE
1.   This is a SECRET BALLOT. DO NOT SIGN YOUR NAME.
2.   Marks in more than one square make ballot void.
3.   Do not cut, mutilate or otherwise spoil this ballot. If you should accidentally do so, you may return the spoiled ballot at once to the Mediator and obtain a new one.

☆U.S. GPO: 1989—246-341

employees' right of organization and representation to such an extent that they made the normal procedure invalid.

The RLA, unlike the NLRA, does not provide the NMB with specific authority to make a finding of unfair labor practices in federally supervised elections. Creation of the Laker and Key ballots is the method employed by the board's presidential appointees to provide what amounts to redress of unfair labor practices in RLA cases. The Laker ballot (see figure 4-5) was the NMB's first attempt to provide a modified ballot for cases where management interference or coercion of employees was found.

Figure 4-5. National Mediation Board Laker ballot

```
                    UNITED STATES OF AMERICA

          OFFICIAL BALLOT OF NATIONAL MEDIATION BOARD

                                      CASE NO.
                   Involving


                   Employees of


_____

        A dispute exists among the above named craft or class of
   employees as to who are the representatives of such employees
   designated and authorized in accordance with the requirements of
   the Railway Labor Act.  The National Mediation Board is taking a
   SECRET BALLOT in order to ascertain and to certify the name or
   names of organizations or individuals designated and authorized for
   purposes of the Railway Labor Act.

                      INSTRUCTIONS FOR VOTING

        No employee is required to vote.  The majority of valid
   ballots actually cast will determine the outcome of the election.
   Mark an "X" in the appropriate square:


                                              YES    ┌─────┐
                                                     │     │
                                                     └─────┘

   Do you desire to be represented by
   the                                   ?

                                              NO     ┌─────┐
                                                     │     │
                                                     └─────┘
_____

                            NOTICE

   1. This is a SECRET BALLOT.  DO NOT SIGN YOUR NAME.
   2. Marks in more than one square make ballot void.
   3. Do not cut, mutilate or otherwise spoil this ballot. If you
      should accidentally do so, you may return the spoiled ballot
      at one to the Mediator and obtain a new one.
```

In the Laker case, the NMB found that management had influenced the certification election by telling all eligible employees to return the ballots to the director of human resources instead of mailing them to the NMB. Management also sent letters and held meetings telling employees not to vote for representation. The offenses on the part of Laker's management lead to the creation of the Laker ballot.

Unlike the standard ballot in figure 4-4, which includes boxes for write-ins, the Laker ballot, which was created in 1981, contains no space for write-in choices and contains only one question: "Do you desire to be represented by . . . ?" and the name of a specific union or employee group. It is not necessary, under the Laker ballot, for a majority of employees to cast ballots for the election to be declared valid, and the majority of valid ballots actually cast determines the outcome of the election.

In the Key case, the NMB said that events surrounding the election in question were "disturbingly similar" to a 1986 case involving the carrier. In that earlier Key Airlines case, the board had also issued a finding that management was guilty of illegal interference and coercion of employees in a unionizing effort. To provide the Teamsters with redress in that 1986 case, the NMB ordered use of the Laker ballot in a subsequently ordered election, which was lost by the union. Board members essentially decided that even stronger measures were required to redress these new instances of management interference and created the Key ballot (see figure 4-6). Key Airlines indicated that it would challenge the NMB's decision on the basis of violation of management's "constitutional rights of free speech and due process."

In a Key election, all eligible employees who fail to cast a ballot are automatically counted by NMB officials as having voted "yes" for representation by the union seeking to represent. The opposite is true for the normal ballot. Employees in this case who want a specific union representative have to cast a ballot in favor of the union of their choice. For the election to be declared valid, a majority of the eligible employees have to cast ballots. The winner is the party receiving the majority of the votes cast. The election would be declared invalid if fewer than a majority of the employees cast votes, and the board has ruled in the past that the employees then would not be represented by any union, because they failed to produce a majority interest in any representation.

The actual balloting under a Key ballot election is conducted by all eligible employees receiving a ballot marked, for example, "Are you opposed to representation by the International Brotherhood of Teamsters-Airline Division?"

The employee, if opposed, places an *X* next to the question and mails the ballot back to the NMB. This procedure considers all eligible employees as voting in favor of the union unless a ballot is returned to the board. Under these guidelines, for the union to be disavowed, the union seeking to represent would have to do something that caused the rank-and-file employees to vote against them.

This form of voting does not follow the traditional method of "one man, one vote." Instead, it stacks the deck in favor of the union. "One man, one vote" only applies to a dissenter. The remainder of the employees, if apathetic to the entire affair, are considered in favor of unionization.

Another indication of the NMB's authority in this area occurred more recently in a representation dispute at America West Airlines. In that case, the board found that the Phoenix-based carrier violated its employees right to freedom of choice. The board held that during an election campaign, the company contaminated the "**laboratory conditions**" necessary for a fair election. According to the board, America West "improperly interfered with, influenced, and coerced its flight attendants in their freedom of choice by the 'totality' of its conduct, by announcing and implementing certain work rule changes, by implementing increases in layover benefits and distributing profit-sharing bonuses during the election." The board ordered that the election be rerun, distributed to all employees special notices concerning the company's conduct, and sent new ballot materials to each affected employee.

Mergers and Acquisitions

Since the Airline Deregulation Act of 1978, the element of mergers and takeovers has dominated the industry. Comparing the names of the airlines in existence before deregulation with the names of those flying today reveals that a variety of well-known carriers have vanished or have been acquired by others. In mergers and takeovers, the NMB has followed a policy of acquiescing to the

Figure 4-6. National Mediation Board Key ballot

UNITED STATES OF AMERICA

OFFICIAL BALLOT OF NATIONAL MEDIATION BOARD

Involving   CASE NO. _____

Employees of

A dispute exists among the above named craft or class of employees as to whether such employees desire representation in accordance with the requirements of the Railway Labor Act. To resolve this dispute the National Mediation Board (NMB) is taking a SECRET BALLOT in order to ascertain and to certify the name of the organization or individual, if any, designated and authorized to represent said employees for purposes of the Railway Labor Act.

INSTRUCTIONS FOR VOTING

You may exercise your choice in either of the two following ways. If you wish to be represented by the United Transportation Union, do not return your ballot to the NMB. Should less than a majority of the eligible employees return valid ballots, the
will be certified.   However, if you are opposed to representation by the
, mark an "X" in the box below and return your ballot to the NMB before
p.m.,   . Should a majority of employees return valid ballots opposing representation, no representative will be certified.

If you are opposed to representation by the
_____

Mark an "X" in this space . . . .

NOTICE

1.   This is a SECRET BALLOT. DO NOT SIGN YOUR NAME
2.   Do not cut, mutilate or otherwise spoil this ballot. If you should accidentally do so, you may return the spoiled ballot at once to the Board representative to obtain a new one.
3.   Ballots to be counted must be received at the NMB before   p.m.,

union or nonunion status of the surviving carrier. For example, when one carrier was merged into another and the result was a mixture of union and nonunion employees in a particular craft or class, the board determined that the new class was to be either totally union or totally nonunion. When the majority of the merged classification was nonunion, the union status of the merged carrier was abolished. Likewise, when the majority of the merged classification was

unionized, the nonunion status was abolished, and the labor union representing the majority of the employees became the representative for all.

This approach was evident in the Delta Air Lines and Western Airlines merger. Delta was the surviving carrier and employed larger numbers of nonunion employees than did Western, a unionized carrier. Western's unions were decertified. In the same case, Western's pilots and Delta's pilots were both unionized, so the Air Line Pilots

Association continued as the certified representative.

More recently, the board has shifted its position away from its precedent. In two cases of merger, USAir and Piedmont, and Federal Express and Flying Tiger, the board, citing inability to determine precise numbers, did not decertify any unions, and the surviving carriers were forced to consider the possibility of having their workforce unionized or, worse yet, having a payroll split by craft. This occurred in the FedEx–Flying Tiger merger, despite the statistics provided by Federal Express that indicated FedEx, the surviving carrier, had almost two hundred more nonunion pilots than Flying Tiger, the merged carrier. In both cases, the NMB ruled that the mix of union and nonunion employees would be temporary until arrangements could be made for an election among all the employees. One close observer of airline labor relations said, however, that "the actual numbers [of union and nonunion employees] could have been determined for the purpose of deciding the representation issue. The mediation board decision was considered 'a back door way to keep the pilots' union alive.'"[41]

These actions, coupled with the board's actions in the Laker and Key cases, indicate a major difference between the NLRA and the RLA. In theory, at least, the NLRB is structurally forced to be impartial. Such is not the case with the NMB under the RLA. In a 1988 federal court of appeals decision, the board's partiality was at issue. In the decision rendered, the appeals judge upheld the NMB's right to be biased, noting that "there is no expressed statutory duty of neutrality."[42]

The Process under the National Labor Relations Act

Employees Subject to the NLRA

Section 2 of the Taft-Hartley Act defines *employee* as a person currently on an employer's payroll and also a person whose work has ceased because of a current strike or an unfair labor practice. The definition specifically excludes

1. Agricultural laborers
2. Persons employed in the domestic service of a family or persons at their home
3. Independent contractors
4. Supervisors
5. Persons covered under the RLA

Employees who fall under the jurisdiction of the act and who appeal for union coverage may still be ignored by the NLRB, because the board limits the cases it will accept based on established employee standards.

Supervisory Personnel Subject to the NLRA

The most unique personnel definition under the NLRA is that of *supervisor*. Prior to the 1947 Taft-Hartley amendments, a supervisor was not excluded from the definition of *employee*, and the employer could not discriminate against him or her for engaging in union activities. Since 1947, however, supervisors have not been protected under the act. Supervisors still may join unions, but they may be discharged for doing so. Additionally, there are no provisions in the law that compel an employer to deal with any union designated by the supervisors to represent them.[43] *Supervisor* is defined in section 2 of the NLRA as a person with the authority "to hire, transfer, suspend, lay off, recall, promote, discharge, assign, reward, or discipline other employees, or responsibly to direct them, or to adjust their grievances, or effectively to recommend such action . . . [that] requires the use of independent judgment." The NLRB, in the case of *Ohio Power Company v Utilities Workers Union of America*, ruled that the responsibility to direct other employees is enough in itself to classify a person as a supervisor.[44]

Managerial Personnel Subject to the NLRA

Other personnel, such as "managerial" and "confidential" personnel are not specifically excluded by the Taft-Hartley Act. But the Supreme Court ruled that a managerial employee is not covered by the act if he or she "formulates and executes management decisions."[45] Furthermore, the NLRB has ruled that confidential workers, defined as those workers with access to personnel and labor relations records and files, must also be excluded from employee bargaining units.[46]

Employers Subject to the NLRA

Employer is defined in Section 2 of the Taft-Hartley Act as an organization or its personnel—other than "employees"—who act in behalf of the organization and whose operations affect, or fall within, the definition of interstate commerce. Specifically exempted from the act are the following organizations:

1. The federal government or any wholly owned government corporation or any federal reserve bank (except the U.S. Postal Service)

2. Employers subject to the RLA

3. Any state or political division of a state

4. Labor organizations, except when acting as employers

In 1958, the NLRB revised its own standards to establish basic guidelines for employees and employers falling under the act. This was done in an effort to reduce excessive case loads. The following year, amendments under the Landrum-Griffin Act forbade the board from changing these standards solely as a way of reducing its workload. These standards are based on the annual amount of business done by the employer—the amount of its sales or purchases. They are stated in terms of total dollar volume of business, and the amounts differ for various kinds of businesses.[47] Table 4-1 lists the various business and dollar amounts necessary for coverage under the NLRA.

Procedures of the National Labor Relations Board

The NLRA provides that the NLRB is responsible for the certification of elections only when a petition requesting one has been filed. A peti-

tion for certification may be filed by an employee, a group of employees, a union, or an employer. The petition must be signed, sworn to, or affirmed under oath at the regional office of the NLRB. Figure 4-7 shows an NLRB representation petition, figure 4-8 shows the various steps required for certification of a union under the NLRA, and figure 4-9 shows typical NLRB authorization cards.

Union Petition. A union may file a petition when it seeks recognition as exclusive bargaining agent and the employer refuses to recognize the union or when it has been recognized by the employer but desires to obtain the benefits of certification by the board.[48] Accompanying the petition should be proof that at least 30 percent of the employees in the unit are interested in having the union represent them.

Individual Petitions. Individuals, excluding supervisors, may file petitions. Such petitions must also be backed by proof that 30 percent of the employees are interested in having the nominated bargaining agent represent them.[49]

Employer Requests. A formal request by an employer is not required. Employer requests are generally made when confronted by a union who contends that the majority of employees desire representation. The board will direct an election even if it is claimed that no reasonable basis exists for questioning the unions majority.[50]

Investigation. Upon receipt of a petition, the NLRB is required to determine if a question of representation actually exists. The investigation is to determine

1. If the board has jurisdiction to conduct the election

2. Whether there is enough showing of employee interest in a collective bargaining representative to justify an election

3. Whether there actually is a question about representation

4. Whether the election is sought in the appropriate unit of employees

Figure 4-7. National Labor Relations Board representation petition

FORM NLRB-502
(5-85)

FORM EXEMPT UNDER 44 U S C 3512

UNITED STATES GOVERNMENT
NATIONAL LABOR RELATIONS BOARD
PETITION

DO NOT WRITE IN THIS SPACE	
Case No.	Date Filed

INSTRUCTIONS: Submit an original and 4 copies of this Petition to the NLRB Regional Office in the Region in which the employer concerned is located. If more space is required for any one item, attach additional sheets, numbering item accordingly.

The Petitioner alleges that the following circumstances exist and requests that the National Labor Relations Board proceed under its proper authority pursuant to Section 9 of the National Labor Relations Act.

1. PURPOSE OF THIS PETITION *(If box RC, RM, or RD is checked and a charge under Section 8(b)(7) of the Act has been filed involving the Employer named herein, the statement following the description of the type of petition shall not be deemed made.)* **(Check One)**

☐ **RC-CERTIFICATION OF REPRESENTATIVE** - A substantial number of employees wish to be represented for purposes of collective bargaining by Petitioner and Petitioner desires to be certified as representative of the employees.

☐ **RM-REPRESENTATION (EMPLOYER PETITION)** - One or more individuals or labor organizations have presented a claim to Petitioner to be recognized as the representative of employees of Petitioner.

☐ **RD-DECERTIFICATION** - A substantial number of employees assert that the certified or currently recognized bargaining representative is no longer their representative.

☐ **UD-WITHDRAWAL OF UNION SHOP AUTHORITY** - Thirty percent (30%) or more of employees in a bargaining unit covered by an agreement between their employer and a labor organization desire that such authority be rescinded.

☐ **UC-UNIT CLARIFICATION** - A labor organization is currently recognized by Employer, but Petitioner seeks clarification of placement of certain employees: *(Check one)* ☐ In unit not previously certified. ☐ In unit previously certified in Case No. _____ .

☐ **AC-AMENDMENT OF CERTIFICATION** - Petitioner seeks amendment of certification issued in Case No. _____
Attach statement describing the specific amendment sought.

2. Name of Employer	Employer Representative to contact	Telephone Number

3. Address(es) of Establishment(s) involved *(Street and number, city, State, ZIP code)*

4a. Type of Establishment *(Factory, mine, wholesaler, etc.)*	4b. Identify principal product or service

5. Unit Involved *(In UC petition, describe **present** bargaining unit and attach description of proposed clarification.)*	6a. Number of Employees in Unit:
Included	Present
	Proposed *(By UC/AC)*
Excluded	6b. Is this petition supported by 30% or more of the employees in the unit? * ____ Yes ____No *Not applicable in RM, UC, and AC

(If you have checked box RC in 1 above, check and complete EITHER item 7a or 7b, whichever is applicable)

7a. ☐ Request for recognition as Bargaining Representative was made on *(Date)* _____ and Employer declined recognition on or about *(Date)* _____ *(If no reply received, so state).*

7b. ☐ Petitioner is currently recognized as Bargaining Representative and desires certification under the Act.

8. Name of Recognized or Certified Bargaining Agent *(If none, so state)*	Affiliation
Address and Telephone Number	Date of Recognition or Certification

9. Expiration Date of Current Contract, If any *(Month, Day, Year)*	10. If you have checked box UD in 1 above, show here the date of execution of agreement granting union shop *(Month, Day, and Year)*

11a. Is there now a strike or picketing at the Employer's establishment(s) Involved? Yes _____ No _____	11b. If so, approximately how many employees are participating?

11c. The Employer has been picketed by or on behalf of *(Insert Name)* _____ , a labor organization, of *(Insert Address)* _____ Since *(Month, Day, Year)* _____

12. Organizations or individuals other than Petitioner *(and other than those named in items 8 and 11c)*, which have claimed recognition as representatives and other organizations and individuals known to have a representative interest in any employees in unit described in item 5 above. *(If none, so state)*

Name	Affiliation	Address	Date of Claim *(Required only if Petition is filed by Employer)*

I declare that I have read the above petition and that the statements are true to the best of my knowledge and belief.

_____
Name of Petitioner and Affiliation, if any

By _____   _____
(Signature of Representative or person filing petition)   *(Title, if any)*

Address _____   _____
(Street and number, city, State, and ZIP Code)   *(Telephone Number)*

WILLFUL FALSE STATEMENTS ON THIS PETITION CAN BE PUNISHED BY FINE AND IMPRISONMENT (U. S. CODE, TITLE 18, SECTION 1001)

Figure 4-8. National Labor Relations Act representation process

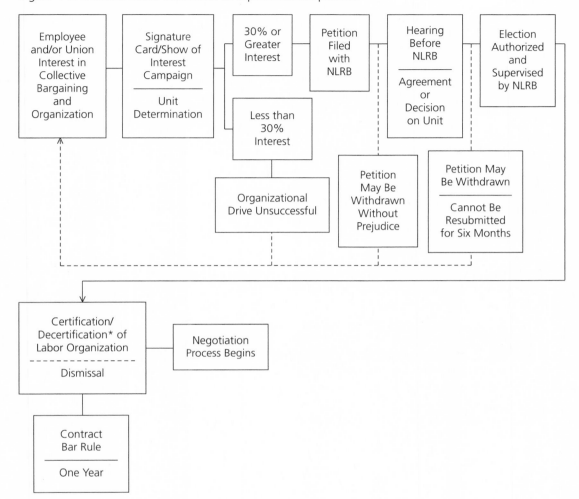

*Process may also be used to decertify an existing union or to change union representation.

5. Whether the representative named in the petition (ordinarily a union) is qualified

6. Whether there are any legal barriers to an election

Often, a legal barrier to an election takes the form of an existing bona fide collective bargaining agreement covering the employees in question. Such an agreement may constitute a contract bar to an election. Another legal impediment is the certification by the NLRB of a bargaining

unit within the previous year. Such a certification bars an election, as does a previous election within the prior twelve months.[51]

Determining Bargaining Units

Subject to certain limitations, Section 9(B) of the NLRA provides that the NLRB determine the bargaining unit: "in order to assure to employees the fullest freedom in exercising the rights

Figure 4-9. *Top,* National Labor Relations Board union authorization card; *bottom,* International Association of Machinists authorization card

---

_____ UNION AUTHORIZATION CARD

WE BELIEVE THAT ONLY THROUGH COLLECTIVE BARGAINING CAN WE HAVE A VOICE IN OUR WORK PLACE, ACHIEVE FAIR TREATMENT FOR ALL, ESTABLISH JOB SECURITY AND FAIR BENEFITS, WAGES AND WORKING CONDITIONS. THEREFORE, THIS WILL AUTHORIZE THE _____ UNION, AFL-CIO TO REPRESENT ME IN COLLECTIVE BARGAINING WITH MY EMPLOYER.

PLEASE PRINT:

NAME

EMPLOYER NAME   DATE

ADDRESS

CITY   STATE   ZIP   PHONE

SHIFT   DEPARTMENT

SIGNATURE

NOTE: This authorization to be signed and dated in employee's own handwriting. Your right to sign this card is protected by by Federal Law.

YES, I WANT THE IAM

I, the undersigned employee of

(Company)

authorize the International Association of Machinists and Aerospace Workers (IAM) to act as my collective bargaining agent for wages, hours and working conditions. I agree that this card may be used either to support a demand for recognition or an NLRB election, at the discretion of the union.

NAME (print)_____ DATE_____

HOME ADDRESS_____ PHONE_____

CITY_____ STATE_____ ZIP_____

JOB TITLE_____ DEPT._____ SHIFT_____

SIGN HERE X _____

NOTE: This authorization to be SIGNED and DATED in Employee's own handwriting. YOUR RIGHT TO SIGN THIS CARD IS PROTECTED BY FEDERAL LAW.

RECEIVED BY (Initial)_____

---

guaranteed by this act, the unit appropriate for the purpose of collective bargaining shall be the employee unit, craft unit, plant unit or subdivision thereof . . . " The Taft-Hartley amendments, however, placed limitations on the NLRB's authority:

1. Professional employees may not be included in a unit with nonprofessionals unless a majority of the professional employees vote for this inclusion in a separate self-determination election.

2. Supervisors are excluded from inclusion.

3. Plant guards may not be included in a unit of production and maintenance workers.

4. The extent to which employees have organized a union shall not be controlling. The NLRB may not direct an election among particular employees just because the union has

not been able to organize employees elsewhere in the plant.[52]

In addition, the act requires that certain types of employees be excluded from a unit. The principal exclusions consist of individuals identified with management interests. Excluded are supervisors, domestic servants, independent contractors, and employees covered by the RLA. The NLRB also excludes confidential employees, "who assist and act in a confidential capacity to persons who formulate, determine and effectuate management policies in the field of labor relations."[53] Not excluded are probationary employees,[54] regular part-time employees, employees on vacation or authorized leave of absence,[55] and laid-off employees or those absent because of illness.[56]

The board has generally sought to determine the appropriateness of a bargaining unit on the grounds of common employment interests of the employees involved. Among the principal factors the board considers are

1. The similarity of duties, skills, wages, and working conditions

2. The pertinent bargaining history, if any, among the employees involved

3. The employees' own wishes in the matter

4. The appropriateness of the units purpose in relation to the organizational structure of the company itself[57]

Craft, Departmental, or Industrial Units

A significant and persistent problem has been the desire of craft employees (those possessing specific skill—e.g., carpenters, mechanics, etc.) not to be included, absorbed, or lost in industrial or departmental bargaining units. Because of the trade nature of these positions, many craft employees wish to have their own separate and distinct representation rather than to be covered under an umbrella union that represents a variety of different workers.

In its 1948 *National Tube* decision,[58] the NLRB decided that craft severance elections should not be permitted in the basic steel industry, because of the integrated nature of these business operations and the history of bargaining on an industrial rather than craft basis. Later, in separate decisions, this denial of craft severance election was extended to the aluminum, lumber, and wet milling industries for the same reasons. The NLRB reversed its *National Tube* decision in the 1954 *American Potash* decision,[59] which held that **craft units** must be split off from an established industrial unit when the unit seeking severance was a "true craft group" or the union seeking to represent the unit had traditionally represented that craft. This decision did not extend to the industries previously barred in the 1948 *National Tube* case.

In 1966, the board again changed its position on craft severance. The decision in the *Mallinckrodt Chemical* case[60] is now controlling and applies to all industries, including those eliminated from consideration in 1948. In the *Mallinckrodt* decision, the board stated that it would consider all areas relevant to an informed decision in craft severance cases, including the following:

1. Whether the proposed unit embraces a distinct and homogeneous group of skilled craftspersons performing the functions of their craft on a nonrepetitive basis

2. The bargaining history of employees

3. The extent to which the employees have maintained their separate identity during their inclusion in the broader unit

4. The history and pattern of bargaining in the industry

5. The degree of integration of the employer's production process

6. The qualifications of the union seeking to represent the severed unit

Certification Election

To appropriately conduct an election, the NLRB may require an employer to provide a list of the names and addresses of all employees eligible to vote, so the NLRB may determine if the petitioning unit is appropriate. If the unit in the petition is not appropriate, an election is not

Figure 4-10. National Labor Relations Board notice of election

NOTICE TO EMPLOYEES
FROM THE
National Labor Relations Board

A PETITION has been filed with this Federal agency seeking an election to determine whether certain employees want to be represented by a union.

The case is being investigated and NO DETERMINATION HAS BEEN MADE AT THIS TIME by the National Labor Relations Board. IF an election is held Notices of Election will be posted giving complete details for voting.

It was suggested that your employer post this notice so the National Labor Relations Board should inform you of your basic rights under the National Labor Relations Act.

YOU HAVE THE RIGHT under Federal Law

- **To self-organization**
- **To form, join, or assist labor organizations**
- **To bargain collectively through representatives of your own choosing**
- **To act together for the purposes of collective bargaining or other mutual aid or protection**
- **To refuse to do any or all of these things unless the union and employer, in a state where such agreements are permitted, enter into a lawful union-security agreement requiring employees to pay periodic dues and initiation fees. Nonmembers who inform the union that they object to the use of their payments for nonrepresentational purposes may be required to pay only their share of the union's costs of representational activities *(such as collective bargaining, contract administration, and grievance adjustments).***

It is possible that some of you will be voting in an employee representation election as a result of the request for an election having been filed. While NO DETERMINATION HAS BEEN MADE AT THIS TIME, in the event an election is held, the NATIONAL LABOR RELATIONS BOARD wants all eligible voters to be familiar with their rights under the law IF it holds an election.

The Board applies rules that are intended to keep its elections fair and honest and that result in a free choice. If agents of either unions or employers act in such a way as to interfere with your right to a free election, the election can be set aside by the Board. Where appropriate the Board provides other remedies, such as reinstatement for employees fired for exercising their rights, including backpay from the party responsible for their discharge.

NOTE:

The following are examples of conduct that interfere with the rights of employees and may result in the setting aside of the election.

- **Threatening loss of jobs or benefits by an employer or a union**
- **Promising or granting promotions, pay raises, or other benefits to influence an employee's vote by a party capable of carrying out such promises**
- **An employer firing employees to discourage or encourage union activity or a union causing them to be fired to encourage union activity**
- **Making campaign speeches to assembled groups of employees on company time within the 24-hour period before the election**
- **Incitement by either an employer or a union of racial or religious prejudice by inflammatory appeals**
- **Threatening physical force or violence to employees by a union or an employer to influence their votes**

Please be assured that IF AN ELECTION IS HELD every effort will be made to protect your right to a free choice under the law. Improper conduct will not be permitted. All parties are expected to cooperate fully with this Agency in maintaining basic principles of a fair election as required by law. The National Labor Relations Board, as an agency of the United States Government, does not endorse any choice in the election.

NATIONAL LABOR RELATIONS BOARD
an agency of the
UNITED STATES GOVERNMENT

THIS IS AN OFFICIAL GOVERNMENT NOTICE AND MUST NOT BE DEFACED BY ANYONE

conducted. If the unit is appropriate and there is no present bargaining unit or **contract bar rule**, the board sets in motion the machinery for holding an election. Figure 4-10 shows an NLRB notice of election.

Preparing for an election involves the establishment of polling places, preparation of ballots, and provision of representatives to monitor the election and tabulate votes. The election is conducted through secret ballots tabulated by NLRB personnel. The union or unions seeking certification are listed on the ballots, which also include a section indicating "No Union." Figure 4-11 shows the ballot used by the NLRB in its elections.

If the union wins the election, gaining a majority of the votes, it is duly certified as the exclusive bargaining agent for the workers in the bargaining unit.[61] To be certified as a bargaining representative, a labor union must receive a majority of the votes cast in an election. Majority is 50 percent plus one person. The majority rule does not take into consideration the total unit. Only those employees actually voting are considered. If a clear majority is not received by any party when three or more choices are on the ballot, **run-off elections** are held for the two parties or categories receiving the most votes.

Within thirty days of the election, the NLRB notifies the company of the vote outcome. If a union wins, it is certified as the exclusive bargaining representative of the employees in the unit. Immediately following, the parties meet to engage in the negotiation of the initial agreement. But if the employer prevails, no election petition is honored by the NLRB for a period of one year. In effect, certification guarantees the union or nonunion status of a bargaining unit for a period of at least one year after an election.[62]

Summary

The principal differences between the RLA and the NLRA in handling union certification elections center on the two respective governing bodies, the NMB and the NLRB. The NMB has far greater discretionary power for dictating and manipulating election rules and conditions than the NLRB, and the very fabric of the RLA is prounion, whereas the NLRA legislation possesses a more balanced view of workers' desires regarding unionization. There is no mechanism under the RLA to allow represented airline employees to decertify and work as unrepresented employees. They are only allowed by law to change unions or representatives, not to eliminate them.

Because of this statutory prohibition on decertification, once a craft is unionized under the RLA, that craft, by law, must always remain unionized or represented. Thus, collective bargaining agreements under the RLA are only amendable, not terminable as under the NLRA. In essence, the RLA has created a set of union contracts that are valid in perpetuity. The terms and conditions can be, and are, negotiated every few years, but the existence of the agreement, like union representation itself, can never be eliminated. The financial impact of these provisions of the RLA and the enforcement power of the NMB on the carriers covered under that act are significant.

Figure 4-11. National Labor Relations Board ballot

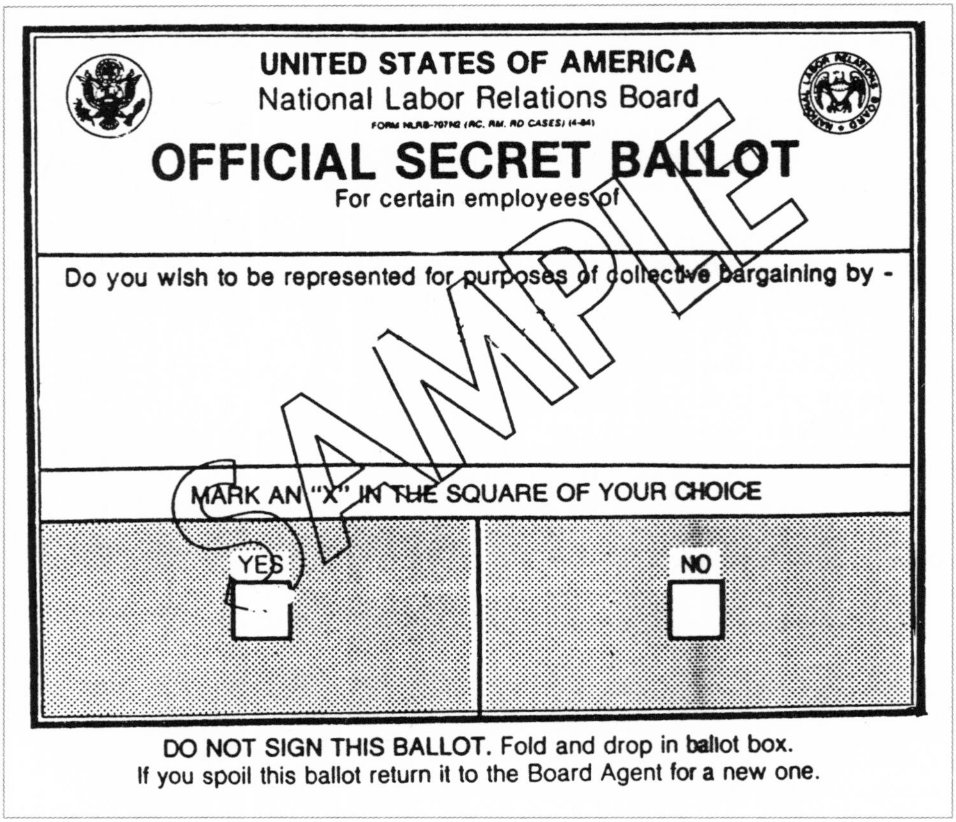

UNITED STATES OF AMERICA
National Labor Relations Board
FORM NLRB-707N2 (RC, RM, RD CASES) (4-84)

OFFICIAL SECRET BALLOT
For certain employees of

Do you wish to be represented for purposes of collective bargaining by -

MARK AN "X" IN THE SQUARE OF YOUR CHOICE

| YES | NO |

DO NOT SIGN THIS BALLOT. Fold and drop in ballot box.
If you spoil this ballot return it to the Board Agent for a new one.

Additional Study Material

Examination of the Events Surrounding the Strike by Trans World Airline Flight Attendants

Contract Continuity under the Railway Labor Act

More than any other case in recent history, the strike action taken against Trans World Airlines by the Independent Federation of Flight Attendants (IFFA) in 1986 points out the perpetuity of relationships that exist under the Railway Labor Act. These events clearly point out that unilateral action on the part of a party to a dispute does not deny a striking union the right to represent the class or craft remaining on the premises.

Introduction

Trans World Airlines is one of the nation's largest and oldest air carriers. It was founded in 1926 and has endured the tests of years, including mergers, takeovers, deregulation, strikes, and corporate spinoffs. In its history, with all the profits and losses taken into consideration, the airline has virtually made no money.

Late in 1985, Mr. Carl Icahn invested $300 million in the company for controlling interest. He became chairman of the board in January 1986, at which time the airline was losing money at the rate of $1 million per day. At the time, Mr. Icahn was trapped, with his prospects riding on a marginal company in a viciously competitive industry.[1]

Recognizing, as have all corporate leaders involved in marginal companies, that the only major variable cost he could attack to reduce his costs was that of labor, he knew that he would have to obtain pay concessions and increased productivity from his employees. His expectations were to receive concessions of $300 million in wage and benefit cost, which would reduce TWA's labor costs approximately 20 percent and its total costs before taxes to about 8 percent. The airline's total losses for 1985 were approximately $150 million.

The members of the Air Line Pilots Association and the International Association of Machinists and Aerospace Workers provided the wage concessions Icahn sought. The pilots agreed to roughly 30 percent, approximating $100 million; the machinists provided 15 percent, or approximately $50 million. In reaching agreements with these unions, Icahn promised a profit-sharing plan and the eventual **Employee Stock Ownership Plan**. Additionally, Mr. Frank Lorenzo of Texas Air Corporation, who has been reputed to be a "union buster" had recently attempted to purchase the airline. The unions desired and received an agreement from Icahn that he would not sell the airline to Lorenzo for at least three years.

Halfway to his goal, Icahn expected to get the remainder of the needed concessions from the airline's flight attendants, management, and other nonunion employees. Mr. Icahn was obliged by his agreement with the pilots to seek pay cuts of 20–22 percent from the flight attendants. The pilots had resented the 15 percent cut the machinists had finally settled for and did not want the flight attendants to "get off" so easily. The pilot's association said that, in addition to the pay cut in January, they had taken one of 11 percent in 1983. Another important element of the pilot's contract was that they agreed not to honor the picket lines of other unions. The machinists refused to make a similar commitment.[2]

The head of the flight attendant's union, Victoria Frankovich, said they would not accept pay cuts greater than the machinists. Ms. Frankovich and Mr. Icahn could not reach an agreement before the takeover. Ms. Frankovich's lawyer, William Jolley, suspected that Mr. Icahn was somewhat sexist. According to the lawyer, Mr. Icahn argued that the flight attendants were not breadwinners in the same sense that the mechanics were and could therefore afford to take deeper pay cuts.[3]

Responding to these allegations, Icahn stated: "I never said they weren't bread winners; that's completely untrue. What I do say is that we can't compete with airlines that are paying half what we are for flight attendants. Our average cost is $35,000 to $40,000. Peoples Express and Continental are paying around $18,000. I tell you categorically that TWA would have gone into Chapter 11 if I hadn't come along and gotten wage concessions. They're losing $150 million this year even with a Pan Am strike helping them."[4]

Icahn insisted that the flight attendants had to make $100 million in concessions if TWA was to become competitive. He originally asked for a 22 percent pay cut but finally agreed to settle for 17 percent. He also demanded a two-hour increase in the workweek, which at that time consisted of some twenty in-flight hours per week. The IFFA agreed to 15 percent wage reductions but refused to work as many hours as TWA demanded. Both sides were determined to get what they wanted. Ms. Frankovich replied to Icahn's demand of work rule changes by stating: "Mr. Icahn says all he wants is a few more hours a week of flying time from us. But he doesn't understand that every added hour of work means six hours away from home. My members already are away 60 hours a week."[5]

Icahn stuck to his position, saying he had trimmed his demand for a 22 percent wage cut to 17 percent but that he would stick to his demand for changes in work rules: "For TWA to exist, we must have this. We're asking for a TWA that can be competitive."[6] Work rules deal with the most fundamental labor related issues, such as how long an employee must work, how much rest they receive between work assignments, and how many hours they must put in during the standard workweek or, in this case, work month.

If TWA received all the work rule changes it demanded, the airline would need far fewer attendants; the number employed could decline by more than 41 percent. From TWA's standpoint, the new rules would make its flight attendant workforce more productive and the airline more cost competitive with other carriers. At this time, the airline needed 6,000 attendants, but under the new regimen, they would need only 5,000.

The attendants were therefore fighting for their livelihoods, and according to the union, it was also "a fight to preserve the occupation as one suitable for mature adults." The union contended that the new rules were too physically demanding and that only extremely healthy people could live up to them, and even they could do so for only a short period of time.[7] According to the union, most of the flight attendants were in their thirties and had families who depended on them as breadwinners; 45 percent had dependent children. If the new work rules were put in effect, these people would be forced from work.

In 1985, the average attendant worked sixteen or seventeen days a month. To work those days, an attendant spent about 75 hours a month actually working flights (hard time) and about 240 hours away from home (trip time). Trip time is time spent waiting at airports between flights and time spent staying overnight in cities away from their domicile. It does not include hard time.

Under the existing contract, the work rules precluded TWA from scheduling attendants for more than 75 hard hours a month. Employees could work more if they wanted to and were paid overtime after the 65th hour. Now, TWA was demanding more flexibility. They wanted to be able to schedule people for anywhere from 70 to 85 hours and would pay overtime for the last 10 hours only.[8] The union said that an 85-hour schedule would translate to about twenty-one days a month and would force members to be away as much as 320 hours a month.

TWA also wanted to be able to schedule attendants for longer days, with shorter rest periods. The airline wanted to be allowed to schedule people on its domestic system to work thirteen hours at a time, which is thirty minutes more

than the present rules. And the airline wanted to reduce the minimum rest time from eight hours to about six and a half hours.[9] The union stated that the rest period demanded by TWA was not enough because of the unhealthy conditions under which the flight attendants work. They argued that flight attendants work, sleep, and eat at irregular hours; are exposed to large numbers of people; and breathe the stale air of airplanes day in and day out.[10]

In addition to the time demands, TWA desired to reduce the number of flight attendants it used on various aircraft. It sought to cut vacation time by 20 percent, so that employees with eight to twenty-four years of service would have a maximum of twenty-four days of vacation a year. The airline also wanted to drop the eight-in-twenty-four rule, which required the company to provide extra rest if an employee worked more than eight hours hard time in any twenty-four-hour period.

The Strike

The National Mediation Board declared a **thirty-day cooling-off period** in February 1986. On March 6th, the cooling-off period ended, and the negotiators for the IFFA declared a strike. In separate press conferences, Ms. Frankovich and Mr. Icahn both blamed each other for provoking the strike. "We're going to shut this place down," Frankovich said after final talks ended. "We went as far as we could . . . ," she continued, "far beyond what other groups on this property were required to do." In response, Icahn declared: "We intend to stay in business. Within three or four days from now, we hope to be up to full capacity."[11]

As a result of the work stoppage, TWA had to cancel all sixty of its early-morning flights from St. Louis, the domestic hub of the airline. This occurred on March 6th. They did manage to start flying again around noon of that same day. Systemwide, the airline had to cancel about half its domestic flights and four of its twenty-three international routes. Icahn estimated that the strike would cost the company $45 to $50 million. TWA had already expected to lose $125 million in the first three months of 1986, even without the strike. Nevertheless, stockholders did not appear to be frightened. Instead, confidence in TWA stock seemed to grow. The day after the **walkout**, the trading on the New York Exchange rose an eighth of a point to $16.25 per share.

In anticipation of the possibility of a strike, TWA had been training new flight attendants at its training facility in Kansas City, Missouri. TWA had operated a training school, charging tuition to learn to become a flight attendant, without offering any assurance that the assumption of a position would actually take place. TWA had fifteen hundred immediate replacement attendants who had paid TWA for the opportunity to become flight attendants. Additional recruits were provided by ticket agents and other employees of the airline who had been trained in flight attendant safety procedures.

THE INTERNATIONAL ASSOCIATION OF
MACHINISTS AND AEROSPACE WORKERS

The IFFA had a better chance of winning the strike if the International Association of Machinists and Aerospace Workers, who represented mechanics, stores clerks, and baggage handlers, would honor their picket line. TWA lost its first major battle when a federal judge in Kansas City, Missouri, denied the airline's request for a temporary restraining order that would bar the machinists from honoring the attendant's picket lines throughout the country. U.S. District Judge Howard Sachs did, however, set a date for another hearing on a similar TWA request for a preliminary injunction against the union's sympathy action.[12] Airline analysts claimed that the absence of the machinists could shut the airline down and that the strike would not succeed without their support.

In the interim period, the machinists were acting independently around the country. Some locals were honoring the picket lines and some were not, but as time continued, more and more sup-

port was being gained. By March 11, 1986, about 80 percent of the union's ten thousand members were respecting the line. Support was very strong in St. Louis and Kansas City, where TWA has located their major hub and overhaul bases.

In an attempt to scare the machinists and attendants into returning to work, Icahn threatened to dismember the airline and sell the individual pieces. He stated: "We need to have these cuts. We must be competitive. If we don't, we will sell the airline. The only way they [IFFA] can win is with the machinists. But then it's a no-win situation for both of them because I'd be reluctantly forced to sell the airline."[13] Analysts said that the airline's domestic system international routes and computer reservation system could all be sold separately. Icahn claimed that he could make a $200 million profit if he sold the airline that way.

Icahn's threat was not necessary, because Federal Judge Sachs issued the preliminary injunction, and the machinists were ordered back to work on March 12th. The attendants were then expected to settle promptly, but the stoppage Frankovich stated: "It's our battle. It's something we have to win with or without the support of other unions."[14]

Judge Sachs's decision was based on his interpretation of the language contained in a contract the machinists had signed on January 3rd of the same year of the attendants' strike. The language of the three-year contract provided: "The union will not authorize or take part in any work stoppage, strike, or picketing of company premises during the life of this agreement, until the procedures for settling disputes involving employees covered by this agreement, and as provided by the Railway Labor Act, have been exhausted."

The machinists argued that this language applied only to direct strikes by the machinist's union and that it had no bearing on sympathy strikes. TWA argued that it did have a relationship to sympathy strikes. Sachs believed that TWA would prevail in a grievance it had filed against the machinists with the System Board of Adjustment, the arbitration panel set up under the Railway Labor Act.

Judge Sachs ordered the machinists back to work until this issue could be arbitrated, because a continuation of the strike would harm TWA. The order stated that the machinists would be subject to discipline by the airline if they disobeyed the return order. It also established penalties if the machinists attempted to thwart TWA with lethargic or poor work.

REPLACEMENT FOR STRIKING ATTENDANTS

Since the beginning of the strike, TWA had been drafting into service hundreds of newly hired attendants. The replacements were being paid approximately $12,000 per year and were working under the rules Icahn was demanding of the IFFA. As of March 12th, 400 attendants, out of a force of 6,000, had crossed the picket line. Along with the 1,200 replacements, TWA needed only another 2,300 to enforce its new work rules, which would leave approximately 3,300 of the striking attendants out of work if the union did return, because Icahn promised to keep the new attendants on the payroll.

TALKS RESUME

On March 13, 1986, talks were held in Philadelphia for the first time since the walkout. The talks were under the supervision of a National Mediation Board mediator and a board commissioner. The talks lasted for three and a half hours, after which Meredith Buel, a spokesperson for the National Mediation Board stated: "We will call for further talks when appropriate. The parties expressed their current positions and we see no basis for further discussions at this time."[15]

The flight attendants would not change their position. They argued that they could not be fired—that this was a legal strike and the union could call it off whenever they wanted and go back to work. Icahn also would not change his demand of a 17 percent pay cut and an 18 percent productivity increase. He reiterated that he would retain the now 1,750 new nonunion flight attendants hired since the strike began. By April,

TWA was operating at or near 100 percent and was in the process of replacing all the unionized attendants.

New Attitudes on Labor Strikes According to the Media

In response to the IFFA strike, the news media reported the development of new national attitudes toward labor strikes, which were in general harsher toward union organizations. One such report appeared in the *St. Louis Post Dispatch* in April 1986:

> The strike by the Independent Federation of Flight Attendants against Trans World Airlines demonstrates the new and harsher labor environment in which airline unions have been operating since deregulation. It also demonstrates the negative turn which the nation as a whole has taken towards unions in recent years.[16]

Earlier that year, in January, the *Minneapolis Star Tribune* reported that

> strikes in general have become so difficult to win that labor leaders are reluctant to wage them. Ever since the strike by the Professional Air Traffic Controllers Organization in 1981, what was once taboo has become an increasingly common management tactic. The government fired the strikers, hired replacements and barred the former union members from getting their old jobs back. Employers have had the legal right to replace strikers in contract disputes since 1983, when the U.S. Supreme Court interpreted the federal labor law to say that employers could replace strikers as long as the employers did not discriminate against union activists.[17]

Finally, in July 1986, the *Akron Beacon Journal* reported on the increasing costs incurred by airline strikes after deregulation:

> Before deregulation, struck airlines routinely shut down. In 1973, a strike by TWA flight attendants caused the airline to halt operations for 43 days. But in those days, a shut down was not as worrisome to management as it is now. The airlines had Mutual Aid Pacts that funnelled the excess revenue received by competing carriers back to the strike-bound airline.

Regulation stopped new carriers from jumping in and taking over business.

Also, before deregulation, organized labor's overall strength and popularity restrained airlines and other industries from exercising their legal rights to hire strikebreakers.

Now with the dissolution of mutual aid pacts and the new era of cutthroat competition, the airlines find it crucial to stay in business during a strike. There is also a definite declining popularity of organized labor, which hurts the union's positions. The public does not care as much as it used to.

After deregulation, there was a high potential for strikes in the airline industry because of the pressure put on airlines to cut labor costs. During the 40 year period when the government regulated airlines, the union would bargain for a better contract and the airlines would pass the costs along in higher rates. If TWA mechanics received a raise, United mechanics would receive a better raise in their next round of negotiations and so forth. To offset these added costs, the airlines would go to the Civil Aeronautics Board (CAB) and ask for an across-the-board fare increase, which generally would be granted. Costs, today, can not be passed on to the customers as easily as before because of the high competition that the airlines are in with each other.[18]

A LOST BATTLE?

Analysts claimed that the IFFA was in an especially weak position because flight attendants were the group airlines could most easily replace. TWA said it was training new flight attendants in eighteen days and graduating nearly twenty a day. But by the end of April, TWA had stopped hiring replacements. The union thought that may have been a sign that the airline was interested in settling the dispute, but TWA stuck to its proposals. The carrier did say that it expected to have four thousand flight attendants to replace the strikers and to staff its flights by May, which would be all that were required at that time of the year. For the peak summer months, they estimated they would need a maximum of five thousand attendants.

The Fight to Regain Union Status

TWA filed suit in late April to stop union flight attendants from forcing the carrier to (1) identify or collect union dues from nonstriking flight attendants or (2) discharge nonstriking attendants for lack of dues payments because of the **union security clause** in effect between the carrier and the IFFA. TWA took the position that the union was trying to enforce security provisions of an expired contract. Shortly before the strike, the union had filed a lawsuit asking Judge Sachs to rule that the company had not negotiated in "good faith." The union contended that the period in which neither side could change the contractual obligations had not expired. Sachs denied the request but set the union's case for trial on June 30, 1986, at which time TWA requested that its suit also be considered; their position was that the union security clause had expired March 7, 1986, and that the airline had no obligation to the union under those provisions.[19]

On May 17, 1986, the union unconditionally volunteered to return to work. By this time, TWA had already filled many of their positions with replacement employees. They did however, accept 198 of the senior union members, who returned with a 22 percent pay cut and an increase in working hours. In the previous month, 1,284 IFFA members had unilaterally decided to return to their former positions and were flying under the same terms and conditions. The remainder of the striking employees were placed on a waiting list until positions opened in the company. Icahn reiterated that he would keep the replacement employees, but he said that he might attempt an early retirement buyout for more than 1,000 of the veteran strikers.

On June 30, 1986, Judge Sachs ordered all of TWA's 4,500 attendants to begin paying dues to the striking union (IFFA). TWA sought to block the order in the U.S. Circuit Court of Appeals. Sachs, however, would not stay his order pending appeal: "The flight attendants must begin paying dues to the union by the beginning of

September 1986. Also, TWA must, within two weeks of the order, implement a system for withholding dues from the flight attendant's paychecks and forwarding the money to the union." Addressing the perpetuity of agreements in the airlines, Sachs ruled that the union security clause, like other contract provisions that were not subject to prestrike bargaining, continued in full force. He stated, briefly, "The portions of the contract not subjected to renegotiation still exist."[20]

Sachs's decision was based on a 1966 U.S. Supreme Court decision written by Justice William O. Douglas in a case concerning the amendability of an airline contract under the Railway Labor Act. Douglas had written that collective bargaining agreements are "the product of years of struggle and negotiations and are not destroyed by a strike that represents only an interruption in the continuity of the relationship. A strike is not the occasion for the carrier to tear up and annul the collective bargaining agreement. . . . to do so, labor-management relations would revert to the jungle."[21] Sachs said that the Railway Labor Act prevented parties to a contract from destroying a contract by simply proposing changes.

The order of June 30, 1986, meant that the newly hired flight attendants would be forced to pay dues to the union that had been trying desperately to replace them. The nonunion members would have to pay $100 initiation fees and $36 a month in dues. Union members who had crossed the picket line and returned to work would be required to pay the monthly dues.

This ruling had no effect on pay cuts and work rule changes implemented by management or the fate of the former strikers who had not been recalled. About the ruling, Ms. Frankovich stated: "This is a first of a string of victories that we will win in court. We are very, very pleased. This will give us some money to operate on."[22] But on August 6th, Sachs's decision on union dues was appealed. The airline asked the circuit court of appeals to stay Judge Sachs's ruling and to hear the arguments on the appeal the week of Sep-

tember 8, 1986. The appeal said that under the order, TWA would have to collect approximately $161,000 a month in union dues. The airline felt that the money would be available to the union in support of its economic boycott of TWA.[23]

By the end of August, Sachs made another important ruling. He ruled that strikers with seniority could replace the 1,284 union members who had crossed the picket lines. He said, "In my judgement all permanent employees working during an economic strike [strike held to pressure an employer to give in to economic negotiating demands] are safe from replacement."[24]

IFFA held fast to its belief that its members with seniority were entitled to be placed in the active workforce. It again filed suit, challenging the job statutes of three groups. Union members who did not strike, 1,200 new attendants who were prospective employees before the strike and placed on the payroll after the walkout, and 463 trainees hired after the union unconditionally agreed to return to work.

The central issue of the dispute was whether TWA clearly told new employees that they were permanently replacing the strikers. TWA maintained that under federal labor laws, it had the right to hire replacements. The company contended that there were no jobs available for the former strikers. The union contended, however, that labor law allows strikers to be reinstated if a company can afford it and that TWA was unfairly refusing to hire former strikers. A ruling made by the Supreme Court during a recent strike by the Teamsters had stated that an employer was liable for two payrolls if it told replacements they would be permanent and then offered union members their jobs back in settlement.[25]

During the first week of September 1986, Sachs ruled that TWA did not have to replace 2,500 of its flight attendants with the former strikers. But he also ruled that the airline had to reinstate 463 senior union members whose positions had been filled by trainees after the union had agreed to return. This reinstatement was required within thirty days, with **back pay** and interest retroactive to May 17, 1986. According to this ruling, TWA could either replace 463 new attendants or add 463 union members to its workforce in other than flight attendant positions, as long as striking employees were available to return. The judge agreed with the union that once the union made an unconditional offer to return to work, its members should have been recalled to fill any remaining openings. The 463 new flight attendants should not have been put on the payroll. In deference, TWA offered the 463 other positions within the company. With regard to the 1,280 flight attendants who refused to strike, Sachs ruled that they could not be bumped by those that did strike. The previously placed 198 senior union members were not affected by the decisions.

As of this writing, all the striking flight attendants have returned to the payroll. No agreement presently exists between the parties other than the old agreement and the new implemented changes made by management, who was free—once the cooling-off period expired—to implement any change they had proposed in negotiations. Interestingly, because the parties have been unable to reach an agreement, there has not been a negotiated settlement, nor is there a contractual expiration date. One can only conclude that under this situation, any attempt to modify the present "limbo" agreement may require a **Section 6 notice**, obligating the parties to renegotiate the present terms and conditions.

The outcome of the IFFA strike against TWA provides evidence that contracts are amendable under the Railway Labor Act. The provisions of the parties' old agreement that had not been a subject of bargaining—or that, in labor parlance, were not "**openers**"—remain in full force. One of these provisions, the seniority provision of the scheduling policy, awards those returning from a strike better bid opportunities based on seniority. The IFFA is the designated sole bargaining representative of all the employees, which will remain so until the majority of the employees seek a change to another representative.

Conclusion

Conditioned by the days of regulation in the airline business, the IFFA and other unions have failed to recognize that times have changed and the old rules no longer apply. In round after round of negotiation in which this author has been involved, the unions have steadfastly maintained the position that (1) they were protected by the Railway Labor Act and virtually could not be replaced and (2) if economics did play a part in the possible demise of a company, the government would stop a certified airline from going out of business or a merger would take place to work to the benefit of the union.

These attitudes were not confined to the unions alone but were also harbored by management. The airlines were an island by themselves, sheltered by the Civil Aeronautic Board, bolstered by the security of the Railway Labor Act, and secure in the belief that this atmosphere would last. We in the business, this author included, believed that the attitudes, the approaches, and the legislated sparring would always be a part of our personal industry and that despite them, Camelot would not die. Vickie Frankovich must have believed that and, in some way, probably still wonders what happened to change the ground rules established over the years. It's unfortunate that, like King Arthur, we must eventually atone for our shortcomings.

Rarely in the modern history of the American labor movement has a union walkout backfired so powerfully against its participants. IFFA suits have variously charged TWA with bad-faith bargaining and with sex and age discrimination. The union also reported to the Federal Aviation Administration (FAA) many incidents of alleged safety violations by inexperienced attendants. The FAA had said it had found no unusual problems with the airline.

Harry Hoglander, former president of TWA's pilots' union said about the IFFA: "The cabin attendants are seen by labor to be out to lunch. They really aren't dealing with the realities of the airline business."[26] Many people in the industry believe that Ms. Frankovich mismanaged the negotiations from the beginning and may not have kept the union members fully informed. F. Lee Bailey, the lawyer who advised all unions at the outset of talks in 1985, said: "Their bargaining power was minimal. They were replaceable. Any experienced negotiator would have told them this was not the time to strike."[27]

Despite all the epitaphs written about the end of the IFFA, because of the perpetuity of unions under the terms of the Railway Labor Act, they still exist on the premises of TWA, and their future is secure until another union seeks to take their place through a reelection procedure under the auspices of the National Mediation Board. Many believe the perpetuity aspect of the Railway Labor Act is obsolete and deserves to be reconsidered. The industry has seen profound changes and has been totally deregulated in almost every aspect of its existence save one, the labor law. In the recent past, many calls have been made among industry officials to seek alternate legislation, because they believe the act to be anachronistic and prolabor. This attempt seems to be gaining greater momentum than ever before.

Fortune Magazine highlighted the prolabor aspects of the National Mediation Board:

Easily the strangest federal agency in our country's capital these days is the National Mediation Board. Nobody can explain this animal to us. For openers, nobody can make clear how it has managed to remain totally, unabashedly pro-union after more than eight years of Reaganism. Both members of the board were appointed by Ronald Reagan (a third position is vacant), the guy who made his day by gleefully breaking a strike by the air traffic controllers. But the NMB members and staffers go right on acting as though nothing has changed since Frances Perkins was Secretary of Labor. The board members even had the liberal *New York Times* calling for their skin a while back, based on their obvious commitment to the Machinists Union, which itself was bent on destroying the Lorenzo regime at Eastern Airlines.[28]

The other side of the picture is best related by middle-of-the-roaders and staunch supporters of the act. The following excerpts from letters to the editor of the *Wall Street Journal* highlight those positions:

... your suggestion to strike down the anachronistic Railway Labor Act may not be the thing to do. There is a lot more at stake and more to this law than the Supreme Court decision (concerning secondary picketing). This is not to say that critical reexamination is out of order. It is appropriate to ask whether, in our contemporary, deregulated transportation environment, the law promotes or encumbers public interest considerations: whether nothing more is needed than to transfer the two industries to the other law; or whether, in an attempt to change, the collision of special interests in Congress might reshuffle the deck in some unpredictable way that would not serve either the public or the industries. For people who have invested their careers in one or the other of the Railway Labor Act industries, these are profound questions that deserve more than a throwaway line in what is otherwise a constructive editorial.

Charles I. Hopkins, Jr.
National Railway Labor Conference
Washington

The Railway Labor Act has provided a legislative base for maintaining labor peace and stability in the railroad and airline industries during periods of severe stress and crises—namely deregulation and fare/rate wars. Despite a relatively few instances of interrupted service due to strikes, the law has achieved settlements without strikes in 97% of the cases handled in the airline and railroad industries. Neither the railroad carriers nor the labor organizations seek to abandon the law in favor of the National Labor Relations Act.

Walter C. Wallace, Member
National Mediation Board
Washington[29]

5

Contractual Negotiations

Introduction

Management and labor are mutually dependent for their continued existence, but within this dependent relationship is a pervasive philosophic conflict. One of management's primary objectives is to minimize costs, particularly labor costs. Naturally, labor seeks the highest wages and fringe benefits possible. Furthermore, management believes that it has the duty and responsibility to make all decisions concerning the business, but labor argues for a voice in these decisions.

Management's view is founded on the argument that the ownership of capital carries with it the right and responsibility of deciding how that capital is used.[1] Management argues that they bear the risk of loss if capital is used unwisely. Labor claims the right to participate in business decisions founded on the philosophy of industrial democracy.[2] This philosophy argues that employees have an inherent right to participate in the decisions that directly affect their work lives, especially those that involve wages, work hours, and employment conditions. Labor also argues that capital owned by the business is of little value without the services of its employees.

Historically, this basic conflict between labor and management has led to the disruption of the free flow of commerce and to many social and economic problems for society. In disputes between labor and management, a third party to the dispute is often overlooked: the general public. All labor law must be designed to reflect the conflicting concerns of all three parties.[3]

The present labor laws were crafted to resolve these disputes and to protect the public from undue harm through the provisions for emergency boards. These boards, contained in both the RLA and the NLRA, are the legislative tools to protect the public from damaging and protracted labor disputes. Emergency boards are particularly important because both the RLA and the NLRA legislation encourage collective bargaining and the settlement of disagreements by negotiation, and the emergency boards promote negotiation by providing for the suspension of self-help options until they become absolutely necessary.[4]

Issues about and attitudes toward negotiations in the airline industry have changed dramatically following the passage of the Airline Deregulation Act of 1978. This act and other labor-oriented developments in the air transport sector—the Professional Air Traffic Controllers Strike, the first bankruptcy of Continental Air Lines, and the demise of Eastern Airlines, to name a few—have altered the traditional approaches taken by both management and unions at the negotiating table. But the negotiation procedures and statutory time constraints remain the same.

This chapter compares the contract negotiation procedures that must be followed under the RLA and the NLRA. Before delving into these issues, however, it is necessary to identify several terms used frequently in the labor negotiations environment that are often used incorrectly by the news media in reporting on those very same negotiations: *arbitration, conciliation, mediation, lockout,* and *strike.* The glossary provides the correct statutory definition for each of these terms.

Negotiation Procedures under the Railway Labor Act

Contractual Status

One of the most striking differences between the RLA and the NLRA is that contracts under the RLA are not terminable but continue in perpetuity unless replaced by another contract from a competing union or an individual certified as such,[5] but contracts negotiated under the NLRA expire at their termination date unless they are renewed. Although contracts under the RLA are negotiated for a specified period of time and have **amendable dates**, they continue in existence after their amendable dates, with all provisions of the existing contract remaining in effect until settlement or modification. This statutory contractual aberration under the RLA is generally unknown to the public and is often misrepresented by the news media, who routinely announce that airline employees are working without a contract. This misinterpretation often occurs in reports on the airline industry, where it is common for negotiations to extend beyond the amendable date of contracts negotiated under the RLA. This media spin interpretation could not be further from the truth, because under the RLA, no self-help action may be taken by either party during the negotiation process. The terminology used by the news media is in reference to contractual activities under the NLRA, not the RLA.

The statutory procedures for opening renegotiation under the RLA are given in Section 6 of the act:

> In case of a dispute . . . it shall be the duty of the designated representative or representatives . . . , within ten days after the receipt of notice of desire on the part of either party to confer in respect of such dispute, to specify a time and place at which such conference shall be held: Provided, (1) That the place so specified shall be situated upon the line of the carrier involved or mutually agreed upon; and (2) that the time so specified shall allow the designated conferees reasonable opportunity to reach such place of conference, but shall not exceed twenty days from the receipt of such notice.

The party seeking renegotiation must serve notice, at least thirty days prior to the contract amendable date of the existing agreement, of their intent to negotiate changes in the contract. Thirty days is the required minimum notification period under the RLA. It is important to understand that under Section 6, notice of desire to renegotiate can be given at any time during the life of the contract whenever a party is interested in reopening negotiation on the rates of pay, work rules, or working conditions. Figure 5–1 shows the required steps for contract negotiation under the RLA.

The Negotiation Time Frame

Once negotiations have begun, the RLA places no time constraint on either party. The contract under negotiation continues in force until either the existing contract is amended or an impasse is reached and mediation by the National Mediation Board (NMB) is requested by the parties. Section 6 provides that during the negotiation time period, "rates of pay, rules or working conditions shall not be altered by the carrier." The carrier must maintain the status quo and may not alter working conditions, and the union must not engage in any strike activity.

Because of the timeless nature of the negotiating process at this point, both the unions and the carriers have a well-established tendency of bringing wish lists to the negotiating table, sometimes consisting of hundreds of items. If this situation occurred under the NLRA, with contract termination dates coming due within short periods of time, such wish lists would increase the likelihood of strikes or lockouts. But strikes are unlawful under the RLA until the parties are released by the NMB. So the parties under the RLA often seek as many concessions as they can get during forced negotiations.

Unfortunately, wish lists generally lead to a

Figure 5-1. Railway Labor Act collective bargaining process

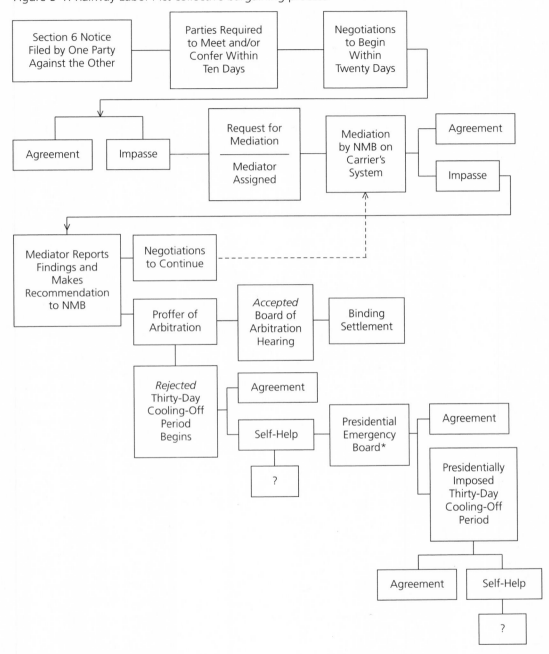

*May occur if the NMB notifies the U.S. President that the dispute threatens interstate commerce, a large portion of society, or national securtiy.

protracted negotiation period. For example, the Air Line Pilots Association and United Air Lines agreement, which had an amendable date of October 1988, was not actually amended until September 1990. Because of this delay, new aircraft (747-400's) were not flown until they were covered under the terms of the amended contract.

A further example of protracted negotiation under the RLA occurred between Ozark Air Lines and their mechanics, who were represented by the Aircraft Mechanics Fraternal Association (AMFA). In May 1978, the agreement between the parties was due for renegotiation. After the proper notices had been filed, negotiations began in April, with more than three hundred issues placed on the table by the union and forty-five by management. Small issues were settled through the first four months of direct negotiation, to eliminate the possibility of an impasse. Neither party wanted to invoke mediation, for fear that an ultimate release to self-help would ensue.

With capital low and the new deregulation act about to curtail the ability of the carrier to pass its increased labor cost on to the public, Ozark Air Lines feared that a strike would devastate its competitive ability. The union, wishing to receive the "best" industry contract, wanted to wait for all other airlines in negotiations to sign agreements, so they could use those airlines' wage increases as leverage against Ozark. Though agreements that had been made prior to deregulation were negotiated on a carrier-by-carrier basis, the union based their negotiation of new demands on the most recent settlement favorable to the union. This process is known as **pattern bargaining**.

The parties agreed to nonbinding interest arbitration to eliminate the prospect of mediation and a possible release to self-help. Ozark believed that any reasonable arbitrator would agree with their position, especially since the union was seeking wage increases in excess of 25 percent, while the industry standard was 9–10 percent. According to O. V. Delle-Femine, the national director of the AMFA, "Since we didn't want a re-

lease from the Board at that time because of too many other airlines in negotiation and since every agreement I've been involved with in the industry has only gotten better, we felt we had nothing to lose. If the decision was good for us we could always agree to it. If it was bad, we could just refuse it and wait for the other agreements to be settled. In any event we get the time we want."[6]

Contrary to the company's belief, the arbitrator in this decision awarded the union the wage increases and a change in work rules that would have severely penalized the company. The decision was refused by the company, and the parties returned to the table. The union wasted no time before pressing for the awards of the decision, however, and an impasse occurred. A NMB mediator was assigned to the case, and negotiations continued for another eight months. Mediation in this particular case did not provide a solution, and the eventual outcome was a release by the NMB and a strike by the AMFA.

The parties eventually came to terms, eighteen months after the amendable date of the original contract. Because the new contract provisions were retroactive to the original amendable date of the previous contract, which continued in force during the entire negotiation and mediation period, and because the new contract, like most airline contracts, was only valid for a period of three years, the parties were again in negotiation within a year and a half.

Mediation

Mediation is a fundamental procedure under the RLA. Unlike the NLRA, which offers optional mediation by the Federal Mediation and Conciliation Service (FMCS), the courts have established that under the RLA, mediation is mandatory under the guidance of the NMB. If the parties are unable to reach an agreement in direct negotiations and conclude that a deadlock or impasse has been reached, either party is free to request mediation by the board.

In *Machinists v National Mediation Board*, the court held the following:

The legislature provided procedures purposefully drawn out, and the Board's process may draw them even to the point that the parties deem them almost interminable.

What is voluntary about mediation, including mediation under this Act, is the decision to accept or reject the result available from the mediation process. What is involuntary about mediation under this Act is the obligation to engage in the mediation process even though a party is not unreasonable from his point of view in his conviction that further mediation is futile. The court's inquiry cannot go beyond an examination of the objective facts and determination thereon whether there is a reasonable possibility of conditions and circumstances (including attitudes and developments), available to the Board, consistent with the objective facts, sufficient to justify the Board's judgment that the possibility of settlement is strong enough to warrant continuation of the mediation process.[7]

Mediation is mandatory under the RLA, but no time frame is mandated. The length of negotiation is at the sole discretion of the NMB and the assigned mediator.

The Mediation Process. When an application for mediation is received in Washington, it is docketed and reviewed by the NMB to verify that an actual impasse has been reached. When the NMB believes that such is the case, a mediator is assigned to the dispute. Mediators are generally assigned on an availability basis. There are approximately twenty full-time mediators employed by the NMB, and they are based throughout the country. A mediator can be of invaluable service to the negotiation process if the parties are willing to utilize the mediator's services and experience. The mediator does not settle the bargaining impasse. The bargaining parties (union and management) must agree to do that. The mediator's role is to assist the parties in reaching an acceptable agreement. This assistance may involve one or more of the following functions:

1. Arranging and scheduling joint or separate meetings between the bargaining parties or the mediator

2. Presiding over and maintaining order at meetings (e.g., determining issues to be discussed, order of speaking, record keeping)

3. Influencing the duration or location of bargaining meetings

4. Facilitating the adoption of procedures for contract extensions or postponement of **strike deadlines**

5. Continuing negotiations between the parties after a strike has occurred

6. Keeping communication channels open

7. Exploring the underlying interests behind each party's position (e.g., How realistic are the party's expectations regarding an acceptable settlement? Is the party aware of the potential costs involved with nonsettlement relative to settlement? How flexible is each party's position?)

8. Helping the parties to define or redefine their respective bargaining priorities

9. Offering creative suggestions on a specific issue or alternative settlement terms

10. Offering creative suggestions to one or both parties on how each might "save face" or create opportunities for settlement that might allow their opponent to agree and still save face in the eyes of constituents, other employers, a union, or the general public[8]

If and when the mediator concludes that his or her efforts are failing to produce results (length of time is solely at the mediators discretion) and an impasse occurs where the parties are no longer talking, the mediator may inform the board of the situation by a private report based on his or her conclusions drawn from the meetings with the parties.

If and when the board concludes that further mediation would be pointless, it works to obtain the parties agreement to submit the dispute to **binding arbitration** by submitting to each party a formalized proffer of arbitration. A proffer of arbitration, made by the NMB under Section 7 of the RLA, is an offer to submit the deadlock or impasse to a neutral judge to decide the conditions of the final agreement.

If either of the parties reject the arbitration proffer, the board notifies both parties, in writing, that its mediation efforts have failed, and it releases the parties from the procedure after a thirty-day cooling-off period. The cooling-off period is designed to allow both parties the opportunity to reevaluate their positions. Nothing precludes the parties from reconvening negotiations during this period.

Supermediation. As a final effort to resolve an issue, the NMB will usually request the parties to attempt to reach an agreement through supermediation. This procedure, although not a statutory part of the RLA, is often employed to avert a strike. The offer of supermediation is rarely refused by either labor or management.

In supermediation, the parties generally meet with one of three members of the NMB who are appointed by the president of the United States. This meeting is designed to bring visibility and political pressure on the parties to reevaluate their positions one final time. If a breakdown in this procedure becomes eminent, the board may again suggest arbitration before withdrawing from the case and effectively leaving the parties to their own devices. Withdrawal at this point does not mean that the NMB can never again reenter the dispute, even after a strike or lockout has occurred. Section 5 of the act indicates they may reenter at any time they, the NMB, deem necessary.

After the thirty-day cooling-off period, the parties are free to resort to self-help, unless the president of the United States establishes an emergency board (discussed in the following section). Self-help includes strikes, lockouts, a company's implementation of its final offer, or any other legal means available to the parties.

The length of the negotiation period is critical to an airline, because a number of unions are present on the property to represent the many craft and class determinations. Theoretically, with protracted negotiations, a contract dispute may be resolved only to become the subject of immediate renegotiation, because agreements under the RLA are retroactive to the amendable dates. Because of protracted negotiations and the number of unions on the property, a company or its labor relations department can be, and often is, in labor negotiations with a variety of unions on a nonstop basis.

Emergency Boards

The RLA, like the NLRA, has provisions for assisting in the settlement of disputes that "threaten substantially to interrupt interstate commerce to a degree such as to deprive a section of the country essential transportation service."[9] This provision permits the president of the United States to intervene and create an emergency board to investigate the dispute and report on it to the president within thirty days from the date of the board's establishment. During that thirty days, and for thirty days following the report, no change in status, except settlement, may be made by the parties to the dispute.

Once the recommendations of the emergency board are submitted to the president and to the parties, the parties have the option, under the RLA, of rejecting the emergency board's recommendations. The situation is left to the parties to resolve, no matter how long it takes. Thus, the emergency board provisions of the RLA provide the president with little more than a method of postponing a strike or lockout for a period of at least sixty days, during which time the parties may make no change to the conditions that prompted the dispute, other than by agreement. Once this time frame passes, the act is silent on further government intervention.

The creation of emergency boards to handle disputes in the airline industry was common during the 1950s and 1960s. Since that time, government has made it clear that threatened or actual strikes will not result in the invocation of the

RLA emergency board procedures, particularly since the transporting of most goods and people can be accomplished by other carriers in the market. Because of the economic impact of deregulation, a reevaluation of this procedure may be necessary in the future if a return to protracted negotiations occurs.

The president does have one other alternative available under executive privilege. He or she may introduce legislation in the Congress, which if passed by both the Senate and the House and signed, would bind the parties in the dispute to the terms of the legislation. Such legislation would generally follow the emergency board's recommended solution.

In late 1993, President Clinton used his office to intercede in a strike by flight attendants against American Airlines. The president telephoned both union and management and asked both to reconsider their positions, stressing quick settlement. Management and the union agreed to send the dispute to binding arbitration. Whether presidents will intercede in this fashion in future airline strikes remains to be seen.

Strikes

The vast majority of self-help action in the airline industry has centered around the strike, which represents the unions' ultimate weapon to resolve the issues when the parties are unable to agree. It has been far more prevalent in the air transport sector than the lockout, primarily because an airline requires a highly sophisticated workforce of specialists (i.e., pilots, aircraft mechanics, reservationists, etc.), all of whom must have some degree of aviation-related knowledge to perform their appointed tasks. Because replacements may be hard to get, a lockout could result in economic suicide, a total loss of cash flow. Consequently, the strike by employees is the dominant form of self-help activity, which is not to say that only the unions are responsible for strikes. In many instances, the company has literally forced the unions to strike.

The Mutual Aid Pact. Prior to deregulation in 1978, there was a distinct advantage to the carriers for forcing a strike rather than become involved in a lockout. In 1958, the airlines formed the Mutual Aid Pact, designed and structured as a form of air carrier strike insurance. The provisions of the pact included recovery by struck carriers of a portion of the windfall revenue profits experienced by other carrier members of the pact. Windfall revenue was the increased revenue of the carrier member of the pact that was attributable to the strike minus the added expense of carrying the additional traffic. In return, the carrier struck was required to make every reasonable effort to provide the public with information concerning air service offered by other carriers in the pact.

Labor tried unsuccessfully to have the courts set the Mutual Aid Pact aside or to have Congress outlaw it. Finally, in 1978, with the passage of the Airline Deregulation Act, all existing mutual aid agreements were declared void. During their twenty-year history, over half a billion dollars in mutual aid was paid under the agreements.[10]

Until deregulation, the outcome of strikes was relatively predictable. It was just a matter of time until the parties reached some sort of agreement on terms and conditions. The cost of any wage or benefit increases could be passed on to the consumer in the form of fare increases granted by the Civil Aeronautics Board. Since the industry was highly regulated, competition by fares was virtually nonexistent and was not a factor in a particular market or airline. Since deregulation, however, all aspects of the air transport labor environment have changed, but none more so than the negotiating approach taken by management in the event of a strike.

Deregulation. The RLA places many limitations on a company during a strike or lockout, but with a one-week notice, a company can hire either temporary or permanent replacement workers.[11] Until deregulation, the thought of replacement workers was foreign to airline management for many reasons. Hiring replacement workers would deny the carrier the opportunity to partake in revenue sharing under the Mutual Aid Pact. More significantly, a sufficient pool of labor to accomplish replacement hiring was virtually nonexistent. Deregulation and the subsequent demise of many carriers and craft positions changed this equation by creating a previously unavailable pool of skilled labor.

In August 1983, the International Association of Machinists and Aerospace Workers struck Continental Air Lines. Continental replaced many of the strikers with permanent employees. A new union contract was negotiated very quickly, and the event ushered in a new era and approach to airline labor relations. Another new element was added later, when Mr. Frank Lorenzo, chairman of the board for Texas Air Corporation and the owner of Continental Air Lines, declared a Chapter 11 bankruptcy. No case brings the post-deregulation changes of labor relations in the air transport sector into sharper focus than the actions of Continental. The effects of this dispute were so profound that the government was forced to change the bankruptcy rules regarding the abrogation of existing contracts. The activities by Continental are discussed further in chapter 9.

Negotiation Procedures under the National Labor Relations Act

Bargaining Topics

The NLRA declares it the policy of the United States to encourage collective bargaining. Section 8(a)(5) makes it an unfair labor practice for an employer to refuse to bargain collectively with the employees' representatives. Similarly, Section 8(b)(3) requires the employees' representatives to bargain with the employer's representative. Section 10(c) provides the National Labor Relations Board (NLRB) the authority to enforce these provisions.

Additionally, the act requires the parties to

meet and confer in "good faith," at "reasonable times," with respect to wages, hours, and other terms and conditions of employment. Defining "good faith" has been the subject of many articles, NLRB rulings, and court decisions. The definition generally rests on the interpretation of the action, or lack of action, by either party to the negotiating process. Accordingly, determining the validity of a charge of "lack of good-faith bargaining" rests on interpretation of the particular activity involved. According to *The Labor Board and the Collective Bargaining Process*, a Bureau of National Affairs publication, good faith is attained if both parties have a "sincere" desire to reach an agreement. Three examples of "bad faith" are

1. Failing to give negotiators sufficient authority to bind the employer

2. Refusing to sign an agreement already reached

3. Unilaterally granting wage increases or changing other benefits without consulting the union[12]

Under the NLRA, certain topics are, by law, the subject of mandatory negotiations, others have been declared illegal, and a third group are the subject of voluntary negotiations. Illegal topics of bargaining are those mentioned directly in the NLRA statutory language. These topics are expressly forbidden, and attempts to bring them to the negotiating table are subject to fines and penalties. Examples of prohibited topics are closed shops, featherbedding, and a union security clause in a right-to-work state. Voluntary topics of bargaining become a part of negotiations only through the joint agreement of both parties. Neither party can be compelled, by law, to negotiate over voluntary subjects. Adamant refusal to bargain about a voluntary subject or to include it in the final agreement is not illegal under the rules of the NLRA.[13] Nor do these subjects have to be bargained in good faith.[14] Mandatory topics of bargaining are those over which the parties must bargain if they are introduced by either party at the table. The courts and the NLRB have placed seventy items into this category. Table 5-1 lists the subjects assigned to each of the three categories by the NLRB.

The Contract Negotiation Process

The Labor Management Relation Act requires that for an existing contract to be legally opened for renegotiation under the NLRA, the party requesting renegotiation must serve written notice to the opposing party sixty days prior to the termination date of the existing contract. The sixty-day notice is a minimum requirement. If a timely notice has not been served by the party seeking to renegotiate, the other party has no obligation, under the NLRA, to bargain, modify, amend, or extend the existing contract. The contract can be allowed to lapse. The company can then implement any changes it wishes with regard to wages, benefits, or work conditions; and any workers who continue to work must accept these new, unilaterally introduced terms and conditions.

The NLRA places certain limitations on employers and unions during the negotiating process. Neither party has the option to strike or lockout at will. No party to a collective bargaining agreement can terminate or modify a contract, unless the party desiring the termination or modification complies with the following procedure:

1. The party must notify the other party to the contract in writing about the proposed termination or modification sixty days before the date on which the contract is scheduled to expire. If the contract is not scheduled to expire on any particular date, the notice in writing must be served sixty days before the time when it is proposed that the termination or modification take effect.

2. The party must offer to meet and confer with the other party for the purpose of negotiating a new contract or a contract containing the proposed changes.

3. The party must, within thirty days after the notice to the other party, notify the FMCS of the existence of a dispute if no agreement has been reached by that time. Said party must also notify at the same time any state or territory where the dispute occurred.

4. The party must continue in full force and effect, without resorting to strike or lockout, all the terms and conditions of existing contracts until sixty days after the notice to the other party was given or until the date the contract is scheduled to expire, whichever is later.[15]

Self-Help

Under the NLRA, the ability to strike or lockout is contingent on a request for mediation or arbitration and also faces the possibility of presidential intervention. Should the president of the United States determine that a strike and or lockout will threaten "an entire industry or substantial part thereof engaged in trade, commerce, transportation, or communication among the several states or with foreign nations, or engaged in the production of goods for commerce" or that it "will, if permitted to occur or continue, imperil the national health or safety,"[16] the president may appoint a review board to study the strike or lockout. If it is determined that the national health is indeed affected, the president, through the U.S. attorney general, may seek an injunction ordering a suspension of the strike or lockout.

The strike or lockout is delayed for a period of eighty days if the injunction is granted, during which time the FMCS works with the two parties to resolve the dispute. Should the reconciliation effort fail and the injunctive cooling-off period expire, new hearings may be held by the NLRB, at which time the final company offer to the union is presented. The members of the union are allowed to vote on this final management proposal. If they vote for the proposal, the dispute is over, and work continues under the new terms and conditions. If the employees vote

Table 5-1

Categories of Bargaining Subjects Assigned by the National Labor Relations Board

Compulsory Subjects

Agency shop	Merit wage increases	Safety
Arbitration	Negotiation Arrangements	Section 125 cafeteria
Bonus payment	**No-strike clause**	programs
Change of payment	Nondiscriminatory hiring hall	Seniority
Schedules	Overtime pay	Severance pay
Change in insurance carriers	Partial plant closing	Shift differentials
Checkoff	Pension plans	Sick leave
Discharge	Piece rates	Solicitation on company property
Discounts on company products	Plant closing	Stock purchase plans
Dues checkoff	Plant relocation	**Subcontracting**
Duration of agreement	Plant rules	**Superseniority** for stewards
Employee physical exams	Price/company provided	Transfers
401(k) programs	meals	Transportation over company lines
Grievance procedure	Profit-sharing plans	Union security
Group insurance	Prohibition of supervisory	Vacations—paid
Holidays	work promotions	Vended food products
Hours of work	Quality circles	Wages
Income tax withholding	Reclassification of workers	Work loads
Layoff	Reinstating economic strikers	Work assignments
Layoff plans	Relocation	Work rules
Lunch periods	Rest periods	Work schedules
Management Rights Clause	Right to enforce arbitration	

Examples of Permissive Subjects

Corporate organization
Size and composition of
   supervisory work force
General business practices

Examples of Illegal Subjects

Closed shops
Preferential treatment of
   union employees
Featherbedding issues

against the proposal, they may then be called out on strike by the union. The strike may continue indefinitely until the disagreement is resolved or until other arrangements are made by the parties. Figure 5-2 shows the steps in the NLRA's collective bargaining process.

This type of cooling-off period and injunctive suspension of self-help options is not used in all situations; it is statutorily limited, under the NLRA, to national emergency disputes. The vast majority of strikes or lockouts do not receive or deserve this level of attention. Consequently, at the termination of a contractual agreement, most parties are able to utilize self-help immediately.

Figure 5-2. National Labor Relations Act collective bargaining process

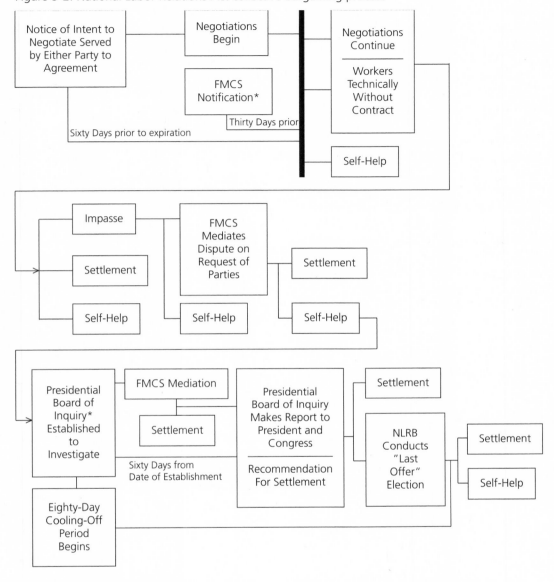

*May occur if dispute threatens interstate commerce, a large portion of society, or national security.

Mediation

Self-help may also be delayed by a request for mediation or arbitration. Mediation is generally the first step. Mediation may begin prior to a contract's expiration. The NLRA does not list a specified time limit for the mediation process but rather follows the doctrine of "reasonable time frame." The FMCS may proffer its services either on its own motion or on the request of one or more parties to the dispute.[17]

Although the FMCS performs a mediation role similar to that of the NMB under the RLA, there are significant differences in their roles. Unlike mediation by the NMB, mediation by the FMCS is a separate function of that service, and mediators do not have any power or authority to make recommendations or determinations on when an impasse between the parties occurs or on whether to force the parties to continue negotiations. Moreover, the time frame for mediation is broadly defined under the NLRA, but no such time frame exists under the RLA, where a mediator could literally hold the parties in mediation, against their will, for as long as he or she desired.

Under the NLRA, the mediator acts only as a guide to assist the parties. If, within a "reasonable time frame," mediation fails, other courses of action may be suggested, such as arbitration. Mediation is not binding in any way, and a rejection of mediation procedure by either party is not deemed a violation of the NLRA or an unfair labor practice.[18]

Arbitration

There are major differences between mediation and arbitration. Arbitration is defined as "a process by which an answer is provided for issues in a dispute."[19] The focus in mediation is to bring the parties to an agreement. Arbitration determines exactly what the actual agreement will be. Even though arbitration is a quasi-legal procedure, it can be accepted or rejected.[20] And to be accepted, it requires both parties' approval.

Under the NLRA, two types of arbitration may be entered into by the parties. Final arbitration settles the dispute on the basis of the arbitrator's decision. Advisory or interest arbitration provides a decision that the parties will use as a guideline in the negotiation process.

Arbitration is conducted by a neutral party, and the process has no specified time limits. Arbitration is usually used as a last resort to settle disputes. Final or binding arbitration will end the dispute. Advisory or interest arbitration may not settle the dispute, and if it does not, a strike or lockout may commence or continue.

Actions During a Strike or Lockout

The intent of either a strike or a lockout is to apply economic pressure on the opposing party and to bring that party to agreement at the negotiating table. Both activities are legal under the NLRA, after the administrative procedures have been exhausted.

Hiring Replacement Workers under Employer Lockout. An employer may lockout its employees only after the bargaining agreement has terminated. After doing so, if the company desires to continue operations, it can continue on a reduced scale, with temporary employees not covered by the terminated contract.[21] When the dispute is resolved, the temporary replacement workers, being temporary, are expected to end their employment relationship with the company.

Permanently replacing employees that have been locked out questions the very fiber of the NLRA, particularly in the area of unfair practices. In a decision rendered in a lockout at Johns-Manville Products Corporation, the NLRB held that a company's lockout becomes illegal when, during the lockout, the employer unilaterally decides to hire permanent replacements without first consulting the union. This unilateral act violates Section 8(a)(3) of the NLRA. Furthermore, permanently replacing all employees in a bargaining unit who are locked out is a violation of Section 8(a)(5), because it completely destroys the bargaining unit and constitutes an unlawful withdrawal of recognition of a duly designated union. The board also noted and cited the absence of evidence that the union had engaged in an in-plant strike or other improper statutory conduct that might justify the employer's hiring of permanent replacements.[22]

Hiring Replacement Workers under Union Strike. The hiring of replacement workers during a strike is treated differently. The hiring of replacement workers on either a temporary or a permanent basis by the employer is legal when the employees are engaged in a strike solely designed to bring economic pressure on the employer to resume negotiations with the striking union. The only condition is that the employer did not cause the strike by engaging in an unfair labor practice, in which case the hiring of replacements is prohibited.

Because permanent replacements are permitted when a union strikes for economic purposes, the strikers may never return to work. The major strikes that unions have lost in the United States in recent years share the characteristic that the employer has been able to obtain replacements and operate indefinitely despite the strike. Examples of this phenomenon include the Florida East Coast Railway Strike—against an intrastate rail carrier covered under the NLRA—the Washington Post Pressmen Strike, and the Caterpillar Strike in 1991–92.

Summary

The issues surrounding contract amendability under the RLA versus contract terminability under the NLRA and the difficult and pervasive question of permanent replacement worker status represent the most troublesome points of contention between management and labor today. That contracts under the RLA remain in force even after their amendable dates essentially means that management, at best, can only achieve a maintenance of the status quo. Under the RLA, the unions have a tremendous bargaining advantage over management, both because highly specialized skill levels are inherent in the air transport industry and because prounion language is extant in the RLA. Under the RLA, the best-case scenario for management, maintenance of the status quo, is the worst-case scenario for unions. The worst a union can do under an RLA-governed dispute is achieve what it already has. There is little downside statutory risk to the union under the RLA. This statutory concept of a "contract in perpetuity" represents management's "crown of thorns" under the RLA and significantly impacts their self-help options.

Equally problematic for management under the RLA is the lack of statutory privilege to hire permanent replacement craft workers under terms different from the existing contract. The RLA expressly states, and the NMB and the courts have expressly held, that any replacement craft workers are "automatically represented by the very union that is on strike" and "must be compensated under the terms of the contract that is being negotiated."

This later issue presents a very different set of concerns when viewed through the legislative lens of the NLRA. Employers under the NLRA can and do hire permanent replacement workers, and they do so under terms decidedly different from the striking union's terminated contract. Under the NLRA, replacement workers are the "crown of thorns" for unions. So important is this issue to labor that heavy lobbying efforts are taking place in Washington to prevent management from hiring permanent replacements during strikes under the NLRA. Airline and railroad management is also lobbying in Washington, to be allowed to utilize permanent replacements under the RLA.

Round one of this issue took place in mid 1993, when Congress considered legislation that would bar employers from permanently replacing employees who walked off the job for economic reasons. It was argued by both the secretary of labor and the American Federation of Labor and Congress of Industrial Organizations that the Workforce Fairness Act, as the issue became titled, would level the playing field between management and labor. According to an article in *Aviation Daily*, the bill had strong support in the House of Representatives, with at least 162 cosponsors.[23] Thus, in June, the House of Representatives passed the Cesar Chavez Workplace Fairness Act, renamed after the hero of the California agriculture union movement. The fate of the Senate version of the same bill (S. 55), known simply as the Workplace Fairness Act, is uncertain because the measure was held up by a Senate filibuster and never reached the Senate floor for vote.[24] Twice before, in 1992, the threat of a Senate filibuster blocked action on a striker replacement ban.

The issue is unquestionably foggy and needs some finality. The NLRA is unclear on procedural application, the RLA has questionable applicability, and the Supreme Court has never really addressed the question except left-handedly. In 1938 a decision was reached in *NLRB v Makay Radio & Telegraph Co.* that has some relevance.[25] In that two-sided ruling, the court decided that it is illegal to fire strikers but that it is not illegal to fail to rehire them. Such a nonsensical position leaves both management and unions in a quandary as to interpretation.

Airline and labor officials say that the fate of the striker replacement bill will set the stage for labor-management relation in the airline industry for the remainder of this century and well into the next. Should it eventually pass both houses of Congress and receive presidential approval, it would make it an unfair labor practice for airlines to give hiring preference to employees who worked or were willing to work during a legitimate walkout (e.g., TWA flight attendants in 1986). Airline officials fear that such a provision would threaten an already weakened industry. Some labor experts argue that the issue is moot because none of today's megacarriers is in a position to withstand a strike.[26]

6

Grievance Procedures

Introduction

Grievance procedures are a fundamental component of any union contract. The grievance machinery of the RLA, which includes an arbitration process, is a mandated procedure. The NLRA lists grievance procedures as one of the mandatory bargaining issues, but the language of the NLRA is not explicit about the procedures that must be employed in resolving grievance disputes.

Under the NLRA, a union has a statutory duty to represent the employees fairly in both contract negotiations and contract administration. This duty is derived from the unions exclusive representative rights in Section 9(a) of the Wagner Act. In Section 203(d) of the Landrum-Griffin Act, Congress declared that "Final adjustment by a method agreed upon by the parties is the desirable method for the settlement of grievance disputes arising over the application or interpretation of an existing collective bargaining agreement."

Statutory Alternatives

Several pieces of federal legislation have had a significant impact on grievance procedures under both the RLA and the NLRA. Grievances that were adjudicated solely under the agreed provisions of the NLRA or under the statutory mandates of the RLA now have alternative means of redress. Of major significance is the legislation passed in the areas of Equal Employment Opportunity and the Occupational Safety and Health Act. When an employee files a charge with either of these agencies, company and union policies and even the grievance procedure itself are subject to outside scrutiny. The existence of statutory alternatives inserts the government as a fourth party to the proceedings and makes the entire process more formalized and legalistic. The parties must be more objective in their relationship regarding those areas where a statutory alternative exists.[1]

In cases of discharge, the employee can seek statutory relief if there is the least indication that the discharge is discriminatory. The employee has the right to enjoin the union as a codefendant if the union refuses to arbitrate the discharge,[2] which puts an added burden on the union to arbitrate even if it does not feel the case has merit.[3] Statutory or contractual grievance machinery and outside agency review can occur simultaneously. These simultaneous reviews can place the grievance adjudicator in an awkward position when deciding complaints, because the adjudicator's decision may be overruled or looked on as not reaching a reasonable decision by the outside government agency considering the same complaint.

Grievance Definition

Generally, a grievance exists when an employee or union alleges that there has been

1. A violation of the agreement

2. A violation of the law (for which a statutory alternative is available)

3. A violation of rules or regulations contained either specifically in the agreement or in other company action

4. A change in working conditions

5. A violation of past practice

6. A violation of health or safety standards (for which a statutory alternative is available)

Many contracts specifically limit the grievance procedure to matters involving the "meaning and application" of the contract. But when matters not directly related to the meaning and application of the contract are brought up, it is permissible to hear these types of complaints and grievances. Both management and the union can use the established grievance procedures to handle these noncontract issues, and by doing so, they may possibly avoid early appeal to arbitration or external statutory investigation. The early steps of the grievance procedure provide for factual discussion, factual exchange, and factual consideration of the issues. Although time may be wasted dealing with these noncontract issues, "it is better to waste time than leave a sore spot unattended."[4]

Contract Administration

When agreements are reached in contract negotiations, the parties generally announce, through informal and formal statements, that a new understanding between the parties exists and that "peace and harmony" will again prevail. In airline negotiations, the **ratification** process is lengthy because the membership is generally spread throughout the country. Because the ratification process is prolonged, the company allows the unions to make the first announcements about what they attained during negotiations. To do otherwise may work against the ratification process and cause an agreement hammered out at the table to become moot.

With all the exuberance and enthusiasm generated by the signing of a new agreement, an aura of optimism is established concerning the workings of the new agreement. It takes some period of time, however, before it is determined whether this optimism is justified. Once the contract is signed, management and union officials have the job of implementing it in the workplace.

The new agreement establishes the framework for which labor relations are to exist during the term of the contract. Although the negotiators, through compromise and statesmanship, believe they are totally aware of what was negotiated, questions of interpretation and application develop almost immediately. To minimize these questions, negotiators sometimes keep "minutes of negotiation" for reference at a later date. But these documents tend to lose their value by the time the contract is finalized, especially in protracted negotiations, which are often found in the airline industry. Therefore, both the company and the union must begin to administer the contract on a daily basis.

Normally, management and the unions devote a considerably larger amount of their time to the administration of the agreement than to its negotiation. The formal signing of the agreement, not the negotiating process, identifies the true beginning of union-management relations. Contract administration is not an event that takes place just once or every three years; it is an ongoing process.

Many administrative problems result from the interpretation of the language of the agreement. Because of the nature of the bargaining procedure—clauses and amendments being written in the haste of the eleventh hour, when negotiators compromise, modify, and change position to reach an agreement before the possibility of a work stoppage—many clauses are written in rather broad and ambiguous terms. Consequently, each side to the agreement may have a different interpretation of the meaning and application of these clauses.

It is unrealistic to believe that a labor agreement that fully insures against ambiguous language can be written. At the bargaining table, the parties may have differences of opinion on which they are not willing to compromise. In the interest of reaching an agreement, they may agree on language that is vague, general, and even contradictory. Written agreements only take on shape and operational meaning when management makes decisions about how it intends to apply meaning to the terms and conditions and when the union and employees react to these decisions.[5] Contract administration works through these issues.

Grievance Procedures

Arbitrator Michael I. Komaroff referred to the grievance procedure as the "life blood of a collective bargaining relationship,"[6] and Gerald G. Somers wrote that the grievance machinery "is not a mere adjunct of the collective bargaining process; it is the very heart of the process."[7] In the initial implementation stages following ratification of the contract, the parties meet to iron out differences that may have developed. But because most contracts have a three-year time frame, the interpretation eventually becomes the responsibility of the labor relations department personnel and the union officials (committeemen, **stewards**, etc.), who may or may not have participated in the formal negotiations.

Problems of interpretation are generally handled through the grievance procedure of the contract. Such procedures can be formalized impersonal and may contain a variety of steps allowing for appeal to a higher authority if the complaining party is not in agreement with the decision rendered. The actual number of steps in the procedure and its machinery and formality are subjects of the negotiation process and are mandatory subjects of bargaining under the NLRA.

The grievance procedure provides an orderly approach for union and management to determine whether a contract has been violated. In very few cases are the alleged violations willful or in complete disregard of the terms and conditions negotiated. More frequently, unions and employers pursue a course they believe to be in conformity with that agreed on at the table. Differences between the way labor and management interpret how the contract applies to continued working relationships are the province of the grievance procedure.

Not all collective bargaining contracts provide for the same structural arrangements, as can be seen by comparing the information in the additional study material at the end of this chapter, which contains a typical procedure for airline grievances handled by a system board of adjustment and a typical grievance procedure found in NLRA contracts. Some grievance procedures contain only one step; others have many more. But the basic characteristics of the procedures are similar. A certain time limit is placed on each step for both parties to file, appeal, and answer grievances. Failure to adhere to these time limits could result in the forfeiture of the grievance by the violating party.

Grievance answers can be precedent setting both in the in-house stages and, more importantly, in the arbitration stage. For this reason, the ultimate decision in small-plant operations should rest with a member of the management team who has final and binding authority for the plant. In cases where the organization is large and spread over many work locations, as is the airline industry, the grievance decision makers at the local level should clear their decisions with an ultimate authority, such as the vice president of labor relations, before rendering a decision. This approach maintains consistency and continuity in the process throughout larger companies.

Ultimately, the procedure is exhausted. The party filing the grievance either agrees with the decision or takes the matter to a higher authority. If it has been agreed to in the contract under the NLRA or in the case of the RLA, this higher authority is an arbitrator.

Grievance Arbitration

A typical grievance and arbitration procedure includes several steps. Generally, the employee and his or her union steward present the grievance to the employee's immediate supervisor. Usually, this first step is not formalized—that is, a written complaint is not initiated. If a satisfactory settlement cannot be reached, the union and employee can appeal to progressively higher levels of management. At these higher stages, the union usually has exclusive control over whether to pursue the grievance further, settle it, or dismiss it. At this point, the union is insulated from suit by the employee, unless he or she can establish that any unilateral action by the union amounts to a refusal or breach of the union's **duty of fair representation**.

When the bilateral process of the grievance procedure breaks down and the parties cannot agree, provisions are made between the parties to place the matter with an impartial arbitrator selected by the parties to decide the controversy. The arbitrator determines the outcome of the dispute. The contract invariably stipulates that the arbitrator's decision is "final and binding."

Arbitration typically begins either by a submission agreement or by a demand or notice invoking an arbitration clause in a collective bargaining agreement. The submission agreement generally describes the dispute and the relief sought by the petitioning party and is jointly signed by the parties to the dispute. The document may also include details concerning the procedures to be followed by the arbitrator, the limits of the arbitrator's authority, and the deadline for rendering a decision.

Irrespective of whether arbitration is initiated by submission or demand, the arbitrator frequently requests a statement of the issues in the case at the outset of the hearing. If the parties are unable to agree on the specifics, the arbitrator may simply request separate statements from each party and may infer from these statements the nature of the dispute.

Arbitrator Authority and Limits. Most arbitrators draw their authority to decide on contract issues from the contract they are asked to interpret. If there are limits, they are usually defined in clear and unambiguous terms. Most contracts provide that the arbitrator has no power or authority to alter, change, or modify the provisions or **intent** of the contract.

When a company and union seek arbitration, they have already made an agreement among themselves to disagree on a particular issue.

Consequently, they seek an arbitrator to rule on what the language of the contract means and on whether it has been applied correctly under the circumstances. The parties are not seeking innovative ideas outside the scope of the agreement. Thus, the arbitrator becomes an instrument of the contract, not a decision maker whose award can be rendered in a vacuum. Should a decision reveal flaws in a collective bargaining agreement, the correction of such inconsistencies is the responsibility of the company and the union at the next round of negotiations. It is not a part of the arbitrator's assigned responsibilities in rendering a decision.

Grievance Arbitration under the Railway Labor Act

Arbitration is mandatory under the RLA. Although the RLA is silent with respect to specific grievance procedures between the parties, it does state in Section 3, First, that disputes "shall be handled in the usual manner up to and including the chief operating officer of the carrier designated to handle such disputes; but failing to reach an adjustment in this manner, the disputes may be referred by petition of the parties or by either party to the appropriate Division of the Adjustment Board." In 1934, the act was amended to establish the National Railroad Adjustment Board (NRAB). This amendment required grievances to be handled on the rail carriers property and, when not resolved, to be submitted to the NRAB for final decision.

In 1936, the National Mediation Board (NMB) was empowered to create for the air transport sector an adjudicating authority similar to the NRAB. This grievance authority was to be the National Air Transport Adjustment Board (NATAB) and was to be composed of two members selected by the carriers and two members selected by the unions. A neutral referee was to be the fifth member of the board. The decisions rendered by this board were to be final and binding on the parties to a dispute.

The NMB has never implemented the NATAB.

Instead, the courts have interpreted Section 204 of Title II—which mandates that each air carrier and labor organization establish grievance machinery and a system board of adjustment—to mean that each airline and their unions must establish grievance machinery that fulfill the statutory requirements and scope of the NATAB.[8] A system board's decisions are subject to the same judicial review as those of the NRAB. Consequently, the airlines and the unions evolved their own grievance machinery, similar in concept to the NATAB, but different in its structure. Each airline agreement provides for a system board of adjustment and a negotiated procedure for resolving disputes. Figure 6-1 shows a typical airline grievance procedure under the RLA.

The System Board of Adjustment

When the machinery of grievance resolution is exhausted, a case is eligible for submission to a system board of adjustment. The composition of such system boards varies among airlines. Some system boards are composed of members from management and labor. System boards decide the outcome of grievance hearings on a case-by-case basis. If a majority of the members of the system board agree, the decision is final and binding. If, however, a deadlock occurs, a neutral referee is required. In this case, the par-

ties may ask the NMB to submit a panel of arbitrators from which the parties will select an arbitrator, or they may proceed on their own to select an arbitrator without the assistance of the NMB.

A variation on the provision for a system board of adjustment is the impanelment of a neutral party from the very beginning of the arbitration process, and in some cases, provisions have been made for the system board to be bypassed in favor of a single neutral arbitrator used on a case-by-case basis. The provision to bypass the system board, although not conforming to the language of the RLA or to the court-ordered requirements, has been allowed by the NMB, because it still provides a system for peaceful settlements of minor disputes.

Overruling Arbitration Decisions

The arbitration methodology in the airline sector is varied, but in most cases, it conforms to the spirit and intent of the RLA. The advantage of a board approach is that in an industry with unique practices and nomenclatures, the appointed union and management parties can help a neutral adjudicator understand the issues more clearly so that he or she may reach an equitable solution. Occasionally, however, even with such assistance, an impartial arbitrator reaches a de-

Figure 6-1. Railway Labor Act airline grievance procedure

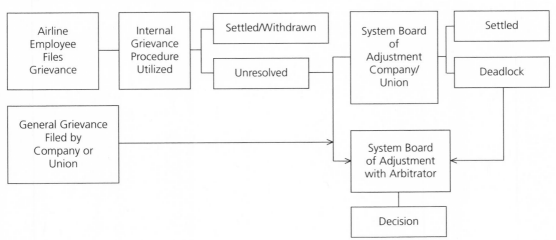

cision that is clearly "out in left field." When this happens, the management and union board members may agree to dissent from and overrule the arbitrator's decision. But when a system board of adjustment is not convened and only an arbitrator is making the final and binding decision, no appeal for judicial review may be made unless language contained in the contract stipulates that the arbitrator may not exceed the intent of the parties to the agreement.

Prior to the 1966 amendment to the RLA, a carrier that disagreed with an arbitration decision could unilaterally set the decision aside and refuse to comply. The union involved could accept the carrier's decision and let the award go unenforced, or they could bring action in federal court to enforce the award. In addition, prior to 1956, the union could strike to force the carrier to honor the decision. But in 1956, in *Brotherhood of Railroad Trainmen v Chicago River & Indiana Railroad Co.*, the Supreme Court eliminated the ability of a union to strike to enforce a decision by stating: "Congress had intended Section 3, First, to be a mandatory comprehensive and exclusive system for resolving disputes over grievances and claims."[9]

The 1966 amendment also provided that the award of a system board was enforceable in federal court. This amendment thus limited the courts' power to review the decisions of the arbitration machinery and required the courts to use the same standards for reviewing awards under the RLA as employed in the *Enterprise Wheel & Car* decision affecting the NLRA. In the *Enterprise Wheel* decision, the court stated that as long as the arbitrator's award drew its essence from the collective bargaining agreement, a court could not set aside the award.[10]

In 1969, the United States Circuit Court of Appeals construed the 1966 amendment to imply that the power of judicial review was limited to awards that had no foundation in reason or fact. The court further held that an award could not be overruled because the court's interpretation of contractual language was different from that of the arbitrator. In a decision similar to that in the *Enterprise Wheel* case, the court concluded that "the parties had bargained for the arbitrator's construction of the contract rather than the court's."[11]

Arbitration Costs

Costs associated with arbitration in the airline sector depend on the arbitrator selected and his or her background and notoriety. It is not unusual for fees to exceed $800 per day plus expenses. The arbitrator's fee and the costs of witness transportation, hotel expenses, time away from work, conference room expense, and other incidentals can make a grievance arbitration very expensive. The size and makeup of the system board creates additional expenses.

An interesting aspect of the RLA is that arbitration held under the NRAB is paid by the government. Although this expense has been under attack by various government agencies and presidential administrations in recent years, the railroad unions have argued that government coverage in this area was part of their agreement to accept statutory, mandated, binding grievance arbitration as a part of the 1926 act.

The RLA provided the airline industry with the NATAB, and one might logically and correctly assume that grievance arbitration in the air transport sector would be at the government's expense if the NMB ever authorized its use. Mediators accustomed to the railroad industry and involved in airline negotiations have espoused the virtues of the NRAB and have suggested that airline management press for the installation of the NATAB, if for no other reason than to reduce expenses. But enactment of the NATAB is highly unlikely for two reasons. First, the system presently utilized by the airline industry and its unions, albeit expensive, is comfortable and familiar. Second, because of the pressures of a massive federal budget deficit, the government is not likely to approve the additional expenditures by the NMB.

Grievance Arbitration under the National Labor Relations Act

Under the NLRA, no statutory language exists to force the parties to a dispute into arbitration. Without specific contractual language to the contrary, usually embodied in a provision to submit unresolved grievances to arbitration, the parties might use strikes or lockouts to settle such problems. Because these methods are costly to both parties, most negotiated contracts contain some method for "final and binding" arbitration. At the present time, some 96 percent of all U.S. labor agreements provide for arbitration as the final step in the grievance procedure.[12] Figure 6–2 shows a typical grievance procedure under an NLRA contract.

Although the NLRA does not contain language requiring arbitration, the Supreme Court has stated: "In the absence of any express provision excluding a particular grievance from arbitration, we think only the most forceful evidence of a purpose to exclude the claim from arbitration can prevail, particularly where, as here, the exclusion clause is vague and the arbitration clause quite broad."[13] Consequently, the courts may impose arbitration if the parties do not specifically exclude it in contractual terms.

Overruling Arbitration Decisions

In many decisions rendered by arbitration, one of the parties may contend that the arbitrator overstepped his or her authority in the interpretation of the contract. Contention is less likely to occur in airline disputes than in those of other industries, because in the airlines' board of adjustment approach, more than one party is involved in the final and binding decision. In some situations where contention has occurred, companies have ignored the decisions. In others, both management and the unions have jointly petitioned the courts to set the decisions aside. The arbitrator's decision-making authority and the binding nature of the arbitrator's decision was outlined in the 1960 decision by the Supreme Court preserving the integrity of the arbitrator's award. Upholding an arbitration decision, the Court stated: "Interpretation of the collective bargaining agreement is a question for the arbitrator. It is the arbitrator's construction which was bargained for; and so far as the arbitration decision concerns construction of the contract, the courts have no business overruling him because their interpretation of the contract is different from his."[14]

The importance and significance of this de-

Figure 6-2. National Labor Relations Act grievance procedure

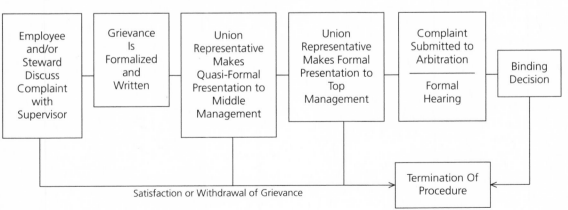

117

cision is clear. Unions and/or management may not use the courts to set aside an arbitrator's award. In an attempt to alleviate this problem, for both union and management, some agreements contain contractual language stating that in the arbitration process, the arbitrator cannot interpret the contract beyond the intentions of the parties to the agreement. But this language itself can be subject to interpretation. The simplest and most common method of dealing with a decision that is contrary to both union and management interpretation is for them to decide among themselves to disregard the finding.

Selecting an Arbitrator

Most labor agreements provide for the method in which an arbitrator will be selected by the parties. This process generally utilizes the services of the Federal Mediation and Conciliation Service or the **American Arbitration Association**. When called on, these organizations provide a list of arbitrators, complete with a brief description of their background and a quote of their daily fees. Often, the parties are familiar with several arbitrators on the list, making the selection procedure less troublesome. If the arbitrators are unknown, useful information concerning their prior decisions on similar issues may be available from a number of sources, including legal and labor relations services or reporters. Reports from these sources review arbitrator's decisions and provide an analysis of the arbitrator's idiosyncrasies, methods, and decisions on an issue-by-issue basis.

If the parties cannot agree on an arbitrator that is mutually acceptable, they may resort to a variety of different methods for selection. The most common is the "first strike" method, which employs the flip of a coin. The party that wins the coin toss is allowed to eliminate the name of the arbitrator least desirable to it, and then the opposing side makes the second strike. This process continues until only one name remains. This method, although not scientific, sometimes employs a degree of gamesmanship and maneuvering to obtain the choice most suitable for each party.

Arbitration Costs

Costs associated with the arbitration process under the NLRA do not vary much from those under the RLA, which are listed earlier in this chapter. But under the NLRA, the parties must pay for arbitration out of their own pockets. Usually, these costs are divided equally between the parties.

Summary

Grievance procedures under the RLA are a matter of law. Under the NLRA, they are purely a matter of contract. Under the RLA, air carriers and their unions must have a system board of adjustment or some other formal, NMB-accepted mechanism for resolving grievances. Over 96 percent of all NLRA-based contracts have some formal grievance resolution provisions.

When a grievance exhausts the available procedures under the RLA, the issue is submitted to binding arbitration by statute. Arbitration is optional under the NLRA. The arbitration decision can be set aside by agreement of the parties, but not through the courts, because the Supreme Court has ruled that such decisions are beyond the scope of the courts to interpret.

The cost of grievance resolution and arbitration for the railroads under the RLA is borne by the federal government through the NRAB. But grievance and arbitration costs for the airlines and their unions is not government sponsored under the RLA, because the duly authorized NATAB has never been activated by the NMB. Consequently, the cost of grievance resolution and arbitration is borne by the carrier and the union equally. The situation is identical for grievance resolution and arbitration costs incurred under NLRA contracts.

Additional Study Material

Grievance Procedure Contained in the Contract Between the International Association of Machinists and Trans World Airlines*

ARTICLE 11
GRIEVANCE PROCEDURE

(a) Representation

The representation of presentation and adjustment of disputes or grievances that may arise under this agreement shall be: The Union will be represented by properly designated stewards, one in each department or section thereof, for each shift at each point on the system. In addition, the Union will be represented by full-time committees at those points listed in (b) below, one of whom shall be designated as chairman. In addition, the Union will be represented by a local committee consisting of not more than three (3) members at EWR, IND, LAS, and PHX; of not more than two (2) members at ABQ, CMH, CVG, DAY, DEN, and IAD and one (1) member at all other points. One (1) member of the local committee shall be designated as Local Chairman. Where a metropolitan area with more than one location is involved, there may be separate stewards and separate committees.

(b) Full-Time Committees

Such committeemen shall be the sole committee members under the terms of Article 11(a)1, unless during the term of the current agreement the parties otherwise mutually agree.

Full-time committeemen will be paid by the Company for a maximum of forty (40) hours per week at their hourly rate of pay including afternoon shift premium. The Union will notify the Company of the individuals who will serve in these positions and the designated area of representation for each committeeman. Normally each committeeman will participate in handling complaints, disputes and grievances in his designated area. The committee may represent the Union on any complaints, disputes or grievances below Step 3 level.

Full-time committeemen will be assigned to various shifts where needed using a base forty (40) hour work week which shall be determined by the Local Committee Chairman, IAMAW, who in turn will advise the Regional Director-Personnel or his/her designee in writing of each committeemen's work assignment. Committeemen will normally "check in" and "check out"

Line Stations/Overhaul Bases	Committees	Committeemen
Kansas City Overhaul Base	7	3
Kansas City Line Station†	2	1
JFK and LGA	6	3
Chicago	2	1
SFO	2	1
LAX	4	1
STL	2	1
Bos	1	1
PIT	1	1
PHL	1	1

†The Kansas City Line Station full-time committeemen will represent all IAM staffed facilities in the Kansas City Metropolitan Area, excluding the Overhaul Base.

*Reprinted by permission of Trans World Airlines, Inc.

when arriving or leaving Company premises. Committeemen will submit time cards in accordance with existing time card procedures.

Each committeemen will represent the Union in handling Step 2 grievances, disputes and complaints with the ranking Company official at the point. In order to facilitate the conduct of union-management business in an orderly and businesslike manner, it is agreed:

(1) The Company will provide the full-time committeemen with space for a single office with an intra-base telephone in an acceptable area.

(2) Stewards and committeemen will be empowered to settle all local grievances or disputes not involving changes in policy or intent and purposes of this agreement.

(3) Full-time committeemen may leave the premises during their working hours without loss of pay for the purpose of conducting union-management business with the President-General Chairman and/or General Chairman of District Lodge 142. When leaving the premises for these purposes, the President-General Chairman and/or the General Chairman shall advise local management.

(4) The Company and the Union will make every effort to keep to a minimum the actual time spent in disposing of grievances, disputes and complaints.

(5) All committeemen will be eligible for overtime in their respective departments. While working overtime, committeemen will not function as Union representatives. If a committeeman does not desire to work overtime, he will request that his name be removed from the overtime list.

(6) All committeemen will be allowed free access and availability to all work areas and shops within their respective areas of representation in order to conduct their business in a proper, efficient and expedient manner. In so doing they will contact appropriate management personnel.

(7) The Union will be further represented by a President-General Chairman and/or his designated representative(s) for dealing with regional or general officials of the Company.

(8) The Company will be represented at each seniority point by an authorized official who will be empowered to settle local grievances or disputes, but such settlement may not involve any change in the intent and purpose of the agreement. The Company will be further represented on a regional and system basis for dealing with the Union President-General Chairman and/or his designated representative(s).

(9) The Union and the Company will, at all times, keep the other party advised through written notice of any change in authorized representatives.

(10) The President-General Chairman and/or his designated representative(s) and a reasonable number of Grand Lodge Representatives of the Union shall be permitted at any time to enter the facilities of the Company for the purpose of representing employees covered by this agreement, after notifying the Company official in charge.

(11) It is agreed the Union and the Company will make every effort to keep to a minimum the actual time spent in disposing of grievances, disputes or complaints. When stewards and committeemen are required to leave their work for the purpose of investigating, processing, presenting and adjusting grievances or to attend meetings as provided for in this article, they will first notify their immediate supervisor or his designee, if available, before leaving their work and will again report to him upon their return. In the event it is necessary to go to another area, they will report in with the foreman or supervisor of that area. It is recognized that stewards and committeemen are not required to obtain permission from their supervisors before leaving work in order to attend Union business; they are merely required to notify their supervisor, who, upon being notified, must inform the steward or

committeemen of the specific contingency which makes his departure at the time stated impractical, if such should be the case. The steward or committeemen are then under an obligation to seek a satisfactory time for such business that will not frustrate the needs of the Company.

(c)Procedure

The procedure for presentation and adjustment of disputes, complaints, or grievances that may arise between the Company and the Union with reference to interpretation or application of any provision of this agreement shall be:
STEP 1

(1) Any employee having a complaint or grievance in connection with the terms of employment, application of this agreement, or working conditions, will, with the steward, discuss the matter with his immediate supervisor. If unable to secure satisfactory adjustment in this manner, the employee may present his complaint or grievance in writing to the department steward, who in turn will, if in his opinion the complaint or grievance is justified, present the written grievance to the Company's designated representative at the particular point or in the department. Subject to operational requirements and the time remaining on a particular shift, a hearing shall be convened on that shift for the purpose of rendering a decision in the matter. In no event shall the hearing be postponed beyond the next regular shift of the grieving employee. A decision in writing shall be rendered not later than three (3) work days following such a hearing.
STEP 2

(2) If the decision in Step 1 is not satisfactory, the Grievance Committee may refer the matter to the appropriate chief operating official for the point or his designated representative. The appeal must be made in writing within five (5) work days after the Step 1 decision, and the actual appeal must be presented at a hearing within seven (7) work days from the date of the

appeal to Step 2. A written decision will be rendered by the Company within four (4) work days after adjournment of the hearing.

At points on the system where a Grievance Committee is not established by the IAMAW (District 142) appeal may be made by the President-General Chairman and/or his designated representative(s) to Step 3, and the time limits for Step 3 shall apply.
STEP 3

(3) If the decision in Step 2 is not satisfactory, the Union's President-General Chairman and/or his designated representative(s) may refer the matter to the Company's Vice-President of Maintenance and Engineering (for Maintenance and Engineering grievances) or the Vice-President of Field Sales and Service (for Sales and Service grievances). The notice of intent to appeal the matter to Step 3 must be made in writing within fifteen (15) work days after the Step 2 decision. Within forty-five (45) days after the Step 3 appeal date, the Vice-President of Maintenance and Engineering or his designee or the Vice-President of Field Sales and Service or his designee will meet with the Union's President-General Chairman and/or his designee and endeavor to reach a settlement of the issues involved in the matter appealed. If unable to resolve the issues, the Company shall issue a written decision setting forth its position on the issue(s). In no event shall such written decision be issued later than five (5) work days.

(4) If the decision in Step 3 is not satisfactory to the Union, the matter may be referred by the Union's President-General Chairman to the System Board of Adjustment.

(5) Grievances relating to matters general in character, which cannot be settled by an immediate supervisor or local Union representative shall be discussed by the appropriate Corporate Vice-President and the Union's President-General Chairman, if such grievances are submitted in writing by either of them. If a satisfactory settlement is not reached within

ten (10) work days after the grievance is submitted, such matters may be referred, within five (5) work days after the expiration of said ten (10) day period, to the President of the Company or his designated representative if submitted by the Union, or to the International President of the Union or his designated representative, if submitted by the Company.

(6) Individual grievances must be filed promptly after the cause giving rise to the grievance is evident, and no individual grievance will be valid if not filed within thirty (30) days of the date the employee knew or could reasonably be expected to have known of the grievance. Grievances filed under paragraph (5) above which involve wage claims must be filed promptly after the cause giving rise to the grievance is evident, and such wage claims will not be collectible for a period earlier than thirty (30) days prior to the date of the filing of the grievance or the date the grievance arose, whichever is more recent.

(7) Disciplinary Time Off

No employee who has been in the service of the Company ninety (90) days or more shall be assessed a disciplinary layoff until he has been given the opportunity to discuss with a Union representative the circumstances involved and to attend an investigation meeting with a representative of the Union, conducted by the charging supervisor, and presented with a written statement copy to his Union representative of the precise charges and the penalty imposed. The employee and his authorized representative will be advised of the purpose of this investigation before it is convened.

Discharge

No Mechanic who has been in the service of the Company one hundred and eighty (180) days or more as a mechanic, and no other employee who has been in the service of the Company for ninety (90) days or more shall be discharged without a fair hearing (and no such hearing shall be conducted without the duly authorized Union representative present) before a designated representative of the Com-

pany, other than the one bringing the complaint against the employee. If an employee is suspended, pursuant to Article 11(d)(4), the Company will advise the employee and/or his duly authorized Union representative in writing of the precise charge(s) preferred against him not later than one (1) work day from the time of suspension.

A discharge hearing will be held not later than five(5) days after the employee and the Union are notified of the precise charges and a written decision will be issued within three (3) work days after the close of the hearing. Prior to the hearing, the employee and his duly authorized representative will be given reasonable opportunity to secure the presence of necessary witnesses. If the decision is not satisfactory, then the appeal may be made in accordance with the procedure prescribed in Step 3.

If the above mentioned provisions are not adhered to, the employee and his duly authorized Union representatives shall be notified in writing advising him of his reinstatement in accordance with Article 11(c)(8) of this Agreement.

The notification of the decision of the discharge hearing is mailed and postmarked not later than three (3) work days after the close of the hearing.

(8) If it is found that an employee has been unjustly suspended or dismissed from the service, such employee will be reinstated with his seniority rights unimpaired, compensated for all wages lost, and his service record cleared.

(9) The Company will not discriminate against any witness called to testify in any hearing or investigation under this Agreement, and if any employee witness is located at some point other than at the point of hearing, employee witnesses and Union committeemen will be furnished necessary free non-positive transportation over Company lines.

(10) Except as specifically provided in this Article, all hearings, meetings, and investigations will be conducted during regular day shift working hours insofar as possible. Union

representatives and necessary employee witnesses shall not suffer loss of pay while engaging in the provisions of this Article.

If grievance hearings or investigations are held during other than regular day shift working hours, at the Company's written request, or if Union representative spends in excess of eight (8) hours per day attending such hearings, at the Company's written request, such Union representative shall be paid at his regular straight time rate for time so spent.

(d) General

(1) It is understood that either or both the President-General Chairman or his authorized representative and the Vice-President of Labor Relations or his authorized representative may intervene and participate in the handling of a grievance or dispute at any level of the grievance procedure.

(2) Probationary employees (mechanics with less than one hundred eighty (180) days service as a mechanic and other employees with less than ninety (90) days service) covered by this agreement shall not have recourse to the grievance procedure in the event of discharge within the probationary period.

(3) For the purposes of computing work days in connection with provisions of the Article, only the calendar days Monday through Friday each week shall be counted.

(4) In meetings for the purpose of investigation of any matter which may eventuate in the application of discipline or dismissal, an employee will be entitled to Union representation, if he so desires.

Regardless of any other provisions of this Article, an employee will not be suspended from the service of the Company, pending a hearing unless the Company determines that its employees, property, or operation is seriously jeopardized.

The Union recognizes the right of the Company supervisors to manage and supervise its work force of employees, individually or collectively in the normal course of work.

(5) The Union's decision to withdraw grievances, not to process or appeal a grievance to the next step shall not in any way prejudice its position on the issues involved.

(6) In assessing discipline, the Company will consider the gravity of the offense, seniority and the work record of the employee involved.

ARTICLE 12
SYSTEM BOARD OF ADJUSTMENT

(a) In compliance with Section 204, Title II, of the Railway Labor Act, as amended, there is hereby established a System Board of Adjustment for the purpose of adjusting and deciding disputes of grievances which may arise under the terms of this Agreement and which are properly submitted to it after exhausting the procedures for settling disputes, as set forth under Article 11.

(b) The System Board of Adjustment shall consist of three (3) members; one (1) appointed by the Union and one (1) appointed by the Company, one (1) selected by the parties from a standing panel of six (6) Referees. Each of the parties shall name three (3) individuals who shall serve on this panel. In addition, an Alternate panel of four (4) Referees shall be established by each of the parties hereto naming two (2) individuals.

(1) Either party may cause the services of a Referee on the six (6) member standing panel to be terminated at anytime (except as to cases already scheduled for hearing), after thirty (30) days written notice to the other party and to the Referee whose services are being terminated by naming a replacement who must be one of the Alternate panel members appointed to said panel by the party making change. Each party is limited to two (2) such replacements in accordance with the above. Thereafter, thirty (30) days prior to the expiration date of the Agreements the parties must name members to the six (6) member standing panel and the four (4) member Alternate panel as provided in paragraph (b) above.

(2) In the event a vacancy or vacancies on

the six (6) member panel of Referees exists, prior to the expiration date of the Agreements, both parties shall within ten (10) working days agree upon replacement panel member(s). Should the Company and the Union be unable to agree upon said replacement member(s) they shall make joint request to the National Mediation Board to name interim Referee(s).

(3) The foregoing notwithstanding, the parties may agree to select a Referee who is not a member of the six (6) member panel to hear a case with the Company and the Union Board members and such panel will, for such, case, constitute the System Board of Adjustment. Such "Ad Hoc" arbitrator will be selected from a list of seven (7) arbitrators submitted, in alternate turns from case to case by one party to the other, the party receiving the list taking the first turn at striking a name from the list. The remaining name on the list shall be the Referee for the case; however, if he is unable to serve in timely fashion, then the parties will make joint request to the National Mediation Board to name a Referee.

Unless the Company and the Union agree upon a combination of cases to be presented to a Referee, each case presented to the Board shall be treated as a separate case; except those grievances involving more than one (1) employee or incident concerning an alleged violation with similar facts and circumstances which shall be treated as on case. The Company and the Union member of the Board shall serve until their successor is duly appointed.

(4) Secretary to the Board

The Office of "Secretary to the Board" shall alternate January 1st of each year between the Company member of the Board and the Union member of the Board with the Union member serving on even numbered years and the Company member serving on odd numbered years.

The Secretary shall give written notice to the Board members and the parties to the dispute in connection with the scheduling of Board matters.

(c) The Board shall have jurisdiction over disputes between any employee covered by this Agreement and the Company growing out of grievances, interpretation or application of any of the terms of this Agreement. The jurisdiction of the Board shall not extend to propose changes in hours of employment, basic rates of compensation, or working condition covered by this Agreement or any amendment hereto.

(d) The Board shall consider any dispute properly submitted to it by the President-General Chairman of the Union or his authorized representative, or by the chief operating official of the Company or his authorized representative, when such dispute has not been previously settled in accordance with the terms provided for in this Agreement, provided that notice of the dispute is filed with the Company and the Union members of the Board, with copy to the Company or Union, as may be appropriate, within forty-five (45) days after the decision in the last step of the grievance procedure. The date of notice shall determine the order for considering cases, unless the parties mutually agree otherwise.

(e) The neutral member (Referee) shall preside at meetings and hearings of the Board and shall be designated as Chairman of the System Board of Adjustment. It shall be the responsibility of the Chairman to guide the parties in the presentation of testimony, exhibits, and arguments at hearings to the end that a fair, prompt and orderly hearing of the dispute is afforded.

(f) The Board shall meet in Kansas City, Missouri, unless a different place of meeting is agreed upon by the Company and the Union.

In the event either of parties is of the opinion that a System Board of Adjustment hearing should be held at a site other than Kansas City on the grounds that the Board would better appreciate the circumstances of the case by being afforded an on-site inspection, such party will notify the other party and if both parties agree, the System Board hearing will be conducted at the site agreed upon.

Should the parties fail so to agree, then the party desiring the change of site shall put the determination of the site to the Arbitrator selected to hear the case, setting forth that party's reasons, in writing, for requesting the change with a copy to the other party who will be afforded an opportunity to oppose such change, setting forth his reasons in writing. The Arbitrator's decision as to such site shall be final.

(g) The notice of disputes referred to the Board shall be addressed in writing to the Company member and the Union member jointly and shall include a statement of:

(1) The question or questions at issue

(2) Statement of facts

(3) Position of appealing party

(4) Position of other party

A copy of the notice of dispute shall be served upon the other party.

(h) Upon filing the notice of dispute, the Company and Union Board members shall within five (5) work days, select a Referee to sit with the Board to settle the dispute and the Secretary of the Board shall advise the appealing party and other party of the name and address of the Referee. If the Board members are unable to agree upon a Neutral Referee within the five (5) work days, a joint request will be directed to the Chairman of the National Mediation Board for the appointment of a Neutral Referee. A copy of the notice of dispute shall be forwarded by the Secretary of the Board to the Neutral Referee who has been appointed or selected to serve in this matter. All subsequent documents filed with the Board shall be addressed to all three members, with copy to the other party or parties.

(i) The Neutral Referee shall set a date for hearing scheduled within thirty (30) days after his appointment. If the Neutral Referee is a member of the standing panel and cannot serve during this, the parties may agree to another member of the standing panel who is available during this same period or the parties shall jointly petition the Chairman of the National Mediation Board to assign a Neutral Referee.

(j) If neither party or the Chairman request a hearing, such hearing shall be waived. If either party desires a hearing to present evidence or oral argument to the Board, or if the Referee desires that evidence or arguments be presented by either party, request for hearing shall be made to the Board and served on the parties within fifteen (15) days after the appointment of the Neutral Referee. If such request is served, the hearing shall be held within thirty (30) days of the date the request is served at a time mutually satisfactory to the Chairman and the Company and Union members of the Board.

(k)(1) Immediately following the hearing, the Board shall convene in Executive Session, unless the parties mutually agree otherwise. The Board shall issue its decision at the conclusion of the Executive Session, if possible. However, a written award will be rendered to the parties not later than ten (10) work days following the Executive Session.

(2) In no event shall a decision be issued until after an Executive Session has been held if either the Company or the Union Board member has requested such session. In the event there is to be no hearing, the Chairman shall set a date which is agreeable to the Board members, for an Executive Session of the Board. The Board shall issue its decision at the conclusion of the Executive Session, if possible. However, a written award will be rendered to the parties not later than ten (10) work days following the Executive Session.

(l) The time limits expressed in this Article may be extended by mutual agreement of the parties to this Agreement. The expenses and reasonable compensation of the Referee selected, as provides herein, shall be borne equally by the parties hereto.

(m) Employees covered by this Agreement may be represented at Board hearings by such person or persons as they may choose and designate, and the Company may be represented by such person or persons as it may choose and designate. Evidence may be presented either orally or in writing or both. The Board may, at the request of either the Union member or the Company member thereon, call any witnesses who are employed by the Company and who may be deemed necessary to the dispute.

(n) A majority vote of all members of the Board shall be competent to make a decision. Decision of the Board in all cases properly referred to it shall be final and binding upon the parties hereto.

(o) If the parties mutually agree, a stenographic report will be made. The costs of such report shall be borne equally.

(p) The Chairman's copy of any transcripts and/or all records of cases will be filed at the conclusion of each case in a place to be provided by the Company, and will be accessible to Board members and to the parties.

(q) Each of the parties hereto will assume the compensation, travel expense, and other expenses of the Board member selected by it.

(r) Each of the parties hereto will assume the compensation, travel expense, and other expenses of the witnesses called or summoned by it. Witnesses who are employees of the Company shall receive positive free transportation over the lines of the Company from the point of assignment to the point at which they must appear as witnesses and return, to the extent permitted by law.

(s) The Company and the Union member, acting jointly, shall have the authority to incur such other expenses as in their judgment may be deemed necessary for the proper conduct of the business of the Board, and such expenses shall be borne one-half by each of the parties hereto. Board members who are employees of the Company shall be granted necessary leave of absence for the performance of their duties as Board members. Board members shall be furnished positive free transportation over the lines of the Company for the purpose of attending meetings of the Board, to the extent permitted by law.

(t) It is understood and agreed that each and every Board member shall be free to discharge his duty in an independent manner, without fear that his individual relations with the Company or with the Union may be affected in any manner by any action taken by him in good faith in his capacity as a Board member.

(u) Nothing herein shall be construed to limit, restrict, or abridge the rights or privileges accorded either to the employees or to the Company or to their duly accredited representatives, under the provision of the Railway Labor Act, as amended.

(v) Regardless of any of the foregoing provisions of this Article 12:

(1) Either party may elect to revert to the procedure set out in Article 12 of the Agreement between the parties dated December 9, 1958, by written notice to the Company and Union Board members and the other party to this Agreement. If the procedures of the December 9, 1958 Agreement have been resumed as the result of such election, they shall continue to apply unless and until modified by mutual agreement.

(2) In any case where the procedure of Article 12 of the December 9, 1958 Agreement applies, paragraph (b) of said Article 12 shall be considered as modified to provide that the Board of Adjustment shall consist of one (1) Company and one (1) Union member.

(w) (1) Discharge Boards of Adjustment are hereby established in New York for those stations located in the eastern time zone; Los Angeles for those stations in the western time zone; and Kansas for those stations in all other time zones. A two (2) member panel shall be established by each of the parties naming one (1) individual with offices in the areas where Discharge Boards are to be established. The parties will make every effort to avoid a conflict in the scheduling of such Boards. The jurisdiction of each such Board shall be limited to dismissal cases.

(2) Each Discharge Board shall be composed of one (1) member appointed by the Company, one (1) member appointed by the Union,

and a Neutral Referee who shall serve as Chairman. Hearings will be held off Company premises at a location in the cities where they are to serve. The rules of procedure, applicable to the System Board of Adjustment, including those pertaining to the sharing of expenses shall apply. Either party may cause the services of a Neutral Referee to be terminated (except as to cases already scheduled for hearing) by giving written notice to the other party and to the Neutral Referee.

(3) If the Company and the Union are unable to agree upon a replacement or on the selection of a Neutral Referee, within three (3) days after the Union elects to engage the Discharge Board in lieu of the System Board of Adjustment, the parties shall promptly make joint request to the National Mediation Board for the appointment of a neutral.

(4) A decision by a majority of the members of a Discharge Board shall be final and binding as to the cases properly before that Board.

Grievance Procedure Between the Communications Workers of America and Southwestern Bell Telephone Company*

ARTICLE XX
GRIEVANCES

Section 1. The Union shall be the exclusive representative of all the employees in the bargaining unit for the purposes of presenting to and discussing with the Company grievances of any and all such employees arising from such employment; subject always, however, to the provisions of this Agreement, the current Agreement of General application between the Union and the Company and of any applicable law.

Section 2.

a. Any employee complaint (except those which contemplate treatment or proceedings inconsistent with the terms of a collective bargaining con-

tract or agreement then in effect including proposals for the modification of, or addition to, any such contract or agreement) which is reduced to writing and delivered by a Union representative in accordance with Section 2.b following, within 45 days of the action complained of, shall be considered and handled as a formal grievance.

b. The grievance procedure shall normally consist of three successive steps. Notice of grievances and appeals of decisions made at the first and second steps shall be forwarded in accordance with the following:

Step No.	Company Representative Designated To Receive Grievance

1. Division level manager having supervisory authority over the conditions or circumstances which gave rise to the grievance. (In the absence of a Division level, the notice of the grievance shall be forwarded to the District level manager having the supervisory authority.)

or

Section Head level manager having supervisory authority over the involved conditions or circumstances if the grievance involves employees in more than one Division organization. If the grievance is initially filed at this level, any appeal of such a decision shall be filed at

Step Number 3.

or

Vice President-Human Resources or designated representative if the grievance involves employees in more than one Section level organization. If the grievance is initially filed at this level there shall be no successive steps.

2. The manager who supervises the individual to whom the first-level grievance notice was directed.

3. Vice President-Human Resources or designated representative.

c. If the grievance involves or affects only employees reporting to a single immediate super-

*Reprinted by permission of Southwestern Bell Telephone Company.

visor, a copy of the notice shall also be forwarded at the same time to such supervisor.

Section 3.

a. The decision made at either of the first two levels of the grievance procedure may be appealed to the next higher level of the grievance procedure provided such appeal is submitted within two weeks of the date the decision is communicated to the Union.

b. A decision at the 3rd level of the grievance procedure or default on the Company's part to meet with the Union, as explained in Section 7., at the 3rd level shall be construed as full completion of the Formal Grievance procedure.

c. At the Union's request, the decision of the Company as to grievances submitted shall be confirmed in writing to the Union.

Section 4. So that the Union may present formal grievances to the appropriate Company representative, the Company will notify the Union of changes in Company organization that require a change in the then existing manner of presentation.

Section 5. After a notice as set forth in Section 2.b. above has been received by the Company, the Company will not attempt to adjust the grievance with any employee or employees involved without offering the Union an opportunity to be present.

Section 6. At any meeting held pursuant to Section 2. above, the Company will designate its representative(s) to meet with the aggrieved employees(s), the representative(s) designated by the Union, or both.

Section 7. Meetings at each level of the grievance procedure shall be arranged promptly. If, due to the Company's actions, a mutually agreeable meeting date is not arranged within two weeks of either the Company's receipt of the initial notification or the appeal of the grievance, the Union may present its original grievance to the next higher level of the formal grievance procedure.

Section 8. The place of the meeting at each level

of the grievance procedure shall be mutually agreed upon, with each party giving due consideration to the convenience of the other.

Section 9. Those employees of the Company including the aggrieved employee(s) and the employee representative(s) designated by the Union, who shall suffer no loss in pay for time consumed in, and necessarily consumed in traveling to and from, grievance meetings shall not be more than three at any level of the grievance procedure.

Section 10. At any meeting held under this Article for the adjustment of a grievance or complaint, any party present (including Union or Company representatives) shall be afforded full opportunity to present any facts and arguments pertaining to the matter or matters under consideration. The decision made upon such facts and arguments shall be made as promptly after conclusion of the presentation as may be reasonably and effectively possible.

Section 11. Any complaint which is not delivered in writing by the Union as specified in Section 2. above, shall be handled by the Company as an informal complaint on an informal basis; provided, however, that nothing in this Article shall preclude the Union and the Company from using any other mutually satisfactory and proper method of presentation, discussion, and disposition of grievances.

ARTICLE IV
ARBITRATION

Section 1. If, during the term of this Agreement, with respect to the 1989 Departmental Agreement effective August 13, 1989, between the Union and the Company, and subsequent agreements which by specific reference therein are made subject to this Article, a difference shall occur, between the Union and the Company, and continue after all steps in the "Formal Grievance" procedure established in the 1989 Departmental Agreement shall have been undertaken and completed, regarding,

a. the true intent and meaning of any specific

provision or provisions thereof (except as such provision or provisions relate, either specifically or by effect, to prospective modification or amendments of such agreement), or

b. the application of any provision or provisions thereof to any employee or group of employees, and grievances arising from such application, or

c. the dismissal for just cause of any employee with more than one completed year's net credited service, or

d. the disciplinary suspension for just cause of any employee

then in any such event, either the Union or the Management may submit the issue of any such matter to arbitration for final decision in accordance with the procedure hereinafter set forth or, where applicable, in accordance with Article V of this Agreement.

Section 2. In the event that either party hereto, within 60 days after completion of the Formal Grievance procedure aforesaid, elects to submit a matter described in the preceding section to arbitration the parties agree that the matter shall be so submitted, and agree that such submission shall be to one arbitrator. The parties shall endeavor in each instance within a three weeks' period to agree upon the arbitrator, but if unable to so agree, the arbitrator shall be designated by the American Arbitration Association upon the written request of either party. In either such event, the arbitration shall be conducted under the then obtaining rules of the Voluntary Labor Arbitration Tribunal of the American Arbitration Association. Each party shall pay for the time consumed by and the expense of its representative, and shall be equally responsible for the compensation, if any, of the arbitrator, and any other general administrative expense that may occur. With respect to the filing fee required by the American Arbitration Association, the Company will pay to the Association the entire arbitration case filing fee for the first one hundred

and fifty (150) arbitration requests filed by the Union during the term of the 1989 Labor Agreements. The entire arbitration case filing fee for each arbitration request filed by the Union beyond the first 150 during the term of the 1989 Labor Agreements will be paid by the Union.

After an election to arbitrate, if within 90 days following completion of the "Formal Grievance" procedure no arbitrator has been agreed upon and no written request has been made upon the American Arbitration Association to designate an arbitrator, then no such matter shall continue to be arbitrable.

Section 3. The arbitrator shall be confined to the subjects submitted for decision, and may in no event, as a part of any such decision, impose upon either party any obligation to arbitrate on any subjects which have not herein been agreed upon as subjects for arbitration; nor may the arbitrator, as a part of any such decision, effect reformation of the contract, or of any of the provisions thereof.

Section 4. The decision of any arbitrator, selected in accordance with Section 2. hereof, shall be final, and the parties agree to be bound and to abide by such decision.

Section 5. If and when notice of termination of this Agreement be given as provided in the Duration Article hereof, any existing dispute described in Section 1 hereof as an appropriate subject for arbitration which is in the process of Formal Grievance negotiation of record prior to the service of such notice of termination, or, if such an existing dispute appropriate under Section 1, hereof shall become a matter of record in the process of Formal Grievance negotiation in the manner and within the time limit prescribed for filing Formal Grievances, then in either such event any such matter may be carried to a conclusion under this Article without regard to the termination of this Agreement.

7

Unfair Labor Practices

Introduction

The RLA contains no "unfair labor practice" provisions. The term *unfair labor practice* has statutory meaning only under the NLRA. The Wagner and Taft-Hartley amendments to the NLRA identified certain practices that were deemed unfair and prohibited their use. These two acts also created the National Labor Relations Board (NLRB) to adjudicate unfair labor practice complaints. Despite the absence of unfair labor practice provisions in the RLA legislation, courts confronted with matters requiring interpretation under the RLA have often cited as precedential the NLRB's rulings on unfair practice.

The RLA does contain strict provisions of conduct regarding organizational representation election and collective bargaining activities. The National Mediation Board (NMB) possesses significant investigative and enforcement authority in these areas. Because of the judicial weight afforded NLRB rulings when interpreting RLA activities, it is essential that both air transport management and union personnel be cognizant of the unfair labor practices contained in the NLRA, which provides a solid foundation for practical guidance under the RLA.

Unfair labor practices apply to all components of the labor process, from initial election of a bargaining representative to conditions present under the bargaining agreement itself. This chapter deals primarily with the involvement of such practices in the selection of a representative and in the organizational process.

The Role of the Railway Labor Act

Unfair Labor Practices under the RLA

Because the RLA contains no unfair labor practice provisions, the NMB does not have the investigatory and enforcement power to regulate employer, employee, or union conduct that may violate the tenants or guaranteed rights of the act. It is, however, a federal crime to violate the act's provisions.[1] The penalties for such violations are set forth in Section 2, Tenth: "The willful failure or refusal of any carrier, its officers or agents, to comply with the terms of the third, fourth, fifth, seventh, or eighth paragraph . . . shall be a misdemeanor . . . subject to a fine of not less that $1,000, nor more than $20,000 or imprisonment for not more than six months, or both . . . for each offense, and each day during which . . . [the] carrier . . . shall fail or refuse to comply . . . " The mechanism for enforcement of these provisions is through the federal court system.

The provisions cited in the Third, Fourth, Fifth, Seventh, and Eighth paragraphs of the RLA state that any conduct by a carrier that interferes with, influences, or coerces employees in any manner in the designation of their collective bargaining representative is a violation of the act itself. These provisions do not preclude the carrier from making any comments on organizational activities during a campaign. The weight rests with the truthfulness of company-directed statements.

Influence, Coercion, and Interference. Two cases before the Supreme Court have interpreted the provisions of the RLA in dealing with the question of carrier management influence, coercion, or interference. In *Texas & N.O.R. Co. v Brotherhood of Railway and Steamship Clerks*, the company formed a company union and urged its employees and members of the Brotherhood of Railway and Steamship Clerks to join the new union. The question before the courts was whether the formation of a company union interfered with the employees' exercise of their rights of self-organization.

In the decision rendered in the *Texas* case, the court noted "that the railroad company and its officers were actually engaged in promoting the organization of the association in the interest of the company and in opposition to the Brotherhood, and that these activities constituted an actual interference with the liberty of the clerical employees in the selection of their representatives."[2] With reference to the meaning of the statutory prohibition against influence, interference, or coercion in Section 2 of the RLA, the court held:

> ... the intent of Congress is clear with respect to the sort of conduct that is prohibited. 'Interference' with freedom of action and 'coercion' refer to well understood concepts of the law. 'Influence' in this context plainly means pressure, the use of the authority of power of either party to induce action by the other in derogation of what the statute calls 'self-organization.' The phrase covers the abuse of relation or opportunity so as to corrupt or override the will, and it is no more difficult to appraise conduct of this sort in connection with selection of representatives for the purpose of this act than in relation to well known applications of the law with respect to fraud, duress, and undue influence ...

The decisions in the *Texas* case and another major Supreme Court case—*Virginia Railroad Co. v System Federation No. 40*[3]—provide the majority of judicial weight for interpreting the influence, coercion, and interference provisions

of the RLA. At the very least, these decisions indicate that management efforts to form company unions interfere with the act. But the decisions do not answer other questions of conduct to any degree. Questions concerning communication to employees and other tactics by management during union elections are answered by the administrative decisions of the NMB itself.

Rulings of the National Mediation Board

The NMB is vested with the authority to interpret and enforce the RLA. Consequently, any interpretations by the board carry significant weight—particularly because most board rulings, especially those dealing with certification, are not judicially reviewable. The absence of judicial review grants tremendous power to the NMB.

Interference Through Communications. The original intent of the RLA was to foster collective bargaining between the parties. Given this basic policy goal, it is reasonable to assume that any communication of a negative or hostile nature between a carrier and its employees regarding any aspect of the collective bargaining process, particularly certification elections, would be viewed as running counter to the intent of the act. But would such communications necessarily be illegal under the act?

A partial answer to this question was delivered by the NMB in a ruling on actions by Allegheny Airlines, Inc.[4] The board determined whether communications and conduct of a carrier influenced employees not to participate in a union certification election.

The alleged interference was a letter sent by the carrier to its employees when a union certification vote was about to be taken. Excerpts of the letter stated such things as "Almost every day, from your newspapers or TV, you learn of destructive actions on the part of labor union leaders. Hindrances, shut-downs, strikes, violence, and similar disturbances have been in the news" and "Merit promotions and merit raises are out. . . . Is this what you want? Do you want to be held back in that way? Remember that professional union organizers work to get your dues. Are they really trying to help you? Do they honestly have the welfare of Allegheny employees at heart? Are they the men whom you respect, whom you look up to, and in whose hands you can place your future? Are they the kind of people who would advance through their own abilities, without politics and union pressure?" The letter concluded: "If you vote for the union, your whole future may be altered, the whole future of Allegheny may be altered. An outside minority will seize your rights."

In its decisions, the board dealt with interference as follows:

> In so far as the Carrier's letter to its employees is concerned, we entertain no doubt that it was designed by the carrier to induce its employees to vote 'No Union.' It is equally clear that the employees would read the letter fully appreciative of the power and authority which the Carrier exercised over them with respect to their day-to-day assignments and security of their jobs. It would be completely unrealistic to believe that under such circumstances employees would not be particularly susceptible to the arguments advanced by the carrier against union representation. It was pure and simple pressure to interfere with a free choice of a representative.

In addition to sending the letter, the airline held meetings with the employees who were eligible to vote. At these meetings, the carrier urged employees to vote and then pointed out how to vote "No Union." The board concluded:

> . . . the Carrier's meeting with its employees constituted activity prohibited by the Act. . . . The coercive effect may be subtle, but it is nonetheless present. Such a technique in and of itself is conduct which interferes with a free choice by employees of a representative. When it is supplementary to other conduct already specified, there can be no doubt that the Carriers totality of conduct in the course of this

representation election prevented this Board from fulfilling its obligation under Section 2, Ninth, to insure the choice of representatives by the employees without interference, influence or coercion exercised by the Carrier.

The implications of the *Allegheny Airlines* case were staggering. By determining, without further delineation, that the "totality of conduct" of the carrier was unlawful, the NMB offered little insight about what is permissible by a carrier in an election campaign. Unlike the NLRA, any and all actions on the part of the carrier appear to be highly suspect, which underscores the need for a carrier to exercise caution.

The RLA prohibits conduct or communication by a carrier that "interferes" with employees rights to self-organization. As the Supreme Court noted in the *Texas* and *Virginia Railroad* cases, the act prohibits communication or conduct by a carrier that, in effect, pressures employees into joining or not joining a union. In this respect, the prohibitions of the act are analogous to the prohibitions of the NLRA.

Any communication or conduct that would be an unfair labor practice under the NLRA would also be unlawful under the RLA. Because no specific illegal communications practices are contained in the RLA, interpretation of interference and its extent is open. NLRB decisions appear to have served as precedents for many NMB rulings and have subsequently been reinforced by the federal courts.

But a review of cases decided by the NMB also clearly indicates that a carrier's election communication or conduct may be ruled unlawful even though the NLRB would not find the same conduct and communication unlawful or sufficient to overturn the results of a certification election. Such conduct and communication by an employer as holding meetings, discrediting the union, telling employees its position concerning an upcoming election, and urging employees to vote "No Union" are not permissible under the RLA. But they are permissible under the NLRA.

Interference in Certification Elections. The language of the RLA provides very little guidance on what kinds of election-related conduct are prohibited. Therefore, the NMB has established procedures to insure that elections are conducted fairly and in a manner that restricts both parties from exercising undue influence or coercion over employee voting. As a part of this process, the NMB is also charged with the responsibility of determining the methods and forms used in the election process and in the conduct of the actual election. The NMB has sole jurisdiction over election procedures and has at times exhibited incongruity in applying these procedures.

Several cases regarding carrier interference with certification elections have been decided. Most notable are the rulings in the *Laker* and *Key Airlines* cases, where direct carrier involvement was observed. The additional study material at the end of this chapter contains the full text of the NMB rulings in the *Laker*, *Key*, and *America West* certification election interference cases, as well as two examples of management guidelines that have been used during the election process.

In a 1955 ruling involving an election scheduled for Linea Aeropostal Venexolana, implication, not direct action, was the key factor in determining carrier interference. On May 16 and 17, 1955, voting was to take place for the mechanics of the airline. Prior to the vote, all eligible employees were notified that if they could not be available for the voting process, they would be sent an absentee ballot by mail. On the days scheduled for the vote, no voters (eligible employees) appeared at the polls. In accordance with the previous instructions, ballots were mailed to the eligible employees. Only 8 of the 108 total ballots mailed were returned. The union then filed an objection with the NMB concerning company actions.

According to company records, on the days of the scheduled vote, no mechanics reported for work. The record also indicated that no mechanic suffered loss of pay for the days in question or was disciplined for his of her failure to report for

a scheduled workday. Based on these facts, the board concluded that the employer had tainted the election process and interfered with the employees' rights. The board was convinced "that in view of all of the circumstances surrounding this election that the employees were not afforded an opportunity to freely express whether they desire representation for collective bargaining purposed in accordance with the Railway Labor Act."[5]

In a more recent decision (in April 1990), America West Airlines was cited for election interference during a representation election campaign. At America West, the customer services representatives who were eligible to vote in a representation election contended that the airline violated the rules for a fair election. The union seeking election, the Association of Flight Attendants (AFA), filed an action with the NMB.

On January 16, 1990, the NMB rendered a decision supporting the AFA position. The NMB ruled that America West's conduct in the February 1989 election had interfered with the election process. The NMB also stated that America West influenced many customer service representatives by announcing and implementing certain changes in work rules that were favorable to the employees. The airline implemented increases in layoff benefits and distributed profit-sharing bonuses to the affected class of employees. On June 30, 1990, the NMB ordered a new election.

Court Decisions

In addition to the cases decided by the NMB, the courts have examined the question of the communication process and whether carriers have interfered with or coerced employees in their choice of a bargaining representative. In the *Teamsters v Braniff Airways, Inc.*, heard in 1969, the Teamsters sought an injunction to prohibit the airline from preelection communication. The unions motion for an injunction was denied. In its ruling, the court found the following:

...the Teamsters and Braniff have issued written communications and have had oral communications with the affected employees, designed to communicate to such employees information and their respective positions, arguments and beliefs with respect to the issues in the election.

On the preliminary record before the Court, the communications complained of in the Complaint and Motion for Preliminary Injunction appear to communicate information, Braniff's position, arguments, and beliefs with respect to issues involved in the proposed election and do not contain threats or promises. Such communications, therefore, are not prohibited by the Railway Labor Act. Such communications are protected by the First Amendment to the United States Constitution protecting free speech.

On the preliminary record before the Court, such communications were not shown to be false or misleading or to have had a corrupting or undue effect on the outcome of the election. The Railway Labor Act [does] not prohibit a carrier involved in a representation dispute and election, which is being conducted by the National Mediation Board, from communicating to the affected employees information, its positions, arguments and beliefs with respect to the issues involved in the election.

The Teamsters belief that Braniff had interfered with employees' representative choice was based on certain memo's and alleged oral communications by Braniff management.[6]

In a more recent federal court decision, rendered in Portland, Oregon, it was ruled that Horizon Airlines had "bargained in a manner designed to frustrate negotiations and engaged in illegal bad faith bargaining under the Railway Labor Act." In this case, the court ordered the company to "cease and desist" from any conduct designed to forestall the reaching of an agreement. In addition, Horizon was charged with "intimidation, arrogance and intractability" at the bargaining table and was ordered to pay the attorney's fees and costs incurred by the union during the lawsuit.

The court determined that Horizon Air had strongly opposed the AFA when it conducted an organization drive in 1987. The court found that after the NMB had certified the AFA to represent Horizon's flight attendants, Horizon had repeatedly delayed and canceled negotiations, consistently refused to make counterproposals during the negotiation process for a first agreement, and "engaged in the mere pretense of negotiating with a completely closed mind." The parties remained in negotiations under the auspices of the NMB. AFA sued the airline in April 1989, alleging that the company had engaged in bad-faith bargaining with the union.[7]

Despite the ruling of the court in this instance, the decisions of the NMB are not subject to judicial review. The ruling in this case only came about as a result of the Teamsters' insistence that an injunction be issued outside the NMB's jurisdiction. Consequently, the board's decision concerning the propriety or impropriety of Horizon's conduct may not have reached the same conclusion as the court.

The lack of case law on RLA communication issues makes employer communication uncertain and consequently hazardous. The broad principle that a carrier can communicate with its employees about the choice of a bargaining representative is easily stated and well established. But as the foregoing examples demonstrate, the content of that right is very difficult to define with precision, particularly because of the non-reviewable nature of NMB decisions and the statutory scheme of the RLA, which encourages both unionization and collective bargaining. Because their rights are not clearly defined, carriers have gone to great lengths to advise their supervisory employees of the responsibilities they have during a union organizing campaign.

Penalties for Interference in Elections. When any airline conducts an aggressive election campaign to offset the efforts of an organization attempt, the airline and its officers risk potential criminal prosecution as outlined in Section 2, Tenth, of the RLA:

The willful failure or refusal of any carrier,

its officers or agents to comply with the terms of the third, fourth, fifth, seventh, or eighth paragraph of this section shall be a misdemeanor, and upon conviction thereof the carrier, officer, or agent offending shall be subject to a fine of not less than $1,000 nor more than $20,000 or imprisonment for not more than six months, or both fine and imprisonment, for each offense, and each day during which such carrier, officer, or agent shall willfully fail or refuse to comply with the terms of the said paragraphs of this section shall constitute a separate offense. It shall be the duty of any district attorney of the United States [United States Attorney] to whom any duly designated representative of a carrier's employees may apply to institute in the proper court and to prosecute under the direction of the Attorney General of the United States, all necessary proceedings for the enforcement of the provisions of this section, and for the punishment of all violations thereof and the costs and expenses of such prosecution shall be paid out of the appropriation for the expenses of the courts of the United States: Provided, That nothing in the Act shall be construed to require an individual employee to render labor or service without his consent, nor shall anything in this Act be construed to make the quitting of his labor by an individual employee an illegal act; nor shall any court issue any process to compel the performance by an individual employee of such labor or service, without his consent.

Rather than invoke this section, the NMB has so far either set aside an election, certified a union representative without an election, or taken some action similar to that in the *Key Airlines* case discussed earlier in this chapter. The NMB's failure to institute the actions under Section 2, Tenth, does not imply that such actions will not be instituted in the future.

There is a decided lack of airline case rulings under this provision. Only two have been brought before the board: one was settled before the board sent it to trial, and fines were imposed in the other. In *United States v Taca Airways Agency, Inc.*, defendants G. R. Moody and Rudolph O. Duscoe

were indicted for firing certain employees who had been obtaining employee signatures to authorize a union to act as the legal bargaining representative.[8] Prior to any decision, an out-of-court settlement was reached. In the only other case, *United States v Jerry Winston: Broome County Aviation, Inc. d/b/a/ Commuter Airlines, Inc.*, indictments were issued by the Department of Justice, and the defendants were convicted of "interfering with, influencing and coercing employees in their choice of a representative."[9] Specifically, in a union organization drive in which the pilots had secured the services of the NMB and an election was being conducted, the defendants:

1. Discharged from their services the chief organizers

2. Called a meeting for all pilots and copilots where the employees were told that they, the employees, would have tough **check rides** if they favored organization

3. Requested the employees to deliver their ballots to the employer rather than to the NMB, which in effect constituted a no vote, because the cards were not turned in

As a direct result of these actions, the president, Jerry Winston, was sentenced to a prison term of fifteen days and fined $75,000 on various counts. In addition, the defendant corporations separately received fines of $1,000 on fifteen counts. The total amount of the fines equaled $105,000.

Featherbedding

Unlike the NLRA, the RLA does not contain any provisions for the elimination of featherbedding. The usage of firemen on the railroads years after the technical elimination of the position is a perfect example that the practice exists under the RLA.

Within the air transport industry, the Air Line Pilots Association (ALPA) sought a three-man cockpit crew in MD-80 aircraft. The ALPA pursued this point and ignored the fact that the aircraft manufacturer had designed the aircraft as a two-man cockpit configuration. The air carriers also insisted that a third man would be superfluous. Nevertheless, the ALPA's position remained adamant until a congressional subcommittee decided against the inclusion of the third crew member.

Although the ALPA presented this issue under the guise of safety concerns, the author of *Flying the Line: The First Half-Century of the Air Line Pilots Association* indicated that other motives might be present:

> Featherbedding is an ugly word. It conjures up images of cynical union bosses extorting wages from helpless employers on behalf of lazy, corrupt workers. From the very beginning, ALPA's crew compliment policy has suffered from charges that it was pure featherbedding, merely an attempt to make work for pilots who would otherwise be unemployed. The third man in the cockpit, critics said, might as well be at home in a featherbed. Only a fool would deny that ALPA was worried about technological unemployment when the crew compliment case arose. In an economic sense, airline pilots were attached to the 'Three' because its relatively low productivity meant jobs.[10]

The Provisions of the National Labor Relations Act

Rulings of the National Labor Relations Board

The National Labor Relations Board (NLRB) has two major functions: (1) supervising and conducting representative elections and (2) ruling on employer and union unfair labor practices. In unfair labor practice proceedings, the NLRB, through its general counsel, actually prosecutes the offending party, and the board functions in the role of a judge. After evidence has been considered, and if a belief exists that an unfair practice has taken place, orders to cease and desist are issued, and appropriate affirmative action measures are introduced. The actions taken by the NLRB are remedial, not punitive. Automatic compliance by an offending party is not

always a reality. Consequently, court reviews of decisions are available under the NLRA, with ultimate appeal to the U.S. Supreme Court.

Unfair Labor Practices under the NLRA

With the passage of the Wagner Act in 1935, Congress attempted not only to recognize unions officially but to inject a degree of control into the organization process by making certain actions illegal. These illegal actions were initially, and almost exclusively, aimed at management and were the "thou shalt nots" that management was forced to abide by when dealing with unions, employees, and the collective bargaining process.

To many critics, the language of the Wagner Act provided a one-sided approach to labor relations law. As a matter of public policy, Congress mandated: "It is hereby declared to be the policy of the United States to eliminate the causes of certain substantial obstructions to the free flow of commerce and to mitigate and eliminate these obstructions when they have occurred by encouraging the practice and procedure of collective bargaining and by protecting the exercise by workers of full freedom of association . . . for the purpose of negotiating the terms and conditions of their employment or other mutual aid or protection."[11] Under the Wagner Act, management was required to recognize unions, bargain collectively, and not interfere with an employee's freedom to join a union.

The Taft-Hartley Act corrected the Wagner Act's one-sided approach by holding the unions to the same standards of conduct originally assigned to management in the Wagner Act. These union standards of conduct became incorporated into the NLRA through the Taft-Hartley Amendment of 1947, which "both amended and added to the NLRA of 1935. Its purpose was to bring organized labor to responsibility by law in the same way that employers had been treated in 1935, specifically singling out certain activities of unions for regulation and establishing additional procedures for the resolution of labor-management conflict."[12]

Activities Prohibited under the NLRA

Section 8(a) of the NLRA proscribes certain activities by management. Section 8(b) of the NLRA proscribes certain activities by unions and employees. Table 7-1 lists the activities in which management and the unions are respectively prohibited to engage.

Most issues of unfair labor practice are raised during union organization campaigns, although others can occur outside an organizational drive. The NLRA establishes certain ground rules of conduct and makes certain actions by employers unfair. The law prohibits employers from restraining, interfering with, or coercing employees in their choice of a bargaining representative.

The employer is not legally precluded from informing, persuading, or urging employees to join or not join a union. An employer has the right of free speech under the First Amendment, and this right has been codified in Section 8(e) of the NLRA. Further, the NLRA does not prohibit all employer activities that may obstruct organizing efforts by employees. The act recognizes that an employer has certain rights, including freedom of speech on matters affecting the operation of the business.

Accordingly, section 8(e) provides that the mere expression of views, arguments, or opinion does "not constitute an unfair labor practice ... if such expression contains no threat of reprisal, or force, or promise of benefit." Some of these

Table 7-1
Unfair Labor Practices

Charges Against Employer

8(a)(1)	Interfering with, coercing, or restraining employees in the exercise of their rights to join or assist labor organizations, or not to join or assist
8(a)(2)	Assisting, dominating, or contributing financially to labor unions
8(a)(3)	Discriminating against employees to discourage or encourage union membership, except as provided by a valid union security clause in a collective bargaining agreement
8(a)(4)	Discriminating against employees because they have filed charges or given testimony to the National Labor Relations Board
8(a)(5)	Refusing to bargain in good faith with the representatives of employees

Charges Against Labor

8(b)(1)	Restraining or coercing employees in their choice of a union representative
8(b)(2)	Causing an employer to discriminate in any way in order to encourage or discourage union membership
8(b)(3)	Refusing to bargain in good faith with the employer about wages, hours, and other employment conditions
8(b)(4)(i)	Engaging in certain types of strikes and boycotts
8(b)(5)	Charging excessive or discriminatory dues or initiation fees
8(b)(6)	Engaging in featherbedding, requiring the payment by employers of services not performed

liberties, which would clearly be questionable under the RLA, rest on the methods the employer uses to make his or her position known to the employees. In this context, whether a practice is considered unlawful and/or illegal depends on definition of interference, threats, and behavior designed to eliminate an employee's choice.

Interference. Interference in union elections can take many forms. For example, questioning employees about union activities or union membership in a manner that restrains or coerces is considered interference. Prior to 1967, the NLRB held that questioning employees about their union activities, though not unlawful per se, was subject to very close scrutiny.[13] Under current policy, questioning is still considered unlawful unless its purpose is to determine the truth of a union's claim or to determine if the majority of the employees are in favor of the union. This type of questioning, however, will also be held unlawful unless several other elements are present:

1. The employees are advised that the questioning is solely for polling purposes
2. The employees are advised that there will be no reprisal
3. The question is asked in a secret ballot
4. A coercive atmosphere has not otherwise been created[14]

Threatening to close or move a plant if a union should be certified has been determined an unfair labor practice. An employer has the absolute right to close his or her entire business for any reason. This right includes the employer's right to close because he or she is totally against unionism. But this right does not extend to closing only a part of the business in an effort to thwart unionization; it is an unfair labor practice to close a plant whose employees are seeking representation or are already unionized and transfer that work to another, nonunion facility.[15]

Granting wage increases or unilateral increases of wages or benefits during a union organizing campaign, whether planned prior to the beginning of the campaign or not, is considered a prima

facie case of unlawful interference and an unfair labor practice. Conversely, charges of unfair labor practice could be sought if the postponement of a planned wage or benefit increase were construed as an attempt to chill a unionist movement.[16] In an airline case heard under the auspices of the NLRB in which the carrier operated intrastate and was covered under the NLRA, not the RLA, it was ruled that the employer may not withhold a general wage increase customary at a specified time each year because the employees had elected to seek union representation.[17] But an employer may be permitted under section 8(c) to announce during a campaign, to influence the election, benefits that would take effect later, as long as the benefits were planned or in motion prior to the beginning of the campaign.[18]

Sending a management or supervisory employee to a union meeting, asking employees particulars about union organizing meetings, and other types of surveillance have been found unlawful interference of union activities.[19] So has the use of spies or informers in connection with any phase of the employees' right to self-organization.[20] The pre-1966 attitude of the NLRB was that if an election was lost by a union due to allegations of surveillance, the election could be set aside.[21] A subsequent decision indicates that proof must exist that the employer both authorized and conducted the surveillance.[22]

Threatening employees with loss of jobs or benefits should they join a union or vote for a union is a direct violation of Section 8(a).[23] An employer may not hire or fire an employee on the basis of the employee's membership or lack of membership in a union or to encourage or discourage union membership.[24] A violation of section 8(a)(3) has been found in one case in which an employer discharged a nonunion employee solely because the employee attended a union organizational meeting[25] and in another in which the employer discharged an employee who refused to join a company-dominated union.[26] An exception to this provision does exist where agreements that permit an employer (at the request of the union) to discharge an employee for non-payment of dues or initiation fees are allowed.[27]

Establishing rules that forbid union solicitation by employees during nonworking time, even if such rules are limited to working areas, may also be considered an unfair labor practice, depending on the past practices of the employer.[28]

Penalties. The penalties set against management for engaging in an unfair labor practice can range from a minor cease and desist order to reimbursing a union and the NLRB for their expenses in investigating, preparing, presenting, and conducting a case,[29] to certification of a union representative without the necessity of an election. The theory behind certification without election is that a union would win an election if not for the unfair practice of management. In 1969, in *NLRB v Gissel Packing Company*, the Supreme Court sustained the right of the NLRB to certify a representative without an election, holding that because of the actions of the company, an election would not reflect the actual sentiment of the employee.[30]

Summary

Though there are differences between the RLA and the NLRA, a carrier can work on the assumption that what is applicable under the NLRA

concerning unfair labor practices will also have application and weight under the RLA. Both management and labor are responsible for dealing fairly with one another. Air carriers and their unions, though subject to no legislation describing unfair labor practices, are in essence bound by the precedents of the NLRB cases, because they have significant weight in the eyes of the courts.

This relationship between NLRB precedents and RLA cases was specifically emphasized in a 1967 district court decision involving Pan American Airways and the Teamsters. In that case, covered by the RLA, the court attempted to provide an analogy between the activities specifically proscribed by the NLRA and the actions of the Clerks Union (IBT) and the airline under the RLA. The court stated: ". . . cases under the NLRA are not controlling under the Railway Labor Act which is different in scheme, structure and enforcement machinery. However, they offer cogent analogy in the solution of similar problems arising under the RLA and the courts have frequently drawn on NLRA cases for guidance."[31]

Additional Study Material

National Mediation Board Rulings in Laker, Key, and America West Certification Elections

8 NMB No. 79
FINDINGS UPON INVESTIGATION; ORDER
CASE NOS. R-5131 and R-5132
February 24, 1981

**In the Matter of the Application of the
INTERNATIONAL BROTHERHOOD OF
TEAMSTERS
alleging representation disputes
pursuant to Section 2,
Ninth, of the Railway Labor Act
involving employees of
LAKER AIRWAYS, LTD.**

On August 21, 1980, the International Brotherhood of Teamsters (IBT), filed applications pursuant to Section 2, Ninth, of the Railway Labor Act, 45 U.S.C. § 152, Ninth, alleging the existence of representation disputes among personnel described as "Office Clerical Employees" and "Passenger Service Employees", employed by Laker Airways, Ltd. (Laker). Said applications were docketed as NMB Case Nos. R-5131 and R-5132, respectively.

At the time the applications were received, these employees were not represented by any individual or organization.

Investigation disclosed that disputes existed among the subject employees, and by order of the Board, secret ballot elections were conducted. Ballots were mailed on December 19, 1980. Tabulation of the ballots was originally scheduled for January 23, 1981.

On January 5, 1981, the IBT protested certain conduct on the part of Laker, and requested that the election be cancelled and that certain other remedial actions be taken. Specifically, IBT alleged

that Laker officials had collected employees' ballots, made promises of benefit or threats of reprisal, and had otherwise interfered with the election. On January 16, 1981, the IBT submitted an additional Statement of Position, and on January 19, 1981, the IBT submitted an affidavit in support of its Statement.

On January 19, 1981, the Board ordered that ballots in both elections be impounded pending further investigation, and ordered that Laker file a response to the IBT Statement of Position. In addition, Laker was ordered to turn in any ballots collected, as well as a list of employees who turned in ballots. 8 NMB No. 65.

On January 22, 1981, Laker informed the Board that, while it had collected ballots, all such ballots had been destroyed, and that no list was maintained. On February 3, 1981, Laker submitted a Statement of Position and fifteen affidavits of carrier officials.

During the period of January 5, 1981, to the present time, Chief Hearing Officer David M. Cohen and Hearing Officer Roland Watkins conducted an investigation on behalf of the Board. Mr. Watkins interviewed a number of employees and other witnesses with respect to the IBT's allegations.

Based upon the investigation, the Statements of Position, and the affidavits, the Board finds as follows:

ISSUE

The issue in these cases is whether Laker interfered with, influenced, or coerced its employees in their choice of a representative pursuant to Section 2, Ninth, of the Act.

CONTENTIONS

The IBT contends that Laker has violated the Act by carrying out a "comprehensive and coercive campaign to restrict employees' right to vote by collecting their ballots." In addition, the IBT asserts that Laker has "dramatically" increased wages and benefits during the course of the organizing campaign for the purpose of influencing the employees.

Laker characterizes the IBT Statement as "gross exaggerations and misrepresentations", and asserts that it acted in accordance with the Act. Laker additionally accuses IBT of improper actions.

FINDINGS OF LAW

Determination of the issue here involved is governed by Section 201, Title II, and Section 2, Title I, of the Railway Labor Act, as amended, 45 U.S.C. §§181, 152. Accordingly, the board finds as follows:

I.

Section 201 of the Act, extends all of the provisions of Title I of the Act, except the provisions of Section 3, thereof, 45 U.S.C. §153, to "every common carrier engaged in interstate or foreign commerce . . . and every air pilot or other person who performs any work as an employee or subordinate official of such carrier, subject to its or their continuing authority to supervise and direct the manner or rendition of his service."

II.

Laker Airways, Ltd, is a common carrier by air as defined in Title II, Section 201 of the Act, 45 U.S.C. §181.

III.

Section 2, Fourth, of the Act, U.S.C. §152, Fourth gives employees subject to its provisions " . . . the right to organize and bargain collectively through representatives of their own choosing. The majority of any craft or class of employees shall have the right to determine who shall be the representative of the craft or class for the purposes of this Act." Section 2, Fourth, also allows employees the right to select representatives without carrier influence or interference. That particular subsection reads as follows:

> No carrier, its officers or agents, shall deny or in any way question the right of its employees to join, organize, or assist in organizing the labor organization of their choice, and it shall be unlawful for any carrier to interfere in any way with the organization of its employees, or to use the funds of the carrier in maintaining or assisting or

contributing to any labor organization, labor representative, or other agency of collecting bargaining, or in performing any work therefor, or to influence or coerce employees in an effort to induce them to join or remain or not to join or remain members of any labor organization . . . (Emphasis supplied).

IV.

Employee-carrier isolation with respect to an employees' choice of a collective bargaining representative is expressed in Section 2, General Purposes Clause. The subsection states that one of the purposes of the Railway Labor Act is "to provide for the complete independence of carriers and of employees in the matter of self organization."

V.

Section 2, Ninth, of the Act, 45 U.S.C. §152, Ninth, requires the National Mediation Board to investigate disputes which arise among a carrier's employees over representation, and to certify the duly authorized representatives of such employees. In determining the choice of the majority of employees under this section, the Board is "authorized to take a secret ballot of the employees involved, or to utilize any other appropriate method of ascertaining the names of their duly designated and authorized representatives in such manner as shall insure the choice of representatives by the employees without interference, influence, or coercion exercised by the Carrier." (Emphasis supplied).

FINDINGS OF FACT

I.

Laker is a British carrier operating low-fare air service between the United States and Great Britain. Initially a charter carrier, Laker now operates as a scheduled carrier between London and New York, Los Angeles, and Miami. Future service to Tampa is planned.

Laker employs approximately 300 persons in the United States in four locations: John F. Kennedy International Airport in New York, the

Laker Travel Center in New York, Miami, and Los Angeles. Employment has increased rapidly since scheduled operations began in 1977.

II.

IBT alleges that Laker actively solicited employees to turn their ballots in to carrier officials; provided stamped, pre-addressed envelopes for this purpose; and kept a record at which employees turned in their ballots.

Laker admits that it told its employees that the most effective way to vote against representation, in view of the form of the ballot used by the Board, was to turn the ballot in to the carrier.

In a letter dated December 15, l980, addressed to all United States employees, Charles Maxwell, Manager USA, and the carrier's highest official in this country stated:

> If you send back a ballot marked, "No union," or "Laker Airways," "Sir Freddie Laker," "Charles Maxwell," or the like, or if you deface the ballot or indicate you don't want any union to represent you, then your ballot will be marked "Void" and not counted. Casting a "void" ballot amounts to the same thing as not voting at all.
>
> This fact again makes it imperative for you not to vote at all if you don't want the Teamsters.
>
> I am aware that many employees have decided they want to have a "ballot-burning party" in order to keep ballots from being cast for the Teamsters. I am extremely gratified that this means so many of you believe we are on the right track here at Laker and that you want to keep any outsiders from coming in and disrupting our work environment while they take your money to sustain the lifestyle and fat salaries of Teamster bosses.
>
> On the other hand, I am concerned that some of you, while agreeing in principle with the ballot-burners, would like to keep your opinions private and to refrain from publicly displaying your views. You <u>could</u> simply tear your ballot up and throw it away.

That would be just as effective as going to a ballot-burning party.

> However, you could also send your ballot anonymously to Mark Hammer. This would probably be the most effective thing to do with your ballot, and would provide a safe solution if you are uncomfortable with destroying an official ballot. If Mark had a majority of the ballots we'd know for sure the Teamsters couldn't possibly win. Therefore, each of you will receive with your paycheck this week a stamped envelope addressed to Mark. Your name will not be on the envelope. If you don't want to go to a ballot-burning party or to destroy your ballot, when you get your ballot you can just put it in the envelope and mail it to Mark.
>
> In any event, no matter how you decide to dispose of your ballot, you must remember that for the reasons I have described the only sure way to keep the Teamsters out is NOT TO VOTE AT ALL. Unlike elections for public office, in an election like the upcoming one the important thing is that you <u>DON'T VOTE.</u>

Mark Hammer is Laker's personnel manager. Envelopes were, in fact, distributed to employees with their paychecks.

On December 22, 1980, Sir Freddie Laker, Chairman and Managing Director of Laker Airways, sent a letter to employees in which he stated:

> I earnestly urge you to demonstrate your continued support by <u>NOT VOTING FOR THEM!</u> Please hand your ballot in to us or destroy it, but <u>DON'T SEND IT BACK</u> to the Government. We all have too much to lose!

Laker supervisors received a number of ballots from employees, which they then forwarded to Hammer. Including those returned in the envelopes and those turned in to supervisors, Laker officials gained possession of 135 of the 189 ballots mailed to Passenger Service Employees, and 38 of the 51 ballots mailed to Office Clerical Employees. Thus, prior to the count date, carrier officials were in actual possession of 73% of the ballots in the two cases.

In view of the fact that Laker supervisors actually received ballots from individual employees, and in view of the Board's conclusions below, it is unnecessary to determine whether Laker kept a list of names of employees who turned in ballots, or actively solicited ballots through personal interviews with employees.

III.

IBT contends that Laker officials sent employees home to retrieve their ballots, with pay. Laker asserts that any employee who went home with pay for this purpose did so without its knowledge, but notes that in any event employees received a paid lunch hour.

In view of the Board's conclusions with respect to the other evidence in this case, it is unnecessary to determine whether employees were sent home to retrieve ballots.

IV.

IBT further alleges that a Laker supervisor contacted an employee at home to ask about his ballot.

Laker, in its affidavits, admits that a supervisor did ask an employee whether the employee had received this ballot, "as several employees had not received ballots and I wanted to be sure [the employee's] had reached him in his absence." The supervisor suggested that the employees either destroy the ballot or return it to the carrier.

V.

Wages, benefits, and working conditions have improved dramatically at Laker in 1980. Salaries increased by some 40%, including a 12 ½% increase just prior to the mailing of the ballots.

In December 1979, Laker announced a policy of automatic increases in wages every time the consumer price index (CPI) rose 5%, plus merit increases on an individual basis each June 1 and December 1.

The December 1, 1980, increase was composed of 5% for the CPI and 7 ½% for "merit." The merit increase for that month, unlike earlier merit increases, was given to all employees across-the-board. The carrier concedes that this represented a conscious change in policy on the part of Laker.

VI.

Laker alleges or implies that the IBT harassed supervisors, broke into its offices on several occasions, and stole lists of employee names and addresses and employee performance evaluations. These allegations are irrelevant to the issue presented, and no evidence of any kind has been presented to link the IBT to the break-ins and thefts.

Laker further asserted that it collected ballots because of a fear that the IBT or its supporters would get hold of and cast ballots from employees who did not wish to vote. In spite of a request by Mr. Watkins for evidence of any such activity, Laker produced nothing to support this fear. Following Mr. Watkins' request, counsel for Laker filed a Freedom of Information Act (FOIA) request for the names of employees who had requested duplicate ballots "to determine whether fraudulent requests for duplicate ballots have been made . . . ." This request was denied in order to preserve the confidentiality of the employees' representation desires. FOIA File No. CF-5099 (1981).

DISCUSSION

I.

The Railway Labor Act gives employees of carriers the right to organize and select a representative with interference, influence, or coercion by the carrier.

The Board has the duty, under Section 2, Ninth, of the Act, when ascertaining who shall represent employees in any craft or class for the purposes of the Act, to "insure" that the method used is such as to guarantee to the employees the opportunity to make such choice free of interference, influence, or coercion by the carrier. Whether the Board uses the device of a secret ballot or any other means to determine the desire of the employees as to who should represent them, the Board must conduct such proceedings in an atmosphere free of any interference or other conduct by the carrier that would tend to interfere with, influence or coerce the employees in their choice.

The terms "interference," "influence," and "coercion" were defined by the Supreme Court shortly after the Act became law. In <u>Texas and New Orleans R. Co. v. Bro. of Railway and Steamship Clerks,</u> 281 U.S. 548 (1930), the court stated:

It is thus apparent that Congress, in the legislation of 1926, while elaborating a plan for amicable adjustments and voluntary arbitration of disputes between common carriers and their employees, though it necessary to impose, and did impose, certain definite obligations enforceable by judicial proceedings. The question before us is whether a legal obligation of this sort is also to be found in the provisions of subdivision third of Section 2 of the act providing that "Representatives, for the purposes of this Act, shall be designated by the respective parties . . . without interference influence, or coercion exercised by either party over the self-organization or designation of representatives by the other".

It is at once to be observed that Congress was not content with the general declaration of the duty of carriers and employees to make every reasonable effort to enter into and maintain agreements concerning rates of pay, rules and working conditions, and to settle disputes with all expedition in conference between authorized representatives, but added this distinct prohibition against coercive measures. This addition can not be treated as superfluous or insignificant, or as intended to be without effect. While an affirmative declaration of duty contained in a legislative enactment may be of imperfect obligation because not enforceable in terms, a definite statutory prohibition of conduct which would thwart the declared purpose of the legislation cannot be disregarded. The intent of Congress is clear with respect to the sort of conduct that is prohibited. "Interference" with freedom of action and "coercion" refer to well understood concepts of the law. The meaning if the word "influence" in this clause may be gathered from the context. Noscitur a sociis. The use of the word

is not to be taken as interdicting the normal relations and innocent communications which are a part of all friendly intercourse, albeit between employer and employee. <u>"Influence" in this context plainly means pressure, the use of the authority or power of either party to induce action by the other in derogation of what the statute calls "self-organization". The phrase covers the abuse of relation or opportunity so as to corrupt or override the will, and it is no more difficult to appraise conduct of this sort of connection with the selection of representatives for the purpose of this Act than in relation to well-known applications of the law with respect to fraud, duress and undue influence.</u> If Congress intended that the prohibition, as thus construed, should be enforced, the Courts would encounter no difficulty in fulfilling its purpose, as the present suit demonstrates.

In reaching a conclusion as to the intent of Congress, the importance of the prohibition in its relation to the plan devised by the Act must have appropriate consideration. <u>Freedom of choice in the selection of representatives on each side of the dispute is the essential foundation of the statutory scheme.</u> All the proceedings looking to amicable adjustments and to agreements for arbitration of disputes, the entire policy of the Act, must depend for success on the uncoerced action of each party through its own representatives to the end that agreements satisfactory to both may be reached and the peace essential to the uninterrupted service of the instrumentalities of interstate commerce may be maintained. There is no impairment of the voluntary character of arrangements for the adjustment of disputes in the imposition of a legal obligation not to interfere with the free choice of those who are to make such adjustments. On the contrary, it is of the essence of a voluntary scheme, if it is to accomplish its purpose, that this liberty should be safeguarded. The definite prohibition which Congress inserted in the Act can not therefore be overridden in the view that Congress intended it to be ignored. As the prohibition was appropriate to the aim of Congress, and is capable of enforcement the conclusion must be that enforcement was contemplated.

· · · · · · ·

Congress was not required to ignore this right of the employees but could safeguard it and seek to make their appropriate collective action an instrument of peace rather than of strife. Such collective action would be a mockery if representation were made futile by interferences with freedom of choice. Thus the prohibition by Congress of interference with the selection of representatives for the purpose of negotiation and conference between employers and employees, instead of being an invasion of the constitutional right of either, was based on the recognition of the rights of both. . . . The Railway Labor Act of 1926 does not interfere with the normal exercise of the right of the carrier to select its employees or to discharge them. The statute is not aimed at this right of the employers but at the interference with the right of employees to have representatives of their own choosing. As the carriers subject to the Act have no constitutional right to interfere with the freedom of the employees in making their selections, they cannot complain of the statue on constitutional grounds. (Citations omitted, emphasis supplied).

The weaknesses of the 1926 Act led to the enactment in 1934, of certain amendments, including Section 2, Third, Fourth, and Ninth. In Virginia Ry Co. v. System Federation No. 40, 300 U.S. 515 (1937), the Supreme Court discussed the impact of these amendments on the right of self-organization.

The prohibition against such interference was continued and made more explicit by the amendment of 1934. [The carrier] does not challenge that part of the decree which enjoins any interference by it with the free choice of representatives by its employees. . . . That contention is not open to it in view of

our decision in the [Texas and N.O. Ry. v.] Railway Clerks case, supra, and of the unambiguous language of §2, Third, and Fourth, of the Act as amended.

Cases since then have limited the scope of judicial review of the Board's actions under Section 2, Ninth, of the Act. Switchmen's Union of North America v. NMB, 320 U.S. 297 (1934). At the same time, the right and power of the Board to insure free representation elections has been affirmed.

Thus, in Aircraft Mechanics Fraternal Assn. v. United Airlines, 406 F. Supp. 492 (ND Cal. 1976), the court held that a complaint of interference was properly a matter for the Board, not the Federal courts. In addition, the Court noted that a finding of illegal influence by the board is binding on the courts. id. at fn. 11. See, also, Texidor v. Ceresa, 590 F. 2d 357 (1st Cir. 1978).

Thus, the problem before the Board is to determine whether or not there was conduct on the part of the Carrier in this proceeding that prevented the employees from participating in a representation election free from interference, influence, coercion. The test in any case of alleged interference in a Board election is whether the laboratory conditions which the Board seeks to promote have been contaminated. Zantop International Airlines, 6 NMB No. 1247 (1979). The essential facts to such a determination were established by the parties' statements and affidavits, and are not in dispute.

II.

We turn now to a discussion of the specific actions of Laker and its officials.

A.

In all mail ballot elections conducted by the Board, ballots are sent to the home address of the employees using address labels supplied by the carrier. Employees are free to vote in the privacy of their own homes, without being subject to pressure from carrier or union officials. No one except employees of the National Mediation Board knows who voted in the election. No one, including the Board's employees, knows how the voters who do cast ballots actually marked their ballots. To vote for representation the employee simply marks the ballot and returns the properly-attested envelope with the ballot enclosed to the Board. To vote against representation, the employee need only refrain from voting.

Laker admits that it actively solicited employees to turn in their ballots to the carrier. Stamped envelopes were provided with employees' paychecks for this purpose. Supervisors collected ballots from individuals.

Laker asserts that these actions were necessary to prevent IBT officials and supporters from collecting and returning ballots of non-supporters, which ballots would be marked in favor of the IBT. It asserts that this Board would not cooperate to prevent this fraud because it would not check each signature on the attest portion of the return envelope.

The rationale given by Laker to support its conduct is patently transparent. No proof has been forthcoming which indicates even the threat of tampering by the union, in spite of a request by a Board representative for evidence of any election fraud. Instead, the carrier has created the specter of fraud and forgery out of whole cloth.

The Board mails ballots to employees' homes in order to avoid the problems envisioned by Laker. Given this safeguard, it is no business of the carrier or the organization whether or how any employee votes or does not vote. Nothing submitted by Laker indicates that employees were subject to undue influence from the union which would amount to election fraud. Had any evidence been produced, the Board would have undertaken an appropriate investigation, including a comparison of signatures.

Employees cannot exercise their right to self-organization in an atmosphere where their employer seeks to control the outcome through the pressure evident in this case. Even employees who would otherwise simply throw their ballots in the trash feel compelled to turn them in as an act of "loyalty." The coercive effect of the carrier's actions is heightened when the FOIA request for names of employees requesting duplicate ballots is considered.

Furthermore, the actions of a supervisor in calling an employee at home to be sure he had received a ballot, because of the supervisor's concern

that some employees had not received ballots, indicates that the carrier was keeping a close watch on the employees. If the supervisor knew who had not received ballots, the Board must conclude that she had that knowledge because she was keeping track of that information. See, e.g., General Shoe Corp., 77 NLRB 124 (1948).

Given the procedure used in Board election requiring that the majority of eligible employees cast valid ballots for representation in order for there to be a certification, soliciting employees to turn in their ballots to the carrier is analogous to polling employees about their views. The National Labor Relations Board has developed a test for the lawfulness of polling which is helpful in considering Laker's conduct. The NLRB held, in Struksnes Construction Co., 165 NLRB 1062 (1967), that:

> Absent unusual circumstances, the polling of employees by an employer will be violative of Section 8(a)(1) of the Act unless the following safe guards are observed: (1) the purpose of the poll is to determine the truth of a union's claim of majority, (2) this purpose is communicated to the employees, (3) assurances against reprisal are given, (4) the employees are polled by secret ballot, and (5) the employer has not engaged in unfair labor practices or otherwise created a coercive atmosphere.

The NLRB adopted this test in order to balance employer-employee interests. However, the Board went on to hold that:

> . . . a poll taken while a petition for a Board election is pending does not, in our view, serve any legitimate interest of the employer that would not be better served by the forthcoming Board election. In accordance with long-established Board policy, therefore, such polls will continue to be found violative . . . of the Act.

The NLRB's reasoning applies with even greater force when an election is actually under way and employees are deciding whether they wish to be represented. In the circumstances of the cases before us, nothing justified any form of polling. See, also, NLRB v. J. M. Machinery Corp., 410 F. 2d 587 (5th Cir. 1969), fn. 3.

The Board holds that it is a per se violation of the Railway Labor Act for any carrier or its officials to solicit employees to turn their ballots in to the carrier. It is, furthermore, a per se violation to provide mailing envelopes for this purpose, and this violation is compounded when such envelopes are distributed with paychecks. It is a violation of the Act, under the circumstances present here, to keep track of which employees do or do not have ballots, and to thereby give the impression of surveillance. It is a per se violation to poll employees during a representation election conducted by this Board. Finally, it is a per se violation for a supervisor to personally receive a ballot from an employee under any circumstances, and without regard to the "voluntariness" with which it is turned over.

B.

In December 1980, Laker granted all employees a 5% cost of living increase and a 7½% "merit increase." While the cost of living increase was consistent with a year-old carrier policy, the merit increase was a radical departure from past policy. Instead of giving individual merit increases based upon employee evaluations, Laker made a conscious decision to give all employees a significant, across-the-board increase. Since counsel for Laker was in almost daily contact with the Board, Laker must be deemed to have known that a craft or class determination and finding of a dispute were imminent. In addition, counsel for Laker knew that ballots would likely be mailed in December 1980.

Under the circumstances, the Board concludes that the timing, amount, and nature of the merit increase were deliberately set to influence employees and to convey the idea that a union was unnecessary.

The offer of benefits to influence the outcome of an organizing campaign is a violation of the Railway Labor Act. As the court held in Union of Professional Airmen v. Alaska Aeronautical Industries, 95 LRRM 2868 (D. Ak. 1977):

The court further finds that the offer to the employees of increased benefits during their organizational process may well interfere with their union efforts. While the benefits were not mandatory it is the mere offer

which tends to undermine their activity. Accordingly, these activities on the part of [the carrier] also appear to be in violation of the Railway Labor Act, supra, and must cease. (Emphasis supplied).

If the mere offer of benefits during an organizational campaign violates the Act, a fortiori, the granting of benefits almost contemporaneous with an election violates the Act.

This holding is consistent with the longest established precedents of the National Labor Relations Board and the Supreme Court. In NLRB v. Exchange Parts Co., 375 U.S. 405 (1964), the Court found the employer guilty of an unfair labor practice where it granted a permanent, unconditional wage increase in order to affect the outcome of the representation election, even though the employer was not charged with any other unfair labor practices. The court held:

We think the Court of Appeals was mistaken in concluding that the conferral of employee benefits while a representation election is pending, for the purposes of inducing employees to vote against the union, does not "interfere with" the protected right to organize.

. . . We have no doubt that [the National Labor Relations Act] prohibits not only intrusive threats and promises but also conduct immediately favorable to employee which is undertaken with the express purpose of impinging upon their freedom of choice for or against unionization and is reasonably calculated to have that effect . . .

The danger inherent in well-timed increases in benefits is the suggestion of a fist inside the velvet glove. Employees are not likely to miss the inference that the source of benefits now conferred is also the source from which future benefits must flow and which may dry up if it is not obliged. The danger may be diminished if as in this case the benefits are conferred permanently and unconditionally. But the absence of conditions or threats pertaining to the particular benefits conferred would be of controlling significance only if it could be presumed that no question of additional benefits or renegotiation of existing benefits would arise in the future; and, of course, no such presumption is tenable.

. . . The beneficence of an employer is likely to be ephemeral if prompted by a threat of unionization which is subsequently removed. Insulating the right of collective organization from calculated good will of this sort deprives employees of little that has lasting value.

See, also, NLRB v. Crown Can Co., 138 F. 2d 263 (8th Cir. 1943); cert. denied 321 U.S. 769 (1944).

III.

Having determined that Laker has violated the Act in at least six ways, the question of an appropriate remedy must be resolved.

A.

The Board is not unmindful of Laker's constitutional right to communicate its views to its employees. However, this right is not without limit, and even conduct which is otherwise lawful may justify remedial action when it interferes with a representation election. General Shoe Corp., supra.

The federal government has successfully prosecuted, under the criminal provisions of the Act, a carrier and its officials for, inter alia, soliciting the employees to turn in their ballots. Although the convictions were reversed on a legal technicality, U.S. v. Winston, 558 F. 2d 105 (2nd Cir. 1977), the case illustrates the serious nature of this type of conduct.

The Board views Laker's admitted conduct as among the most egregious violations of employee rights in memory. Rarely has a carrier waged such a deliberate campaign designed to override employee free exercise of the rights guaranteed by the Act. Extraordinary remedies are required to overcome Laker's violations and to restore conditions which will permit a free election.

B.

It is obvious that the original elections must be set aside. Since Laker collected almost three-quarters of the ballots mailed by the Board, counting those ballots which were returned would be futile. New elections must be conducted in an atmosphere free of unlawful conduct.

In addition, steps must be taken to provide both the employees and the carrier with an incentive to comply with democratic procedures. The new election must therefore encourage maximum employee participation, and provide complete safeguarding of ballots and polling procedures.

The Board has traditionally required that a majority of eligible voters cast valid ballots in order for a representative to be certified. However, it is clear that such a procedure is not required by the Act. For example, in 1935 the Board stated:

. . . the Board interpreted [Section 2, Fourth of the Act] as requiring a majority of all those eligible rather than a majority of the votes only. The interpretation was made, however, not on the basis of legal opinion and precedents, but on what seemed to the Board best from an administration point of view. Where, however, the parties to a dispute agreed among themselves that they would be bound by a majority of the votes cast, the Board took the position that it would certify on this basis, on the ground that the Board's duties in these cases are to settle disputes among employees, and when an agreement is reached the dispute as to that matter is settled.

First Annual Report of the National Mediation Board (Fiscal Year 1935), at 19.

The Board then noted, id. at 20, that a court challenge had been made to the voting procedure it had adopted. When that challenge reached the Supreme Court, the Court held that a union need not receive the votes of a majority of those eligible in order to be certified. Virginia Ry Co., supra. The Court reasoned that those who do not participate are presumed to assent to the expressed will of those who do, and that "[t]here is the added danger that the absence of eligible voters may be due less to their indifference than to coercion by their employer." id. Later decisions involving the National Labor Relations Board held that less than a majority of eligibles could elect a representative where the organization certified received a majority of the votes cast. See, NLRB v. Standard Lime & Stone Co., 149 F. 2d 435 (4th Cir. 1945); cert. den. 326 U.S. 723 (1945).

In 1947, in response to challenges to the Board's requirement that a majority of those eligible cast valid ballots, the Board sought the opinion of the Attorney General as to whether it had the power to certify a union where less than a majority of eligibles voted. The Attorney General replied:

> . . . it is my opinion that the National Mediation Board has the power to certify a representative which receives a majority of the votes cast at an election despite the fact that less than a majority of those eligible to vote participated in the election. While the National Mediation Board has this power, it need not exercise it automatically upon finding that a majority of those participating were in favor of a particular representative. Op. Atty. Gen. (September 9, 1947).

The Board continued its prior practices, which were upheld in Radio Officers Union v. NMB, 181 F. 2d 801 (D.C. Cir. l950), relying in part on the Attorney General's opinion in order to foster the stability in labor-management relations which the Act contemplates.

In BRAC v. Assn. for the Benefit of Non-Contract Employees, 380 U.S. 650 (1965), the Supreme Court upheld the form of the Board's ballot and the majority rule as being within the Board's discretion, noting that a failure to participate was treated as a vote against representation, under the Board's procedures in effect at that time.

Mail ballot elections have been favored because the voting population is generally a mobile one in the railroad and airline industries. In the instant cases however, the employees are permanently based in only three cities, so that a ballot box election is feasible.

Under the circumstances of the present case, the Board finds that its usual election procedures will be unable to determine the true desires of Laker employees. This is because the factors normally existing in representation cases which support those procedures have been upset here by employer action. Therefore, exercising our discretion in representation matters. the Board concludes that a ballot box election is necessary and that the following ballot should be used:

Finally, to vitiate the clear violations of the law by Laker and to insure that there will no longer be incentives in cases such as this one for the employer to interfere with the free choice of its employees, the desires of the majority of those actually casting valid ballots will determine the outcome of the elections, whether or not a majority of those eligible participate in the elections. The action we take here should not be considered a precedent for the usual election situation, but is limited to situations where there is gross interference with a Board conducted election.

C.

Finally, employees must be reassured of the Board's determination to conduct a free election, and they must be fully informed of their rights under the Act and of the nature of the violations leading to the new elections. Copies of these "Findings Upon Investigation; Order" will be provided to all eligible employees. In addition, the carrier will be required to post notices assuring employees of their rights. The Notice is provided as an appendix to this decision.

D.

The remedies ordered in these cases are broad and, to some extent, innovative. However, like the NLRB, this Board has a statutory mandate to protect the right to self-organization. As the Court of Appeals stated in Teamsters Local 115 v. NLRB, Nos. 79-1619 and 79-2018, (D.C. Cir. 1981):

> The [National Labor Relations] Board has long struggled to accommodate the interests of employers and employees while assuring free choice of bargaining representatives. When one side or the other destroys the balance and creates a climate inimical to an untrammeled selection process, Congress intended the Board to exercise broad discretion in fashioning a remedy. The remedies chosen may or may not be sufficient to the task, but the Board is entitled to

UNITED STATES OF AMERICA
OFFICIAL BALLOT OF NATIONAL MEDIATION BOARD
Involving   CASE NO. _____

Employees of
LAKER AIRWAYS, LTD.

A dispute exists among the above named craft or class of employees as to who are the representatives of such employees designated and authorized in accordance with the requirements of the Railway Labor Act. The National Mediation Board is taking a SECRET BALLOT in order to ascertain and to certify the name or names of organizations or individuals designated and authorized for purposes of the Railway Labor Act.

INSTRUCTIONS FOR VOTING

No employee is required to vote. The majority of valid ballots actually cast will determine the outcome of the election. Mark an "X" in the appropriate square:

Do you desire to be represented by the
INTERNATIONAL BROTHERHOOD OF TEAMSTERS,
AIRLINE DIVISION?

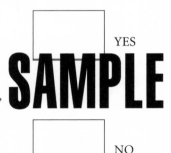

YES

NO

NOTICE

1. This is a SECRET BALLOT. DO NOT SIGN YOUR NAME.
2. Marks in more than one square make ballot void.
3. Do not cut, mutilate or otherwise spoil this ballot. If you should accidentally do so, you may return the spoiled ballot at once to the Board representative and obtain a new one.

try all reasonable measures. The boundaries within which the Board may reasonably exercise its discretion will vary with the severity of the conduct and the needs that conduct creates. Quoted at <u>BNA Daily Labor Reporter,</u> February 6, 1981, at E-7.

This Board need not consider what other action may be required if the new elections are tainted. We trust they will be conducted under the democratic conditions required by the Act.

CONCLUSION

The Board finds that Laker has violated the right of its employees to self-organization free of interference, influence, or coercion.

It is Hereby Ordered That:

1. The prior elections in Case Nos. R-5131 and R-5132 are set aside.
2. Ballot Box elections are hereby authorized using a cut-off date of September 14, 1980. No follow-up mail ballot will be used.
3. The form of the ballot will provide "Do you desire to be represented by International Brotherhood of Teamsters, Airline Division?" with boxes marked "Yes" and "No." No write-in space will be provided. The majority of valid ballots actually cast will determine the outcome of the elections.
4. A copy of these Findings Upon Investigation; Order will be mailed to each eligible employee.
5. The carrier will immediately post the Notice attached hereto, and the Notice of Election, when issued, on each employee bulletin board. These materials will be posted until the next business day after the election.

By direction of the NATIONAL MEDIATION BOARD.

Rowland K Quinn, Jr.
Executive Secretary

Copies furnished to:

Dennis A. Lalli, Esq.
Epstein Becker Borsody & Green, P.C.

Ronald M. Green, Esq.
Epstein Becker Borsody & Green, P.C.

Sir Freddie Laker, Chairman and
 Managing Director
Laker Airways, Ltd.

Mr. Charles Maxwell, U.S. General Manager
Laker Airways, Ltd.

Mr. Mark Hammer, Director of Personnel
Laker Airways, Ltd

Wilma B. Liebman, Esq.
International Brotherhood of Teamsters

Roland Wilder, Esq.
International Brotherhood of Teamsters

Mr. Norman Greene, Director National
 Airline Division
International Brotherhood of Teamsters

Copies furnished to:

Mr. William Genoese, Assistant Director
Teamsters Local Union No. 732

Mr. Alex Calder
Teamsters Local Union No. 732

All eligible employees in
Case Nos. R-5131 and R-5132

RKQ/dca

NOTICE TO ALL EMPLOYEES

PURSUANT TO FINDINGS UPON INVESTIGATION AND ORDER OF THE NATIONAL MEDIATION BOARD AND IN ORDER TO EFFECTUATE THE POLICIES OF THE RAILWAY LABOR ACT, AS AMENDED, WE HEREBY NOTIFY OUR EMPLOYEES THAT:

After an investigation conducted by the National Mediation Board in which we had the opportunity to present statements and evidence, the

National Mediation Board found that the Carrier's conduct, taken as a whole, improperly interfered with employees' choice of representative under Section 2, Ninth, of the Act. It is unlawful for a carrier to interfere with the organization of its employees.

Section 2, Fourth of the Act, 45 U.S.C. §152, allows employees the right to select representatives without carrier influence or interference. That particular subsection reads as follows:

> No carrier, its officers or agents, shall deny or in any way question the right of its employee to join, organize, or assist in organizing the labor organization of their choice, and it shall be unlawful for any carrier to interfere in any way with the organization of its employees, or to use the funds of the carrier in maintaining or assisting or contributing to any labor organization, labor representative, or other agency of collective bargaining, or in performing any work therefor, <u>or to influence or coerce employees in an effort to induce them to join or remain or not to join or remain members of any labor organization. . . .</u>

Employee-carrier isolation with respect to an employee's choice of his collective bargaining representative is expressed in Section 2, General Purposes Clause of the Railway Labor Act. The subsection states that one of the purposes of the Railway Labor Act is "to provide for the complete independence of carriers and of employees in the matter of self organization."

Since the Board has found that the Carrier improperly interfered with the employees' choice of representation under the Railway Labor Act and has ordered re-run elections in NMB Case No. R-5131 (Office Clerical Employees) and NMB Case No. R-5132 (Passenger Service Employees) using a ballot box election:

> WE WILL NOT influence, interfere or coerce employees in any manner in an effort to induce them to participate or refrain from participating in the upcoming elections.

All of our employees are free to express their desire to be represented by a labor organization or remain unrepresented.

LAKER AIRWAYS, LTD.

Dated: _____

By _____
Carrier Representative

This notice must remain posted until the first business day following the elections, and must not be altered, defaced or covered by any other material.

If any employees have any question concerning this notice or compliance with its provisions, they may communicate directly with the National Mediation Board, 1425 K Street, N. W., Washington, D.C. 20572, Telephone 202-623-6920.

16 NMB No. 88
FINDINGS UPON INVESTIGATION—
ORDER TO SHOW CAUSE
CASE NOS. R-5850, R-5855 AND R-5869
April 19, 1989

In the Matter of the Application of the INTERNATIONAL BROTHERHOOD OF TEAMSTERS-AIRLINE DIVISION alleging representation dispute pursuant to Section 2, Ninth, of the Railway Labor Act involving employees of KEY AIRLINES

On December 9, 1988, the Board received an application filed by the International Brotherhood of Teamsters-Airline Division (IBT) pursuant to

45 U.S.C. § 152, Ninth, alleging a representation dispute among Flight Attendants of Key Airlines Inc. (Key). The application was docketed as NMB Case No. R-5850. Subsequently on December 22, 1988 the Board received a representation application from the IBT for Flight Deck Crew Members at Key. This application was then amended to pertain to Pilots and Co-Pilots and Flight Engineers and these cases were respectively docketed as NMB Case Nos. R-5855 and R-5869.

At the time these IBT applications were filed, these employees were not represented by any organization or individual.

Mediator Joseph E. Anderson was assigned to investigate the case and during the investigation the IBT submitted evidence of carrier interference. A written response to the charges was filed with the Board by Key. Mediator Anderson and Hearing Officer David J. Strom were subsequently directed to examine the interference charges through interviews with certain Key employees as well as members of management.

ISSUE

The issue before the Board is whether Key violated the Act by interfering, influencing or coercing employees in their choice of a representative.

CONTENTIONS

The IBT alleges that Key has engaged in "a pervasive pattern of interference, influence or coercion" which has "tainted the laboratory conditions for a fair election." IBT further contends that "this conduct is deliberate, well planned, and orchestrated by high management officials" and that a Laker ballot procedure[1] is necessary to remedy the adverse effects of such carrier interference.

Key "denies the Teamsters['] allegation of carrier interference and requests that they be summarily dismissed."

The specific IBT allegations and Carrier responses are described below:

The IBT claims that the Carrier "has sought to make examples of one flight attendant and one pilot, both active and visible union adherents. The pilot was discharged by Key assertedly because he was discussing the benefits of unionization with

two new flight attendants. The flight attendant was removed from flying the line and transferred from her duty station in Las Vegas, Nevada to a clerical assignment in Herndon, Virginia. It is alleged that the purpose of this transfer and change of assignment was to "isolate an active union supporter from fellow flight attendants during this election period" and to make an example of her "to intimidate others to refrain from union activities".

The Carrier admits that the pilot was discharged as a result of his conversation with certain flight attendants but asserts that the pilot was "discharged for disparaging the Carrier while on duty in violation of Carrier policy and for unprofessional conduct." Key claims that its decision to remove the flight attendant from flying the line and to reassign her to a different duty station "was based solely on objective business considerations."

The Organization alleges that Key has conducted numerous one-on-one and group meetings with the flight attendants, pilots and flight engineers. Key management is accused of having questioned certain employees about their own and other employees' "union sentiments or activities"; threatened that if the flight attendants unionize Key will merge with World Airways, its sister subsidiary, and that such merger would result in a loss of jobs for Key's flight attendants; threatened that if the flight attendants vote to unionize when the company starts its DC-10 operations, flight attendant work will be contracted out; and solicited and discussed employee grievances with flight attendants, flight engineers and pilots.

Key claims that it did not conduct one-on-one meetings with employees concerning the union but rather "discussed the union situation with employees in voluntary, non-coercive settings." Key acknowledges that it "has discussed with employees the possibility of a merger of World Airways and Key, including the feasibility and efficiency of maintaining two carriers in the event of Teamsters representation at both carriers." Key maintains that these statements are "predictions based on objective facts" and are "unrelated to any retaliation for support of representation." With regard to the subcontracting of flight attendant DC-10 work, the Carrier states "the flight attendants have been told that subcontracting of DC-10 flight attendant duties was an option being considered because of the complications related to the shifting of bases necessary in the first year of operations." Concerning the charge of solicitation of grievances Key asserts that it has "discussed grievances with employees without promising any resolution thereof."

IBT also alleges that a pay raise, granted to pilots and flight engineers, was withheld from the flight attendants in order to discourage unionization and to send a message that flight attendants would have had a raise had they not filed a representation application. IBT further claims that Key has engaged in numerous acts of unlawful surveillance in a calculated effort to discourage organizing activity.

The Carrier responds that once it "had knowledge of the [flight attendants'] application, it might have been unlawful to grant a pay raise which had not previously been decided upon." Key distinguishes the raises granted to the pilots and flight engineers on the basis that "the new pay scale for flight deck crew members was restructured and finalized prior to the time the Company learned that an application [for these individuals] had been filed . . ."

Concerning the IBT's contention of improper surveillance of employee organizing activities, the Carrier "denies that it has engaged in any form of unlawful surveillance of the employee's union activities . . ."

On March 27, 1989 after the Organization's unsuccessful election results in R-5855 and R-5869 involving pilots and co-pilots and flight engineers, respectively, were known, the IBT renewed its earlier request for Laker balloting procedures in these cases. The Organization contends that in addition to the prior evidence submitted to the Board on carrier interference "the result of the elections demonstrate that the carrier effectively undermined the union's organizing campaign."

Key is opposed to re-run elections in R-5855 and R-5869 because it believes the record does not support a finding of carrier interference.

FINDINGS OF LAW

Determination of the issues in this case is governed by the Railway Labor Act, as amended, 45

U.S.C. §151, et seq. Accordingly, the Board finds as follows:

I.

Section 201 of the Act, extends all of the provisions of Title I of the Act, except the provisions of Section 3, thereof, 45 U.S.C. §153, to "every common carrier engaged in interstate or foreign commerce . . . and every air pilot or other person who performs any work as an employee or subordinate official of such carrier, subject to its or their continuing authority to supervise and direct the manner of rendition of his service."

II.

Key is a common carrier by air as defined in 45 U.S.C. §181 of the Act.

III.

IBT is a labor organization and representative as provided by 45 U.S.C. §151, Sixth and §152, Ninth of the Act.

IV.

Employee-carrier isolation with respect to an employee's choice of collective bargaining representative is expressed in Section 2, General Purposes Clause. The subsection states that one of the purposes of the Railway Labor Act is "to provide for the complete independence of carriers and of employees in the matter of self-organization."

V.

45 U.S.C. §152, Third, provides:

Representatives . . . shall be designated . . . without interference, influence, or coercion. . . . (Emphasis added)

VI.

45 U.S.C. §152, Fourth, gives employees subject to its provisions " . . . the right to organize and bargain collectively through representatives of their own choosing. The majority of any craft or class of employees shall have the right to determine who shall be the representative of the craft or class for the purposes of this chapter." This section also provides as follows:

No carrier, its officers or agents, shall deny or in any way question the right of its employees to join, organize, or assist in organizing the labor organization of their choice, and <u>it shall be unlawful for any carrier to interfere in any way with the organization of its employees . . . or to influence or coerce employees in an effort to induce them to join or remain or not to join or remain members of any labor organization . . .</u> (Emphasis added)

VII.

45 U.S.C. §152, Ninth, provides that the Board has the duty to investigate representation disputes and shall designate who may participate as eligible voters in the event an election is required. In determining the choice of the majority of employees, the Board is "authorized to take a secret ballot of the employees involved, or to utilize any other appropriate method of ascertaining the names of their duly designated and authorized representatives by the employees <u>without interference, influence, or coercion exercised by the carrier.</u>" (Emphasis added)

FINDINGS OF FACT

I.

Key Airlines and World Airways (World) are subsidiaries of World Corp., and all three companies are based in Herndon, Virginia. Key's prior home office was in Las Vegas, Nevada which to this date remains a major base of operations. The other primary base of Key's operations is Philadelphia, Pennsylvania.

Thomas Kolfenbach, who has been a Key employee since early 1986, is the Vice President and General Manager. His affidavit submitted to the Board states that "my responsibilities include primary authority for conduct of the Carrier's campaign resisting the Teamsters' organizing efforts."

II.

The IBT's organizing effort at Key commenced in May or June of 1988 when the union began holding employee meetings and distributing authorization cards to the Carrier's personnel.

III.

In July of 1988 Key responded to the IBT organizing drive by distributing anti-union literature

and holding employee meetings. A letter from Mr. Kolfenbach dated July 13, 1988 and addressed to "Fellow Key Employees" states in part:

> We had previously planned employee meetings over the next several weeks. During these meetings we will have more to say about the subject of unionization.

One meeting took place on or about July 28, 1988 and was attended by approximately fifteen flight attendants as well as several cockpit crew members. Other smaller meetings, which were primarily attended by flight attendants, took place at various times over the course of the summer.

The meetings, which were convened by senior management officials, were held for the express purpose of discouraging Key's employees from organizing. Among the subjects discussed by the Carrier at the meetings was the possible merger of Key with its sister subsidiary World Airways should Key's employees vote for IBT representation. In the event of such merger, Key has indicated at several of the meetings that its employees may well be adversely affected by the merger of seniority lists, as there are presently a number of senior World employees on furlough. It should be noted that the IBT represents flight deck crew members and flight attendants at World.

Additionally, in a letter from Mr. Kolfenbach dated July 21, 1988 to all Key flight crew members the carrier makes the following statements:

> In closing, I would ask each of you to carefully consider whether or not you want to be a partner with an organization that has such a sordid reputation as the Teamsters. Ask yourself the following questions: Why do the Teamsters have an interest in you? Is it because they want you to grow within the organization? Do they want to see you retain your job? (Several hundred people are currently on furlough at World.) Do they want to see you upgraded? . . . Is it really a fair deal for you or do they want to help the unemployed crew members at World Airways at your expense?

Another subject discussed by the Carrier during these meetings was the possible subcontracting of DC-10 flight attendant duties when that new service commenced. At the time these statements were made the Carrier indicated that the final decision was pending. Subsequently, on March 1, 1989 the Carrier decided to allow its flight attendants to bid on the DC-10 work.

IV.

Since December of 1988 and through January, February and into March of 1989 Key has repeatedly sent senior management personnel, including its Vice President, to meet with employees during their layover. Approximately eight such meetings took place. These meetings were typically conducted in informal settings and the subjects discussed have included the potential merger with World Airways and the sub-contracting of DC-10 flight attendant work, should Key's flight attendants vote to unionize. The express purpose of the meetings, which were a result of the IBT organizing drive, was to discourage unionization. In addition, Key has continued to communicate with its flight deck crew employees by letters including one dated February 22, 1989 which contain sharp criticism of the "Teamsters". The Board notes the conspicuous involvement of Key's highest officials including the Vice President and General Manager in these activities.

V.

The Carrier denies that any one-on-one employee meetings have taken place. However, the IBT has submitted evidence to the contrary.

VI.

On December 21, 1988 Key called an employee meeting in Herndon, Virginia which was attended by roughly 30 flight attendants, flight engineers and pilots. At the meeting Key's General Manager and Vice President, Tom Kolfenbach, stated that pay raises would be given to all flight deck crew members, except the flight attendants.[2] Mr. Kolfenbach announced that the flight attendants would not receive pay raises because of the pending IBT representation application and because such raises could constitute unlawful interference. In explaining why the flight attendants would not be granted a raise, Mr. Kolfenbach singled out and pointed to flight attendant Mary Cook and sug-

gested that the employees ask her as she was an avid union supporter. Mr. Kolfenbach admits to making such statements.

On December 22, 1988, one day later, Key convened a similar meeting at its Las Vegas, Nevada base. With the exception of the flight engineers, this was the first pay raise granted by Key in well over two years and the raise was not part of a regularly scheduled program of salary increases.

VII.

On December 16, 1988 flight attendant Mary Cook, who has been employed with Key for 6 years, was reassigned from her Las Vegas base to Herndon, Virginia to perform certain office "projects." At the time the assignment was made the Carrier knew that Mary Cook was "one of the leading union adherents". Key states that Mary was chosen because of her experience with the company. This assignment consisted of such tasks as "revision of flight attendant recurrent training examinations, creation of policies for morale enhancement and motivational slogans, revision of weight and grooming programs . . . and proofreading of the revised flight attendant manual." Mary Cook was not pleased with the transfer and according to the Carrier "from the time she arrived in Herndon, Cook began complaining about her assignment, and was unproductive and uncooperative." Despite the fact that in the Carrier's own words Mary Cook did not seem to be working out at this assignment, Key acknowledges to making "numerous subsequent attempts to have Cook . . . complete her assignment" in Herndon.

Before the assignment was completed, Mary Cook was put on medical leave and returned to Las Vegas, Nevada. As of the present time she remains on medical leave. It is not clear whether the tasks assigned to Mary Cook in Herndon have subsequently been completed by another individual.

VIII.

Tony Russell, a pilot with 20 years experience, has served as a co-pilot at Key for eighteen months. In mid-1988 Mr. Russell was recommended for an upgrade to Captain by the Chief Pilot and other Captains who had flown with him. Without prior warning and on the day the NMB mediator conducted his field investigation of the instant case, January 12, 1989, Mr. Russell was discharged.

The Carrier states that Russell was fired because on January 8, 1989 he engaged in a discussion with two new flight attendants which "upset the flight attendants and left them with a negative overall impression of the Carrier." The IBT has submitted evidence which indicates that Mr. Russell and the flight attendants were discussing how the union could be helpful to establishing such practices as duty time limits. No members of the public were present when this conversation took place.

Mr. Russell had no prior disciplinary record with Key Airlines and appears to have been held in high regard by his colleagues. There is no evidence in the record that any Key employee other than Russell has been discharged for a similar infraction. A reinstatement action, which alleges that Mr. Russell was improperly discharged for organizing activities, has been filed in Federal court.

IX.

On February 13, 1989 the Organization requested that the Board proceed and conduct elections in the pilot and co-pilot and the flight engineers crafts or classes (R-5855 and R-5869), notwithstanding the pending charges of carrier interference. This request was made "without prejudice to our right to raise the Laker arguments at the conclusion of the elections, should that be necessary." On March 23, 1989 the ballots were counted in R-5855 and R-5869 with the following results:

Number of Employees Voting (R-5855)

	IBT	ALPA	Number of Employees Eligible
Pilots and Co-pilots	9	1	39

Number of Employees Voting (R-5869)

	IBT	Number of Employees Eligible
Flight Engineers	8	22

Subsequently, on March 27, 1989 the Organization filed a letter with the Board which stated in relevant part:

The results of the elections demonstrate that the carrier effectively undermined the Union's organizing campaigns.

Accordingly, the Union hereby requests that the Board conclude its investigation of the carrier's interference, invalidate those elections, whose results were tainted by carrier misconduct, and order new elections utilizing Laker balloting procedures.

In support of its request for re-run elections by Laker ballot, the IBT's letter of March 27, 1989 incorporated by reference its earlier allegations, with supporting documentation, of carrier interference.

DISCUSSION

I.

These cases are disturbingly similar to a prior Board action concerning this Carrier involving charges of improper carrier interference. Just three years ago in Key Airlines, 13 NMB 153 (1986) the Board found that Key had violated the pilots and co-pilots and flight engineers' freedom of choice of a representative when, among other things, two individuals involved in union activities were summarily forced to resign and employees were polled on their support for the union. As a remedy for carrier interference in the prior case the Board conducted elections by Laker ballot, but the organization was unsuccessful in garnering sufficient votes for certification. The Board's consideration of all the facts and circumstances present here in view of the applicable legal standards strongly supports the conclusion that Key has again engaged in a carefully designed and calculated campaign to interfere with, influence and coerce its employees in their choice of a representative.

II.

The employees' right to organize and select a representative without interference, influence or coercion is expressly provided in at least three provisions of the Railway Labor Act - Section 2, Third, Fourth and Ninth as well as the General Purposes Clause, Section 151a(3). In the context of a representation dispute and pursuant to Section 2, Ninth, of the Act the Board is specially empowered with the authority for assuring that employees are provided the opportunity to choose a representative free from the taint of carrier interference. See Mid-Pacific Airlines, 13 NMB 178 (1986); Key Airlines, 13 NMB 153 (1986); and Laker Airways Ltd, 8 NMB 236 (1981).

The test used by the Board in evaluating instances of alleged carrier interference is whether the "laboratory conditions" which the Board seeks to promote in representation elections have been contaminated. See, Metroflight, Inc., 13 NMB 284 (1986); Key Airlines, supra; Mid-Pacific Airlines, supra; Laker Airways Ltd, supra; and Zantop International Airlines, 6 NMB 834 (1979). Where the Board finds interference in the employees' freedom of choice, the NMB has devised remedies to purge the taint and ensure a fair election. In the past the Board has used the Laker ballot to remedy such infractions. However, the Board's remedial powers are not limited to such ballot procedures. See Norfolk & Portsmouth Belt Line Railroad, 16 NMB 162 (1989). See generally Metroflight, supra; Key Airlines, supra; Rio Airways, 11 NMB 75 (1983); Mercury Services, 9 NMB 312 (1982); and Laker Airways Ltd, supra. The Board is mindful that in an appropriate case reliance on authorization cards alone could result in certification. See NLRB v. Gissell Packaging Co., 395 US 575 (1969).

From this vantage point the Board turns to the case at hand.

III.

With respect to the discharge of Tony Russell and the reassignment of Mary Cook, the Board does not find the Carrier's explanation credible. Key states that the reason for terminating Tony Russell was that he expressed negative opinions about the company to other employees. These statements occurred in the context of a union organizing drive. Tony Russell had a solid employment record and no history of prior disciplinary action with the company. He received the maximum punishment possible, discharge, for an alleged violation of Carrier policy for which no other employee has ever been similarly disciplined. As in the prior Key case the termination occurred in the midst of the Board's field investigation, just before formal NMB election procedures were to commence, and at a crucial juncture in the em-

ployees' organizing campaign. The effect was to send a threatening message to all Key employees concerning the possible consequences of voicing support for a union.

Only a few days after the IBT's representation application was filed, Mary Cook was reassigned from one of Key's major bases of operation, Las Vegas, Nevada, to an office job in Herndon, Virginia. Cook's transfer had the effect of severely limiting her exposure to other flight attendants. The carrier admits that it knew Mary Cook was an "avid union supporter" and even singled her out as such at a company meeting on December 21, 1988. While Key has gone to elaborate lengths to economically justify her reassignment, the Board finds that the Carrier intended to isolate this union supporter from her co-workers and thus interfere with its employees' organizing efforts.

IV.

The Carrier's explanation that it was denying a pay raise to the flight attendants because it did not want to engage in improper interference during an election campaign, but was granting such a raise to pilots and flight engineers who had not yet filed an application, is under these circumstances implausible. The raises were not part of a regularly scheduled increase. Just as the offer of benefits during an organizing campaign may constitute improper interference so may the denial of benefits. In the flight attendant situation the impact of the Carrier's actions was to place the blame on the union for the denial of the pay increase. The pay increase for the pilots, co-pilots and flight engineers, one day before the representation application for these individuals was filed, was a calculated attempt to improperly undermine the union's organizing drive and curry the employees' favor. The key distinction in each case is that a representation application for the flight attendants had already been filed whereas the petition for the pilots and flight engineers had not yet been filed. Thus the denial of the wage increase to the flight attendants could naturally be expected to be seen as a penalty for showing union support; whereas the granting of wage increases to the pilots and flight engineers could be expected to be seen as a benefit for not filing and a threat against filing.

The evidence is clear that Key was aware of the IBT's organizing drive since at least early July of 1988, well before the wage increases were given on December 21, 1988. From that date onward until the conclusion of the election laboratory conditions must be maintained.

In NLRB v. Exchange Parts Co., 375 US 405 at 409 (1964), the United States Supreme Court explained the impact of such a grant of benefits:

> The danger inherent in well-timed increases and benefits is the suggestion of a fist inside a velvet glove. The employees are not likely to miss the inference that the source of benefits now conferred is also the source from which future benefits must flow and which may dry up if it is not obliged.

Thus Key's handling of the pay raises amount to improper interference in the employees' representation drive.

V.

The Board is deeply troubled by Key's repeated statements concerning the possible merger with World Airways and the sub-contracting of flight attendant work should Key's employees vote to unionize. Implicit in these statements is the thinly veiled threat that the future job security of Key Airlines' employees would be at stake should they vote to be represented. While the carrier maintains that such statements "are based upon objective facts related to economic efficiencies," the Board finds otherwise. Indeed, these communications reasonably tended to convey the impression that a vote for unionization by Key's employees could lead to the loss of jobs by Key personnel.

VI.

The Board finds that Key's conduct here amount to egregious interference and that the NMB's usual election procedures will be ineffective for determining the true representation desires of Key's employees. This is the second time in three years that Key has engaged in improper interference and, indeed, Key has here repeated many of the same coercive acts taken in the prior case. The effects of the Carrier's interference on a workforce as small as Key's are certain to have pervaded the entire complement of flight crew employees. Based on the foregoing determinations of carrier interference, the Board finds that re-run elections are necessary for NMB Case Nos. R-5855 and R-5869 involving pilots and co-pilots and flight engineers, respectively, and that special election procedures are required in all three crafts or classes in order to protect the rights of the employees to exercise their franchise rights independent of carrier interference.

The Board notes that the Laker ballot procedure has not proved to be an effective remedy for cases where there is serious and repeated carrier interference such as this. That is because in those situations the Laker ballot does not restore to the voters the desired "laboratory conditions". While the Laker ballot may still be an appropriate remedy in certain instances of carrier interference, it has not been effective in egregious cases. The Board's remedial authority in this area is expressly provided in Section 2, Ninth of the Act which states that in investigating representation disputes the Board "shall be authorized to take a secret ballot of the employees involved, or to utilize <u>any other appropriate method . . . as shall insure the choice of representatives by the employees without interference, influence or coercion exercised by the Carrier.</u>" (emphasis added)

Therefore, further remedial steps beyond the Laker ballot may be necessary to help provide a climate where the employees can freely express their representational desires. Towards this end the Board hereby issues an order to show cause why it should not utilize a ballot procedure in which the IBT-Airline Division will be certified unless a majority of the eligible voters return votes opposing IBT representation. No space for write-in votes would be provided. This is the first time such a ballot procedure will be utilized and in the interest of soliciting the participants' views, the Board is issuing a show cause order. Responses to the show cause order should be limited solely to the question of the Board's proposed ballot procedure and not to the aforementioned findings of carrier interference.

The Board will further require that the Carrier post, and each flight attendant, flight engineer, and pilot and co-pilot receive, a notice which states that the NMB has found that Key has engaged in improper carrier interference. Such notice will state that the employees have a right to organize free of carrier interference and that Key will not interfere with such rights. The notice is intended to inform the employees of their rights under the Act, of the Board's determination to conduct a free election, and of the nature of the Carrier's violations.

Under Section 2, Tenth of the Act conduct described herein may be the subject of criminal prosecution. Accordingly, the Board, as it has traditionally, weighs its responsibilities with respect to those who have prosecutorial authority.

CONCLUSION

The Board finds that Key has violated the rights of its employees to self-organization free of interference, influence or coercion.

It is Hereby Ordered That:

(1) An all-mail ballot election is authorized for the craft or class of flight attendants using a cut-off date of December 28, 1988. Re-run elections for the flight engineers and pilots and co-pilots are authorized as well using the same cut-off date.

(2) The participants respond within ten calendar days of this decision to show cause why the Board should not use a ballot which will provide "Are you opposed to representation by the International Brotherhood of Teamsters-Airline Division" with a box for the employee to so vote if he or she chooses. An employee that desires representation by the IBT need not return a ballot. No write-in space would be provided. Unless a majority of the eligible employees vote <u>against representation</u> by the IBT, that organization would be certified. Responses to the show cause order must be limited to the form of the ballot and not to the merits of the Board's findings of carrier interference.

(3) The Carrier will provide the Board with a set of gummed, alphabetized address labels for all eligible flight attendants, flight engineers and pilots and co-pilots within three business days of receipt of this decision.

(4) The designated Carrier official shall sign and return the attached notice by pre paid express

mail to the NMB within three business days of its receipt. Copies of the notice and Findings Upon Investigation will be mailed to each eligible flight attendant, flight engineer and pilot and co-pilot with their ballot.

(5) The Carrier will immediately sign and post the attached notice as well as the Notice of Election, when issued, on each employee bulletin board. These materials will be posted until the next business day after the election.

By direction of the NATIONAL MEDIATION BOARD.

Charles R. Barnes
Executive Director

—Attachment—

Copies to:

Mr. Clifford E. Farnham
Mr. William F. Genoese
Mr. Marvin L. Griswold
Mr. Ray Benning
Bruce Friedman, Esq.
Wilma Liebman, Esq.
Mr. Thomas Kolfenbach

NOTICE TO ALL EMPLOYEES

PURSUANT TO FINDINGS UPON INVESTIGATION AND ORDER OF THE NATIONAL MEDIATION BOARD AND IN ORDER TO EFFECTUATE THE POLICIES OF THE RAILWAY LABOR ACT, AS AMENDED, WE HEREBY NOTIFY OUR EMPLOYEES THAT:

After an investigation conducted by the National Mediation Board in which we had the opportunity to present statements and evidence, the National Mediation Board found that the Carrier's conduct, taken as a whole, improperly interfered with employees' choice of representative under Section 2, Ninth, of the Act. It is unlawful for a carrier to interfere with the organization of its employees.

Section 2, Fourth of the Act, 45 U.S.C. § 152, allows employees the right to select representatives without carrier influence or interference. That particular subsection reads as follows:

> No carrier, its officers or agents, shall deny or in any way question the right of its employees to join, organize, or assist in organizing the labor organization of their choice, and it shall be unlawful for any carrier to interfere in any way with the organization of its employees, or to use the funds of the carrier in maintaining or assisting or contributing to any labor organization, labor representative, <u>or other agency of collective bargaining, or in performing any work therefore, or to influence or coerce employees in an effort to induce them to join or remain or not to join or remain members of any labor organization. . . .</u>

Section 2, General Purposes Clause of the Railway Labor Act, states that one of the purposes of the Railway Labor Act is "to provide for the complete independence of carriers and of employees in the matter of self organization."

WE WILL NOT influence, interfere or coerce employees in any manner in an effort to induce them to participate or refrain from participating in the upcoming elections.

All of our employees are free to express their desire to be represented by a labor organization or remain unrepresented.

KEY AIRLINES, INC.

Dated: _____

By: _____
Thomas Kolfenbach
Vice President/
Manager

This notice must remain posted until the first business day following the elections, and must not be altered, defaced or covered by any other material.

If any employees have any question concerning this notice or compliance with its provisions, they may communicate directly with the National Mediation Board, 1425 K Street, N.W., Washington, D.C. 20572, Telephone 202-523-5920.

16 NMB No. 38
FINDINGS UPON INVESTIGATION—
AUTHORIZATION OF ELECTION
CASE NO. R-5817
January 5, 1989

**In the Matter of the Application of the
ASSOCIATION OF FLIGHT
ATTENDANTS
alleging a representation dispute
pursuant to Section 2,
Ninth, of the Railway Labor Act, as
amended involving employees of
AMERICA WEST AIRLINES, INC.**

On September 9, 1988, the Association of Flight Attendants (AFA) filed an application pursuant to the Railway Labor Act as amended, 45 U.S.C. §152, Ninth, alleging a representation dispute among "Flight Attendants (Customer Service Representatives)", employees of America West Airlines, Inc. This application was docketed as NMB Case No. R-5817.

At the time the application was filed, these employees were unrepresented.

The Board assigned Mediator John B. Willits to the case. The cut-off date for purposes of eligibility was established as of September 30, 1988. During the investigation, the carrier raised the issue of the appropriate craft or class of the employees in question.

The carrier filed a position statement on September 21, 1988, and a "Motion for Hearing and Determination of Customer Service Representative craft or class" on September 28, 1988. AFA filed a response on October 3, 1988. America West filed a reply brief on October 14, 1988 to which AFA replied on October 31, 1988. The carrier filed a final brief on November 16, 1988.

ISSUES

There are several issues before the Board in this case. The primary question is whether there is a distinct craft or class of Flight Attendants on America West, or whether the individuals AFA seeks to represent are part of a larger craft or class of "Fully Cross-Utilized Customer Service Representatives." A second issue is whether the carrier has interfered with the employees' freedom to select a representative. A third issue is whether the use of a preponderance check is appropriate in this case to determine eligibility. Additionally, AFA questions the eligibility of trainees, and the use of recurrent training time in a preponderance check. A final procedural question is whether a hearing should be held in order to resolve these issues.

CONTENTIONS

AFA maintains that there is a distinguishable group of employees on America West who spend a majority of their time performing flight attendant functions. In support of its contention, the organization cites the Board's previous craft or class determination involving this carrier, in which the Board found appropriate a craft or class of Flight Attendants.

AFA also takes the position that trainees are not eligible voters and that recurrent training time should not be counted in the NMB's preponderance check. Further, the organization alleges that the carrier has interfered with the employees freedom of choice by manipulating the September bid awards, which would affect voter eligibility. AFA proposes as a remedy a ninety-day preponderance check.

The carrier takes the position that due to extensive cross-utilization and cross-training there is no identifiable craft or class of Flight Attendants. America West contends that the more appropriate craft or class is "Fully Cross-Utilized Customer Service Representatives" (CSRs). According to the carrier, these individuals regularly perform in-flight functions, passenger service functions, and fleet service functions. It is the carrier's position that the Board's prior determination is not binding, both because the Board makes its decisions on a case-by-case basis and because "the facts have

changed considerably in the intervening two years."

America West contends further that a preponderance check should not be applied, and that trainees should be included in the craft or class. If the Board does use preponderance, America West urges that all recurrent training days be counted. Finally, the carrier claims that AFA's allegations of interference are unsupported by evidence and that the carrier has not engaged in any activity which interferes with the employees' freedom of choice.

FINDINGS OF LAW

Determination of the issues in these cases is governed by the Railway Labor Act, as amended, 45 U.S.C. §15l, et seq. Accordingly, the Board finds as follows:

I.

America West Airlines, Inc. is a common carrier by air as defined in 45 U.S.C. §181 of the Act.

II.

AFA is a labor organization and representative as provided by 45 U.S.C. §151, Sixth and §152, Ninth, of the Act.

III.

45 U.S.C. §152, Fourth gives employees subject to its provisions " . . . the right to organize and bargain collectively through representatives of their own choosing. The majority of any craft or class of employees shall have the right to determine who shall be the representative of the craft or class for the purposes of this chapter."

IV.

45 U.S.C. §152, Ninth, provides that the Board has the duty to investigate representation disputes and shall designate who may participate as eligible voters in the event an election is required.

FINDINGS OF FACT

I.

America West Airlines is a national air carrier operating from the dual hubs of Phoenix, Arizona and Las Vegas, Nevada. The airline currently serves

46 cities in the U.S. and Canada. According to the carrier, all employees who are in the portion of the work force which deals directly, or indirectly, with customers . . . are designated as [CSRs]." CSRs are divided into three categories: Fully Cross-Utilized, Cross-Utilized, and Non-Cross-Utilized. There are approximately 1700 Fully Cross-Utilized CSRs, virtually all of whom are stationed in Phoenix, Arizona.

II.

According to the carrier, Fully Cross-Utilized CSRs perform the following functions: ramp, ticket counter and gate, reservations and in-flight services. All Fully Cross-Utilized CSRs are paid at the **same** rate, receive the same benefits, and are subject to the same terms and conditions of employment. These individuals are all FAA-certified and are all subject to an annual recurrent training program. Fully Cross-Utilized CSRs are part of a separate supervisory structure, CSR Resources.

III.

Job assignments for Fully Cross-Utilized CSRs are made through a bidding process. The bid schedule, which contains several hundred bid lines, includes ramp, reservations, in-flight, and ticket counter and gate assignments. According to the carrier, in some instances, "job assignments are entirely in one area (i.e. 100% in-flight or 100% reservations). Most commonly, the bid lines involve a combination of duties." Since bids of the most senior Fully Cross-Utilized CSRs are given preference, the senior employees generally receive the schedules they bid. Job assignments may be traded under certain circumstances, and adjustments may be made due to illness or vacations. If a CSR is outbid by a more senior CSR and has not bid alternative lines, that CSR will not receive any bid line.

According to AFA, "bid period after bid period, senior CSRs perform the duties of a flight attendant . . . ", due to a "CSR-wide preference for flight attendant time."

IV.

There are approximately 1,300 Cross-Utilized CSRs who are stationed at locations other than Phoenix. These individuals perform ticket counter and gate duties (including reservations duties), and ramp functions. They are neither trained to perform in-flight functions nor are they FAA-certified. Cross-Utilized CSRs are on a different pay scale than Fully Cross-Utilized CSRs and are not under the CSR Resources supervisory structure.

V.

In addition to the Fully Cross-Utilized CSRs, in Phoenix there are approximately 1,600 Non-Cross-Utilized CSRs who either perform exclusively ramp functions or exclusively reservations functions. Neither in-flight-trained nor FAA-certified, these individuals are on a different pay scale than Fully-Cross-Utilized CSRs and are part of a different supervisory structure.

VI.

The carrier provides a recurrent training program for Fully Cross-Utilized CSRs. This training encompasses all of the functions performed by the Fully Cross-Utilized CSRs. According to the carrier, the four days include training for all CSR functions.

VII.

The training program for newly-hired CSRs at America West involves both classroom training and on-the-job training. While undergoing the on-the job-portion of the training programs, trainee CSRs are paid at the same rate of pay as regular Fully Cross-Utilized CSRs, receive the same benefits and are subject to the same supervisory structure and carrier policies. However, trainees are not paid during the time they undergo classroom training which accounts for approximately 50% of the training time. According to the carrier, of the 53, trainee CSRs in question, approximately 50 were already employed by the carrier in other capacities. All trainees who successfully complete their training are guaranteed a position at America West."

VIII.

A comparison of the bid periods in July, August, and September reveals no significant discrepancy in either the number of CSRs performing in-flight functions or bid awards to junior CSRs versus senior CSRs in each month. However, according to the carrier, an error in the October 15–October 31 bid period resulted in the creation of additional awards and a limited opportunity for rebidding. The Board did not use bid periods beyond September 30, 1988, in making its determination of potential eligible voters.

DISCUSSION

I.

Two years ago the Board found there was an identifiable craft or class of Flight Attendants on America West. America West Airlines, 13 NMB 259 and 346 (1986). The Board's determination was based upon the limited amount of information provided by the carrier.

In the present case, the carrier has provided the Board with more information including bid assignment. and actual work schedules for the Fully Cross-Utilized CSRs. Further, the carrier has provided the Board with information regarding both the trainee program and the recurrent training program. The carrier and AFA have submitted several briefs in support of their respective positions.

II.

A.

The National Mediation Board makes its craft or class determination on a system-wide basis. Simmon Airlines, 15 NMB 124 (1988).

In determining the appropriate craft or class on a particular carrier, the Board examines a number of factors. These factors include functional integration, work classifications, terms and conditions of employment and work-related community of interest. USAir, 15 NMB 369 (1988), British Airways, Inc., 10 NMB 174 (1983), Air Canada, 6 NMB 1216 (1979). The factor of work-related community of interest is particularly important. USAir, supra, Airborne Express, Inc., 9 NMB 118 (1981).

The carrier argues that the "Fully Cross-Utilized" CSRs constitute an appropriate craft or class. The carrier asserts that Fully Cross-Utilized CSRs share a work-related community of interest, and main-

tains that if the Board should find otherwise, the carrier's business would suffer significantly.

The Board has been presented with similar arguments on several previous occasions. In USAir, supra, the carrier asserted that its "Customer Service Agents" performed both fleet service and passenger service functions on a regular basis. USAir maintained that if the Board found a separate Fleet Service craft or class, the carrier would lose the flexibility necessary for the airline to function efficiently.

The Board found, based upon its investigation, that a separate Fleet Service craft or class did exist on USAir. One of the factors in the Board's decision was that there was a group of individuals who regularly performed Fleet Service functions.

America West argues that it is unique among air carriers in that certain of its employees are part of a non-traditional cross-utilized craft or class. The investigation establishes that a significant number of individuals bid and work as flight attendants 100% of their time. For example, during the month of September, at least 580 Fully Cross-Utilized CSRs worked 100% of their time as flight attendants. In addition, several hundred individuals work as flight attendants a preponderance of their time. Few CSRs work an equal percentage of their time in two or more functions.

Further, although the carrier argues that seniority is not a basis to determine a craft or class, both the carrier and the organization agree that the more senior CSRs are more likely to regularly bid for, and regularly be awarded, flight attendant duties. The craft or class determination in this case, however, is based not upon seniority, but on the fact that there is an identifiable craft or class of flight attendants who share a work-related community of interest.

B.

Section 5.313 of the Board's Representation Manual provides, in part:

> On many carriers, employees may hold seniority rights or work regularly in more than one craft or class and work back and forth between these crafts and classes. . . .
>
> Additionally, when the [mediator] finds that employees not considered eligible by

virtue of their assignment on the cut-off date, do work a preponderance of their time in the craft or class involved, a preponderance check may be used. . . .

The investigation in this case reveals that there is an identifiable group of individuals who work a preponderance of their time in flight attendant functions.

III.

AFA takes the position that a 90 day preponderance period should be used to remedy the carrier's interference. In support of its allegation of carrier interference, AFA has submitted affidavits from two senior CSRs who maintain that they were not awarded in-flight bid lines in September, and one individual who maintains that the "Crew Scheduling Department" stated that "the September bid lines were not designed to utilize the entire work force" . . . and that therefore, America West was short 80 lines. AFA alleges that as a result "when the bids were awarded the eighty most junior CSRs held preponderantly in-flight lines." In response, the carrier has submitted company records and states that the two senior CSRs were either outbid by more senior CSRs or had bid improperly. Further, the carrier has submitted evidence that there were no irregularities in the September bidding periods, but admits there were errors in October. However, since the cut-off date is September 30, 1988, the October bid awards were not taken into consideration by the Board.

The Board finds insufficient evidence of carrier interference to warrant any remedial action. Nevertheless, the Board finds that a 90 day preponderance period, which includes all those CSRs working in in-flight functions on the cut-off date, as well as those CSRs who worked a preponderance of the 90 days as flight attendants, is the most effective method of ensuring that as few individuals as possible are inadvertently disenfranchised. The 90 day preponderance check is one option provided under Section 5.313 of the Board's Representation Manual, supra.

IV.

Although the carrier has argued that preponderance should not be used to determine eligibil-

ity, America West urges the Board to consider all the "recurrent training days" if preponderance is used. AFA requests that the Board use none of the days. The record reveals that the training for the Fully Cross-Utilized CSRs includes FAA required flight attendant training as well as training for non-flight attendant functions: However, it is virtually impossible to segregate the time allotted to training for flight attendant and non-flight attendant functions based upon the nature of the training program. CSRs who receive recurrent training are compensated as if they actually work those days, and this training is mandatory. The Board, finds, therefore, that recurrent training will be counted towards preponderance.

V.

In several recent decision, the Board has considered the question of whether flight attendant trainees are eligible. In Simmons Airlines, 15 NMB 228 (1988) the Board stated its policy on this subject:

> For the Board to find trainees eligible, the Board must be presented with evidence that the individuals in question have performed line functions in the craft or class as of the cut-off date. Factors such as accrual of seniority and receiving pay and benefits are not determinative of employee status absent substantive evidence of performance of line work in the craft or class.

See, also, Westair Commuter Airlines, 15 NMB 213 (1988), Midway Airlines, 15 NMB 26 (1987) and Horizon Air, 14 NMB 406 (1987).

Until individuals training for in-flight functions have successfully completed their IOE, they have not performed line functions and therefore are not eligible. The 50 individuals whom the carrier, alleges have been employed in other functions are not eligible to participate in an election among the craft or class of Flight Attendants unless they have performed work as Flight Attendants as of the cut-off date.

The Board finds that only those individuals who had completed their IOE and performed line functions as Flight Attendants as of September 30, 1988, will be eligible.

CONCLUSION

The Board finds that there is an identifiable craft or class on America West consisting of individuals who regularly and preponderantly perform flight attendant functions. Therefore, the Board finds a dispute to exist among the craft or class of Flight Attendants on America West and authorizes an all-mail ballot election using a cut-off date of September 30, 1988. The count will take place in Washington, DC. The list of eligible voters shall include all individuals working as flight attendants on the cut-off date, as well as those who worked a preponderance of their time during the 90 day period ending September 30 on in-flight functions. Recurrent training time will be counted. Trainees are not eligible to vote. The Board further finds that there is insufficient evidence that the carrier has interfered with the employees' freedom of choice. Finally, the Board denies the carrier's request for a hearing, based upon the sufficiency of the record and the absence of unique facts and issues.

By direction of the NATIONAL MEDIATION BOARD.

Charles R. Barnes
Executive Director

Copies to:

Michael J. Conway
Martin J. Whalen
Susan Bianchi-Sand
Deborah Greenfield, Esq.
David J. Hamilton, Esq.
John B. Willits

16 NMB No. 62
February 15, 1989

Deborah Greenfield, Esq.
Edward J. Gilmartin, Esq.
Association of Flight Attendants
1625 Massachusetts Avenue, N.W.
Washington, DC 20036

Mr. Martin J. Whalen
Senior Vice President
Administration and General Counsel
America West Airlines
4000 E. Sky Harbor Boulevard
Phoenix AZ 85034

Re: NMB Case No. R-5817
<u>America West Airlines</u>

Gentlemen and Ms. Greenfield:

This will address the January 30, 1989 objections and challenges to the list of eligible voters filed by the Association of Flight Attendants (AFA). The individuals whom AFA alleges are eligible have been sent "challenged" ballots. The carrier submitted evidence and argument in response on February 7, 1989. Final submissions were received on February 13, 1989.

I.

A.

AFA asserts that five individuals on medical leave during the 90 day preponderance period used to determine eligibility in this case are eligible to vote. The carrier maintains that these individuals are ineligible. The organization contends that Martha Jones was on maternity leave from the craft or class of Flight Attendants between April and September of 1988. According to the carrier, however, Ms. Jones was working as a secretary from June 4 through June 29, 1988, although prior to that time she was working as a fully cross-utilized Customer Service Representative (CSR).

AFA also contends that Barbara Foster, Linda Summers, and Mitzi Loretz were on maternity leave, and that Valerie Paulson was not working in the craft or class due to an "on the job injury" from July 29, 1988 to October 22, 1988.

According to the carrier's records, Barbara Foster went on leave from September 15, l988. However, she worked as a CSR from July 1, 1988 to September 15, 1988, but did not work a preponderance of that time performing flight attendant functions. The carrier's records also indicate that Mitzi Loretz was not on leave at all, but in fact worked "passenger service duty" through August 27, 1988, when she was assigned "to a desk position." Finally, the carrier states that Valerie Paulson worked as a CSR from July 1 through July 28, 1988, but did not work a preponderance of that time as a flight attendant.

The carrier states that its records indicate that Linda Summers worked as a flight attendant prior to taking leave commencing June 3, 1988.

B.

AFA also asserts that Scott Fallentine was on medical leave from June 13, 1988 to July 15, 1988, and restricted to ground duties from July 21, 1988 to August 30, 1988. The organization further contends that Theresa Rivera was "forced to work reservations in July and August 1988 due to illness."

In response, the carrier states that Mr. Fallentine last worked as a flight attendant on May 10, 1988, was on leave through July 19, 1988, and performed "ground assignment" functions through September 11, 1988. The carrier also states that Theresa Rivera last worked as a flight attendant on April 28, 1988, "was assigned to the reservations functions because her right to bid was revoked for disciplinary reasons" from May 26, 1988 through August 26, 1988, and continued to perform reservations functions through September 11, 1988.

C.

Section 5.306 of the Board's Representation Manual provides, in part:

> An employee on authorized leave of absence . . . from the craft or class in dispute, who is neither working in another craft or class [nor] working for the carrier in an official capacity . . . will be considered eligible. . . .

In determining whether an individual on leave is eligible, the Board frequently examines whether or not that individual was working in the craft or class involved in the representation dispute prior to taking leave. However, in this case eligibility in the craft or class was determined using a 90-day preponderance period, from the beginning of July 1988 to the end of September, 1988. Individuals either working in the craft or class as of September 30, 1988, the cut-off date, or who worked a preponderance of their time as flight attendants during the 90-day period, were found eligible, pursuant to Section 5.313 of the Board's representation Manual, <u>America West Airlines, Inc.,</u> 16 NMB 135 (1989).

As eligibility to vote in this case was determined by preponderance of days worked in the craft or class, the Board must have substantive evidence that the individuals in question worked preponderantly in the craft or class of flight attendants or worked their last day in the craft or class prior to taking leave in order to find these individuals eligible. Therefore, the Board finds that none of the individuals discussed above is eligible, with the exception of Linda Summers, who is eligible.

II.

AFA challenges the eligibility of six other individuals on the basis that they are "supervisory". In support of this allegation, AFA cites Section 5.312 of the Board's Representation Manual, which provides, in part:

> If an individual is determined not to be an employee-subordinate official, the individual shall be considered ineligible. The Board representative shall consider, in the investigation, whether the involved individual has the authority to discharge and/or discipline employees or to effectively recommend the same; the extent of supervisory authority; the ability to authorize and grant overtime; the authority to transfer and/establish assignments; the authority and the extent to which carrier funds may be committed; whether the authority exercised is circumscribed by operating the policy manuals; the placement of the individual in the organizational hierarchy of the carrier; and, any other relevant factors regarding the individual's duties and responsibilities.

AFA has not provided the board with substantive evidence in support of its contentions regarding these six individuals. The carrier responds that Kay Rzonga is an in-flight supervisor, Sabrina Anderson a CSR trainer, Richard Canfield a gate supervisor, John White a Customer Service Supervisor, Brent Boyd a pilot scheduler and Kimberly Romine a "supervisor" in CSR resources.

According to information provided by the carrier, an Inflight Supervisor on America West "works closely with Inflight CSRs onboard . . . flights ensuring quality/consistency of . . . Inflight procedures and adherence to [FAA] Regulations." Responsibilities include: conducting inflight evaluations; observing CSRs with reported problems and counselling or recommending corrective action; monitoring inflight CSR appearance; maintaining inflight CSR activity records; and reviewing passenger feedback and following through with "appropriate action." Inflight Supervisors report to the Staff Manager, Inflight Line Operations.

CSR Trainers on America West perform various functions. CSRs who work in inflight service training are "responsible for the classroom and hands-on training segments of Inflight Service for all cross-utilized CSR trainers . . . "

CSR Resource Supervisors supervise fully cross-utilized CSRs. Responsibilities include: providing support and assistance to CSRs including career counseling, and authorization of pay increases/anniversary awards; administration of company guidelines, including "ensuring that the availability, appearance and job performance standards established by the company are maintained and accurately reflected in CSR performance records." CSR Resource Supervisors also "interface with CSRs in sensitive matters relating to leaves of absences, transfers, promotions, resignations and terminations."

The evidence presented, when viewed in light of Board policy, establishes that none of the individuals in question possess the authority of carrier officials. However, the record also establishes that only the position of In-Flight Supervisor falls within the craft or class of Flight Attendants. Therefore, Kay Rzonga is eligible, but Sabrina Anderson, Richard Canfield, John White, Brent Boyd, and Kimberly Romine are ineligible. Further,

Suzanne Nilges, who transferred to Supervisor, CSR Resources, in July, is also ineligible.

On February 10, 1989, the carrier took the position that all In-Flight Service Supervisors (and CSR Resource Supervisors) should be considered eligible. The list of eligible voters in this case is comprised of individuals working as Flight Attendants on September 30, 1988, and those individuals who worked as Flight Attendants a preponderance of the time during the 90-day period in question. Therefore, as there is no substantive evidence that any of the twelve other In-Flight Supervisors alleged by the carrier to be eligible met either criterion used in this case, none of those individuals is eligible.

III.

AFA maintains that six individuals are ineligible because they have resigned. According to the carrier, however, only two of the six have resigned. Of the other four, two are on medical leave, one is an active CSR, and one is a CSR trainer.

The Board finds that Jodi Mizell and Michelle Ducusin are ineligible as they are no longer employed by the carrier. Deanna McFarland, who is a CSR trainer, is ineligible because she is not working in the craft or class of Flight Attendants. John Shurr, as an active member of the craft or class is eligible. Janet Yarner and April Ballard are on authorized medical leave. Both individuals previously had been determined to be eligible in the craft or class of Flight Attendants; therefore, they are eligible voters.

IV.

AFA contends that Virginia Gulden, Guy Muhammed, and Nancy Merkle are ineligible because they no longer work in the craft or class. The carrier's records confirm this contention. These individuals are, therefore, ineligible.

V.

Finally, AFA asserts that two individuals, Elizabeth Robinson and Dorothy Gaber, worked a preponderance of the period in question as flight attendants. As America West's records confirm this, these individuals are eligible voters.

VI.

The ballot count will take place as scheduled at 10:00 a.m., Wednesday, February 15, 1989. No further challenges to the list of eligible voters will be considered prior to the count without substantive evidence in support.

By direction of the NATIONAL MEDIATION BOARD.

Charles R. Barnes
Executive Director

17 NMB No. 24
FINDINGS UPON INVESTIGATION—ORDER
CASE NO. R-5817
January 12, 1990

**In the Matter of the Application of the
ASSOCIATION OF FLIGHT
ATTENDANTS
alleging a representation dispute
pursuant to Section 2,
Ninth, of the Railway Labor Act,
as amended involving employees of
AMERICA WEST AIRLINES, INC.**

On September 9, 1988, the Association Of Flight Attendants (AFA) filed an application pursuant to the Railway Labor Act, as amended, 45 U.S.C. §152, Ninth, alleging a representation dispute among "Flight Attendants (Customer Service Representatives) (CSRs)", employees of America West Airlines, Inc. This application was docketed as NMB Case No. R-5817.

At the time the application was filed, these employees were unrepresented. The Board assigned Mediator John Willits to investigate.

During the investigation, an issue arose concerning the appropriate craft or class of the employees covered by AFA's application. The carrier took the position that all of its fully cross-utilized CSR's constituted an appropriate craft or class. AFA maintained that there was an identifiable group of CSRs who preponderantly worked as Flight Attendants.

On January 5, 1989, in 16 NMB 135, the Board determined that the appropriate craft or class was that of Flight Attendants. The Board also found a dispute to exist and authorized an all mail ballot election using a cut-off date of September 30, 1988. The eligible electorate consisted of CSRs who worked a preponderance of their time as flight attendants during the 90 days prior to the cut-off date, and those who worked as flight attendants on the cut-off date. Ballots were mailed on January 17, 1989, and the count was scheduled for February 15, 1989.

On February 13, 1989, AFA filed a "Motion for Board Determination of Carrier Interference." The organization requested that the Board defer resolution of its Motion pending the count of ballots.

The results of the ballot count conducted on February 15, 1989 were as follows: 1193 eligible voters; 301 votes for AFA; 10 "void" ballots; and 2 votes for IBT. The votes ruled "void" were those cast for the carrier's CSR Panel.

On March 2, 1989, the carrier filed a Response to AFA's Motion. AFA filed a Reply to the carrier's Response on March 17, 1989. Both AFA and America West filed affidavits or declarations and exhibits in support of their arguments. On June 5, 1989, AFA requested that the Board use a "Key" ballot as a remedy for carrier interference. The carrier filed a position statement opposing a "Key" ballot on June 15, 1989.

ISSUES

The issue before the Board is whether the laboratory conditions which the Board is required to ensure in representation elections were tainted by the carrier's actions and if so, what remedy shall be applied.

The final issue is whether votes cast for the CSR Panel discussed infra should have been ruled void.

CONTENTIONS

AFA contends that the carrier's actions at various points during the organizational campaign and election have tainted the laboratory conditions necessary for a fair election. The organization alleges that the carrier "illegally conferred benefits" on eligible voters, and provided funds to assist in an anti-AFA campaign; that carrier officials used mandatory work-rule meetings as a forum to discuss the election; that during these meetings carrier officials "used threats, distortions, and untruths about AFA to discourage CSRs from voting"; that despite the fact that CSRs were prohibited from wearing AFA insignia, America West supervisors were encouraged to wear anti-AFA insignia.

Additionally, the organization maintains that the carrier circulated anti-union propaganda designed to influence employees in their choice of representative, which contained "false" statements and "deliberate mischaracterization of the Board's statutory duties." AFA's final contention is that the carrier failed to post the Board's official Notices of Election.

The carrier denies AFA's allegations. Specifically, the carrier asserts that the "conferred benefits" had been planned and announced well before AFA filed its application; that carrier officials did not make any statements during the work rule meetings which constituted "threats, promises, or misrepresentations" and that the carrier's campaign literature "merely" stated the carrier's opinion; that its policies prohibit the wearing of insignia on company uniforms; that the Board's election notices were posted; and that it did not provide funds "to support an anti-AFA labor organization."

FINDINGS OF LAW

Determination of the issues in this case is governed by the Railway Labor Act, as amended, 45 U.S.C. §151, et seq. Accordingly, the Board finds as follows:

I.

America West Airlines, Inc. is a common carrier by air as defined in 45 U.S.C. §181 of the Act.

II.

AFA is a labor organization and representative as provided by 45 U.S.C. §151, Sixth and §152, Ninth, of the Act.

III.

45 U.S.C. §152, Third, provides:

Representatives . . . shall be designated . . . <u>without interference, influence, or coercion</u> . . . (Emphasis added)

IV.

45 U.S.C. §152, Fourth, gives employees subject to its provisions " . . . the right to organize and bargain collectively through representatives of their own choosing. The majority of any craft or class of employees shall have the right to determine who shall be the representative of the craft or class for the purposes of this chapter." This section also provides as follows:

No carrier, its officers or agents, shall deny or in any way question the right of its employees to join, organize, or assist in organizing the labor organization of their choice, and <u>it shall be unlawful for any carrier to interfere in any way with their organization of its employees . . . or to influence or coerce employees in an effort to induce them to join or remain or not to join or remain members of any labor organization . . .</u> (Emphasis added)

V.

45 U.S.C. §152, Ninth, provides that the Board has the duty to investigate representation disputes and shall designate who may participate as eligible voters in the event an election is required. In determining the choice of the majority of employees, the Board is "authorized to take a secret ballot of the employees involved, or to utilize any other appropriate method of ascertaining the names of their duly designated and authorized representatives by the employees <u>without interference influence, or coercion exercised by the carrier.</u>" (Emphasis added)

FINDINGS OF FACT

I.

America West, headquartered in Phoenix, Arizona, commenced operations in 1983. The carrier employs approximately 9,000 people. The Chairman of the Board and Chief Executive Officer is Edward R. Beauvais. Michael J. Conway is the President and Chief Operating Officer. The Senior Vice-President and General Counsel is Martin J. Whalen, and the Senior Vice-President of Customer Services is Thomas P. Burns.

II.

AFA filed its application in this case on September 9, 1988. However, according to AFA, the organization's campaign commenced in February, 1988. As stated previously, ballots were mailed in January 1989 and the ballot count took place on February 15, 1989.

III.

America West's CSR Panel consists of six CSRs and one "designated manager." Thomas Burns is the official under whom the Panel operates. According to documents submitted by the carrier, the objectives and functions of the Panel are:

> To provide an ongoing and effective method of communication between America West [CSRs] and management.
>
> To facilitate the development, refinement and application of the CSR job function.
>
> The Panel will . . . review and present to management various matters on suggestions such as, but not limited to compensation, scheduling and cross-utilization. . . .

The term of office for each panel member is one year. While Panel members are elected by the CSRs, the carrier has established several eligibility requirements which must be met to qualify for election. The carrier reserves the right, in joint agreement with the Panel members, to remove from the ballot "any individual significantly deficient in meeting the determined criteria." The final decision is made by management and management continues to evaluate the performance of Panel members after election.

The Panel functions partially as a grievance resolution body. The Panel periodically issues a newsletter, the "Panel Channel", which provides information about its activities and other matters.

IV.

In July of 1988, the CSR Panel announced in the "Panel Channel" that the panel would develop work rules for the CSRs similar to those previously developed for the pilots and implemented on July 1, 1988. In August of 1988, America West's management authorized the CSR panel to proceed with the formulation of new work rules. Work rule meetings were held in September with Beauvais, Conway, and Burns as "guest speakers" at these meetings.

The work rules were approved on December 1, 1988, and were scheduled to be implemented March 1, 1989. The work rules included monetary and scheduling benefits, with "[i]ncreased compensation for layover time [to] be effective January 1, 1989." According to Thomas Burns, that date was selected because the carrier planned to implement a new per diem rate for the pilots on that same date, and "company practice has always been to provide new benefits both to pilots and to the fully cross-utilized CSRs."

V.

On December 23, 1988, the new work rules were announced. Sixty-two work rule training classes were conducted in January and February of 1989. Each class was attended by 30 or more CSRs. Beauvais, Conway and Burns attended and spoke at several of these sessions. CSRs were required to attend these meetings. Each CSR bid for the meeting they wished to attend, and each CSR was paid time and a half to attend these meetings.

AFA has submitted affidavits from several CSRs who attended these meetings. Each CSR states that the sessions were approximately four hours in duration. Each CSR states further that the first three hours of each session was devoted to the work rules and the CSR bidding system. The fourth hour of each of these sessions was led by a carrier official.

A.

According to AFA's affiants, America West President Michael J. Conway spoke at several of these meetings. CSRs who attended these meetings allege that Conway made a number of remarks concerning the election and AFA. Conway purportedly said that if AFA were certified, the carrier's Employee Assistance Program would be eliminated. Other comments attributed to Conway include state meets that: profit-sharing would be eliminated if AFA won the election; CSR benefits would probably not be as good if AFA was certified; AFA was misleading the CSRs about the possibility of USAir expanding in Phoenix; AFA's radio campaign was causing the carrier to lose business; the carrier's child care program may be at risk if AFA were elected; and CSRs should not vote for the union since it wasn't necessary.

B.

America West Chairman Edward Beauvais also spoke at several work rule meetings. Remarks attributed to Beauvais include: CSRs should throw away their ballots because if AFA won the election it would be detrimental to the carrier; other union carriers were not happy with their flight attendant unions; if AFA won the election, CSRs would start with a "clean slate" with respect to pay and benefits; the benefits now enjoyed by the CSRs would be in jeopardy if AFA won; if AFA won the election, it would ruin America West; and AFA was not necessary for the CSRs.

C.

On January 19, 1989, Senior Vice-President of Customer Services Thomas Burns spoke at a work rule meeting. According to an affidavit submitted by AFA, Burns told the CSRs that America West did not need a union. Burns also allegedly stated that despite AFA's failure to reach an agreement on Midway Airlines, the flight attendants had to pay dues. When a CSR told Burns that his statement about the Midway flight attendants was incorrect, Burns purportedly acknowledged that he may have been wrong. Finally, AFA's affiant contends that Burns said the CSRs would lose everything they had if AFA were certified.

VI.

The carrier has submitted Declarations regarding the work rule meetings (and other matters) from Conway, Beauvais, and Burns.

Conway and Beauvais state that they attended several work rule meetings during which they expressed opinions regarding the election. According to Conway and Beauvais, they never made any statements that CSRs would lose benefits if AFA were elected. They state further that they never suggested that the carrier would not negotiate in good faith with AFA.

Beauvais' declaration states that he did say that AFA's campaign flyer comparing salaries at America West with salaries on other carriers "was inaccurate, because the flyer failed to include the annual longevity bonus which America West CSRs receive." Burns also denies the remarks attributed to him.

VII.

The Declaration submitted by Burns provides details about America West's CSR work rules, profit-sharing plan, and 401 (k) plan.

According to the carrier, the 401 (k) plan, which covers all employees, had been under development for over a year prior to it being announced in April of 1988. On June 15, 1988, the carrier announced that the 401 (k) plan would be implemented on January 1, 1989. The plan was, in fact, implemented on that date.

VIII.

America West has had a profit-sharing plan since the carrier commenced its operations. Profit-sharing checks were distributed in April of 1985 at a party at which Beauvais and Conway were present. According to the carrier, no checks were distributed in 1986 and 1987, because the carrier had not made a profit.

On July 28, 1988, America West announced that if the carrier were profitable for an entire year, its employees would receive profit-sharing checks. The carrier made a profit in 1988 and profit-sharing checks were distributed at a party held on January 27, 1989, in the middle of the election period. Beauvais and Conway were present at this party.

IX.

AFA has submitted an affidavit from an individual who viewed a videotape "purportedly produced" by CSRs who did not support AFA. AFA's affiant watched this tape at the CSR Resources Department in Phoenix. The CSR asserts that the tape was labelled "Live Shoot—1/20/89—Produced by AWA Corporate Communications/ Audio-Visual Department." According to the CSR, the "tape was a prolonged anti-union/AFA tirade." The tape featured several CSRs discussing the election, unions, and AFA in particular. The individual who viewed the tape states, "it was my impression that these CSRs were provided . . . some Company assistance in the production of this video tape."

According to Burns, during the campaign, "a group of CSRs approached America West and requested permission to create a video tape concerning the election." Burns states that the carrier allowed the CSRs to use company equipment in making the tape.

X.

On January 25, 1989, an America West CSR was in the main terminal in Las Vegas, Nevada when he was noticed by Michael Conway. The CSR asserts that Conway, who was standing with a group of people, called out, "I heard from D.C. and they received one ballot and it was yours." According to the CSR, several passengers witnessed this incident.

In response, Conway states that he had conversed with the CSR a few weeks earlier on a flight concerning the election. Conway maintains that the CSR was comfortable in expressing his views as to "why AFA should be elected." Conway states that when he saw the CSR in Las Vegas a few weeks later, he made the remark as a joke in reference to the prior conversation.

There is no evidence that any other CSRs were present during the Las Vegas incident.

XI.

In an affidavit submitted in support of AFA's contentions, an individual states that there did not seem to be any official Notices of Election posted on America West property during the election period.

While investigating another case on the property in January, 1989, Mediator Willits inquired of America West's Senior Vice-President of Administration and General Counsel Martin J. Whalen as to whether the carrier had posted the Board's Notices of election. Whalen submitted a letter to Mediator Willits on January 30, 1989 stating that

Notices were posted on January 9, 1989. Attached to Whalen's letter were copies of letters from two members of Whalen's staff who stated that the Notices were posted at various locations on the property.

XII.

According to another CSR who has submitted an affidavit, on or about January 17, 1989, the CSR was asked by an America West supervisor, Thomas Marcellino, to attend a meeting of carrier managers. The CSR asserts that Whalen, who was at the meeting, stated that he did not know how AFA had obtained a master list of employees, but that there would be an investigation and "retribution".

Whalen contends that the CSR in question attended the meeting because the CSR requested to speak to America West's managers. Whalen denies that there was any discussion of employee lists or of retribution.

Thomas Marcellino has submitted a declaration in which he states that the CSR asked him if he could meet with carrier managers to discuss issues relating to CSRs. Marcellino further states that the CSR expressed his view to the managers and that "at no time did anyone at this meeting discuss an employee list or threaten retribution . . . "

XIII.

During the election campaign, the carrier and the organization circulated literature and disseminated information regarding their views. Each has accused the other of providing false information to the electorate.

A.

On June 15, 1988, America West issued a letter to its Pilots and CSRs regarding an ALPA/AFA radio announcement. The letter, signed by Beauvais and Conway, characterized the radio ad which mentioned "rumors of merger or acquisition" as a "'Scare Tactic' of the highest order" and concluded that the "unions are in a desperate race against America West's return to profitability."

B.

In a letter dated October 7, 1988, Beauvais and Conway answered questions concerning AFA's campaign. One response dealt with the determination of who was eligible to vote in the election. Beauvais and Conway stated,

> The AFA . . . is attempting to limit the extension of the "voting right" by asking the government to conduct an election involving 947 Fully Cross-Utilized CSRs out of a total of 1700.

C.

In another letter Beauvais and Conway discussed payment of union dues by fully cross-utilized CSRs not eligible to participate in the election, and the situation at Midway Airlines.

> What exactly has taken place at Midway Airlines in the 12 months since the AFA was voted in by a narrow margin. Lawsuits have been filed, nothing positive has happened to the Midway Flight Attendants, and the situation there has gotten outright ugly. Why does the AFA believe things would be any different at America West?

D.

On January 13, 1989, Beauvais and Conway sent a letter to all Fully Cross-Utilized CSRs regarding the impending election. Included in this letter was the following:

> It is very important to keep in mind that all of the time and expense that has been devoted to the 'Who Gets to Vote' issue could have been avoided if the AFA had petitioned the NMB to call an election involving all Fully Cross-Utilized CSRs. We certainly would not have objected to this approach, and the NMB would have sanctioned this, provided the AFA had a sufficient 'showing of interest.'

E.

In another letter from Beauvais and Conway, the Board's craft or class determination was discussed. The carrier officials re-stated their position that all Fully Cross-Utilized CSRs should be eligible to vote. Beauvais and Conway continued,

> It is quite clear to us that the AFA strategy to prevent a large number of Fully Cross

Utilized CSRs from voting stems from the fact that the AFA does not have the support of a majority of the 1700 Fully Cross Utilized CSRs at the Company. The AFA has stated they are only following the 'rules' by soliciting ballots from those CSRs who worked more than 50% Inflight for a given period of time. <u>This is nonsense.</u> The AFA had conducted a <u>malicious and distorted</u> campaign over the past several months, relying heavily on AFA organizers who are employed by airlines who compete against us. Over the next few weeks, we intend to play back to you documented statements made by the AFA which will support our assessment of their behavior. (Emphasis in original)

The letter concluded with . . . "if you receive a ballot and do not want to be unionized by the AFA, the only legal way to vote 'NO' is to destroy your ballot and not vote."

F.

On January 23, 1989, Beauvais and Conway issued another letter to the CSRs which contained statements about the progress of AFA's negotiations at Midway. Beauvais and Conway suggested that the CSRs ask themselves:

> If the situation at Midway is any indication of what it would be like at America West, are you likely to benefit from sending at least $400 of your after tax earnings each year to AFA outsiders from Washington?
>
> Is employee owned America West likely to be a better and stronger Company as a result of AFA outsiders attempting to manage your future for a fee of approximately $500,000 a year (1,200 CSR's x $34.00 per month x 12 months)?
>
> Vote "NO" BY DESTROYING YOUR NMB BALLOT.

The carrier attached "The Midway Chronology" to this letter.

G.

The final piece of America West campaign literature, issued in January 1989, described the results of another election conducted by the NMB as follows:

> [A]t USAir [t]he Teamsters union got 1854 votes . . . 12 less than a majority. The union would have lost the election . . . but then the NMB added 16 write-in ballots and decided that a majority of the employees wanted to be unionized. Next, the NMB decided that the Teamsters union got a majority of the votes for unionization. So now all 3733 employees have been unionized even though the union didn't get a majority of the votes!
>
> AFA is trying to make the same thing happen here. They know that they do not have the support of a majority of the CSRs . . . or even of the smaller group that they didn't argue to disenfranchise . . .
>
> VOTE FOR AMERICA WEST. DESTROY YOUR NMB BALLOT ON RECEIPT.

XV.

AFA has submitted affidavits from CSRs who state that America West supervisors made them remove pro-AFA insignia from their apparel. These individuals allege further that certain supervisors wore anti-AFA insignia during this campaign.

The carrier has submitted sections of its policy manual which indicate that wearing of pins and buttons on uniforms is prohibited.

AFA has also submitted copies of photos showing signs urging CSRs to destroy their ballots which were posted around the outside of the CSR Panel Office.

DISCUSSION

I.

In cases involving allegations of carrier interference, the Board examines whether or not the laboratory conditions which the Board seeks to promote in representation elections have been tainted. Metroflight, Inc., 13 NMB 284 (1986), Key Airlines, 13 NMB 153 (1986), Laker Airways, Ltd., 8 NMB 236 (1981), Zantop International Airlines, 6 NMB 834 (1979). Although the issue of interference has been before the Board many times, the Board does not order remedial action in each case.

In reaching its determination in this case, the Board has relied upon the evidence and arguments submitted by the organization and the carrier, as well upon the Board's own experience with cases of this nature.

The most recent case dealing with the question of carrier interference was Key Airlines, 16 NMB 296 (1989). In Key, the Board found that the carrier had violated its employees' right to freedom of choice in selecting a representative under the Act. This finding was based upon several acts of the carrier: discharge and re-assignment of leading union organizers; denial of a scheduled pay increase to one group of employees immediately after a representation application was filed, but the granting of a pay increase to another group of employees immediately prior to the filing of its application; holding meetings for the express purpose of discouraging organization; and threats to employees' job security should they vote for representation. The carrier issued letters criticizing the organization which included comments such as: "[do] you want to be a partner with an organization that has such a sordid reputation as the Teamsters . . . " and "do they want to help the unemployed crew members at World Airways at your expense?" Significantly, the carrier had violated employee representation rights in a similar manner three years previously. As a remedy for this situation, the Board ordered a new election using a ballot procedure in which the organization would be certified unless a majority of eligible voters returned votes opposing union representation. No write-in space was provided.

The Board has found other election remedies appropriate depending on the extent of the carrier interference found. In Mid Pacific Airlines, 13 NMB 178 (1986), the Board held that the carrier had violated the Act by polling its employees and implying that the carrier's financial future rested on the employees' rejection of union representation. The Board ordered a "Laker" election as a remedy. A "Laker" election involves the use of a "Yes" or "No" ballot. No write-in space is provided, and the majority of votes cast will determine the outcome of the election. In Zantop International Airlines, supra, the Board found that the carrier had contaminated the "laboratory conditions" by misinforming its employees of the Board's voting procedures and by holding meetings with small groups of employees. The Board ordered a re-run election to offset the carrier interference. In Allegheny Airlines, Inc., 4 NMB 7 (1962), the Board found, that the carrier had sent the employees involved in the election a letter, the "obvious purpose" of which the Board found, was "to discredit the [union]." In addition, the Board found that the carrier had mix-represented the Board's ballot and voting procedures. The Board noted that,

> the carrier's totality of conduct in the course of this representation election prevented this Board from fulfilling its obligation under Section 2, Ninth, to insure the choice of representative by the employees without interference, influence, or coercion exercised by the carrier. (Emphasis added)

II.

America West has advanced a number of arguments in support of its position that its actions did not constitute interference with the election. The carrier attempts to justify the timing of the new work rules by citing both legal and factual factors. First, the carrier states that since the new work rules were scheduled well in advance of the election or the filing of AFA's application, to withhold these benefits would have been unlawful. Second, in response to AFA's contention that the carrier was well aware of AFA's organizational drive in the months prior to the filing of the application, the carrier asserts that "America West had had 'organizational campaigns' . . . almost constantly since . . . 1983" and that most of them never proceeded beyond the stage of collection of authorization cards.

The carrier also asserts that the opinions expressed in the work rule meetings and in the campaign literature were protected by the First Amendment of the Constitution.

The Board is persuaded that the carrier did post the Notices of Election as required. Further, the Board finds that the 401 (k) plan had been under development for a substantial period of time, well prior to AFA's campaign.

The evidence presented by the carrier and AFA as to the specific content of the discussions in the work rule meetings, and the meeting on January

13, 1989, was inconclusive. While numerous coercive comments were alleged by several different CSRs to have been made by senior carrier officials, those officials denied making the comments.

III.

The Board finds that the carrier has improperly interfered with, influenced, and coerced its flight attendants in their freedom of choice, by the "totality" of its conduct. First, the Board finds that the timing of both the announcement of the work rule changes, and the implementation of the increase in layover benefits on January 1, 1989, immediately prior to the balloting period, improperly influenced the employees' freedom of choice. The Carrier submitted no evidence which would indicate that these events were scheduled or occurred for reasons independent of the election. As the Board stated in its recent decision in Key Airlines, supra,

> [f]rom that date [the time from which the carrier was aware of the organizing drive] until the conclusion of the election laboratory conditions must be maintained.

The Board gave consideration to the decision of the United States Supreme Court in NLRB v. Exchange Parts Co., 375 U.S. 405 (1964) in its decision.

Similarly, the Board finds that the timing of the profit-sharing party with Beauvais and Conway present, on January 27, 1989, during the balloting period and approximately two weeks before the ballot count, had the effect of improperly influencing the employees. As AFA has pointed out, the last profit-sharing party was held in April 1985. For the carrier to distribute these checks during the election period shows careless disregard of Act's requirements at best and a serious violation of those same provisions at worst.

In Allegheny Airlines, supra, the carrier claimed the First Amendment protected its actions, as America West does here. The Board stated in Alleaheny, "[t]he privilege of free speech, . . . is not absolute. It must be evaluated in the context of the rights of others." As the Supreme Court said in Texas & New Orleans Railroad v. Brotherhood of Railway and Steamship Clerks, 281 U.S. 548 (1930),

The petitioners, the Railroad Company

and its officers, contend that the provision confers merely an abstract right which was not intended to be enforced by legal proceedings; that, in so far as the statute undertakes to prevent either party from influencing the other in the selection of representatives, it is unconstitutional because it seeks to take away an inherent and inalienable right in violation of the Federal Constitution. . . .

The intent of Congress is clear with respect to the sort of conduct that is prohibited. 'Interference' with freedom of action and 'coercion' refer to well understood concepts of the law. The meaning of the word 'influence' in this clause may be gathered from the context. Noscitur a sociis. The use of the word is not to be taken as interdicting the normal relations and innocent communications which are apart of all friendly intercourse, albeit between employer and employee. 'Influence' in this context plainly means pressure, the use of the authority or power of either party to induce action by the other in derogation of what the statute calls 'self-organization'. The phrase covers the abuse of relation or opportunity so as to corrupt or override the will, and it is no more difficult to appraise conduct of this sort in connection with the selection of representatives for the purpose of this Act than in relation to well-known applications of the law with respect to fraud, duress and undue influence. If Congress intended that the prohibition, as thus construed, should be enforced, the Courts would encounter no difficulty in fulfilling its purpose, as the present suit demonstrates.

In reaching a conclusion as to the intent of Congress, the importance of the prohibition in its relation to the plan devised by the Act must have appropriate consideration. Freedom of choice in the selection of representatives on each side of the dispute is the essential foundation of the statutory scheme. All the proceedings looking to amicable adjustments and to agreements for arbitration of disputes, the entire policy of the Act, must depend for success on the uncoerced action of each party through its own representatives to the end that agreements satisfactory to both may be reached and the peace essential to the uninterrupted service of the instrumentalities of interstate commerce may be maintained. There is no impairment of the voluntary character of arrangements for the adjustment of disputes in the imposition of a legal obligation not to interfere with the free choice of those who are to make such adjustments. On the contrary, it is of essence of a voluntary scheme, if it is to accomplish its purpose, that this liberty should be safeguarded. The definite prohibition which congress inserted in the Act can not therefore be overridden in the view that Congress intended it to be ignored. As the prohibition was appropriate to the aim of Congress, and is capable of enforcing the conclusion must be that enforcement was contemplated.

Congress was not required to ignore this right of the employees but could safeguard it and seek to make their appropriate collective action an instrument of peace rather than of strife. Such collective action would be a mockery if representation were made futile by interferences with freedom of choice. Thus the prohibition by Congress of interference with the selection of representatives for the purpose of negotiation and conference between employers and employees, instead of being an invasion of the constitutional right of either, was based on the recognition of the rights of both. . . . The Railway Labor Act of 1926 does not interfere with the normal exercise of the right of the carrier to select its employees or to discharge them. The statute is not aimed at this right of the employers but at the interference with the right of employees to have representatives of their own choosing. As the carriers subject to the Act have no constitutional right to interfere with the freedom of the employees in making their selections, they cannot complain of the statute on constitutional grounds. (Citations omitted, emphasis supplied).

Viewing the carrier's conduct in its totality, including <u>inter alia</u> the timing of benefits, the presence of Beauvais and Conway at the profit-sharing party, as well as the timing of the party, the letters from Beauvais and Conway with their criticism of AFA—leads the Board to conclude that the laboratory conditions necessary for a fair election were contaminated.

CONCLUSION AND ORDER

AFA has requested as a remedy either a re-run election using a <u>Laker</u> ballot or a certification based upon authorization cards or a <u>Key</u> ballot. Based upon the circumstances in this case, the Board finds none of these remedies to be appropriate. The Board finds insufficient basis to use the remedy used in the <u>Key Airlines</u> case. That method, which involves the use of a presumptive "NO" ballot was a remedy for Key's "serious and repeated interference". This was Key's second violation in three years and the carrier had taken adverse action against known union supporters. Further, the carrier's actions in this case do not compare to those of the carriers in either <u>Laker, supra</u> or <u>Mid-Pacific, supra.</u>

The Board hereby authorizes a re-run election among Flight Attendants of America West Airlines. Further, a special "Notice to All Employees" (attached) will be distributed along with the ballot materials to each eligible voter in these elections.

The Board's craft or class determination in this case remains in effect and a mediator will be assigned to continue the investigation and make appropriate determinations that will, in fairness, enable the Board to carry out its responsibilities pursuant to Section 2, Ninth of the Act.

In view of the fact that a new election will be held, the Board makes no finding on whether votes for the CSR Panel in the first election were properly ruled "void". Finally,

[t]his Board need not consider what other action may be required if the new election [is] tainted. We trust [it] will be conducted under the democratic conditions required by the Act.

<u>Laker, supra,</u> at 258.

By direction of the NATIONAL MEDIATION BOARD

Charles R. Barnes
Executive Director

copies:

Mr. Edward R. Beauvais
Mr. Michael J. Conway
Mr. Martin J. Whalen
Robert A. Siegel, Esq.
Tom A. Jerman, Esq.
Edward J. Gilmartin, Esq.
Ms. Susan Bianchi-Sand
Deborah Greenfield, Esq.

NOTICE TO ALL EMPLOYEES

PURSUANT TO FINDINGS UPON INVESTIGATION AND ORDER OF THE NATIONAL MEDIATION BOARD AND IN ORDER TO EFFECTUATE THE POLICIES OF THE RAILWAY LABOR ACT, AS AMENDED, ALL EMPLOYEES ARE HEREBY NOTIFIED THAT:

After an investigation conducted by the National Mediation Board in which the Carrier and the Union had the opportunity to present statements and evidence, the National Mediation Board found that the Carrier's conduct, taken as a whole, improperly interfered with employees' choice of representative under Section 2, Ninth, of the Act. It is unlawful for a carrier to interfere with the organization of its employees.

Section 2, Fourth of the Act, 45 U.S.C. §152, allows employees the right to select representatives without carrier influence or interference That particular subsection reads as follows:

No carrier, its officers or agents, shall deny or in any way question the right of its employees to join, organize, or assist in organizing the labor organization of their choice, and it shall be unlawful for any carrier to interfere in any way with the organization of its employees, or to use the funds of the carrier in maintaining or assisting or contributing to any labor organization, labor representative, or other agency of collective bargaining, or in performing any work therefor, <u>or to influence or coerce employees in an effort to induce them to join or remain or not to join or remain members of any organization. . . .</u> (emphasis added)

Section 2, General Purposes Clause of the Railway Labor Act, states that one of the purposes of the Railway Labor Act is "to provide for the complete independence of carriers and of employees in the matter of self organization."

All employees are free to express their desire to be represented by a labor organization or remain unrepresented. The Carrier is not permitted to influence, interfere or coerce employees in any manner in an effort to induce them to participate or refrain from participating in the upcoming elections.

If any employees have any questions concerning this notice or compliance with its provisions, they may communicate directly with the National Mediation Board, 1425 K Street, N.W., Washington, D.C. 20572, Telephone (202) 523-5920.

17 NMB No. 63
June 6, 1990

Robert S. Siegel, Esq.
Tom A. Jerman, Esq.
O'Melveny & Myers
400 South Hope Street
Los Angeles, Ca 90071-2899

Edward J. Gilmartin, Esq.
Deborah Greenfield, Esq.
Association of Flight Attendants
1625 Massachusetts Avenue, N.W.
Washington, DC 20036

Re: NMB Case No. R-5817
    <u>America West Airlines</u>

Ms. Greenfield and Gentlemen:

This determination will address the carrier's Motion for Reconsideration of the Board's decision in 17 NMB 79 (January 12, 1990), as well as the various documents filed by the Association of Flight Attendants (AFA) in support of the organization's request for a "Laker" election. The Board will also address the question of appropriate cut-off date and other issues which were the subject of the numerous submissions filed by America West and AFA.

I.

In <u>America West Airlines,</u> 17 NMB 79, the Board found that the carrier had interfered with its employees' freedom of choice of a representative in an election involving the craft or class of Flight Attendants. The Board's finding of interference was based upon the "totality" of the carrier's conduct, including but not limited to, timing of the grant of certain benefits, and discussions at work rule meetings.

The Board held the election after receiving an application filed by AFA in September 1988. The election period was from January 17, 1989, to February 15, 1989.

Prior to the election, the Board had undertaken a lengthy and thorough investigation of several issues including the question of craft or class.

The Board, in its January 12, 1990, decision authorized a re-run election using standard ballot procedures to remedy the carrier's interference. The question of appropriate cut-off date was not resolved. Mediator Andrew J. Stites was assigned to investigate this issue, as well as other eligibility issues.

On January 26, 1990, the carrier filed a Motion for Reconsideration of the Board's January 12, 1990, decision. AFA filed a position statement in response on February 5, 1990. AFA also filed letters alleging continuing carrier interference on February 8, 1990, and February 15, 1990.

On February 21, 1990, the carrier filed a Motion for an Expedited Ruling on its earlier Motion for Reconsideration. The Board declined to issue an expedited ruling on February 22, 1990. On that same date, the carrier filed a Supplemental Memorandum in Support of its Motion for Reconsideration. The carrier filed a response to AFA's February 15, 1990 position statement on March 9, 1990.

AFA filed a letter on April 5, 1990 alleging that America West Customer Service Representative (CSR) Kevin Gillihan, is an active AFA supporter who had been disciplined due to his union activities. Documents in support of AFA's allegations regarding Kevin Gillihan were filed on April 12, 1990. On that same date, AFA filed a position statement and affidavit regarding remarks made by America West Manager David Coulson. The carrier filed a position statement on April 23, 1990, and AFA filed additional submissions on April 27, 1990. The organization also submitted a videotape April 5, 1990, in support of its request for a "Laker" election. The carrier submitted a final response to AFA's allegations regarding Coulson and regarding the videotape on May 16, 1990.

The carrier and the organization also filed several position statements and other documents with Mediator Stites on the question of the cut-off date.

II.

A.

The carrier argues that the Board should reconsider several aspects of its January 12, 1990, decision. It is America West's position that the Board's findings of fact "preclude" a determination of interference and that the Board's decision is a violation of the First Amendment. America West also contends that the level of interference found by the Board was <u>de minimis.</u>

Should the Board decide to proceed with the re-run election, the carrier requests that the Board "clarify" its rules on carrier interference. The carrier also argues that the Notice to Employees which the Board has ordered appended to the ballots is not justified. In the alternative, the carrier proposes a revised version of the Notice. Finally, the carrier continues to insist that the Board conduct a hearing on the question of interference.

B.

In support of its Motion for Reconsideration, the carrier has submitted an affidavit from Raymond T. Nakano, Vice President and Controller for America West. Nakano states that it is the car-

rier's policy to distribute profit-sharing checks in the month following a profitable quarter.

On February 8 and 15, 1990, AFA filed letters with the Board regarding a profit-sharing party scheduled for February 23, 1990. (America West had informed the Board of this event in its Motion for Reconsideration). The organization contended that the planned party was another example of the carrier's "illegal conduct" which required a "Laker"[1] election as remedy.

C.

AFA takes issue with the carrier's Motion for Reconsideration on all points, and characterizes the carrier's request for Board "rules" on carrier conduct in representation elections as a request for an advisory opinion.

As support for its position that a "Laker" election should be used, AFA cites a videotape dated June 16, 1988, which features three carrier officials: Senior Vice President for Customer Service Thomas Burns; General Counsel Martin J. Whalen; and Senior Director of Human Resources Alan Koehler. The topic of discussion is unions. The three participants discuss the merits of joining unions. (At this time, AFA was collecting authorization cards, but had not yet filed its application). Burns, Whalen and Koehler also discuss seniority integration, Board election procedures, and AFA. AFA asserts that the most "disturbing statement" is that of Koehler who, in essence, states that once employees vote for a union the union is there forever. AFA contends that this videotape is "still available for viewing at many [America West] locations . . .". According to the carrier, the tape was available for viewing in CSR breakroom for approximately 60 days in the summer of 1988. The carrier asserts that all but one copy of the tape (which is still missing) were collected and that the carrier's records indicate that "the library copy of the . . . tape has never been viewed or checked out by anyone."

AFA also refers to a newsletter sent by Michael J. Conway, President of America West, dated January 18, 1990. According to the organization, Conway "distorts" Board rules and "mischaracterizes" the Board's January 12, 1990 decision. The organization contends that Conway's memorandum and the carrier's announcement of the February

23, 1990, profit-sharing party have "already . . . tainted" the laboratory conditions necessary for the re-run election.

AFA has submitted an affidavit from a CSR who attended a recurrent training class in February of 1990. According to the CSR, the carrier's Manager of CSR Administration, David Coulson, asked the CSRs a series of questions during the session, including, "Is the NMB a union?". The CSR states further that most of the CSRs indicated their belief that the "NMB is a union." The CSR states that Coulson's response was that the Board was a federal agency "but 'traditionally its sympathy is with labor and it tends to side with labor.'"

In addition, the affiant states that Coulson referred to "Frequent Flier", a publication of CSRs who support AFA, as "filled with inaccuracies and distortions."

In its March 8, 1990, response to AFA's allegations, the carrier, as in the past, asserts that Conway's statements in the January 18, 1990, newsletter are protected by the First Amendment. The carrier also disputes AFA's assertion that any profit-sharing party violates the Railway Labor Act. America West re-states its position that the February 23, 1990, party was consistent with its past practice of holding such parties four to six weeks after the end of each profitable quarter. Finally, in response to AFA's position statement regarding David Coulson, the carrier asserts that Coulson's statements were true and that what Coulson actually said about the Board was that it "was created to protect the rights of employees and unions at a time when such protection was particularly needed . . .".

D.

The final basis for AFA's request for a "Laker" election is the series of disciplinary actions involving America West employee Kevin Gillihan. The personnel actions in question took place between March 13, 1990, and April 5, 1990. AFA contends that these actions were taken against Gillihan because of his union activities. Gillihan has appeared on local television in Phoenix, and has been listed as an AFA supporter on "almost all the literature sent to the Company's CSRs." Therefore, the organization maintains that the carrier's actions constitute "egregious" violations of the Rail-

way Labor Act, which must be rectified by a "Laker" ballot.

In response, the carrier states that there was no anti-union motivation behind the actions taken against Gillihan. America West asserts that Gillihan was disciplined due to his engaging in various violations of company policy, which were detailed in the carrier's filings as discussed below.

III.

AFA urges the Board to use the cut-off date used in the last election, which was September 30, 1988. In support of this position, the organization cites previous Board interference cases where the original cut-off date was retained in the second election in order to restore the requisite laboratory conditions.

America West takes the position that the Board should use December 31, 1989, as the cut-off date. This date represents the last day of the last payroll period prior to the Board's January 12, 1990, decision. The basis for the carrier's position on this issue is that use of the original cut-off date would disenfranchise a substantial number of individuals. Despite the Board's express statement in 17 NMB 79 that it would not reconsider the craft or class issue, the carrier continues to argue that there is no Flight Attendant craft or class on America West. Instead, America West contends that the appropriate craft or class is all Fully Cross-Utilized Customer Service Representatives (CSR's). As of December 31, 1989, there were 2307 such individuals employed by America West.

IV.

A.

The Board has carefully reviewed and considered the carrier's Motion for Reconsideration and finds no basis to reverse or alter its decision in 17 NMB 79. Absent new substantive evidence presented in support of such requests, the Board generally does not reverse its decisions upon request for reconsideration. USAir, Inc., 17 NMB 22, (1989), Air Wisconsin, 16 NMB 290 (1989), USAir, 16 NMB 194 (1989).

The Board remains unpersuaded that the timing of the January 26, 1989, profit-sharing party, which occurred in the middle of the balloting period, was not intended to influence the employees' decision regarding representation. The evidence submitted by the carrier in support of its request for re-consideration is insufficient to support a finding that there was either an established historical pattern or that this was a regularly scheduled benefit at the time the January 26, 1989 party was held.

In addition, the Board finds that the carrier's First Amendment arguments have been previously presented, considered, and rejected by the Board. As the Board stated in Laker, supra, at 253,

> [t]he Board is not unmindful of Laker's constitutional right to communicate its views to its employees. However, this right is not without limit, and even conduct which is otherwise lawful may justify remedial action when it interferes with a representation election. General Shoe Corp., supra (77 NLRB 124 (1948).

Although the carrier maintains that the Board did not find "egregious" violations of the Act, but only de minimis "interference which could not possibly have had an effect on the outcome of [the] election," such is not the case. Nowhere in the Board's decision did the Board refer to the carrier's conduct as "de minimis." While the level of interference found was insufficient, in the Board's view, to grant the relief requested by AFA ("Laker" election, "Key"[2] election or certification based upon showing of interest), neither was the interference found so minimal as to warrant no relief at all.

The Board also denies the carrier's request for clarification of "the rules for carrier conduct." It is the Board's policy to decline to issue advisory opinions on any subject. Overseas National Airways, 12 NMB 269 (1985). Further, the Board makes its representation decisions on a case-by-case basis. The Board's finding of whether carrier interference has occurred depends upon the particular facts and circumstances of each case. Certain conduct which is proscribed in all cases has been discussed by the Board in previous decisions.[3] Finally, the Board takes note of the decision of the United States Supreme Court in NLRB v. Gissell Packing Co., 395 U.S. 575 (1969), where the Court stated,

> . . . an employer, who has control over [the employer-employee] relationship and therefore knows it best, cannot be heard to complain that he is without an adequate guide for his behavior.

The Board also declines to either rescind or revise[4] the Notice to be attached to the ballots in the re-run election. It is not true, as America West asserts, that the "notice was developed for, and has been used only in, cases involving . . . egregious misconduct . . .". As a remedy for the interference found in Laker, supra, and Key, supra, the Board ordered the use of a Notice to the employees. Since Key, it has been Board policy to require the Notice to be used in all cases where there has been a finding of interference and an order of remedial action. For example, in Florida East Coast Railway Company, 17 NMB 177 (1990), the Board found that the interference was not at the level of the interference found in Laker or Key. Nevertheless, the Board ordered a re-run election with the Notice in question to be attached to each employee's ballot.

B.

The Board also denies AFA's request for a "Laker" ballot. With the exception of the June 18, 1988, videotape, the organization has not presented any new evidence regarding the previous election which could persuade the Board to reconsider or alter the remedy ordered in 17 NMB 79.

The majority of AFA's allegations in support of the request for a "Laker" election deals with actions taken subsequent to the Board's January 12, 1990, decision. After a review of the arguments and evidence before it, the Board finds that there is insufficient basis to conclude that the laboratory conditions for the forthcoming election have been tainted.

C.

The carrier has presented evidence that it has held profit sharing parties within four to six weeks of the end of a profitable quarter since the last election (for at least five quarters). The Board finds that the February 23, 1990, party, delayed due to a change in the carrier's payroll system, was consistent with past practice. The Board's finding that the timing of the January 26, 1989, profit sharing party constituted carrier interference does not mean that the carrier may never hold a profit-sharing party. We merely find here that the timing of such actions as the granting of benefits must not be with a blind eye toward the Act's requirements for "laboratory conditions."

AFA argues that the carrier's newsletter of January 18, 1990, "Executive Report", is an example of "illegal conduct". In the newsletter, Conway states, <u>inter alia</u>:

> In 1988, the NMB made a determination that based on the specific urging of the AFA, there is a 'craft or class of flight attendants' at America West.
>
> • • • •
>
> Despite our protests that nearly half of the affected employees were being disenfranchised by not being allowed to participate in the voting process, the NMB, nevertheless, conducted an election among the group that the AFA and it considers to be 'flight attendants'
>
> • • • •
>
> The NMB's decision . . . does not find any threats, intimidation or other egregious misconduct on the part of America West, but only quarrels with the timing of work rule changes, benefits and profit-sharing. Apparently, the AFA and NMB believe we should have delayed our pre-existing plans to implement improvements until after the election . . this makes no sense to us at all.
>
> • • • •
>
> To say the least, we are extremely disappointed by the NMB's decision to hold another vote and we find the entire process leading up to their decision to be bizarre.

AFA maintains that the newsletter "distorts the Board's Rules", attacks the Board's integrity and "its very legitimacy as the agency charged with supervising representation elections . . . " and "mischaracterizes" the Board's January 12 decision.

The carrier argues that "[t]here is absolutely nothing in the "Executive Report" which is not either an accurate statement of fact or a clearly labeled statement of opinion." America West asserts further that while it "has vigorously disagreed with several of the Board's rulings in this case. . . . [it] has never attacked the integrity of the Board."

The Board finds that the newsletter of January 18, 1990, does not provide a basis for a "Laker" election.

D.

David Coulson has submitted an affidavit in response to AFA's allegations regarding the remarks he made during a recurrent training class held in February 1990. Coulson, who is the Manager of CSR Administration, states that it is his practice to give a written quiz at the beginning of each recurrent training session. According to Coulson,

> [t]he purpose of this quiz is to demonstrate that the CSRs may have misconceptions . . . [o]ne question that I have asked in the past is whether the [Board] is a union organization. . . . I have [o]n all occasions made it clear to the class that the Board is Federal government agency organized to protect the rights of employees for representation and not a union.
>
> • • • •
>
> As historical background, I have informed training classes that the NMB is an agency which was created in the early 1900s to ensure that all employees in the railroad and airline industries were allowed to freely engage in collective bargaining. I also informed the class that agencies like the NMB were created . . . in order to protect employees from abuses by employers which were occurring at the time.

Coulson states further that the statements he made in regard to the "Frequent Flier" newsletter were true. The carrier has attached copies of issues of this publication in support of its May 16, 1990, position statement.

The Board has carefully reviewed the arguments and evidence regarding the remarks made by Coulson during the recurrent training session, and finds insufficient basis for ordering a "Laker" ballot. The question remaining therefore, is whether Kevin Gillihan was disciplined due to his union activities, which would constitute a serious violation of the Act.

E.

Gillihan has been employed by America West since June of 1986, and has preponderantly performed Flight Attendant functions for the past three years. Since July of 1988 Gillihan has been an active supporter of AFA's efforts to represent America West's Flight Attendants.

On March 13, 1990, Gillihan was issued a letter of "Formal Warning" and restricted from performing In-Flight functions for 90 days. This action was triggered by a complaint filed against Gillihan by another Flight Attendant who worked with him on a series of flights in February of 1990. The complaint alleged that Gillihan had violated FAA and company policies. (There is no evidence or even any allegation that the Flight Attendant who filed the complaint was motivated by anti-union animus). Both Gillihan and another individual have submitted affidavits stating that a member of the review board which upheld the disciplinary action, Scott Ramsey, told them that the carrier did not like Gillihan's outspoken support of AFA. Ramsey has submitted an affidavit denying the remarks attributed to him.

A second incident took place on March 14, 1990. Gillihan reported for work to perform his ground assignment but could not perform his ground functions because he did not have his computer password. Given the option of obtaining his password personally from another area of the carrier and losing pay for part of the day, or losing pay for the whole day (going home) Gillihan chose the latter. A "letter of concern" was issued to Gillihan on March 15, 1990.

The third incident resulting in disciplinary action occurred on March 31, 1990. One of Gillihan's supervisors reported that Gillihan had left at least 45 minutes before the end of his shift. On April 5, 1990, Gillihan was issued a "Letter of Final Opportunity."

The carrier has submitted several documents and affidavits relating to Gillihan, including the original complaint filed against him, and pertinent pages of the Company Policy Manual. Also submitted were affidavits from several individuals involved in the three incidents, including Gillihan's supervisors.

F.

In Transkentucky Transportation Railroad. Inc., 8 NMB 495 (1981), the Board, in finding that the carrier had interfered with its employees' freedom of choice of a collective bargaining representative, noted the decision of the United States District Court for the Eastern District of Kentucky, Hughes v. Transkentucky Transportation Railroad, Inc., Civ. No. 81-40.

The court found that after its evaluation of the evidence, it could only conclude that individuals who had been terminated were terminated because of their union activity. The court stated, however that

> . . . this doesn't mean that there can't be any discharges . . . This means only that nobody can be discharged for union activities.

This Board has reviewed the record before it regarding the disciplinary actions taken against Kevin Gillihan and finds insufficient evidence to conclude that Gillihan was disciplined due to his union activity.

Based upon the foregoing, the Board does not find a basis for using a "Laker" ballot in the forthcoming election.

V.

The cut-off date for purposes of eligibility in the prior election was September 30, 1988. The Board determined in 16 NMB 135 (1989) that the list of eligible voters included all individuals working as Flight Attendants as of September 30, 1988 and all those who worked a preponderance of the 90 days prior to September 30, 1988 as Flight Attendants. On the date of the count, there were 1193 eligible voters.

As of December 31, 1989, there were 1522 individuals who preponderantly performed Flight Attendant functions for America West. Of the 1193 individuals eligible to vote in the last election, approximately 107 were no longer eligible as of December 31, 1989, with 1086 of the 1193 remaining potentially eligible. Application of the September 30, 1988, cut-off date would therefore result in the eligibility of over 71% of the employees in the craft or class of Flight Attendants. The Board finds no basis to revise its previous craft or class finding or to accept the carrier's argument that the 2307 Fully Cross-Utilized CSRs should be eligible.

A recent Board determination involving the issue of changing the cut-off date was USAir, 17 NMB 117 (1990). There the Board stated,

> [o]nce the Board establishes a cut-off date for purposes of eligibility, it changes that date only in unusual circumstances.

The carrier has cited two Board decisions, in support of its position that the cut-off date should be changed, USAir, 10 NMB 495 (1983), and Piedmont Airlines, 9 NMB 41 (1981). In each case the cut-off date was changed due to "unusual circumstances." The unusual circumstance in the USAir case was that there had been a 100% turn-over in the craft or class. In Piedmont, there had been a five year delay between the original cut-off date and the election due to protracted litigation.

In USAir, 16 NMB 63 (1988), the Board retained the original cut-off date despite the addition of 197 individuals into the craft or class during the five month period between the establishment of the cut-off date and the Board's authorization of election.

The Board's investigation of this issue reveals no "unusual circumstances" which would warrant changing the cut-off date. In addition, the Board finds neither substantial turn over nor lengthy delay, the only two bases found in the past for changing the cut-off date. Therefore, the list of eligible voters in the re-run election authorized on January 12, 1990, will consist of all employees eligible to vote in the last election, with the exception of those individuals no longer employed by the carrier or no longer working in the craft or class.

CONCLUSION

Upon reconsideration, the Board finds that neither America West nor AFA has provided sufficient basis for granting the various forms of relief requested. The election will proceed forthwith. Should the Board find that the laboratory conditions which are required for a fair election have been tainted, the Board will use any method within its discretion as a remedy. Finally, as the result of

its investigation, the Board finds that the appropriate cut-off date is September 30, 1988.

By direction of the NATIONAL MEDIATION BOARD.

William A. Gill, Jr.
Executive Director

Copies to:

Mr. Martin J. Whalen
Senior Vice President
America West Airlines, Inc.
4000 East Sky Harbor Boulevard
Phoenix, AZ 85034

Mr. Andrew J. Stites
Mediator

Sample Management Guide to Permissible Campaigning under the Railway Labor Act

The Railway Labor Act makes it unlawful for any carrier, including its management and supervisors, to interfere with, coerce, or influence employees in the choice of a bargaining representative. *Influence* has been defined by the Supreme Court to mean "undue influence or pressure." These statutory prohibitions apply to verbal and written communications. All written material must be carefully reviewed for compliance before distribution and usage.

Permissible Management Control

Management may do the following:

1. Enforce company rules on solicitation and distribution, so long as even enforcement is followed at all times. The solicitation and distribution rules

a. Must be applied in the same manner whether the activity involves unions or is totally unconnected with union organizational activity

b. Must be applied uniformly among competing unions

c. Must be applied in exactly the same way to employees who are engaging in antiunion activity.

2. Prevent its facilities, including mail, telephone, and company records, from being used for organizational purposes.

3. Take steps to safeguard information. Do not give anyone a list of employees' names, phone numbers, addresses, job descriptions, etc. Anyone requesting such information, whether it is an employee of the company or not, should be referred to the personnel office. You should also inform the personnel office of the specifics of the incident.

4. Provide complete factual information about the union and unionization. Management may

a. Tell employees the facts about any misleading statements made by a union organizer or appearing in handbills or other literature distributed by union organizers.

b. Tell employees what benefits they have already received and how they compare favorably with organized employees.

c. Tell employees they will take on certain obligations if they are union members, that they will be controlled by the union constitution, bylaws, and resolutions whether they agree with them or not. Tell them they are subject to the union's leadership with respect to union matters and that union leadership is not necessarily confined to company employees but includes the union's national leadership.

d. Tell employees about the necessity of paying union dues and initiation fees if there is a union security agreement. Tell them how much these dues are currently and what increases have occurred. Tell them that under union security agreements, retention of their jobs can be conditioned on payment of union dues or equivalent service fees. Tell them they are subject to union assessments to pay, for example, strike benefits to employees of other carriers.

Tell them they are subject to union-imposed fines if they cross picket lines contrary to union dictates.

e. Tell employees that if a union represents them, their conditions of employment will be established by the union, and they will lose their individual bargaining rights.

f. Emphasize that once a union is certified as the employees' representative, there is no procedure to return to unorganized status. It is a one-way street with no return.

g. Tell employees that even if they signed an authorization card, they are not obligated to vote in the election. Explain the voting procedure and inform employees that if they do not want union representation, they should not vote at all. (But do not tell or direct employees not to vote.)

h. Stress the positive side of being unorganized. Tell the employees they are currently compensated based on individual ability.

i. Tell employees about the strike record of the union; but do not excessively emphasize this fact to induce employees into believing that a strike is inevitable if a union is successful in organizing them.

j. Bring to the employees' attention any unfavorable *factual* publicity that the union or its representatives have received as a result of the Senate Committee hearings, court proceedings, newspaper reports of picket line violence, corruption, theft, etc.

k. Reassure employees, if the union has threatened that employees will be discharged unless they support it, that the union has no way of carrying out these threats and that the company will not permit it.

5. Point out that if any union makes lavish promises to employees to obtain their votes, none of the promises can be fulfilled except by agreement of the company. In doing so, the company must be careful not to portray an image that the employees are wholly dependent on the company so as to convey the power and authority exercised over them by the com-

pany. This kind of communication is particularly sensitive.

6. Point out that federal law forbids a union or its agents from restraining or coercing employees in the exercise of their rights, including the right not to support a union.

In communicating with employees under the Railway Labor Act, several cautions must be emphasized:

1. The tone of all communications should be moderate, certainly never making inflammatory statements to disparage or discredit the union.

2. Communications should be as factual as possible, avoiding inflammatory statements to disparage or discredit the union.

3. Minimize small group meetings, particularly in managers' or supervisors' offices. Most communications will be in writing. If large group meetings are held, a written record or outline should be used to guide the discussion. This outline should be approved by the personnel office before the meeting.

4. Do not explicitly tell employees not to vote. Rather, explain that if they do not wish union representation, they can express their wishes by not voting. Emphasize that the choice is theirs and that the company respects the rights of its employees to make that choice.

Nonpermissible Management Conduct

During a union organizational campaign under the Railway Labor Act, management is under the following restrictions:

1. Company representatives may not make any statement, whether by direct conversation, letter, bulletin board posting, or speech, that contains either explicitly or implicitly a promise of benefit or threat of reprisal. Nor may management attempt to influence employees by use of superior management position, pressure employees, or contribute funds to defeat unionization. Thus, for example, it is not permissible to:

a. Promise or hint that employees will get a wage increase, a better job, or any other similar benefit if they vote against the union or if the union is defeated in an election

b. Threaten or hint that employees will receive a wage cut, a less desirable job, or any other loss of benefit or privileges if the employee supports the union or if the union wins the election

c. Threaten or hint that employees will be discharged, demoted, laid off, or otherwise discriminated against if the union succeeds in organizing employees

d. State or hint that the company will close down its entire operations, move the work location, or drastically reduce operations if the union succeeds in organizing the employees

e. State or hint that the company will refuse to bargain with the union if the union is successful in organizing the employees

2. The company may not interrogate employees at any time, including during hiring, regarding their union sympathies or union activities.

3. The company may not solicit or suggest that employees demand the return of their union authorization cards or assist employees in attempts to secure the return of authorization cards.

4. Company representatives may not call employees individually or in small groups into the *private offices* of management or supervisory personnel for the purposes of making statements in opposition to the union or unions involved. Company representatives may, however, discuss unionization in places where usual employee communication takes place (work areas, briefing rooms, etc.).

5. The company may not permit employees to engage in antiunion activities or distribute antiunion literature on company time and premises while denying pro-union employees similar rights to engage in pro-union activities. This applies, also, when there are one or more competing unions.

6. The company not keep union meetings under surveillance for *any* purpose or create the impression of surveillance.

7. Management or supervisory personnel may not visit employees in their homes for the purpose of discussing matters relating to union organizational activities.

8. Management cannot

a. Discharge, discipline, or lay off an employee because of legitimate activities on behalf of the union

b. Discriminate against employees actively supporting the union by intentionally assigning undesirable work to the union employees

c. Transfer employees prejudicially because of union affiliation

d. Engage in any partiality favoring nonunion employees over employees active on behalf of the union

e. Discipline or penalize employees actively supporting a union for an infraction that nonunion employees are permitted to commit without being likewise disciplined

f. Make any work assignment for the purpose of causing employees who have been active on behalf of the union to quit their jobs

g. Ask employees for an expression of thoughts about a union or its officials

h. Ask employees how they intend to vote or if they intend to vote

i. Give financial support or assistance to a union or its representatives or to employees who oppose unionization

j. Ask employees about the identity of the instigator or leader of employees favoring the union

k. Make any misrepresentations about the union

Rules on Solicitation and Distribution

Company rules on solicitation and distribution are long-standing and appear in the TWA General Rules of Conduct and in the union contracts. Rule 16 of the General Rules of Conduct states:

No employee shall make an unauthorized appearance on Company property nor shall he solicit funds or services, sell tickets, distribute petitions or literature for any purpose on Company property at any time without the prior consent of his supervisor.

The pertinent section of the IAMAW agreement states:

There shall be no general distribution or posting by employees of advertising or political matter or of any kind of literature upon the Company's property. No employees covered by this agreement, shall during working hours, engage in solicitation of membership for any union, collection of dues or other Union activity not provided for in this agreement.

It has long been the company's policy to effect strict control over unauthorized persons and unauthorized conduct on company time and property. This is particularly important in light of the intensified concern in our industry over all aspects of airline security. Activity that compromises, or even might lead to compromise of, airline security or safety is critical. To be specific:

1. We must apply our rules in a uniform and firm manner. You cannot, of course, give consent to antiunion solicitation activity without also giving consent to pro-union solicitation activity. If you are not absolutely certain what is the proper course of action, contact the personnel office immediately.

2. You should refuse to permit outside solicitors or union organizers to talk to employees on company time or on company property, which includes all property controlled by the company, such as cafeterias, parking lots, ramp offices, etc. Union organizers have the same right to enter such public facilities as ticket offices and terminal areas as does any member of the public. But they do not have the right to solicit membership, either verbally or through the distribution of literature, or to interfere with the conduct of company business. An off-duty employee who has entered company premises for the purpose of conducting solicitation activities should be required to leave. If

solicitation activities are conducted in such instances in conjunction with company business, the off-duty employee should be instructed to complete his or her business expeditiously and then leave.

3. Working time is for work. Employees may not engage in union solicitation during working time. This rule against solicitation applies to the working time of the employee doing the solicitation and the employee being solicited. Employees may discuss nonwork matters, including unionization, on their own time on company premises (lunch and break periods), so long as one employee does not unduly disturb or interfere with the rights of others.

4. Distribution of union literature, buttons, etc. may not be done on company time or premises.

5. Unions are not permitted to post on union or company bulletin boards notices or information that go beyond the specifics permitted in their contracts with the company. If such posting is made on union bulletin boards, contact the union official at the time of the posting and get him or her to remove it. If posting is made on company bulletin boards, or if the union official refuses to remove such posting from a union bulletin board, you should remove such posting and forward it with an explanation to the personnel office.

6. Any contacts of the type described above should be reported to the personnel office immediately.

Sample Materials Provided to Frontline Managers During an Antiunion Campaign under an NLRA Environment

Sample Statement to Employees Concerning Labor Unions

In this plant, it is almost certain that one or more labor unions will try to gain additional members by aggressively soliciting you and conducting organizing activities over the months and years ahead. For this reason, it is appropriate that you understand management's position concerning unions. We are against a union coming into the plant because we sincerely believe that it would not be good for you or the business. You will not need a union to get fair treatment. It is our companywide policy to provide fair treatment in pay, benefits, and working conditions for all employees alike—union or nonunion.

Signing a union card is a serious thing. Your signature is valuable, because it may indicate to a union your desire to be represented. As with any agreement, before signing, understand the total particulars and what you are getting into. We feel strongly that it is in your best interest not to sign a union authorization card. In any event, do not sign a card just to please someone else or get the union organizer to leave you alone.

At most of our plants, when the issue has been raised, employees have decided against having a union represent them. We think you will feel the same way. Our request is that you give us an opportunity to demonstrate to you that a union is not needed here.

Your plant management has pledged itself to high standards of treatment and respect for all employees. You can be certain that we will constantly seek to achieve and maintain this fairness of individual treatment for your best interests and long-term job security. As far as your complaints are concerned, we want you to feel free to express them to us. We know we are not perfect, and that mistakes will be made. Through our problem-solving procedure, which can get your complaint all the way to the plant manager, we stand ready to investigate and, when warranted, adjust any decision that personally affects you and that you believe has not been handled fairly. It is a good thing to know that you have a complaint system available to you that even permits you to go around your supervisor to get an answer if you feel that he or she has not been fair.

Summing up, we ask that you not be persuaded that signing a union authorization card is the thing to do and that you always carefully consider the many benefits of your job that are yours without the need to pay union dues and risk the loss of your pay through strikes, work stoppages, fines, and other costs of union membership.

Disadvantages of union representation from the company's point of view include

1. Negative effects on customer service and satisfaction. A union is a third party that has no legal obligation to provide service. Naturally, its objectives will differ from those of the company. As a result, the union may

a. Demand work rules that detract from the quality or quantity of service

b. Demand special privileges, such as the right to conduct union business in the facility

c. Call a strike and engage in picketing

These are only a few examples of how unionization could interfere with the service we provide.

2. Lack of managerial flexibility. The company now has the flexibility to adjust to meet changing company needs.

3. Wasted management time. With unionization, supervisors may spend a great deal of time dealing with petty union gripes and grievances. With a union, consultation with the union steward becomes standard procedure before changing duties, assignments, or schedules or before taking other actions affecting employment conditions. Time-wasting decisions and horse trading become a part of many management decisions.

4. Divided loyalty of employees. Unionization often means that management cannot get wholehearted cooperation and support from employees in solving problems.

5. Higher operating costs. Due to delays, time wasting, work rule restrictions, grievances, arbitration, etc., the cost of operating the company will go up. This rise in cost reduces the amount of money available for investing in new equipment, new programs, new facilities, and wages.

Disadvantages of union representation from the supervisor's point of view include

1. Restrictions on the supervisor's freedom

and authority. Union shop stewards will be constantly looking over your shoulder—second-guessing your decisions. Since the union can effectively override many supervisory decisions by threatening arbitration, the individual supervisor loses prestige and authority.

2. Difficulties in dealing with employees. Unions often generate feelings of distrust toward supervisors. They may also create an uncooperative attitude among employees by telling them that they are untouchable. This attitude is especially prevalent among union delegates or stewards.

3. Time involved in handling petty grievances. Again, your time may be wasted in dealing with stewards over petty grievances.

4. Overemphasis on seniority. Many union contracts require that employment decisions be based solely on seniority, rather than on skill and ability.

5. Internal bickering. Unions often increase dissension, and a less friendly, more formal work atmosphere results.

Disadvantages of union representation from the employee's point of view include

1. High cost of union membership. Union representation has a hefty price tag. A few examples of the financial obligations employees will encounter with membership in the union are

a. Union dues

b. Initiation fees

c. Special assessments

d. General assessments

e. Reinitiation fees

f. Union fines

2. Loss of personal freedom. Because of union disciplinary rules and procedures (e.g., trials, fines, suspension, expulsion, etc.), employees will lose personal freedom.

3. Loss of individuality. Though employees will have the right to talk to management individually, the union will probably discourage this communication and insist that employees only use the union's formal grievance procedure. Under the labor law, the union has a right to be present at any supervisor-employee

conference whether the employee likes it or not.

4. Incentives are limited. Merit increase and individual incentives for extra effort and skill are contrary to trade union philosophy.

5. Possibility of strikes. Despite these costs and disadvantages, employees have no guarantee that they will get more or better wages or benefits. In cases where the union is unable to achieve what it has promised at the bargaining table, unions sometimes draw employees into costly and unsuccessful strikes. While on strike, employees do not receive wages, benefits, or unemployment compensation. They may even be *permanently* replaced in an economic strike.

Recognizing the Early Warning Signs of Union Activity—Recognizing Unexplained Change

It is extremely important that supervisors react in a quick, positive, and aggressive manner following the first signs of union organizing. A delayed reaction is almost always damaging and often fatal to company efforts to remain union-free. But before the company can react to the attempted unionization of its employees, it must be aware of the attempt to organize. It is a tragic but all-too-common fact of labor relations that many employers are totally unaware of organizing until the union declares itself either in the form of a demand for recognition or a petition for an election filed with the NLRB. Should that happen, the company will have already lost the first battle in its fight to retain its freedom.

The key is to be aware of the early warning signs of union activity and how they can be recognized. The signs in the following list may or may not appear at the company; but if you recognize any of the activities in the list, you should report them immediately to the designated member of management who handles union-related concerns. You may have discovered important evidence of an attempted organization of employees if you notice

1. A change in the nature of employee complaints and an increase in their frequency

2. Employees forming into groups that include individuals who do not normally associate with each other

3. A large number of policy inquiries, particularly on pay, benefits, and discipline

4. Employees in work areas they do not normally visit

5. Avoidance of supervision—employees clamming up

6. Argumentative questions being asked in meetings

7. Exit interview information indicating that people are attempting to escape an unpleasant environment

8. News items placed on bulletin boards about union settlements in local companies or other industries

9. Cartoons or graffiti that direct humorous hostility toward the organization, management, or supervision

10. A significant change in the rate of turnover, either upward or downward

11. A number of people applying for jobs who do not have relevant experience and appear to be willing to work in a job with lower status and pay than a job for which their record qualifies them

12. An unusual interest on the part of vendors and subcontractors in communicating with employees

13. Nonunion people beginning to meet and talk with known union members

14. Complaints beginning to be made by a delegation, rather than by single employees

15. Strangers appearing and lingering on the company premises or in work areas

16. Employees or strangers showing unusual curiosity about company affairs and policies

17. Employees adopting a new, technical vocabulary that includes such phrases as "protected activity," "unfair labor practices," and "demands for recognition"

18. Union authorization cards, handbills, or leaflets appearing on the premises or in parking areas

19. Union representatives visiting or sending

mail to employees at their homes

20. Any factor that is out of the ordinary and seems to be separating management from the workforce

Conditions that cause union organizing include

1. Lack of ability or care in screening applicants

2. Failure to remove misfits, preferably during introductory period

3. Expecting overqualified or higher paid employees to do lower qualified or lower paid work

4. Lack of continuing courtesy, respect, and fair consideration from managers, supervisors, and others

5. Lack of effort to motivate employees

6. Failure to listen to and understand employees before making decisions or responses

7. Failure to persuade employees that wage and benefit terms are fair and competitive

8. Lack of attention to employee facilities— lavatories, eating areas, parking, etc.

9. Failure to give employees a sense of security and a feeling that they have a job the others want

10. Handing out nasty little surprises in work schedules, time off allowances, work assignments, pay cuts, or other changes

11. Failure to truthfully communicate what employees need to know about the company and their jobs

12. Making or implying promises that are not kept

13. Making vague promises that are subject to misinterpretation by employees

14. Failure to persuade employees that criticism or discipline is for their benefit, not solely for company benefit

15. Having a "small" person for a boss—a supervisor who sets a bad example, is snobbish, and/or has a little clique or favorites

16. Failure to respond to employee questions, problems, and complaints

17. Generally, absence of an effective em-

ployee communication program

18. Absence of effective problem-solving procedures

19. Absence of an effective mechanism for monitoring employee complaints

20. Absence of an employee evaluation procedure

21. Presence of supervisory favoritism— "different strokes for different folks"

22. Absence of clear and consistent employee policies and procedures

23. Absence of fair, equal, and nondiscriminatory disciplinary procedures

The following steps are recommended for handling a demand for recognition:

1. If you are contacted in person by anyone purporting to represent your employees, follow the guidelines below:

a. If the person is already in your presence or knows of your presence, do not refuse to talk with him or her. Get the person's business card.

b. Get a witness, preferably another member of management or your secretary.

c. If the union representative claims that the union represents a majority of the employees, state that you do not believe it.

d. Do not look at any list of employees.

e. Do not look at any cards with names on them.

f. Do not accept, touch, or examine in any way cards presented to you. If the cards are left on your desk, request that the union representative take the cards with him or her. If the representative refuses, have an employee place the cards in an envelope without looking at them, seal the envelope, and mail the cards back to the union.

g. Do not discuss with the union representative any alleged complaints regarding employee grievances or other employee matters. State clearly: "I have no authority with respect to union matters. I will refer this to my superiors, who will be in touch with you immediately."

h. Escort the union representative off the

premises.

i. Contact the designated management representative responsible for union-related matters and report what occurred.

j. Record what transpired, in writing, and have your witnesses do the same.

2. If you are contacted by mail, use the following guidelines:

a. Do not accept from a union any bulky, certified mail that might contain authorization cards.

b. If, however, cards are received by mail, do not touch or examine them.

c. Have your secretary place the envelope containing the cards in another envelope, without looking at the cards, and mail them back to the union.

3. If you are contacted by mail with a letter requesting recognition from a union, forward it immediately to the designated management representative.

4. Immediately report any demands for recognition to the designated management representative. If he or she is personally unavailable, contact a previously designated alternate.

Part 3

8

The Labor Relations Environment

Introduction

Between the passage of the Title II RLA amendment in 1936 and the passage of the Airline Deregulation Act of 1978, the airline industry and the air transport unions developed a workable set of procedures for handling disputes. During this time period, agreements between the carriers and the unions, although at times acquired only after protracted strikes, were negotiated on generally very favorable terms for the unions in the areas of wages, benefits, and work conditions, but without undue financial impact on the carrier. This latter point seems paradoxical but in fact was the result of a public policy decision to heavily regulate the air transport sector and the unique nature of that regulation.

The Civil Aeronautics Board

Air transport regulation had its formal beginnings with the passage of the Civil Aeronautics Act of 1938. This act created the Civil Aeronautics Authority, the Administrator of Aeronautics, and the Air Safety Board. In 1940, the Civil Aeronautics Authority and the Air Safety Board were combined into the Civil Aeronautics Board (CAB). The CAB was granted broad economic regulatory power, and until the board began moving toward a deregulated posture in 1976, it controlled virtually every aspect of airline economic operation.

Certificates of Public Convenience

In 1938, when industry regulation began, the Civil Aeronautics Authority granted only sixteen Certificates of Public Convenience and Necessity, to airlines that the authority felt were financially strong enough to survive. Under the 1938 act, a carrier was required to have such a certificate before it could operate scheduled air service or carry U.S. Mail. A regulated and controlled airline environment was put in place.

The authority to issue and rescind operating certificates and the other economic policy tools available to the CAB allowed the organization to (1) control the number of carriers permitted to operate in the U.S.; (2) control the entrance or exit from a particular city pair market—no carrier could enter or stop serving a market without CAB approval; (3) control fares by approving, modifying, or rejecting the fare requests of individual carriers or by directly setting the exact fare or a narrow range of permissible fares in each city pair market; and (4) regulate the rate of return and profit an airline could earn. In addition, only the CAB could award new routes, and it had absolute authority over mergers and acquisitions. In general, the CAB took a restrictive view of mergers, and often, instead of allowing a financially distressed carrier to merge, it would grant monopoly route awards to that airline in an attempt to strengthen the carrier and maintain stability in the industry.[1] According to Nawal K. Taneja, this regulation had a profound impact on labor-management relations in the industry, specifically in the areas of certification rejection, mergers, fare provisions, and the existence of the Mutual Aid Pact, which was a CAB-authorized program.[2]

Certification Rejection. The CAB's powers were enhanced substantively by the passage of the 1958 Federal Aviation Act, which contained the provision that a carrier holding a Certificate of Public Convenience and Necessity had to be in full compliance with the RLA. This provision had great impact on the labor relations process and placed the CAB in the position of deciding whether a carrier was acting in good faith in terms of the RLA. A carrier's failure to bargain in good faith with its unions could allow the CAB to rescind the carrier's operating certificate. For example, in 1962, the Air Line Pilots Association presented arguments to the CAB that Southern Airlines had failed to engage in good-faith negotiations. In that case, the board demanded that Southern begin negotiating in good faith with the Air Line Pilots Association or face the consequences of losing its operating certificate.

This broad discretionary power remained a part of the CAB until it ceased operations, or sunset, in 1984. It placed the collective bargaining efforts of the carriers under the scrutiny of not only the National Mediation Board and the union itself but also a third party, the CAB. The CAB could independently consider whether the carrier's negotiating styles were in good faith and thus enforce statutory remedies that were not available to the National Mediation Board through the RLA.

Mergers

The CAB controlled not only whether carriers could merge but also the terms and provisions of any mergers and/or route transfers. Consequently, the board could, and often did, provide job protection for the employees and the unions affected by any mergers. These CAB-managed mergers and transfers provided an umbrella of protection for craft positions, wage and benefit levels, and seniority rights during mergers. For example, in the 1961 merger of United Air Lines and Capital Airlines, provisions for integration

of seniority lists, based on length of service, were standardized.[3] Thus, an employee of an acquired airline could bump employees of the surviving airline if they had more seniority in a particular craft or class determination.

Fare Provisions

The CAB was given the dual role of both regulating and promoting the air transportation industry. Therefore, if the industry faced cost increases because of high wage settlement agreements with the unions, these cost increases would usually be passed on to the consumers through a tariff adjustment application—submitted to the CAB by the carrier—for a series of fare increases that would cover the increases in labor costs. The existence of this financial security blanket tended to increase the bargaining power of the unions.[4]

The Mutual Aid Pact

The Airline Mutual Aid Pact, approved and supported by the CAB, was designed to increase the bargaining power of airline management by increasing the ability of a carrier to withstand a strike. Prior to the existence of the pact, consensus among airline management was that labor had far greater bargaining power than management. This opinion was based partially on the nature of the industry and partially on the language of the RLA. To shift the balance in favor of management, the airlines began as early as 1947 to look for ways to cooperate among themselves. By 1958, Capital Airlines, faced with a strike by the International Association of Machinists, convinced six airlines to agree to the initial Mutual Aid Pact, which was a form of strike insurance.

The provisions of the Mutual Aid Pact included recovery by the struck carrier of "windfall revenues" to other carriers if the strike resulted from

1. Union demands in excess of those recommended by the emergency board

2. A strike called prior to the exhaustion of prestrike procedures under the RLA

3. An otherwise unlawful strike

Windfall revenue is the increase in traffic and revenues received by the unaffected carriers. The Mutual Aid Pact was designed to return to the struck carrier a portion of the increased revenue received by the pact carriers attributable to the strike less the added expense of carrying the additional traffic. The carrier struck, in return, was to make every reasonable effort to provide the public with information concerning air service offered by the other carriers in the pact.[5]

The Transition to Deregulation

In 1976, the CAB, under the chairmanship of John Robson, began to move away from the restrictive policy posture of the previous thirty-eight years. Under Robson, the board reversed its policy of not allowing discount fares and permitted Texas International to begin its "Peanuts" fare and American Airlines to begin its "Super-Saver" fare. These discount fares were quickly followed by similar discount fares offered by other airlines. Robson also became the first CAB chairman to advocate airline deregulation.

When Alfred E. Kahn became CAB chairman on June 10, 1977, the board accelerated its move toward less economic regulation. The CAB gave airlines even wider latitude to experiment with discount fares. In addition, the CAB expressly stated and stressed fare reductions as an important factor in the selection of applicants for new route authorities—a major shift from the CAB's previous policies.

Under Kahn, the CAB also no longer considered a carrier's financial need in making route awards. The board no longer forced cross-subsidization by awarding long-haul routes to subsidized short-haul carriers. The CAB shifted the burden of proof in route proceedings from the applicant to those opposing the new route authorities. Diversion of traffic and revenue from an incumbent carrier was no longer a sufficient reason for denying new route authority in markets with little or no competition. Kahn suggested that the CAB eventually allow all applicants found "fit, willing, and able" to compete on any routes they wished to serve.[6]

Deregulation

A general move away from excessive government regulation of industry began to emerge in the early 1970s. Proponents of industry deregulation cited the banking industry, the telecommunications industry, and the transportation industry—more specifically, the trucking and the airline sectors—as industries in which government regulation actually worked to the disservice of the American public.[7] Conceptually, the proponents of deregulation cited consumer welfare and freedom of choice as the driving factors, believing that free and competitive markets would provide more and better products, promote greater efficiency, and lower prices for comparable competitive services. In some instances, this belief was correct, as the deregulation of the telephone industry has proved. Certainly the antithetical result was the banking industry, where unbridled, undisciplined, and illegal activities resulted in a bailout that cost the taxpayers $500 billion dollars. Whether these expanded services and products have improved the lot of the average citizen is a point of conjecture and continuing argument.

Whatever the rationale or intent behind the push for deregulation, on October 24, 1978, Congress enacted the Airline Deregulation Act, which ended the economic regulation of the airline industry. If the case for deregulation stressed concerns for the welfare and choices of the public, it had little or no concern with the affected labor markets or collective bargaining agreements in the industry. In the intellectual world, the case was established for deregulation of product markets—for example, fares, rates, entry, and quality of service—but there was no consideration of its consequences or impact, in the short run or over a longer term, on labor markets, the collective bargaining process, wage and benefit levels, unemployment, and so on. This lack of foresight had significant impact in the years to come.[8] A highly sophisticated system had developed under regulation. The failure to manage the transition from regulation to deregulation led to a fragmented labor relations system.

Deregulation and the plethora of nonunion new entrants to the industry were not the only factors that destabilized the labor relations process. It was further damaged by the strike of the Professional Air Traffic Controllers (PATCO); the Chapter 7 bankruptcy of Braniff Airways; the Chapter 11 bankruptcy of Continental Air Lines; and the formation of nonunion airlines by former unionized carriers, through the use of holding companies. Carriers, as a result of this increased competition, began fighting for their economic survival by implementing draconian cost-cutting measures.

Deregulation has now passed its sixteenth anniversary, and numerous articles have been written, both pro and con, about its impact and effectiveness. Initially, most carriers were against passage of the act, but several perceived it as a competitive godsend. In many cases, those who fought the change lost the ultimate battle because of an inherent inability to manage costs effectively in the new environment, partly because of the long-standing CAB security blanket of guaranteed profits. Some of the existing management teams were unable to play hardball. They had been brought up playing only softball.

In 1980, New York market analyst Robert J. Joedicke wrote one of the most insightful and accurate assessments of the impact of deregulation, an analysis titled "The Goose That Laid Golden Eggs."[9] Although the analysis was written for the benefit of investors interested and concerned about the future financial outlook of the air transport sector, Mr. Joedicke had no way of knowing the profound impact deregulation would have.

His observations were based only on the first two years of the deregulated environment. Mr. Joedicke did not know how accurate his predictions would turn out to be.

Excerpts of Mr. Joedicke's analysis follow. This analysis provides the student not only with an appreciation of Mr. Joedicke's views but also with an understanding of the historical developments that impact the air transport industry. Aside from providing a snapshot overview of the industry in 1980, it examines the industry's responses to deregulation as the airlines moved from the closed environment of stringent economic regulation to a laissez-faire, open-market environment. This article also serves as a backdrop for examining the status of the industry as it exists in the mid 1990s.

THE GOOSE THAT LAID GOLDEN EGGS

Once upon a time, so the story goes, a goose that laid golden eggs was killed by its owner who hoped to get all the gold at once. The moral of this parable might aptly be applied to the airline industry today. The major losers could be management and employees of the large carriers. In fact, they may find their goose is cooked, if a new industry danger is not faced squarely. Meanwhile, many shareholders in recent times have been receiving only goose eggs as far as dividends are concerned.

Nor is the gold flowing to produce necessary profits, since cash flow has already dried up to a mere trickle. This financial weakness is sharply restricting funds available for most carriers to modernize their capital plant for greater efficiency.

The problem is productivity and the only long-term solution is greater effort by the work force and better utilization of existing capital plant. More efficient new generation jets of medium size will become available within a couple of years, but these planes will have a high capital cost per seat as a result of inflation, as well as inclusion of advanced technology equipment. As a result, increasing debt commitments must also be served.

THE AIRLINE INDUSTRY TODAY

The transportation area has always provided a labor of love for some, ever since lads ran away to sea on sailing ships. Then the railroads had their day when boomers roamed the High Iron throughout America. More recently, transportation buffs were attracted to the airlines following the derring-do of early aviators in the era of the leather cap, goggles and white silk scarfs.

Much of the romanticism in conquering the skies is long gone and the airline field is now big business, generating $35 billion of annual revenue for U.S. carriers. The entire industry currently employs close to 350,000 people, with a wage bill that exceeds $10 billion per year, while tens of thousands more work for ancillary and support operations. The U.S. Travel Data Center estimates that the overall travel field provides employment for over five million people, or 9% of all jobs in the United States.

Service industries are very labor intensive. Employee costs in the airline industry account for over 35% of cash operating expenses, and the average annual compensation per employee reached $33,580 by the end of September 1980. A majority of the work force has been unionized for some time; several craft unions, such as the 33,000 member Air Line Pilots Association (ALPA), trace their founding back to the early 1930s.

As a result, the organized airline labor field is also big business, with total union membership near the quarter million mark. Union officers administer noteworthy assets and executive type jets are available to whisk them to meetings around the country.

Much has already been written about changes following the Airline Deregulation Act of 1978 as it has affected route networks and fare structures, since these trends actually began to emerge before passage of the Act. Little has been said about the way in which the new climate is markedly altering the airline labor picture. The intent of deregulation was to foster competition in the airline industry, with the result that the number of carriers on many important routes has increased over the past two years and pricing flexibility is evident on all fronts.

However, few industry observers appreciate the fact that this legislation has also produced a competitive labor situation as a result of the emergence of new nonunion airlines. In this regard, CAB Chairman Kahn stated in a recent speech in New York that "There is a revolution at hand, and that revolution has been made possible by deregulation." He also noted that "The combined effect of government intervention, in all its forms, permitted labor costs to increase at a rate which, while within the productivity gains made possible by technological advances, was far in excess of the market for comparable skills."

We expect the industry may well face a peck of trouble in this area over the next several years until a new modus vivendi is achieved in labor relations, one based on management and union leadership working together.

THE LATEST INDUSTRY CHALLENGE

Adjustment to the changed circumstances under deregulation is proving particularly difficult for all parties since the airline industry is already encrusted with some diehard traditions. In addition, the problem of transition is being exacerbated by rampant cost inflation, paced by price escalation of fuel which now accounts for 32% of industry cash operating expenses. This dilemma is necessitating an acceleration in retirement of fuel-inefficient jets at a time when cash flow is inadequate to meet the massive capital expenditures required for their replacement.

Sagging traffic demand, accentuated by erosion of discretionary income for the populace, is also another important factor at the moment. Passenger volume in 1980 was down around 5% from the prior year. Records back to 1927 indicate only two years of decline (1948 and 1975), but these annual downturns were both less than one half of one percent. No one expects a sharp upturn of volume in the near future.

This story may not be a tale wherein "everyone lives happily ever after," since we foresee a period of major labor unrest for the airlines until the realities of the new order are recognized by unions and management alike. Some union leaders have belatedly been petitioning the Federal government to take a critical look at the effects of deregulation, but it is clearly too late to "put Humpty Dumpty back on the wall."

. . . Deregulation can be viewed as a two-edged sword capable of drawing blood. We look for some blood letting affecting most parties involved, but hope that a blood bath will not occur. Nevertheless, some airlines may not survive under the current laissez-faire attitude fostered by Washington, while others are likely to prosper by achieving new peak earnings and we are already seeing indications of this dichotomy. Whichever the case, the astute investor should be interested in the details of the new labor situation since it will become an increasingly important consideration in shaping investment selections within the airline group.

LABOR CLIMATE BEFORE DEREGULATION: THE HISTORY OF UNION ACTIVITY

Since 1936 interstate airlines have come under the jurisdiction of the Railway Labor Act, with its provisions for mediation and arbitration through the National Mediation Board, as well as for "cooling-off" periods before legal work stoppages can take place. Thus, it has not been unusual that union members continue to work for months beyond an amendable contract date until a new accord is achieved. Union agreements under the Railway Labor Act only become amendable, but do not expire as in the case of most other industries, unless a strike occurs.

Organization of the work force within the airline field has traditionally been based on separate representations for most of the major crafts, as opposed to companywide memberships such as exist in the automobile and steel industries. As a result, many of the large trunks have a dozen or more labor contracts in force, with varying renewal dates. The degree of employee membership varies among the established scheduled carriers, but active union organization over the years in this labor intensive

field has produced coverage ranging from around 60% of the headcount to over 90% unionization today.

There are 21 separate unions certified within the airline industry, although several (e.g., Air Line Pilots Association; International Association of Machinists; and the Transport Workers Union) hold broad certification embracing numerous carriers. The 10 trunks alone have a total of 173 individual contracts in effect today, but some are negotiated on a group basis by a single union. This fragmentation of representation has sharply increased the potential for strikes over the years. The average 2–3 year contract period produces incessant labor negotiation for most airlines.

Historically, Delta was the only major exception to this widespread unionization of the airline industry prior to deregulation. The company continues to have very limited union membership, which is restricted to the pilot cadre and a small group of dispatchers. Even its organized flight officers have a unique rapport with the company. This relationship was evident in early 1974 when jet fuel allocation required a major cutback in operations. No layoffs were made but many pilots temporarily took on other chores, including the fueling of aircraft and handling of baggage.

This lack of union representation at Delta may partially reflect a traditional disinclination toward organized labor in the South, particularly since the company has always provided wage levels comparable to or better than those of its peers. However, the main reason was paternalistic guidance in the formative years by the company's founder and unique long-time leader, who molded an esprit de corps among the staff to the point that employees view themselves more as a family working together.

The end result is that Delta has not been faced with the same degree of restrictive and costly contract conditions resulting from work rules and duty assignments embodied in most union agreements. In return, its employees enjoy job security without layoffs and benefit from a policy of promotion from within the ranks. It is of interest to note that a recently retired chief executive officer of Delta was one of the original organizers of its pilots union in the 1930's.

It was no accident that Delta led the industry in profits during 1980, while many other trunk airlines were generating record losses. An entente cordiale with labor is a key factor in its continuing financial success.

There was a rather unique arrangement within the airline industry for 20 years prior to deregulation. The Mutual Aid Pact among a majority of the large scheduled airlines was first approved by the CAB in 1958 to permit financial aid to a struck airline under a formula basis intended to defray the fixed expenses and compensate for diverted traffic during a work stoppage. Over half a billion dollars in mutual aid was paid under this agreement until its demise under provisions of the Airline Deregulation Act of 1978.

THE SUCCESS OF LABOR BARGAINING

Airline labor negotiations involve three distinct considerations. The most visible aspect is basic wage rates, although fringe benefits paid by the employer have increased even more sharply in recent years and are very expensive, particularly when applied retroactively on a length of service basis. The third major area is work rules, but the cost importance of this feature is not widely appreciated. Restrictive work rules do not increase the average compensation per employee but they do inflate the number of employees required to run an operation by decreasing the average productivity per employee—a real concern of American industry today.

In any case, there is no doubt as to the success of airline union negotiators in gaining above average increases for their members, at least up to the time of deregulation. The average annual percentage increase in compensation per employee was 9.9% for the airline industry in the 1969–79 period, as compared with an 8.1% average for all U.S. industry. This differential added $1.5 billion to total airline labor costs in 1979 alone.

Unfortunately, one measure of a successful labor leader is the gains he can achieve for the rank and file, irrespective of whether the company can make sufficient profit to cover the increases. It is more difficult for an airline to accept a strike than for most other industries because of an inability to maintain market presence by selling its products from inventory during a shutdown. . . .

. . . suffice to say at this point that the pervasive deregulation legislation is not protecting those airlines with inordinately high unit labor costs. The CAB does not require uniform fares pegged at levels high enough to compensate carriers with an above average cost structure.

In other words, the "closed shop" situation that existed prior to deregulation has evaporated and the necessary gains in employee productivity now required by unionized carriers cannot be achieved solely by acquisition of more efficient aircraft, if the established carriers are to compete successfully with the newer unorganized entrants. . . .

In spite of continuing wage escalation, it is obvious that fringe benefits have become an increasing proportion of total employee compensation, the expense of which is inflating unit operating costs of the established carriers. In addition, there are sizable liabilities for unfunded but vested past service costs, which totaled around $1.5 billion for the trunk group of airlines at the end of 1979. . . .

The end result of these developments has been a steady gain in the average employee compensation within the airline industry that has outpaced the rise in the Consumer Price Index. It can also be noted that average passenger yields have not increased as rapidly to produce the commensurate gains in revenue required to support these escalating labor costs. . . .

The facts suggest it is high time for a new attitude by all parties to replace the traditional stance of adversaries on opposite sides of the bargaining table with a spirit of cooperation for mutual benefit. Such action has occurred in the past only when individual airlines have been in financial distress to such a degree that union membership has felt threatened as to its very livelihood.

Such brinkmanship indicates a lack of management ability to convey the seriousness of the problem and a lack of willingness on the part of union leaders to face the inevitable, before excessive financial deterioration occurs. Nevertheless, a company cannot solve the problem alone. Management does not negotiate from strength as in the past so it must rely more on creating an appreciation of the critical situation.

Labor officials must exhibit leadership and integrity, even though internal union politics can make an unpopular stand difficult to gain acceptance. Changing union representation to naive candidates who promise unrealistic goals to the rank and file will not change the outcome in the long run since it will be impossible "to get blood out of a stone" under the existing climate. . . .

Thus it should be patently clear that the fallout effect of airline deregulation is now sifting down on labor to becloud its favorable climate of the past that permitted above average gains in total benefits without offsetting increases in productivity.

It is to be hoped that the proverb "None so blind as those who do not want to see" will not prevail in this murky situation.

Make no mistake, the proliferation of non-union airlines is already producing an increasing threat to the financial viability of some mature trunks and further deterioration will take place if steps are not taken promptly to improve profitability. Neither wishing nor blustering will change the inexorable trends, even though some may not be willing to accept the verity of the harsh facts facing the airline industry under deregulation. . . .

Trade unionists may believe that the solution is to organize the labor forces of all new entrants and some success in this is to be expected. However, many of the employees recognize that their financial future depends on gaining market share from the higher-cost incumbents. Managements of the new airlines also understand this threat and are taking great care to relate to their employees in order to retain higher productivity. There are already cases where national certification of union groups within the new carriers has been withdrawn at the request of the local membership.

In any case, it is to be expected under deregulation that new entrants will keep popping up wherever there is an opportunity for a low-cost operation to make profits. Some union leaders may believe that strikes will be necessary to solve the problem, but such action is more likely to hasten the demise of larger airlines with high unit costs if a work stoppage is protracted.

Finally, in our underlying lighter vein of bird lore covering goose and phoenix, we would caution against a stance similar to the ostrich approach of burying its head in the sand when danger is at hand.

Mr. Joedicke's analysis in 1980 was prophetic. His call for new methodologies and a heightened awareness on the part of both management and unions to the necessary changes that deregulation demanded has not been universally answered. Throughout the 1980s, airline executives and labor leaders alike maintained an adversarial labor-management relationship. The parties remained deadlocked, fighting among themselves instead of facing the enemy of change together.

During the sixteen years since deregulation, numerous changes have occurred in fundamental business philosophy. Leveraged buyouts, restructuring and downsizing, and business failures and mergers have modified the relationship between labor and management at the bargaining table. The only constant in this scenario has been the unchanged continuation of the RLA of 1926.

When Congress enacted deregulation, it believed that the competitive capabilities of the industry and the ability to adjust to the new environment would have been tested at the end of ten years.[10] Now, in deregulation's seventeenth year, the modifications are still creating unrest and, in some cases, catharsis in the labor community. In 1989, Eastern Airlines was in the throes of a massive labor dispute driven by these fundamental changes. The carrier experienced a major strike and subsequently filed a Chapter 11 bankruptcy to reorganize operations, presumably so that it might emerge as a nonunion carrier. The carrier was unable to achieve this goal and ceased operations in 1991.

In January of 1985, John T. Dunlop, Lamont University Professor at Harvard University, wrote: "The one word that best characterizes transportation labor relation is fragmented, and an extreme form pervades the airlines. There the separate system groups frustrate stronger national organizations of labor in many crafts. The crafts are isolated and often engage in intense rivalry to capture or to extinction; the carriers are divided along many lines, and government labor policy in the air transportation sector can only be described in recent years as nihilistic and devoid of constructive leadership."[11] Three years prior to this, in a speech delivered at an airline industry conference, the then president of Eastern Airlines, Mr. Frank Borman, stated, "in the final analysis, the Deregulation Act, if nothing else, was the greatest anti-labor act ever passed by an American Congress."[12] Taken together, these statements reflect the industry today and the attitude taken by major carriers in their pursuit of, in some cases, a nonunion operating environment or, at least, an environment devoid of the crippling effect of huge labor costs.

The metamorphosis of the last sixteen years is complex and not easily explained, nor can the final outcome be predicted, because airlines, government, and the unions still grapple with the hows and whys of their deregulated relationships. Management, with its newfound freedoms, has become more entrepreneurial. The government, in its judicial capacity, has reversed many long-standing traditions. The National Mediation Board has seemingly taken a wait-and-see attitude. Many unions are still negotiating in an unenlightened manner, trying to desperately hold on to the ways of the past, while others seek to control their destinies through employee/union ownership of the very airlines with which they negotiate. This atmosphere would seem to indicate that continued labor chaos will be the norm for the foreseeable future.

The Labor Relations Environment: 1978 to the Present

On October 8, 1975, President Gerald Ford proposed legislation that would reduce the authority of the CAB to regulate the airlines. The proposed legislation was based on the premise that the airline industry had outgrown the need for protective regulation by the government. In a message to Congress, President Ford adamantly stated: "the rigidly controlled regulatory structure now serves to stifle competition, increase costs to travelers, makes the industry less efficient than it could be and denies large segments of the American public access to lower cost air transportation."[13] To accommodate the American public, President Ford suggested that the CAB's control over the availability and pricing of airline services be relaxed.

The Airline Deregulation Act of 1978 prescribed the process by which the gradual removal of economic control over the industry was to occur. The 1978 act did not mandate the immediate and total deregulation of the industry that then president Jimmy Carter had suggested. The act was directed toward redesigning the existing regulatory structure to ease the transition to eventual removal of regulatory controls. All the entry and pricing barriers were not eliminated until 1983, and the CAB did not cease operations, or sunset, until December 1984.

Prior to passage of the act, certain compromises were made to satisfy concerns over the consequences of deregulation. There were major concerns that deregulation would have adverse effects on aviation safety. The act's declaration of policy contained a clause emphasizing the preeminence of safety. In addition, many in Congress believed that the abrupt elimination of regulations was too drastic a measure, so the act provided for a slow transition period—for example, by the sunset provision. Small communities feared losing air service. The act guaranteed air service for ten years to all communities served at the time of passage. Lastly, Congress was aware that deregulation could have negative impacts on airline employees who "entered the industry and shaped their careers in reliance on a regulatory system which gave them a measure of job security."[14] Therefore, the legislation contained labor protection provisions to ensure safeguards for employees.

In March 1979, the Department of Labor initiated a program designed to accomplish this policy objective. It provided a ceiling of $1,800 a month for a "protected employee" who lost his or her position due to the effects of deregulation. The Department of Labor defined one group of protected employees as those with four years continuous service who lost their jobs for reasons other than just cause. Benefits would include monthly allotment checks, relocation funds, and first right of hire at another airline. A second group of protected employees included those who worked for an airline that had lost at least 7.5 percent of its workforce or that had filed bankruptcy. To initiate benefits for the latter, the CAB would be required to rule that the layoffs or the bankruptcy had been caused by deregulation before benefits could begin. The program for unemployed airline employees included referrals to state agencies, and the Department of Labor was the focal point for information, compiling lists of those affected for regular release to state agencies.

Immediately prior to the intended implementation date, the program came under fire. Captain John O'Donnell, then president of ALPA, immediately took issue with the $1,800 ceiling for an ex-airline employee. An ALPA spokesman stated, "that amount was simply not enough for a pilot."[15] Moreover, Congress never appropriated money to fund the program, and as a result, the financial assistance was never forthcoming. Finally, carriers were less than enthusiastic about being forced to hire employees of other airlines,

and this portion of the plan met with only moderate success. All these concerns had an impact on the airlines. But the question of job security became the most important and vigorously negotiated item by the employees and their union representatives.

Prior to deregulation, the CAB was responsible for setting fare levels based on actual industry costs. This system enabled the existing airlines to place the expense of each carrier's new labor agreement into the overall rate structure, which allowed the carriers to recover the increased costs. These fares were used by all domestic airlines, and a certain level of consistency and understanding was instilled in the minds of those responsible for running the airline industry. With strict levels of conformity, there was little incentive for a company to resist excessive union demands, which, if not acceded to, could result in a potentially expensive strike for the airline. Because of this management mindset, airlines generally made the allowances requested by the labor organizations and passed the costs through the adjusted general fare level set by the CAB.[16]

With the advent of deregulation, there was no longer a regulated route franchise to protect high-yield domestic routes from free entry by any carrier. Carriers added new routes and city pairs rapidly, because restrictions on entry were lifted and because the CAB had implemented and expedited procedures that significantly opened the air transport route structure. Deregulation also meant the demise of the Mutual Aid Pact. Airline management found themselves with no possible way to compensate for strike losses. The fundamental problem faced by the airlines was the inability, directly or indirectly, to defer the high costs of the labor contract structure per unit, let alone any increases demanded by the unions. With the demise of the Mutual Aid Pact, there was also no way to defer the cost of a strike.

One year after the act was passed, and while the CAB still maintained control over pricing arrangements, the CAB responded to the concerns of the higher unit costs faced by the industry by matching them with increases of the standard industry fare level. But starting in mid-1979, the airline industry suffered serious financial losses that were primarily due to effects beyond the CAB's control or influence. The principal culprit creating sharply reduced airline net profits in late 1979 appears to have been "a managerial lag in reducing capacity offerings and cost structures rather than a regulatory lag. However, this managerial lag is eminently understandable. The industry was confronted with many developments that departed sharply from historical precedents."[17]

Cost Reduction

The new watchword in the industry became cost control. The airlines began to turn inward in search of profits and took an introspective look at their internal organizations and cost structures. To produce a profit, adjustments and reductions needed to be made in operating costs. Fuel and labor costs are the two largest operating expenses for an airline. A variety of internal cost reduction programs were initiated.

Fuel Cost Reduction. The airlines first looked at the need to reduce fuel costs. Short-term responses were to alter flight planning and flight operations procedures. Ozark Air Lines and North Central (later Republic) Airlines, for example, achieved fuel reductions by using only one engine on DC-9s during taxi and initiating complete engine shutdown when departure was delayed by Air Traffic Control. Longer-term responses were to alter route structures and fleet compositions, eliminating the older, less fuel efficient aircraft and acquiring more efficient transports (i.e., the MD-80 or B737-300/400).

The unprecedented fuel price instability extant since 1979 made some of these approaches superfluous and ineffective, and these rapid fuel price fluctuations did not fall on all carriers equally. Competitive advantage and the consequent ability to lower fares were available to those carriers who were able to negotiate more favorable fuel contracts with their suppliers. The big carriers generally got a better price and could use this to competitive advantage.

These fuel cost reduction programs, although generally effective, were insufficient to return the carriers to profitability in and of themselves. Additional cost reductions had to be achieved. Labor costs had to be reduced.

New Entrants

The most significant impact of deregulation on the existing carriers was the gradual removal of the restrictions placed on entry into the marketplace. Smaller carriers began to surface to provide scheduled service on selected routes in direct competition with established operators. Most of these new airlines started their services with smaller, two-engine aircraft. These new carriers for the most part operated on short- to medium-length routes that were in high-traffic areas. This enabled these airlines to generate profitable levels of traffic without having to compete in the long-haul markets with high capital cost. Since these new entrant airlines were almost exclusively nonunion, employee compensation levels were significantly lower for them than for the existing unionized carriers. These lower compensation levels equated directly to lower operating costs and allowed the new entrants to apply tremendous pressure on the larger, established carriers to adjust their fares downward.

Because of the nonunion nature of these new entrants, nontraditional job descriptions were developed, which meant greater efficiency in the use of personnel. Pilots were required to assist in the boarding of passengers and to spend non-flying hours in the airline sales or reservation offices. Ticket and gate personnel were required to assist in loading and off-loading passenger luggage. Flight attendants might assist in making seat assignments and in boarding procedures in the gate areas.

The new entrants did not generally offer the same level of service as did the existing carriers, so there was no need for them to invest in a full complement of ground services required by the larger carriers. These services, such as meal preparation, aircraft cleaning, fueling, and aircraft maintenance, were contracted to fixed-base operators, which reduced fixed costs drastically when compared to the costs of the existing carriers. Another important cost advantage was that without union contracts, the new entrants were at liberty to hire part-time or temporary workers to accomplish their goals. The existing union carriers were not afforded this luxury.

The new entrants were able to choose desired routes, dictate wages, and utilize contracted airline services to their profitable advantage. The smaller aircraft utilized by the new entrants required smaller crews and were much more efficient. The operating economies that the new entrants achieved by the use of smaller, more efficient aircraft was put into perspective by Marvin Cohen, the chairman of the CAB in 1980, who stated:

> Incumbents must either concede many of these point to point markets to the new entrants or find a way to remain competitive. The magnitude of the problem is illustrated by the significant disparity in flight crew costs for the aircraft best suited to these markets as operated by various carriers. The average Boeing 737 labor cost for a trunk carrier in 1979 was about $418 per block hour. For the local service carriers, the cost was about $260. For Southwest, one of the oldest new entrants, flight crew costs were about $163 per block hour in the year ending June 1980, approximately 65 percent below the trunk carrier costs. Southwest has generally lower costs for every phase of its operation. If the incumbents want to remain competitive in these markets they must find ways to reduce costs. It is difficult to predict what will happen in these short-haul markets, but the pressure is now on the incumbents.[18]

This situation placed the trunk carriers in a precarious position. The necessity for lower fares was present, but the new entrants were able to establish fares at lower rates than the trunk carriers and still generate a profit. With their higher operating costs per unit, the larger airlines focused attention on preserving their market share of long-haul routes to fund lower rates on the routes where they competed with the new entrants. This approach did not create a profit, but it did make it more difficult for the new carriers.

Mergers

In one area, however, the trunk carriers held tremendous advantage over the new entrants: they had very deep pockets. The predominant approach ultimately taken by the trunk carriers in dealing with the new entrant problem was given by the philosophy "If you can't beat 'em, buy 'em out." This approach lead to a plethora of mergers and consolidations that effectively reduced competition in the industry.

Since its creation in 1938, the CAB controlled the airline industry with a velvet hammer, not allowing new airlines to enter and attempting to keep existing airlines viable by granting route authorities monopoly in select markets. In the forty years before the enactment of deregulation, not a single new trunk carrier was established, and none went out of business. The early years of deregulation saw an explosion of new airlines. But by 1988, only a handful of these new entrant carriers were still flying. Most went bankrupt; the balance were bought out by the major carriers. The predominant players in the merger game and the survivors of this dynamic period of activity were the remaining trunk carriers that had been in existence prior to deregulation.

Once the inherent inefficiencies in route structure and fare levels began to be corrected, management turned its attention toward labor costs. But just as the management of many airlines felt initially that they could ignore the presence of airlines like Southwest and Midway, labor reacted to deregulation just as passively, and a business-as-usual approach continued. Labor's inability to respond to the new market reality added to the demise of Braniff and Frontier Airlines and weakened both United Air Lines and Trans World Airlines with inflexible behavior. Labor unrest was evident throughout the airline industry.

Initially, both labor and management demonstrated some indifference toward the new concepts of a deregulated environment. This attitude changed very quickly. In 1980, the pilots of Pacific Southwest Airlines (PSA), an intrastate carrier covered under the NLRA, struck for an extended period of time. The pilots, adamant in their demands, rejected several offers made by PSA. The PSA Strike ventured into new territory in labor relations, because the contract between the parties had expired under the NLRA. After seven weeks of strike activity, PSA advertised for replacements of flight deck officers. The company was inundated with applications from unemployed, and very well qualified, pilots. Because of PSA's ability to hire trained pilots in large num-

bers, enough striking pilots crossed their own picket lines that the parties agreed on a contract settlement similar to the original offer made by PSA management. A new approach to contract negotiations had been discovered.

Also significantly influential in the overall labor relations environment was the Professional Air Traffic Controllers Strike of 1981. The activities surrounding the handling and eventual outcome of this situation provided management with a new set of bargaining tools. The PATCO Strike will long be remembered as a milestone in American labor history: "The firing of 11,000 air traffic controllers established clearly in the minds of businessmen and union leaders a pro-management stance by government."[19]

Because of the PATCO Strike, scheduling restrictions were imposed by the Federal Aviation Administration on traffic flow, airport usage, and gate usage at select airports. These restrictions lessened the market impact of the new entrants, but the continued competition for market share caused a considerable erosion in airline prof-

Table 8-1

Impact of Deregulation on New Entrant Airlines from 1979 to 1984

Airline	Year Begun	Still in Operation
Midway Airlines	1979	No
New York Air	1980	No
Peoples Express	1981	No
Muse Air	1981	No
Jet America	1981	No
Pacific Express	1982	No
Northeastern International	1982	No
Hawaii Express	1982	No
Best Airlines	1982	No
Sunworld International	1982	Yes
Air One	1983	No
America West	1983	Yes
Regent Air	1983	No
Frontier Horizon	1984	No
Air Atlanta	1984	No
Florida Express	1984	No

Source: Data from Harry P. Wolfe and David A. NewMyer, *Aviation Industry Regulation,* 1st ed. (Carbondale: Southern Illinois University Press, 1985)

Table 8-2

Airline Bankruptcies from 1979 to 1984

Year of Bankruptcy	Airline
1979	Aeroamerica
	American Central
	Mackey International
	New York Airways
1980	Florida Airlines
	Indiana Airways
1981	Apollo Airways
	Golden Gate Airlines
	Mountain West Airlines
1982	Air Pennsylvania
	Air South
	Altair Airlines
	Braniff International
	Conchise Airlines
	North American
	Silver State Airlines
	Swift Aire Lines
	Will's Airlines
1983	Continental Air Lines
	Golden West Airlines
	Inland Empire Airlines
	National Florida Air
	State Airlines
1984	Air Florida
	Air Illinois
	Air North
	Air One
	Airpacific Express
	Air Vermont
	America International
	Atlantic Gulf
	Capitol Air
	Combs Airways
	Connectair Airlines
	Dolphin Airways
	Emerald
	Excellair
	Hammonds Commuter
	New York Helicopter
	Oceanair Line
	Pacific East
	Wien Air Alaska
	Wright Air Lines

Source: Data from Air Transport Association.

itability. New entrant bankruptcies and mergers followed in rapid succession—a fortunate situation for the existing carriers. Table 8-1 lists all new entrant airlines since deregulation, and Table 8-2 lists the airline bankruptcies since deregulation.

Summary

In 1982, Braniff Airways went bankrupt after several last-ditch efforts at reducing costs. It was the first bankruptcy of a major airline, and it sent shock waves throughout the industry. By 1993, it was quite evident that management had the upper hand in negotiations and that operating costs had to be cut for economic survival. Forty-one thousand air transport workers were already unemployed. If the unions remained standing on principal and continued the ways of the past, more job loss would occur. Chapter 10 discusses how some of the unions responded to the need to cut costs. What has emerged is a "new unionism" in the U.S. air transport sector.

9

Annual Activity

Introduction

Deregulation caused profound changes in the labor relations environment. Prior to deregulation, the negotiation table was not a place of mutual problem solving. Instead, the operative management attitude was "How little of what they want will we have to give them, and how soon can we petition the Civil Aeronautics Board (CAB) to increase fares to recover those increases." The unions, fully aware of the cost-recovery option available to management, generally demanded increases in wages and benefits that far outstripped the increases achieved in other industrial sectors. The unions were not concerned about the carriers' underlying financial condition. These bargaining approaches, fostered by the regulated financial protectionism of the CAB, created an industry with above average wage and benefit levels and an adversarial labor-management relationship. These approaches also set the stage for the complex and disturbing changes that were to occur under deregulation.

The idea of mutual problem solving was anathema to both management and unions. Both factions had grown up together believing that problem solving was someone else's responsibility, namely, the CAB's. With the CAB rapidly backing away from full industry regulation, the carriers found themselves in a fight for survival. They would have to develop new ways of operating their businesses. They would also have to find new ways to resolve labor cost and productivity issues both at the table and with the unions in general. Those carriers that made inroads into this new managerial terrain survived; those that

did not either have vanished or are close to extinction.

The unions also grew complacent under CAB regulation. They had become very big and very myopic businesses in and of themselves and were bureaucratic and trenchant in their responses to change. Also, they were unprepared for the onslaught of change brought about through deregulation. They had to either shift focus from patterned demand increases and seek new paths of negotiating or face catastrophic worker displacement potentials. The realization that airline wages in 1978 were far too high (e.g., \$26,000–\$30,000 a year for janitorial service employees, \$14–\$16 per hour for baggage handlers, and average salaries of \$89,000 a year for pilots) would be a bitter pill to swallow for employees and labor unions. On the other side, viewing the unions and their employees as active and necessary participants in the airline decision process was too great a change for many airline managers to accept.

Economically, deregulation could not have arrived at a worse time. Inflation and interest rates were at very high levels, and the country was heading into a severe recession. The industry was also experiencing extreme instability in the price of aviation kerosene, and some carriers' fuel allocations were being cut back. These factors would have been sufficient in and of themselves to cause disruption and change in the labor-management relationship, but an even more impactive event shook the very foundations of organized labor.

The public policy goal of the Deregulation Act

was "to encourage development and attain an air transportation system which relies on competitive market forces to determine the quality, variety and prices of air services."[1] Regulatory changes were intended to promote more competitive pricing, establish greater flexibility to respond to changing market demands, and improve overall efficiency of the industry. Little attention was paid by the framers of the act to the underlying reality that all collective bargaining agreements in the airline industry were based on the old regulatory system. The unions had captured a portion of, and were equally slaves to, the monopoly profits generated by the CAB regulatory process.[2] Consequentially, deregulating the airlines also meant deregulating the air transport collective bargaining process—a reality evidently noticed or ignored by the act's framers.

Whether deregulation has or has not worked is a moot point. It is, in the final analysis, a fait accompli. Alfred Kahn, the former chairman of the CAB and the "architect" of the act, has, however, had second thoughts regarding this grand experiment in economic theory. As early as 1986, Mr. Kahn stated "that deregulation rather than fostering greater competition has produced a group of mega-carriers with feeder networks offering potentially far less competition than had been intended."[3]

Labor relations in the air transport sector did not change overnight with the passage of the Deregulation Act. Instead, an evolution in labor relations took place, fostered not only by the act but also by the exogenous market and political forces both extant and emerging. This chapter examines the major management-labor and market issues that have occurred in the years since the passage of the act and the significant rulings made on these issues by the National Mediation Board (NMB).

1978

According to data from the Department of Transportation, forty-two Section 401 carriers

were grandfathered into the act in October 1978 as preexisting carriers:

Airlift	Flying Tiger	Reeve
Air Micronesia	Frontier	Rich
Air Midwest	Hawaiian	Seaboard
Air New England	Hughes Airwest	Southern
Alaska	Kodiak	Texas International
Aloha	Munz	Transamerica
American	National	Trans World
Aspen	New York Airways	United
Braniff	North Central	USAir
Capitol	Northwest	Wein
Continental	Overseas National	Western
Delta	Ozark	World
Eastern	Pan American	Wright
Evergreen	Piedmont	Zantop

The implementation of the act caused no noticeable change in the behaviors of these existing major carriers or their unions. The most notable aspects of 1978 are that a few upstart airlines filed for entry into the industry and that the Mutual Aid Pact was abolished.

The passage of the act gave the airline industry many options. Managers were free to restructure their networks and gain control over their product lines. These new freedoms required carriers to make fundamental decisions about their future—decisions that some were willing to make quickly. Others took a wait-and-see attitude.

Most airline management concerns and activities in this first year were directed not at learning how to compete in a deregulated market but at how to prevent the new entrants from eroding market share. The existing majors began to develop defensive marketing plans.

The initial analysis of this first year would seem to indicate that union bargaining power had increased. The Mutual Aid Pact was dead, and a carrier no longer had a guarantee that it could survive a strike. New entrants could now also enter a market during a strike and lure passengers away.

1979

In 1979, nineteen new carriers entered the marketplace. The first wave of mergers took place, with North Central and Southern combining to form Republic, and with National being absorbed by Eastern. Two other carriers, Apollo and New York Airways, ceased operation. Table 9-1 lists the new carriers that entered the marketplace and the old carriers that exited. The new market entries triggered a series of fare wars that had disastrous consequences on income and profitability and directly impacted the collective bargaining process. These fare wars eventually forced the airlines to negotiate aggressively for lowered labor costs.

Table 9-1
Section 401 Carrier Certification Activity in 1979

New Carriers Entering

Aeromech
Air Cal
Air Florida
Air Wisconsin
Altair
Apollo
Big Sky
Empire
Golden West
Mackey
Mid South
Midway
Mississippi Valley
Pacific Southwest
Republic
Sky West
Southeast
Southwest
Swift Aire

Carriers Exiting

Merged/Sold	Waivers	Financial
National North Central Southern	Apollo	New York Airways

Source: Data from Department of Transportation.

In 1979, a massive profit decline driven by this fare competition began. In 1978, the trunk carriers generated operating profits of $1.2 billion. By 1981, the trunk carriers had suffered operating losses of $672 million, a swing of $1.9 billion dollars.

Coming off a fifty-eight-day machinist strike in 1979, United Air Lines initiated a half-fare coupon promotion to try to win back some of the customers it had lost to new entrants. Retaliation followed, as other airlines not only matched fares but created a variety of combinations of reduced fares that made proponents of deregulation smile at the windfall the paying passenger was receiving. With new, low-cost, non-union carriers entering the marketplace, competition in the area of lower fares became increasingly disastrous to the unionized carriers. Price wars became commonplace. Price cutting of as much as 75 percent of prederegulation fares became the norm. With wages established by contract, existing carriers were forced to match the prices of the new carriers without the ability to lower costs. These fare wars, promulgated by the new entrants lower cost structures, caused the unionized carriers to seek immediate solutions. The fare wars set the stage for demands of wage and benefit concessions. Several carriers even formally requested their unions to open negotiations in advance of established contract amendment dates.

As the fare wars continued, market analysts were seeing airline losses so catastrophic that they questioned the ability of some airlines to ever recover. In an article for *Forbes Magazine*, Harold Seneker wrote: "So what this game is really about is: Who will have to draw back from the brink first; Who will have to choose first between owning the routes and owning the more fuel efficient planes the airlines must have in the future? It is a trench war whose Verdun is New York–California. If it long continues without some sort of de-facto truce, even winners may be bled white."[4]

Aside from the price wars that developed, incumbent carriers were forced to adopt new managerial strategies. They now had to manage costs and generate revenues to achieve a profitable return, instead of collecting monopolistic revenues guaranteed by the CAB to return an acceptable profit irrespective of costs. During the initial years of deregulation, the airlines were faced with the challenge of new entrants in the marketplace and had to develop new plans for future viability. No one particular approach was followed by all airlines in answering questions of expansion, maintenance of market share, fares, and route structure. Instead, each airline followed its own path, based on its own management capabilities, experiences, and capital structure and on the conservative or liberal policies held by its management and boards of directors.

The depressed economic conditions and fuel crisis of 1979 were beyond direct control of the airlines, but many members of the industry made crippling strategic errors in other areas. The most prominent error was made by Braniff International Airways.[5] Braniff saw deregulation as an opportunity to expand its route structure. It was the first airline to apply for "automatic market entry" of unused routes made available by the sunsetting CAB. Although other airlines (Texas International, Continental, Pan American, and North Central) also followed an expansion philosophy, no one did so with the same vigor as Braniff. This monomaniacal approach, without consideration for costs, market surveys, and equipment, ended in the nation's first casualty of deregulation: Braniff's Chapter 11 bankruptcy two years later.

Another option pursued by many airlines was to utilize the financial mechanism that became the trademark of Texas International. The airlines began to form holding companies. This financial restructuring allowed the carriers to start up a low-cost nonunion airline, owned by the holding company that also owned a union carrier. Texas International started such an airline, New York Air, in 1980.

Very few contracts were scheduled to open for amendment during 1979. As a result, there were few changes in the collective bargaining process. But the stage was set for massive changes in 1980.

1980

In 1980, fourteen new carriers entered the marketplace, two existing carriers merged, and one airline exited the market (see table 9-2). The most controversial new entrant in 1980 was New York Air, a subsidiary of Texas Air Corporation. The impact of the creating of New York Air as a nonunion entity of Texas Air, a highly unionized carrier, was felt almost immediately. Existing carriers embraced the concept, the NMB was perplexed by the novelty, and the airline unions fought to curtail this approach. They viewed it as a threat by management to transfer bargained work, corporate assets, and jobs through manipulation. This complaint existed into the late 1980s at Eastern Airlines. The chairman of Eastern, Frank Lorenzo, transferred routes, equipment, and assets to Eastern's parent company, the same Texas Air Corporation.

Table 9-2

Section 401 Carrier Certification Activity in 1980

New Carriers Entering
Air North
American Eagle
Cascade
Flagship
Golden Gate
Great American
Imperial
International
New Air
New York Air
Rocky Mountain
Southern Air Trans
Sun Land
T-Bird

Carriers Exiting		
Merged/Sold	Waivers	Financial
Hughes Airwest	None	Mackey
Seaboard		

Source: Data from Department of Transportation.

This **double-breasting**, as it was called, was not a new phenomena in the labor arena. The practice of transferring union work to nonunion companies owned by the same corporation has existed and been addressed numerous times by the National Labor Relations Board (NLRB) in other business sectors. But the concept gained wide acceptance in the airline industry as one airline after another took measures to capitalize on the new windfall, seeing the potential to rid themselves of the unions.

Indicative of the popularity of the approach were some of the changes made and holding companies created. Name changes and corporate identities took on new meanings. Alaska Airlines Inc. became Alaska Air Group, Inc.; American Airlines became AMR Corporation; Northwest Orient became NWA, Inc.; Ozark Air Lines, Inc. became Ozark Holdings, Inc.; Pan Am World Airlines became Pan Am Corporation; Peoples Express and Frontier Airlines became Peoples Express, Inc.; Piedmont Airlines became Piedmont Aviation, Inc.; Trans World Airlines became Trans World Corp.; USAir became USAir Group, Inc.; and Continental Air Lines, New York Air, Texas International, and Eastern Air became Texas Air Corporation.

Although some of the former corporations and holding companies existed in form before the creation of New York Air, the methods were put in place to insure the ability of the corporations to assume new arrangements when and if the time came to form a new, nonunion carrier. Ozark Air Lines formed Ozark Holdings without any intention to operate a subsidiary carrier, intending, instead, to use the ploy as negotiating leverage with all their unions—in particular with the Aircraft Mechanic Fraternal Association (AMFA), who represented the mechanics and who had struck the airline on numerous occasions. So intent was the airline to use such strategy that Ozark Holdings was formalized and signed while the parties were in **direct negotiations**, and within one hour of its birth, the issue was presented at the negotiating table by management.

Texas Air's establishment of the nonunion New York Air was challenged by the unions, particularly by the Air Line Pilots Association (ALPA). The ALPA sought to dismantle the maneuver in federal court, contending that Texas Air Corporation had violated the tenants of the RLA. The ALPA's contention was that they were the certified collective bargaining representative for Texas International Airlines and that New York Air was simply an alter ego or extension of that airline. The ALPA cited transference of landing slots at various airports by Texas Air to New York Air. The ALPA also cited management, technical assistance, financial resources, and cross-leased aircraft as indications that the two airlines were for all purposes one and the same.

The court granted Texas Air's motion to dismiss the case, and this decision was affirmed by a court of appeals, which contended that the issue was one of representation under the RLA and therefore fell within the purview of the NMB. The board was to rule on the issue in case 8 NMB 217. But prior to the ruling, the merger of Texas International Air and Continental and Continental's subsequent filing for bankruptcy protection completely overshadowed the original issue, and no NMB decision was ever rendered.

The failed union challenge to Texas Air's establishment of the nonunion New York Air left the unions with only one viable approach to counter such tactics: to negotiate scope language that would recognize the unions for any alter ego carrier established under the holding company concept. But such negotiations were not accomplished without a price, because management demanded an extensive quid pro quo. The eventual costs were concessions and the establishment of B scales for new employees on a number of airlines.

1981

In 1981, thirteen new carriers entered the market, two existing carriers were sold or merged, and five carriers ceased operation for financial reasons (see table 9-3). The difficult labor relations environment was exacerbated by a continuing economic recession. The financial position of the industry had worsened, with major carrier losses of $550 million for the year. Prospects were also grim for airline employees. Despite union attempts to curtail layoff's, seventeen thousand employees received **furlough** papers that year.

Table 9-3

Section 401 Carrier Certification Activity in 1981

New Carriers Entering		
Air Nevada		
Aerostar International		
American Transair		
Arrow		
Challenge		
Colgan		
Global		
Gulf		
Jet America		
Midstates		
Muse/Transtar		
Peoples Express		
South Pacific		

Carriers Exiting		
Merged/Sold	Waivers	Financial
Aeromech	None	Air New England
Aspen		American Eagle
		Apollo
		Golden Gate
		Swift Aire

Source: Data from Department of Transportation.

The fare wars continued, and as with any war ever fought, the costs to wage the battle had to be funded somehow. Financially vulnerable carriers sought to attack the only variable cost that could offset their losses—labor costs. Labor concessions and lower labor costs became the major focus of contractual negotiations. Management sought concessions and work rule changes for cost reduction. Unions sought to preserve the status quo. In general, neither party concerned

itself with the other's needs or well-being. The "piper" of past negotiations was beginning to be paid.

Several financially vulnerable carriers were able to secure concessions and lower labor costs from unions desiring to reduce expected unemployment losses. As encouraging as these achievements were from a cooperation standpoint, it created a bandwagon effect as the more financially stable carriers were placed at a cost disadvantage. The bandwagon now called for concessions from unions at all carriers, and union concessions became the byline of the management position.

The two events in 1981 that would shape the labor negotiations process for a long period of time in the future were the strike of the Professional Air Traffic Controllers (PATCO) and the bankruptcy of Braniff.

The PATCO Strike

As one contractual negotiator during this time commented, the actions of President Reagan in the unilateral firing of PATCO members was viewed by management with a sigh of relief and respect in anticipation of its impact on airline negotiations: "The firing of 11,000 air traffic controllers established clearly in the minds of businessmen and union leaders a pro management stance by government."[6] The action had two major influences on the negotiating process. First, airline negotiators schooled at preserving the most possible were now on the offensive, and their goal changed to getting the most possible from the union during contractual discussions. This philosophical change, never seen in the airline industry, fueled the demand for increased **concessionary bargaining** and work rule reduction talks and entrenched attitudes promoting management's right to manage. Second, in future negotiations, this new attitude that came about in response to the government's actions, coupled with Frank Lorenzo's seemingly cavalier approach toward unions, created in management a resolve never seen before by union negotiating committees. But PATCO also had its downside, and despite management's newfound freedoms, the scheduling restrictions placed on various airports by the Federal Aviation Administration caused many of the existing carriers, particularly those who followed a path of expansion, severe economic hardship because of their inability to retreat from their costly route expansions.

The Braniff Bankruptcy

The air transport industry received another jolt in 1981 with the loss of a major carrier, Braniff International Airways. In May, Braniff announced the filing of Chapter 11 bankruptcy. In its application, Braniff cited steadily slipping financial conditions amounting to debts of $733 million.[7]

This closure was devastating, because until this point, airlines, unions, and employees believed it could not happen. At the table, comments were often made that the government would not permit an airline to go out of business—that someone would always take over and that most jobs would always be protected. This bankruptcy served notice to the entire industry that it could happen to any airline.

Braniff's demise also reinforced management's position that cost improvements and cash flow were of utmost importance. Immediate survival became the paramount issue. The short run became more important than any long-term strategies demanded by the industry deregulation.

In late 1981, however, the unions achieved two important breakthroughs, and the two issues involved laid a pattern for negotiations that carried through the 1980s. At United Air Lines, who was the industry leader in 1981 in almost all aspects, including labor relations, the ALPA successfully negotiated a letter of agreement concerning alter ego operations. In August 1981, United agreed to broad guarantees for job secu-

rity of the pilots. This agreement addressed the issue of alter ego. Part of the agreement, dubbed the "Blue Sky's" contract, called for a no-furlough clause and an agreement that during the term of the contract, "neither United Airlines, Inc., nor any organization which it or its successors or assigns, control, manage or hold an equity interest in shall conduct commercial flight operation . . . unless such flying shall be performed by pilots on the United Airlines system . . . in accordance with . . . the Air Line Pilots Association, International." This letter of agreement became the benchmark for almost all future negotiations on scope protection where concessions were sought by management, and recognition of it as precedent was demanded by the unions before any agreement would be considered.

The second issue negotiated at the bargaining table was Employee Stock Ownership Plans (ESOPs). This program was initially brought out by Texas Air Corporation's takeover of Continental Air Lines. During the hostile takeover attempt, employees and management of Continental unsuccessfully attempted to prevent the acquisition by bidding for ownership themselves. This unsuccessful attempt planted a seed in the minds of employees at other beleaguered airlines, and several subsequent attempts at ESOP buyouts had a profound impact on negotiations and on the future of some airlines.

1982

In 1982, nine new carriers entered the marketplace, two existing carriers were merged or sold, and four carriers ceased operation on waivers (see table 9-4). In addition, the bankruptcy of Braniff in 1981 resulted in its certification loss in 1982. Concessions remained the watchword in negotiations during 1982. Airlines and employee groups scrambled to preserve their existence.

Among major carrier agreements, both Republic Airlines and Western settled with their

Table 9-4

Section 401 Carrier Certification Activity in 1982

New Carriers Entering

American International
Arista
Best
Emerald
Guy America
Hawaii Express
Jet Charter
Pacific East
Pacific Express

Carriers Exiting

Merged/Sold	Waivers	Financial
Altair	Air North	Braniff
Texas International	Big Sky	
	Imperial	
	Rocky Mountain	

Source: Data from Department of Transportation.

unions on a 10 percent wage reduction for over eleven thousand workers. Pan American reached an agreement with their flight attendants calling for various wage increases followed by a 10 percent reduction that was to last for fifteen months. This agreement followed the lead of four other unions who had accepted 10 percent wage cuts. In exchange for wage reductions and a change in some work rules, Pan American employees received one dollar in company stock for every five dollars of earnings forgone. In addition, the union gained membership on the company's board of directors.

At Eastern Airlines, the airline pilots agreed to a wage freeze for twelve months followed by two wage increases totaling 10 percent. Interestingly, and as an indication of the impact of deregulation, Delta Air Lines, the darling of the industry, suffered its first fiscal loss ($86.7 million) in thirty-six years. This loss led Delta to concessionary talks in the following year.

As the impact of the new entrant carriers increased, the existing major carriers were confronted with a continuing erosion of their market share. The existing carriers attempted to

complicate the ability of these new entrants to compete effectively. So intense was the concern over new entrant competition that carriers such as TWA and Ozark even developed plans to cripple a new entrant, Air One. TWA and Ozark attempted to stall Air One's baggage transfer, gate space, and ticketing agreements. These two carriers also employed "reverse yellow-dog threats," threatening employees with loss of both benefits and eligibility for rehire if they left to go to work for the new carrier.

1983

In 1983, eighteen new carriers entered the marketplace, two existing carriers were sold or merged, and seven carriers ceased operation either on waivers or for financial reasons (see table 9-5). In late 1982, the country began to emerge from a recession that had lasted twenty-six months, but the airline industry continued to struggle. Huge losses occurred in 1982, and the forecast for the industry indicated that the downhill profit picture was unlikely to change. This plight led to a number of concessionary agreements.

Prior to this time, when concessions were given by the unions, the parties generally agreed on "snapback" provisions, or a date when the reductions and work rule changes would be returned. But with the Chapter 11 bankruptcy of Braniff and the September 1983 filing by Continental, management bargained more strenuously, threatening extensive layoff and/or Chapter 11 proceedings if concessions were not agreed on, and allowing no quid pro quo for snapback.

The bandwagon approach to negotiations gained full momentum in 1983. Each time a carrier received concessions, employees and unions at other carriers knew their management's demands would be similar or more intense. This bandwagon style of negotiation was not uncommon in the industry. Prior to deregulation, the unions practiced it with apparent success, seeking more in wages and benefits in the next con-

Table 9-5
Section 401 Carrier Certification Activity in 1983

New Carriers Entering

Aeron
Air Illinois
Air National
Air Niagara
Air One
All Star
America West
Bellair
Bluebell
Galaxy
IASCO
Jet Fleet
Northern Air
Northeastern
Sunworld
Sun Country
Tower
Trans Air

Carriers Exiting

Merged/Sold	Waivers	Financial
IASCO	Air Nevada	Air Niagara
Mid South	Colgan	Golden West
	Midstate	Guy America
		Hawaii Express

Source: Data from Department of Transportation.

tract, based on the figures of negotiations settled earlier.

In seeking concessions, management's approach varied in 1983 from strict wage and benefit reductions to additional demands of cross-utilization of employees, improved productivity, and the use of part-time employees; the latter had been desired for many years by management but had always been thwarted at the table by union negotiators. This state of affairs led unions to lobby Congress for aid. The unions were not able to convince Congress to restore some regulations of the industry. It was apparent that the parties would have to sort out the new environment themselves. The negotiation process would continue to evolve, guided by the only remaining

controlling legislation, the RLA. Management used its leverage to gain concessions from its unions and to weaken the perception of labor's strength. While labor gave significant relief to many carriers during this period, much of it was used by management to subsidize the ongoing fare wars and to continue the corporations diversification strategies rather than to improve airline operations.[8]

Fighting back against the concessionary trend, the unions pursued introduction of ESOPs as a countermeasure. Because of the expense of continuing ruinous price wars, management was failing to improve operations. Labor argued that concessions would not return the carriers to profitability and, as such, were not providing the employee with any hope of future security. The union position was that the carriers could not save their way back to profitability. Demands in return for concessions became commonplace. These returns could only be embraced under the ESOP programs, where the employee received a measure of company stock for his or her contribution. A variety of different programs emerged at this time, including total company buyouts in situations where management had given up hope of winning the ultimate battle of airline viability. Plans of an ESOP nature either had been previously introduced or entered the labor scene at this time at Republic, Trans World, Eastern, Frontier, Western, Pan American, and Pacific Southwest. A host of others were on the union drawing boards for introduction at a later date.

Among the concessions made in 1983, Eastern achieved an 18 percent pay cut (22 percent for pilots) and cost-reducing measures among three unions, Pan American negotiated extended pay cuts of 10 percent, Republic's ten thousand employees approved a 15 percent pay cut to last for nine months, and Western's employees approved 15 percent cuts for almost ten thousand workers. One model of labor-management cooperation stood out in 1983. Delta Air Lines employees, in appreciation for the carriers continuance of a no-furlough policy, purchased a new

Boeing 737 aircraft for the carrier. The costs of this acquisition were financed by an employee agreement to a 2.5 percent pay reduction during the year. Two other events of major significance occurred in 1983 that further improved management's hand at the bargaining table: the development of the **two-tier wage agreement** and the bankruptcy of Continental.

The Two-Tier Wage Plan

In November, American Airlines and the American Pilots Association agreed on a two-year contract that included a provision for reduced rates for new employees. The provision, for B rates or a two-tier pay system, provided that new hired pilots would receive wage rates of approximately 50 percent of current pilot wage rates. The savings generated by such a plan did little to provide immediate cost relief but were thought to be a boon for future years. Since American was an airline that had developed specific strategic plans for deregulated operations, the agreement was seen as having significant consequences.

The unions abhorred the two-tier system, contending that it was both unfair and unhealthy for airlines to give different remuneration to employees who did the same work side by side. According to O. V. Delle-Femine of the Aircraft Mechanics Fraternal Association, this system would "cause chaos and dissension among employees."[9] Delle-Femine's argument fell on deaf ears and did not deter other carriers from pursuing similar plans. Establishment of the B scale, in various forms, became a commonplace concessionary goal. Two-tier wage plans spread rapidly, with eight negotiated in 1983 alone. By 1985, that number had increased eightfold, to 63.

The Continental Bankruptcy

The Braniff bankruptcy in 1981 had sent shock waves through the airline community. The Continental bankruptcy in 1993 sent shock waves not only through the industry but through all labor

relations contracts in general, whether established under the RLA or the NLRA. Continental Air Lines faced losses totaling over $471 million. Under the leadership of Frank Lorenzo, the carrier attempted various approaches, including negotiations with its unions, to find relief. In selecting the Chapter 11 bankruptcy alternative for reorganization, Lorenzo downsized the airline from twelve thousand employees to approximately four thousand, using the protection provisions to reopen as a low-fare carrier operating only a small portion of Continental's former route structure.

Seizing on provisions of the Bankruptcy Code that allowed for the abrogation of contracts, ostensibly designed to repudiate contracts with suppliers of goods and services, Lorenzo informed the unions at Continental that their employment contracts were no longer valid and that the airline would no longer honor the provisions of such previously negotiated agreements. Following this approach, he further advised employees that there were jobs available, but with modified wage rates and working conditions. Pilots were told that if they desired to retain employment, their new salaries would be reduced from the previous average of $77,000 to a flat $43,000; flight attendants' salaries would be reduced from an average of $29,000 to $14,000. Because the International Association of Machinists (IAM), representing mechanics and baggage handlers, had been on strike against the carrier, no provisions were forthcoming for those workers except that the strikers may be rehired at company-approved rates, with selection at the company's discretion.

The bankruptcy of Braniff had released thousands of talented and trained employees, many of whom had not found airline work. This event had provided Continental and all other airlines with a ready supply of personnel from which to draw should their own airlines have need for strike replacements. This availability was not overlooked by existing mangers and was used time and time again as a threat to unions that they were not irreplaceable as many had come to believe. Fully aware of this vast supply of trained workers, Continental also announced work rule changes, including "emergency work rules" calling for increased pilot and flight attendant flight hours and modifications to rest periods.

In response to the company's decisions, the pilot and flight attendant unions joined the striking machinists. This action was not unanticipated, and Continental prevailed, drawing on the pool of available talent to continue operations while the unions and employees looked to the courts for relief. The abrogation of employment contracts was not a new occurrence. In 1980, Bildisco & Bildisco, a New Jersey building and supply company, had employed similar tactics with the Teamsters. But the situation at Continental prompted the first application of those rules in the airline industry.

In October 1983, the Supreme Court concluded hearing arguments in the Continental case. A decision was to be rendered sometime in early 1984. In the first court hearing of the bankruptcy, the U.S. Court of Appeals for the Third Circuit sided with Continental and Lorenzo, holding that an employer need only prove that a contract is a burden, leaving the bankruptcy court to balance the interests of the employers against those of the union-represented employee. The final decision was anticipated by labor to be in their favor, because no activity of this nature had taken place before in the airline industry.

1984

In 1984, eighteen new carriers entered the marketplace, and fifteen existing carriers exited (see table 9-6). The year opened with the awaited Supreme Court decision on *NLRB v Bildisco & Bildisco*, in which the court held that employers filing for reorganization could temporarily terminate or alter labor contracts even before the bankruptcy judge had heard the case. Moreover, the termination or alteration could be made permanent if the employer could persuade the

bankruptcy judge that the agreement burdened chances of recovery.[10]

Considering the *Bildisco* decision a striking blow to labor, the unions set a course of seeking legislation to alter that decision and to amend the bankruptcy proceeding to curtail the unilateral obliteration of negotiated agreements. With union support, amendments were eventually proposed to the Bankruptcy Code, and Section 1113 requiring court approval for any rejection or change to a collective bargaining under Chapter 11 was ultimately added. Further delineation

Table 9-6

Section 401 Carrier Certification Activity in 1984

New Carriers Entering

Air America
Air Atlantic
Airmark
Airpac
Aerial Transit
Braniff
Buffalo
Florida Express
Frontier Horizon
Horizon Air
Key
Midway Express
Midwest Express
Royale
Trans Air

Carriers Exiting

Merged/Sold	Waivers	Financial
T-Bird	Blue Bell	Air Florida
	Sky West	Air Illinois
		Airmark
		Air National
		Air North
		Air One
		American International
		Arista
		Capitol
		Pacific East
		Pacific Express
		Wien

Source: Data from Department of Transportation.

of the requirements for abrogation of collective bargaining agreements was highlighted in a subsequent case in 1986, *Wheeling-Pittsburgh Steel Corporation v United Steelworkers*,[11] which set requirements that must be followed before any abrogation may take place. These requirements include the following:

1. The abrogation cannot be unilateral; it must be discussed with the union, and a proposal must be made to the union permitting them to address the issue before any action may take place.

2. Only those modifications necessary to permit reorganization can be considered and can be subjects of the above proposal.

3. All relevant information must be supplied to the union.

4. The company must meet with the union in an attempt to reach a good-faith agreement.

6. The court can authorize abrogation only if the union has failed to accept the carrier's proposal without good cause.

The amendments to the code and the effects of *Wheeling* and other decisions curtailed the wanton abandon that management had employed and threatened in the heat of labor-management battles. The bankruptcy threat, so often used at the table, had now been neutralized.

Despite these activities, in May 1984, Continental's contract abrogation was upheld by a bankruptcy judge, and Continental later showed a profit of $17.6 million for the third quarter compared with a third quarter loss of $77.2 million one year earlier. During 1984, several airlines operated at a profit. But the continued erosion of profitability continued at most carriers, and the demands for concessions continued.

By this point, the continued concessionary demands were creating solidarity among the industry's unions, and concession requests were invariably met with offsetting demands for ESOP's and alternative compensation programs. The focus of concessionary talks followed the bandwagon approach, and management's goals changed and centered on B-scale relief. Present

or immediate cost reductions were now being slowly replaced by the need for future anticipated cost cuts. A "monkey see, monkey do" mania was replacing the strong push for immediate wage reductions. Industry negotiation practices had not changed appreciably from when the unions were in the catbird seat; they had only changed from one side of the table to the other. A follow-the-leader approach was still prevalent. In defense of the change of strategy, it might be noted that it was anticipated that the economy was going to recover appreciably and that a necessity for increased employment might occur in late 1984 and 1985.

The follow-the-leader approach to two-tier wage scales lacked the thought process that had been employed at American Airlines when the company and its unions agreed on implementation of its B-scale program. Under the aegis of that plan, new hire rates were never intended to merge with current employees, and in return, American management made several agreements concerning job security and expansion to offset the union's agreement to the two-tier permanent arrangements. By the end of 1984, two-tier salary arrangements in the industry reached approximately forty in number, but none had the sophistication or forethought of the original agreement at American. Frequently, competing airlines sought two-tier arrangements because it was the negotiation "pearl" of the times.

Several 1984 settlements included concessionary provisions (which usually resulted in an overall increase in compensation).[12] At United Air Lines, the flight attendants agreed to a thirty-seven-month contract including a two-tier (B-scale) wage agreement for new employees at 25 percent of existing rates, to remain in effect for seven years of hiring, before merging with nonreduced (A-scale) rates; the mechanics agreed to a three-year contract with B-scale rates of pay to be in effect for five years before merging with existing A-scale rates. At Pacific Southwest Airlines, the Teamsters, the Southwest Airline Pilots Association, and other unions called for a 15 percent pay cut in return for a company agreement to place 15 percent of its stock into an employee trust fund. At Northwest Airlines, flight attendants represented by the Teamsters agreed to a six-month wage freeze, followed by a 6 percent increase in July of 1984 and 1985 and a 3 percent increase on July 1, 1986. The contract also established a dual pay system under which newly hired attendants would be paid 30 percent of the current rates for six years, after which the A-scale rates would be applicable.

Piedmont Airlines negotiated contracts with four unions in which two-tier rates became applicable. Republic Airlines negotiated agreements with six unions that provided a two-tier system and an extension through 1986 of 15 percent pay reductions. In exchange, Republic agreed to establish profit sharing and to provide workers with shares of stock, increasing **employee ownership** of the company from 20 to 30 percent. At Western Airlines, four unions agreed to a 22.5 percent pay reduction through 1986. Five contracts negotiated by Western called for changes in work rules to increase productivity. In return, the company agreed to increase employee shares of company stock, engage a profit sharing program, and increase union representation on the board of directors from two to four members. Frontier Airlines consummated agreements among five thousand workers calling for 11.5 percent reduction in wages and a two-tier pay system.

1985

In 1985, the first year of full deregulation, the last vestige of the regulated years, the CAB, ended its existence. Seventeen new carriers entered the marketplace, and eighteen existing carriers exited (see table 9-7). Nineteen eighty-five marked the beginning of a wave of mergers. All prior mergers had taken place under the aegis of the CAB, and its demise left a void in future resolution of labor issues when mergers took place.

Under the CAB's guidance, mergers involving unionized carriers traditionally contained "fence agreements," or agreements that allowed an orderly integration process of seniority and work rules to take place while the air operations continued. Mergers could have a destabilizing effect on workers, and the CAB kept amalgamation problems at a minimum. The CAB followed a policy of establishing labor protective provisions to minimize the potential for severe disruption by providing a "floor," or standard, for employee

Table 9-7

Section 401 Carrier Certification Activity in 1985

New Carriers Entering

Air Hawaii
Atlantic
Five Star
Interstate
JetEast/Express One
Mid Pacific
Million Air
New Wien
Pacific Interstate
Pilgrim
Presidential
Regent
Samoa
Skybus
Skystar
Skyworld
Trans Pacific International

Carriers Exiting

Merged/Sold	Waivers	Financial
Frontier Horizon	Bellair	Airlift
Midway Express	Cascade	Aerostar/Flt Intl
Mississippi Valley	Royale	All Star
New Air		Best
		Global
		Jet Charter
		New Wien
		Northeastern
		Overseas National
		Samoa
		Wright

Source: Data from Department of Transportation.

protection during mergers and acquisitions.[13] This regulatory feature no longer existed. Starting in 1985, the industry underwent major changes due to mergers.

Also in 1985, profitability began to return to many carriers in the industry, resulting in a continuation of their route expansion efforts. Coincident with industry improvement and expansion came the need for more employees. This single factor forced management to review and, in some cases, alter their bargaining approach, particularly with respect to the two-tier wage scale.

In 1985, the two-tier wage scale, in a form similar to that of the original scale established at American Airlines, met its Waterloo at United Air Lines. In negotiations during late 1985, United's management had demanded a non-merging two-tier pay scale for newly hired pilots. The ALPA refused to agree to the nonmerging aspect of the B scale, and the result was a twenty-nine day strike, which, when resolved, led to a two-tier scale that lasted for only a certain amount of years and then returned to the regular pilot pay rates. The nonmerging aspect of B scales had been defeated. Elsewhere in the industry, the ALPA's two-year-old strike against Continental Air Lines ended on October 31, by order of a U.S. bankruptcy judge.[14] The approach taken by the ALPA at United and the return at Continental marked a new beginning of union unity toward management's demands at the bargaining table.

In apparent reaction to its experience in the United and Continental strikes, the ALPA announced plans to build a $100 million "war chest" to repel employer attacks on the wages and benefits of its members. The fund, to be used for such purposes as strike benefits to the union members and loans and grants to other supporting unions,[15] was accumulated by increasing membership dues by 1 percent. This fund later had a major impact in the strike against Eastern Airlines, which ended in the demise of that airline.

The Continental bankruptcy and the strike against that carrier were low points for the unions, but the United pilot's strike and an agreement

that the unions at TWA entered into with Carl Icahn to preclude Frank Lorenzo from purchasing TWA were the most positive events for airline unions. Both situations reflected the renewed ability of unions to fashion strategies to deal with difficult and potentially devastating occurrences. If done properly, unions once again could engage in self-help and effectively shut down a major carrier. Likewise, unions could enter the financial world and make arrangements enabling the employees to determine the question of ownership of their company.[16]

1986

In 1986, seven new carriers entered the marketplace, and eighteen carriers ceased operation (see table 9-8). Most notable were the mergers in which Ozark, Republic, New York Air, and Peoples Express were absorbed by other carriers. The focus of negotiations in 1986 was on meeting competition, particularly in the wake of the continuing fare wars. Key objectives sought by man-

Table 9-8

Section 401 Carrier Certification Activity in 1986

New Carriers Entering

Air Puerto Rico
Challenge Air Cargo
Challenge Air International
Federal Express
McClain
Royal West
Sun West

Carriers Exiting

Merged/Sold	Waivers	Financial
Empire	Pilgrim	Air Hawaii
Challenge	South Pacific	Airpac
New York Air	Trans Pacific	Atlantic
Ozark	International	Frontier
Peoples Express		Galaxy
Republic		Regent
		Skybus
		Transamerica
		Worldwide

Source: Data from Department of Transportation.

agement at the negotiating table remained the same, consisting of wage freezes or small increases, lump sum payments, B scales, increased productivity, fringe benefit reductions, and relief from work rules previously negotiated during the regulatory environment.

Key settlements during 1986 related to Trans World and the strike by the flight attendants' union, Eastern Airlines, and Delta Air Lines. Indicative of the mood of labor relations, settlements were not as easily won. Following the position of the ALPA in the United settlement, Delta pilots agreed on a thirty-month contract involving a two-tier pay system with a merging agreement after five years of B rates. The Delta negotiating session was so intense that, for the first time in the history of the airline, it was necessary to nearly exhaust the procedures of the RLA by calling in a mediator from the NMB.

Corporate moves during the year portended serious problems for airlines' unions in future years. Nineteen eighty-six became the year of the merger. Company after company sought to improve their balance sheets and eliminate competition through consolidation. These mergers fueled union desires to seek protective programs to preserve jobs. One of the most notable of such approaches was the unions' willingness to move from a position of protectionism to entrepreneurialism by attempting to obtain control of various companies through Employee Stock Ownership Plans.

Responding to the rash of mergers and acquisitions, the NMB acted to resolve some of the labor disputes resulting from questions about the bargaining status of unions absorbed in a merger. Rather than allowing questions of representation—that is, whether a carrier would be represented by one union or another or by no union at all—to be resolved with carte blanche based on which group had the largest population at the time of merger, the board ruled that carriers must alert the NMB to possible employee representation disputes before a merger takes place. Up to this time, there were no such requirements, and many airlines made no attempt to notify the NMB

until after the mergers had been solidified. This laid-back approach on the part of airline management had worked toward the advantage of the airlines at the negotiating table.

The new procedure established by the board provided for earlier decision making about the representation status of a particular union. The board further established that when the certification status of a union was terminated, that same union could file for a new election for the combined craft or class within sixty days, if they could obtain union authorization cards from at least 35 percent of the new combined craft and class. This move almost insured a reelection procedure if the absorbed or decertified union had an appreciable number of members.

1987

Five carriers entered and eleven exited in 1987; four of the exiting carriers merged (see table 9-9). Eastern Airlines continued its ongoing dispute with the IAM. At Trans World, the Independent Flight Attendants continued legal maneuvering to regain jobs lost as a result of their work stoppage. At United Air Lines, the pilots proposed the first of many attempts to purchase the airline via an ESOP.

Table 9-9

Section 401 Carrier Certification Activity in 1987

New Carriers Entering		
Amerijet		
Connor		
Florida West		
MGM Grand		
Orion		

Carriers Exiting		
Merged/Sold	Waivers	Financial
Air Cal	Britt	Air Atlantic
Jet America	Mid Pacific	Air Puerto Rico
Muse/Transtar		Challenge Air Intl
Western		McClain
		Skystar

Source: Data from Department of Transportation.

At American Airlines, the original two-tier pay scale approach suffered a setback at the hands of the American Pilots Association. American's original nonmerging B scale in 1985 was renegotiated to a merging scale, and in 1987, new employees hired at the B rates were granted pay increases ranging from 11 to 28 percent during the life of a three-year contract. In other actions at American, the company, after exhausting the procedures of the RLA, imposed the terms of their last contract offer on the flight attendants represented by the Association of Professional Flight Attendants. Although a strike did not take place, it took six months for the parties to come to an agreement after the union membership authorized a strike in December. As in other labor activities during 1987, at issue was the narrowing of the two-tier wage differential.

Merger and representation disputes were accentuated by activities at both USAir and Northwest Airlines. At USAir, the acquisition of Pacific Southwest Airlines (PSA) and Piedmont Aviation, Inc. permitted the Association of Flight Attendants full representation of USAir and the acquired companies after the Teamsters (IBT) withdrew from an NMB election over the flight attendants at PSA. The Teamsters, adamant that no election should be held over the PSA/Piedmont merger until the USAir/PSA merger was actually completed, failed to convince the board of their position. Until that time, the Teamsters had been the certified bargaining agent for the PSA flight attendants.

In the Northwest/Republic merger, the Teamsters gained the right to represent the flight attendants by defeating the Association of Flight Attendants, who represented Republic. Similarly, in the same merger, the IAM were certified to represent approximately twenty thousand Northwest employees. The former Republic employees had lower wage rates than Northwest employees. Because of the wage difference, the IAM sought parity wage increases, but Northwest refused to bargain, insisting that the agreements with these employees were still intact and were not subject to being amended under the RLA.

While Delta Air Lines was completing the acquisition of Western Airlines, the Air Transport Employees Union was in court attempting to stop the merger. At issue was the union's attempt to force Delta into honoring contracts it had previously negotiated with Western. Supreme Court Justice Sandra Day O'Connor vacated a lower-court ruling that mandated arbitration to resolve this dispute, citing that merger preparations were too costly to reverse. The lower-court ruling would have forced Delta to agree in advance to accept arbitration, and the merger would have been delayed until a decision was announced.[17]

Soon after the high-court decision, Delta made it known that the more than six thousand employees of the former Western Airlines would be nonunion after the merger, because they were outnumbered in each respective job class by Delta employees, all of whom were nonunion. The only exception was the ALPA, who represented Western's pilots. That classification would remain union, because Delta pilots were also members of the ALPA.

Later in the year, USAir Group, attempting to thwart a takeover bid by Trans World Airlines, set about acquiring other carriers. The negotiations and plans were put on a faster track when the Teamsters and Pacific Southwest Airlines agreed to drop several provisions of their agreement. A crucial point that would have delayed the process was the Teamsters' right to bargain with any new owner of the airline. Once that provision had been dropped, USAir moved ahead with the purchase of Pacific Southwest.

These events represent examples of how management was able to "wrestle" the unions into positive postures for the carrier. Unions were now used to severe financial problems on the part of the carriers. This financial trouble also had an impact on their members' security. The Braniff bankruptcy had shown the industry that it was not immune to free-market forces.

The buyout of Republic by Northwest led unions to give more attention to the potent power of ESOPs. Republic had been purchased by Northwest in 1986 for $17 per share, up from an original value of $3.50 per share. Employees of Republic in the early 1980s had taken company stock in exchange for wage and benefit concessions. Disbursements totaled $150 million dollars for fifteen thousand employees/stockholders of Republic. The buyout demonstrated the potential of ESOP deals with management.[18]

1988

Four carriers entered and five exited in 1988 (see table 9-10). Eastern Airlines dominated the news of the industry. Eastern posted significant losses, while the three biggest carriers generated record profits. Eastern was also fined $1 million for safety violations and was the subject of a maintenance safety investigation by the Federal Aviation Administration. The Eastern unions were sued by Texas Air Corporation, the Eastern Airlines holding company. Eastern claimed that the machinists and the ALPA were conspiring to destroy the airline.[19] On top of that litigation, the secretary of transportation criticized those unions for filing undocumented safety complaints.

Table 9-10
Section 401 Carrier Certification Activity in 1988

New Carriers Entering		
Air Transport International		
Tropical		
United Parcel Service		
Westair		

Carriers Exiting		
Merged/Sold	Waivers	Financial
Pacific Southwest	None	Interstate
		Royal West
		Sunworld
		Tropical

Source: Data from Department of Transportation.

In October, Texas Air Corporation announced it was selling its Eastern Air Shuttle to entrepreneur Donald Trump for $365 Million. The unions sued to block the sale. Under the proposed sale, the 850 employees would have the option of moving to the new Trump Shuttle with their existing contract benefits or staying with Eastern. Later, in 1988, Eastern announced that it was terminating contracts that called for Continental to train pilots and flight attendants in the event of a strike. Texas Air made it clear that Eastern was not for sale; management was confident it would win contract concessions from the unions.

American Airlines finally ratified a five-year contract negotiated with the Association of Professional Flight Attendants late in 1987. The chief bargaining issue of narrowing the two-tier wage differential was resolved by shifting lower-tier workers to the top rate of the Schedule A scale after eight years of service. USAir and the Association of Flight Attendants negotiated a one-year contract that raised wages for nearly all employees and closed the gap between the two pay scales that had been in existence at USAir since the Pacific Southwest Airlines and USAir merger. Pan American received $118 million in savings after pay and concessionary cuts were received from their unions. The ALPA and the Flight Engineers Beneficial Association settled on three-year contracts calling for a 22 percent reduction in pay in return for equity shares in the company. Pan American imposed an 8 percent reduction in pay on the reservationists, clerks, dispatchers, and gate agents, after the Teamsters refused to accept a proffer of arbitration.

Delta Air Lines took steps to eliminate the two-tier wage scale. Delta's management probably took this action because Delta remained the only major nonunion carrier. The unions were attacking the two-tier plans at almost all carriers, and it was in Delta's best interest to initiate such a move from a management rather than a union position. The move was accomplished by merging the lower scale into the higher, existing scale.

All employees who were under a single scale received a wage increase. A Teamsters official stated that Delta employees were among the highest paid airline employees but that the employees were leaning toward representation in the wake of the Delta and Western Airlines merger.

1989

Five carriers entered and ten exited in 1989 (see table 9-11). The Supreme Court handed down a much anticipated ruling on drug testing. They ruled that employers could test employees for drugs during periodic physical examinations without such testing being first negotiated at the bargaining table or under the terms and conditions of the RLA.

Table 9-11
Section 401 Carrier Certification Activity in 1989

New Carriers Entering		
Casino Express		
Kalitta		
Private Jet		
Trans Continental		
Trump Shuttle		

Carriers Exiting		
Merged/Sold	Waivers	Financial
Florida Express	None	Aeron
Flying Tiger		Braniff
Piedmont		Five Star
		Orion
		Presidential
		Skyworld
		Trans International

Source: Data from Department of Transportation.

Eastern Airlines encountered more problems with its unions when 8,500 employees represented by the International Association of Machinists and Aerospace Workers (IAMAW) walked out of negotiation after Eastern demanded compensation cuts and changes in work rules. Initially, Eastern planned to continue operating without the mechanics and related employees, but that changed when virtually all 3,500 flight and cockpit crew members would not cross the machinists' picket lines. The 6,000 flight attendants represented by the Transport Workers Union also supported the machinists' strike. The unified stand forced Eastern to lay off 1,000 nonunion employees.

Simultaneously, Eastern filed for protection under Chapter 11 of the Bankruptcy Act and attempted to continue operation as it was selling off assets and routes. The ultimate outcome was the finalization of the sale to Donald Trump of the lucrative East Coast shuttle. Eastern began a downsizing campaign of selling off valuable assets that would eventually be its own death knell. While in the mediation process with the IAMAW, Eastern continued to seek relief from the procedure through the self-help process. President Bush vetoed a bill to set up a board to investigate labor relations problems at the troubled carrier.

American Airlines settled with the Transport Workers Union, agreeing to a wage increase of $1.80 an hour for twenty-one thousand employees and to quarterly productivity payments. The carrier also adopted a flexible health insurance plan that permitted employees to select their benefits while sharing the premium costs.

Northwest Airlines was faced with two problems in 1988. Outside investors were bidding to purchase NWA, Inc., Northwest's parent company. Ultimately, NWA, Inc. accepted an offer of $3.6 billion from Wings Holdings, Inc., a group of investors led by William Checci and Gary Wilson. Simultaneously, the airline settled a contract dispute with the ALPA, ending a negotiation process that had lasted two and a half years and was culminated with months of strike threats.

USAir and the Association of Flight Attendants negotiated a contract for 8,500 employees that had been added to the carrier's payroll as a result of the August merger with Piedmont. The contract assured former Piedmont employees of equal pay with those employees previously on the USAir payroll. International flight pay, carryover of accrued sick leave, vacation bids, insurance, and other, seniority-related issues were also resolved.

1990

In 1990, six new carriers emerged, and four carriers exited the marketplace (see table 9-12). The three United unions tried again to purchase United Air Lines. The breakdown of the tentative agreement reached earlier between UAL Corporation and the unions had the board of directors accepting a $4.4 billion offer, or $200 per share.[20] The deal had been put together by the Coniston Partners investment group, UAL's largest stockholder and the instigator behind the Allegis breakup.

Table 9-12
Section 401 Carrier Certification Activity in 1990

New Carriers Entering
Emery
Executive
North American
Trans Pacific International
Universal
Wrangler

Carriers Exiting

Merged/Sold	Waivers	Financial
None	None	Air America
		Gulf
		Independent
		Trans Pacific International

Source: Data from Department of Transportation.

Eastern and the Transportation Workers Union, who was representing the flight attendants, signed a back-to-work agreement stating that flight attendants would have the right to return to work in seniority order as jobs became available. To the liking of most unions at Eastern, Frank Lorenzo, the "Union Buster" was replaced as the operating head by Martin Shugrue, a trustee appointed by the bankruptcy courts. In contract negotiations, Eastern and the pilots reached an impasse, and a proffer of arbitration was made by the NMB. But the company refused to accept the proffer. Though Eastern could not achieve reductions in wage rates and time and work rules through direct negotiations, the bankruptcy court did approve a contract amendment proposed by Eastern that temporarily imposed a 20 percent wage and benefit cut to save the airline $7–9 million monthly.

1991

Nineteen ninety-one will be remembered as one of the saddest, yet most influential, years in airline history. Four carriers entered the market, and six exited (see table 9-13). Two of the six carriers exiting were Eastern and Pan Am, two of the nation's oldest carriers. Midway, one of the deregulation successes, also ceased operation. Proponents of deregulation and free-market forces who viewed the airlines as an overweight and pampered industry and who predicted that only the strong would, or should, survive were having their "I told you so's." Losses totaled over $4 billion for the industry, and the pressures to reduce costs created difficult and complex negotiation issues. Management needed concessions from

Table 9-13
Section 401 Carrier Certification Activity in 1991

New Carriers Entering
Braniff International
Miami Air
Simmons
Trans States

Carriers Exiting

Merged/Sold	Waivers	Financial
Emerald	None	Connor
		Eastern
		Flagship
		Midway
		Pan Am

Source: Data from Department of Transportation.

unions, and the unions demanded some form of quid pro quo.

Eastern Airlines, after a turbulent past, liquidated in January. Pan American World Airways, the premier flag carrier of the United States, closed its doors in December, less than one month after Midway ceased operations in November. On the heels of these liquidations, Continental Air Lines and America West filed for Chapter 11 protection.

American Airlines settled its eighteen-month dispute with the pilots organization, agreeing to a fifty-six-month agreement that would equate American's pilot wages with those at Delta. The NMB had proffered arbitration, with both parties in agreement, to settle unresolved issues. Chief among those issues was health care costs.[21]

United and the ALPA reached an agreement on a forty-two-month contract covering 7,500 pilots. United also reached an agreement with the flight attendants for a fifty-four-month contract after the NMB refused to release the parties and forced them to continue to negotiate. Delta reached an agreement with the ALPA on an extension to the pilots' contract for an additional sixteen months. TWA restored pay rates for the IAM union members under a snapback provision negotiated earlier. USAir announced wage cuts for all nonunion workers and a freeze on promotions for one year. These cuts and freezes would be rescinded after fifteen months if productivity increases were satisfactory.

1992

In 1992, a second wave of new entrant applications emerged. Seventeen carriers filed for entry (see table 9-14). These new carriers focused on finding niches in the point-to-point market and, by and large, chose not to compete directly against the hubbed majors.

TWA filed for bankruptcy protection, joining America West and Continental. Northwest, operating under a tremendous debt load, opened negotiations with all its unions to trade wage and work concessions for equity participation in the

Table 9-14

Section 401 Carrier Certification Activity in 1992

New Carriers Entering
Air Mark
Atlantic Southeast
AV Atlantic
Branson
Business Express
Capitol Express
Express II
Family
International Xpress
Kiwi
Morris
Northeast Express
Patriot
Reno
Ryan International
UltrAir
ValuJet

Carriers Exiting		
Merged/Sold	Waivers	Financial
None	None	None

Source: Data from Department of Transportation.

company. American created a new fare structure that precipitated a massive fare war that drove revenues further downward. American's pilot union formally stated that the carrier should seek to partner with other carriers to preserve Americans competitive edge. The union stated it would be willing to negotiate wage and work rule concessions to assist such an effort.

The unions at United attempted again to buy the carrier under an ESOP program, but the effort failed to win sufficient financial support. As revenues continued to decline to record levels, the air transport unions began to examine in detail the merits of ESOP programs as vehicles for protecting members' jobs and wages. Several carriers and unions entered into formal discussions of trading equities for wages. TWA began a restructuring program that would involve union equity positions and the departure of Carl Icahn as owner. Northwest also began similar discussion with its unions. Continental's plan to emerge from bankruptcy involved union participation as well. These labor relations activities reached critical mass in 1993.

1993

Ten more new carriers entered the market in 1993 (see table 9-15). Revenues began to climb for the first time in three years. The principal activity in 1993 was the emergence from bankruptcy of Continental and TWA. Union equity participation was a key component of the restructuring. Northwest, after several failed attempts, secured wage and work rule concessions from all its unions in return for equity and seats on the board of directors.

Table 9-15
Section 401 Carrier Certification Activity in 1993

New Carriers Entering
All American
Direct Air
Fine
New West
Polar
Renown
Salair
Sunbird
Sun Jet
Trans America

Carriers Exiting		
Merged/Sold	Waivers	Financial
None	None	None

Source: Data from Department of Transportation.

The unions at United restructured their buyout proposal, and the plan moved toward closure. In the fourth quarter, however, the flight attendants backed out of the proposal. The remaining unions, the ALPA and the IAMAW, then sought and received participation commitments

from all nonunion and managerial workers. The buyout plan was set to be presented to the shareholders in March 1994 and was anticipated to be successful.

1994

Seventeen new carriers were activated in 1994. Noteworthy was the reemergence of the name Frontier Airlines. Frontier had been one the carriers 'grandfathered' under the Airline Deregulation Act of 1978, only to cease operations in 1986.

The movement toward unions' stakeholder participation in the airlines continued in 1994 as new approaches to labor relations included contract provisions in exchange for a stake in companies. Unions favored employee ownership po-

Table 9-16
Section 401 Carrier Certification Activity in 1994

New Carriers Entering
Air South
Astral Aviation (Skyway)
Frontier Airline
Great West Air
Jet Train
Jet USA
Katmailand
Mabolo Air
Nations Air Express
Pacific International
Polar Air Cargo
Southeast Express
Sunbird Airways
Trans Continental
Tri Star
USA Jet
Vanguard

Carriers Exiting		
Merged/Sold	Waivers	Financial
International Cargo Express	Air Cargo Hawaii	None

Source: Data from Department of Transportation.

sitions in contractual negotiations more than immediate economic considerations in order to gain a modicum of control in an unstable and turbulent industry.

Due to the nature of the industry's financial problems, President Clinton established the National Commission to Ensure a Competitive Air Line Industry. The report, finalized and presented in September, addressed, from a labor relations perspective, the economic health of carriers, their ability to continue operations, potential work rule changes, employee ownership, and job security. Of special concern were major issues of tax and regulatory relief and the privatization of air traffic control.

In special labor areas, Continental's pilots voted to unionize as the Independent Association of Continental Pilots (Ind.) and begin bargaining for their first contract. This was a setback for the Airline Pilots Association (ALPA) who had previously represented Continental pilots prior to the Chapter 11 bankruptcy inspired by Frank Lorenzo years previously. ALPA's representation standing was given a boost as the pilot employees of Federal Express voted for ALPA certification and representation.

The most distinguishing labor activity of this year occurred at Northwest Airlines, whose financial problems set the stage for a difficult bargaining session. Northwest reopened negotiations to discuss refinancing its debts and lowering its labor costs. The International Association of Machinists, their largest union, was advised the airline would achieve lower labor costs as a result of bankruptcy filing. This threat was conditioned on the premise that if its six unions (including ALPA and Teamsters) did not agree to a $900 million labor cost reduction, bankruptcy would follow. As result of such activity, the pilots settled for $365 million in direct wage reductions and $61 million in cost savings through changes in work rules. The machinists forfeited $346 million in concessions, and the Teamsters, representing the flight attendants, gave up $82 mil

lion. The remainder was made up by the remaining unions. In exchange for these sacrifices, the unions received 30 percent of Northwest's preferred stock, three seats on the company's fifteen-member board, enhanced job security, and a significant voice in the carrier's operations. Additionally, major bank creditors gave Northwest a postponement on the collection of their debts until 1997. Adding to the Northwest deficit reduction, preferred stockholders agreed to reduce annual stock dividends by $36 million over nine years.

At United Airlines the Union Coalition designed to buy UAL away from United Management offered $4 billion over a five-year period in exchange for representation on the board of directors, a 60 percent equity position in the company and restrictions on the present debt structure. The Flight Attendants, however, pulled out of the Coalition talks after learning a new domicile in Taiwan would reduce two hundred flight attendant positions in the United States.

At American Airlines a first in the flight attendant labor relations occurred when President Clinton interrupted a sanctioned strike, forcing management and the union back to the bargaining table. The strike, begun on November 18, was ceased and the parties returned to the table on November 22, agreeing to submit all unresolved issues to binding arbitration.

In the aerospace industry, due principally to commercial aviation's cutback in aircraft orders, thousands of jobs were affected and union retaliation raised the specter of potential job security strikes.

At McDonnell Douglas, within minutes of a machinists strike, the company and the union signed a three-year contract covering eight thousand workers in St. Louis, Missouri. Work rules modifications and job consolidation led to contractual resolution.

The Boeing Company and the International Association of Machinists signed a three-year contract awarding employees with a lump-sum payment equal to 12 percent of the individuals' annual pay for 1992. In addition, the employees received a 3.5 percent pay increase on October 4, 1993 and 1994, and fully paid health care. This contract also included changes to work rules that provided the employees with increased job security.

At Pratt and Whitney in June, the machinists (representing ten thousand workers) agreed to concessions to save twenty-three hundred jobs. Under the new contract, Pratt and Whitney agree to enhance job security by closing only one plant, rather than five it had under consideration.

The Lockheed Corporation and the International Association of Machinists signed a three-year contract covering eleven thousand workers.

1995

The year 1995 saw the introduction of six new carriers and the exit of five previously certified airlines. After four years, the airline industry started showing a comeback. Airlines lost about $11 billion between 1990 and 1993, and a number of carriers left the business. Airlines benefited from comparatively moderate hikes in jet fuel prices, from cuts in work forces and fleets, and by withdrawing from markets that did not prove profitable. The industry was undergoing reconstruction activity to compete with low-cost airlines. Unions routinely cut back wages in exchange for stock in their respective companies.

At United Airline's parent company, UAL corporation was bought out on July 12 by its employees. Included were thirty-one thousand pilots from ALPA and the machinists and seventeen thousand nonunion members. The contract called for 55 percent in the company in exchange for $4.9 billion in wage and work rule concessions over the next six years, three seats on the

Table 9-17

Section 401 Carrier Certification Activity in 1995

New Carriers Entering		
Air 21		
Custom Air Transport		
Eagle Canyon		
Eagle Jet Charter		
Hemisphere International Air		
NavCom Aviation II		
Prime Air		
Seaborne Aviation		
Western Pacific		

Carriers Exiting		
Merged/Sold	Waivers	Financial
None	Air Service	Airmark
	Sky King	Eclipse Airlines
		Patriot Airlines

Source: Data from Department of Transportation.

twelve-member board and restrictions on the new United Shuttle. In exchange, the company would receive wage cuts over the next six years.

The aerospace industry experienced major downsizing as a result of numerous government contracts that had been cut. Total employment declined 5.4 percent from September 1993 to September 1994. A large majority of the contracts that expired in 1995 in the transport industry belonged to aerospace companies. These contracts affected approximately seven unions.

Four major contracts were discussed at Boeing in 1995. Other large companies seeking concessions in 1995 were McDonnell Douglas, United Technologies, and the Aerostructure Division of Textron.

Lockheed and Martin Marietta's merger in August 1994 was finalized in 1995 to form the largest defense company.

Additional Study Material

Recent Rulings by the National Mediation Board and the Courts on Questions Arising under the Railway Labor Act

Arbitration Agreements

A hearing board procedure outlined in an employee handbook constituted "arbitration," even though the procedure was not deemed as such by the manual. Thus, a decision of the hearing board, which upheld the discharge of an employee, constituted an arbitration award subject to judicial confirmation. That the employee handbook stipulated that the decision of the hearing board would be "final and binding" manifested the arbitrative nature of the proceeding and facilitated confirmation of the award. By electing to pursue his grievance through this procedure, the employee tacitly submitted his dispute to arbitration. (*Bakri v Continental Air Lines, Inc.*, DC Cal, 126 LC Sect. 57, 558)

Conflict of Jurisdiction Between Boards

A special board of adjustment, created to resolve labor disputes that arose out of a modified collective bargaining agreement, had jurisdiction to resolve a controversy involving a union and a railroad employer. The authority to do so arose from the parties' modified bargaining contract. Although another special board of adjustment, created by the parties pursuant to their original collective bargaining agreement, had permissive jurisdiction to resolve that type of dispute, it did not have exclusive jurisdiction and thus did not divest the board created by the parties' modified agreement from deciding the issue raised. (*United Transportation Union v Consolidated Rail Corp.*, DC Pa, 126 LC Sect. 10, 935)

Seniority Negotiation Proper

In negotiating a new collective bargaining agreement with an employer, a union properly agreed to a work equity allocation method of calculating seniority rights rather than a straight day-of-hire method. Under the work equity method, some members who worked on busier railway routes received greater seniority than other members who actually had greater years in service. That method of calculating seniority rights was, however, a legitimate and rational means of determining seniority rights. Moreover, the complaining members failed to demonstrate that the union did not fairly consider their seniority interests before executing the contract. (*Allen v United Transportation Union*, CA-8, 122 LC Sect. 10, 305)

Agency Shop Agreement

An agency shop agreement was lawfully entered into between an airline pilots' union and an employer without employee consent. The union's policy manual permitted the union to enter into the agreement without an employees' vote, the union gave affected nonmembers treatment equal to members, and the agreement did not serve to penalize nonmembers for delinquencies in dues payments incurred prior to the date of the implementation of the agreement. (*Miller v Air Line Pilots Assn.*, DC DofC, 126 LC Sect. 10, 807)

Interstate Commerce Commission Lease Approval

The Interstate Commerce Commission, in approving the lease of a small railroad line to a noncarrier subsidiary of a rail carrier, acted properly, because that rail carrier had formed the subsidiary for legitimate business reasons, not to evade labor regulations. The carrier was attempting to avoid unusual administrative delays generally associated with such lease transactions, and the lease involved no exceptional circumstances likely to cause injury to rail employees and calling for protective labor conditions. (*Railway Labor Executives' Assn. v Interstate Commerce Commission*, CA DofC, 125 LC Sect. 10, 798)

Coverage by the National Labor Relations Board Asserted

An employer that furnished ground handling services to airlines or aircraft at an international airport was subject to the jurisdiction of the National Labor Relations Board. Accordingly, a union representation election was ordered. The employer claimed that it was governed by the Railway Labor Act. But the employer was not subject to substantial controls by the airlines that it services, and the National Mediation Board ruled that the Railway Labor Act was inapplicable. (*Caribbean Airline Services, Inc.*, 1992-93 CCH NLRB Sect. 17, 271)

Restoring Jury Verdict

A jury verdict in favor of a wrongfully discharged employee—who sued his employer for violation of a state law, public policy theory—was reinstated by a federal appellate court after a federal district court had granted to the employer a judgment notwithstanding the verdict. The federal appellate court provided that the state would recognize the tort of wrongful termination in violation of public policy, even if other remedies were available to the employee, and even if the employee could be terminated for "just cause." (*Davies v American Airlines, Inc.*, CA-10, 122 LC Sect. 10, 122)

Union Certification Upheld

A certification of an employee representative issued by the National Mediation Board was

proper because, in issuing the certification, the board did not violate the Railway Labor Act or any constitutional principle. Although the NMB refused to stay a representation election at the request of an employer, it was empowered to do so, and the free speech rights of those employees not choosing to be represented by the union were not violated. (*Virgin Atlantic Airways, Ltd. v National Mediation Board*, CA-2, 121 LC Sect. 10, 011)

Jurisdiction of the National Mediation Board

A dispute between a merged employer and unions that represented several crafts among the employees was properly categorized as a representation dispute by the National Mediation Board. Therefore, the NMB had jurisdiction over the matter. (*Maintenance of Way Employees v Grand Trunk Western Railroad Co.*, CA-6, 121 LC Sect. 10, 106)

National Labor Relations Board Declines Jurisdiction

Following an advisory opinion issued by the National Mediation Board that employees of an in-flight catering service would be subject to the provisions of the Railway Labor Act, the National Labor Relations Board dismissed a union's petition to represent those employees. The employer had entered into a partnership with a subsidiary of an air carrier, and the National Labor Relations Act did not provide coverage to persons engaged in the airline industry. (*Dobbs Internations Service, Inc.*, 1992–93 CCH NLRB Sect. 17, 202)

Right-to-Hearing Notice

An employee contended on appeal that the failure of the National Railroad Adjustment Board to provide him with proper notice of a referee's hearing in his case voided the award. The contention was dismissed because the employee had waived his right to an oral hearing before the board. The referee properly decided the employee's case based on written submissions, as requested by the employee; thus, he had no right to notice of the hearing, and the board's decision did not violate due process. (*Bates v Baltimore & Ohio R.R. Co.*, CA-7, 126 LC Sect. 10, 898)

Mandatory Dispute Arbitration

A railroad employer's alleged failure to maintain a nonhostile workplace free of sexual harassment of its employees involved a minor dispute subject to the mandatory arbitration procedures of the Railway Labor Act. Therefore, an employee's claim under the Civil Rights Act, Title VII, was properly dismissed by a federal district court. The RLA's arbitration provisions were required to be liberally construed, and Section 118 of the Civil Rights Act encourages the use of "alternative means of dispute resolution," including arbitration. (*Hirras v National Railroad Passenger Corp. d.b.a. Amtrak*, CA-5 127 LC Sect. 10, 966)

Fair Representation Duty

A union's decision not to extend an agreement with an employer was not arbitrary, discriminatory, or capricious and did not render the union liable for damages in a lawsuit alleging breach of its fair representation duty. The agreement, which bridged the gap between an expiring contract and ratification of a new bargaining contract, was not extended by the union after it expired. The employees' evidence did not raise a genuine issue of material fact as to whether the union's opposition to the employer's proposal to extend the bridge agreement fell outside the wide range of reasonableness in which the union's conduct was required to fall. (*Griffin v Air Line Pilots Assn.*, DC Ill, 126 LC Sect. 10, 913)

Public Board's Discharge Ruling Upheld

A ruling of a public law board that an employee was lawfully discharged was proper, not wholly baseless or completely without reason so as to permit a federal district court to overturn it. The discharge decision was based on a reasonable interpretation of the evidence presented to the board, was not in reprisal for union activities, and followed applicable law under the Railway Labor Act. (*Ruck v Atchison, Topeka and Santa Fe R.R.*, DC Tex, 126 LC Sect 10, 823)

Lack of Preclusive Effect

Determinations made under arbitration mandated by the Railway Labor Act should not be given preclusive effect in a separate action under the Federal Employer's Liability Act. A public law board had arbitrated the propriety of a railroad employee's discharge under the RLA, but in the subsequent FELA action, a jury had returned a verdict in the employee's favor and against the railroad for the employee's personal injuries sustained on the job. Arbitration proceedings did not sufficiently protect the employee's rights under the FELA. Moreover, Congress did not intend to subordinate rights created by the FELA to the restrictions of the RLA. (*Kulavic v Chicago & Illinois Midland Ry. Co.*, CA-7, 125 LC Sect. 10, 783)

National Mediation Board Procedures

Procedures adopted by the National Mediation Board that permitted merged railroad carriers to request the board to conduct an investigation to determine the postmerger representative of employees for collective bargaining purposes were upheld. The Railway Labor Act did not expressly prohibit carriers from requesting a representation investigation. Moreover, the court had no authority to infer a requirement that only employees or representatives may request an investigation. (*Railway Labor Executives' Assn. v National Mediation Board*, DC DofC, 122 LC Sect. 10, 322)

Employment at Will

There was nothing in an employer's rules and regulations indicating a waiver of the employer's right to terminate management employees with or without cause. Moreover, the employee's employment application expressly stated that employment was terminable at will. (*Crum v American Airlines, Inc.*, CA-5, 121 LC Sect. 56, 794)

National Mediation Board as Sole Authority

A federal district court lacked the authority to review a decision of the National Mediation Board in a dispute between a union and a railway carrier. The board correctly determined that the matter before it was a representation dispute over which the NMB had exclusive jurisdiction. (*Brotherhood of Maintenance of Way Employees v Grank Trunk Western Railroad Co.*, CA-6, 121 LC Sect. 10, 166)

Lump-Sum Severance Offer

An arbitrator exceeded his authority in requiring a railroad to show express or implied authority to make a unilateral lump-sum severance offer to certain employees. The arbitrator was required to consider existing common law of the railroad industry, in which railway arbitration awards held that unless a contractual prohibition precludes a carrier from taking a disputed action, there is no authority to find for a union. (*Richmond, Fredricksburg & Potomac R.R. Co. v Trans-*

portation Communications Union, DC Va, 122 LC Sect. 10, 206)

Merger Implementation Agreement

A union did not act in bad faith when it entered into a railroad merger implementation agreement without consulting union members. The agreement consolidated seniority rights on the basis of work equity allocations. In the absence of factual support, a member's allegation that the union contorted the constitution and bylaws was without merit. Interpretation of the relevant constitutional provisions was wholly consistent with the union's prior practice. (*Smith v General Committee of Adjustment of Union Pacific Eastern Region*, DC Mo, 122 LC Sect. 10, 219)

System Board of Adjustment's Authority

A system board of adjustment exceeded its authority in resolving a dispute between an employer and a union concerning the recall rights of former airline strikers. The board drew conclusions regarding the purpose of a paragraph of the collective bargaining agreement and the employer's attitude toward the union. It then used its conclusions to determine that the paragraph violated the Railway Labor Act. (*Machinists v Alaska Airlines, Inc.*, DC Wash, 121 LC Sect. 10, 122)

Federal Preemption

A discharged railroad employee was not allowed to amend his complaint against a railroad employer to avoid preemption by the Railway Labor Act. When a complaint, as amended, would be subject to dismissal, leave to amend need not be granted. Since the employee's libel claim, arising out of a letter written to him by a railroad superintendent, was inextricably intertwined with the grievance procedures of the collective bargaining agreement, preemption was required. (*Fox v Southern Railway Co.*, DC Ga, 121 LC Sect. 10, 112)

Health Plan Changes

Implementation of recommended changes in a railroad's health and welfare plan, under the terms of collective bargaining agreements with a union, was a minor dispute within the exclusive jurisdiction of the National Railroad Adjustment Board. (*Consolidated Rail Corp. v Maintenance of Way Employees*, DC Pa, 121 LC Sect 10, 163)

Coalition Bargaining

A railroad union's bargaining with other unions as a **coalition** and its conditioning of ultimate approval of a collective bargaining agreement on the approval of all the unions was not evidence of bad-faith negotiating. (*Grand Trunk Western R.R. Co. v Sheet Metal Workers*, DC Mich, 121 LC Sect. 10, 044)

Injunction Denied

Union and nonunion airline pilots were denied a preliminary injunction seeking to enjoin a union from implementing an agency-shop agreement entered into by the union without membership ratification. The pilots failed to demonstrate a substantial likelihood of success on the merits of their case or irreparable harm if the injunction was not granted. Moreover, the equities were more in favor of the union. (*Miller v Air Line Pilots Assn., International*, DC DofC, 120 LC Sect. 11, 084)

Retroactivity of Award

Subsequent to issuing a final decision, an arbitrator had jurisdiction to rule on the retroactivity of an award. The parties clearly contemplated raising the issue of retroactivity before the arbitrator; the parties acknowledged that the arbitrator had reserved jurisdiction for the purpose of correcting the effective date of the award; and the arbitrator had the authority under the parties' bargaining agreement to resolve any ambiguity in the contract language. (*Air Line Pilots v Aviation Assn., Inc., d.b.a. Sunaire Express*, CA-120 LC Sect. 11, 095)

10

The View of the Unions

Introduction

The air transport sector has passed through a crucial period of post-deregulation adjustments. One of those adjustments occurred in the relationship between management and the unions that represent the bulk of the industry's employees. One common view of this adjustment maintains that unions are "losers" in this post-deregulation period: "The common wisdom in the U.S. airline industry is that labor unions are the biggest losers from deregulation and the dash into consolidation. Certainly there is plenty of evidence for this view. Deregulation spawned split wage scales, futile strikes at United and Pan American, Chapter 11 bankruptcies, and the emergence of a handful of super-carriers which, on the surface at least, handed management oligopolistic bargaining powers."[1]

This view of how unions have weathered the storm of deregulation is certainly negative. Is it well founded? More important, is it a view shared by the airlines' unions? These questions suggested the direction for a survey questionnaire of union views sent to the air transport unions in late 1991. This chapter reports the results of that survey and provides a subsequent analysis of the direction unions are expected to take in the 1990s. The survey was designed to elicit the union view of the impact of deregulation on their present membership levels and contractual status. It also requested their views of future collective bargaining issues.

Unions since Deregulation

The air transport sector has gone through four basic stages in the deregulation era: expansion, consolidation, concentration, and globalization.

In addition, a new wave of change is emerging. Employee and union equity position in the carrier is gaining popularity as management seeks to control costs in the face of massive losses and unions seek a say in determining the future direction of carrier operations. Trans World Airlines, Northwest Airlines, and Continental Air Lines have given substantial equity positions to their unions in return for equally substantial reductions in labor costs and more flexible work rules. In 1994 after years of attempts by the machinists and pilots to take control of United Air Lines, in a concession-for-equity swap the nation's largest carrier became employee controlled. This takeover, the most recent airline metamorphosis, is the largest employee takeover in U.S. corporate history. The new unionism appears to be directed at participation as opposed to contention. The most interesting aspect of union equity stakes is the impact these ownership positions will have on the collective bargaining process. Each of the four stages have had a different type of impact on the labor unions.

In the expansion phase, for example, many "new entrant" airlines were added to the U.S. system. Because most were initially nonunion carriers and thus operated at a lower unit cost, their ability to provide comparable service at a lower passenger price forced the incumbent carriers to follow suit by matching price and bringing their cost structures under control. This increase in competition and cost cutting pressured airline unions into agreements to reduce wages, benefit levels, and work rules. James Nammack has warned of the affect such an atmosphere may have on the airline industry:

While the average employee wage plus benefits nearly doubled from 1975 to $39,373 in 1982, and now averages $42,000 according to the Air Transport Association, the average wage/benefit package among the new and largely non-unionized carriers is valued at an estimated $22,000 per year. As these new carriers begin larger scale operations, it is clear that the existing carriers will have to adapt to the new cost structures against which they must compete. Unless the larger airlines change their pricing policies to reflect more specifically the cost and demand characteristics of each of their markets, they are going to attract new entry on a great scale.[2]

During the consolidation phase, as airlines moved to improve their balance sheets and reduce threats of competition, mergers and acquisitions became the norm. In 1986 alone, twenty-five airlines were involved in some form of consolidation movement. Union membership either remained constant or decreased depending on the union membership status of the surviving carrier. In most cases in which the surviving carrier was unionized prior to merger, the absorbed employee groups remained unionized, though the union representing them may have changed. If the absorbing carrier was nonunionized, the status of union or nonunion representation depended on the craft or class involved and on which carrier had the largest number of either unionized or nonunionized employees in that craft or class at the time of the merger.

Exclusive of the final union/nonunion outcome of mergers, many contract provisions were either amalgamated with surviving unions or ceased to exist. During this consolidation phase, forty-four contracts were eliminated. Airlines that lost contracts to merger after 1984 were Air California (3 contracts), Air Florida (3), Capitol (4), Flying Tiger (5), Frontier (5), Ozark (5), Piedmont (4), Pacific Southwest (5), Republic (5), and Western (5).

From the beginning of the consolidation phase in late 1985 until 1990, the number of airline industry employees grew 43 percent, to 506,728 (see table 10-1). The result has been the concentration of more airline business among fewer airlines. This unprecedented concentration has increased not only nonunion employee classifications but also the ranks of the airline unions holding contracts with the surviving, growing carriers.

Finally, the globalization phase gives both airlines and airline unions a further opportunity to increase their numbers. Generally, international travel has grown at a faster rate than domestic traffic. Consequently, for some air carriers with the correct fleet mix, there will be more international service and growth in employment to support this service.

Table 10-1

Airline Industry Employment since 1978

Annual Employment Figures

Craft/Class	1979	1985	1989
Pilots/Co-Pilots	29,936	32,960	43,671
Other Flight Personnel	7,141	7,193	8,070
Flight Attendants	52,694	63,496	77,771
Mechanics	44,801	42,781	57,282
Aircraft and Traffic Service	97,953	100,875	225,166
Office Employees	71,374	75,839	42,717
All Other Employees	36,797	31,969	52,051
Total	340,696	151,113	506,728

Source: Data from Air Transport Association of America (1990).

The deregulation period has been a time of traumatic and fundamental changes. Once relatively stable labor relationships have given way to more aggressive and interactive negotiations. The future appears bright for the airlines, who have been able to negotiate uncharted waters and adapt to a variety of heretofore unknown variables. Labor, however, has suffered extremely difficult adjustments and has gained a new awareness of the impact they have on the airlines and their union members, both positive and negative.

Early on, the proponents of deregulation stated that there would only be a handful of survivors when the deregulation dust had cleared and settled. They maintained that to be one of these survivors, extreme measures might have to be taken, but that in the final analysis, the rewards would be worth the sacrifice. In retrospect, that vision has come true. Airline after airline has moved to secure its own survival. Many airlines have died in the attempt. In this quest, management has subscribed to the philosophy of the legendary coach of the Green Bay Packers, Vince Lombardi, that "Winning isn't everything. It's the only thing." But what do the airline unions think of these events? A survey of the airline unions listed in table 10-2 explores these issues.

Table 10-2
Surveyed Airline Unions

AFA	Association of Flight Attendants
APFA	Association of Professional Flight Attendants
ALPA	Airline Pilots Association
APA	Allied Pilots Association
ATDA	Air Transport Dispatchers Association
FEIA	Flight Engineers International Association
IAM	International Association of Machinists
IBT	International Brotherhood of Teamsters
IFFA	Independent Federation of Flight Attendants
PAFCA	Professional Airline Flight Controllers
ROPA	Ramp Operations Provisioning Association
SAEA	Southwest Airline Employee Association
TWU	Transport Workers Union
UFA	Union of Flight Attendants

Results of a Survey of Airline Unions

An analysis of the results of a survey questionnaire sent to airline unions in late 1991 found that 164,652 airline employees were represented in the survey, representing 32.5 percent of all U.S. scheduled airline employees in 1989. More importantly, in comparing unionized employees, this figure represented 55.8 percent of all unionized airline employees and 72.5 percent of the

Table 10-3
Unionized Airline Employees by Craft and Class

Classification	Employees in Unions			Total Surveyed	Total Responses
	1979	1985	1989		
Mechanic	44,801	42,781	57,282		
A/C Services Personnel	97,953	100,875	225,166		
Total	142,754	143,656	282,448	136,364	90, 000
Captain & First Officers	29,936	32,960	43,671		
Other Flight Personnel	7,141	7,193	8,070		
Total	37, 077	40,153	51,741	47,151	41,652
Flight Attendants	52,694	63,496	77,771	43,421	33,000
Grand Total	232,525	247,305	411,960	226,936	164,652
Surveyed as % of total 1989 union workforce				55.1%	39.9%
Response of total surveyed					72.6%

Sources: Air Transport Association of America and Future Aviation Professionals of America

craft and class to which the respondents belonged (i.e., pilots, flight attendants, and mechanics and related employees). Furthermore, 50 of 59 contracts in these crafts and classes were represented in this survey, or 84.7 percent of the available contracts at the major and national airlines at the time of the survey (see table 10-3).[3]

Questions four, five, and six of the survey gave each organization an opportunity to quantify and qualify the change in its membership over the past eleven years. Of the five unions surveyed, three showed increases in membership between 1979 and 1989, and two reported losses. The net gain in membership for the period was 23,852 (see table 10-4).

Table 10-4

Union Membership in 1979 and 1989 and Net Gains/Losses

Union	Membership		Net Gain/Loss
	1979	1989	
IAM	70,000	90,000	+20,000
ALPA	40,000	41,000	+1,000
AFA	21,000	25,000	+4,000
IFFA	9,000	8,000	-1,000
FEIA	800	652	-148

According to table 10-5, the airline unions largely attributed these increases in membership to the initiative of the individual unions in their quest to "organize the unorganized" in the industry (particularly passenger service agents). The International Association of Machinists also found that increased numbers of aircraft in the system after the spring of 1988 forced various airlines to hire additional personnel. These people were targeted by the union in their organizing efforts. On the down side, all the unions surveyed indicated that they thought consolidation in the industry had a major negative affect on their membership numbers. Even those who gained members over the last ten years felt they would have gained many more had it not been for the tumultuous climate of the airline industry.

A further survey question addressed these negative aspects a little more directly. The unions were asked to choose from among the following the post-deregulation development in the airline industry that they thought had the most negative impact on their organization:

1. Individual airline bankruptcies
2. Airline consolidations and mergers
3. Hub-and-spoke airline operations

Table 10-5

Reasons Reported for Changes in Union Membership

Union	Reported Reason
IAM	Organizing the unorganized within crafts and class, airlines' acquisition of aircraft in 1988
ALPA	Little change, lost to business tactics, gained through aggressive organizing effort
AFA	Organizing effort offset by loss to mergers and bankruptcies
IFFA	Hiring of replacements during strike
FEIA	Pan American Airways business problems, downsizing, no domestic routes

Table 10-6

Ranking of Negative Impact of Deregulation Activities on Unions

Activity	Ranking of Negative Impact from Most Negative (l) to Least Negative (4)				
	IAM	ALPA	AFA	IFFA	FEIA
Management's Change in Attitude	1	3	1	1	*
Individual Airline Bankruptcies	4	2	2	*	2
Airline Consolidations/Mergers	2	1	3	*	*
Hub-and-Spoke Operations	3	4	*	*	*

* Not rated or no answer

4. Changes in attitudes toward collective bargaining organizations by airline managements

The last of these developments was chosen by three of the five organizations as the primary factor for negative unionism. Table 10-6 gives each organization's ranking of the negative impact of each development.

Although the unions' further rankings were sprinkled randomly among the remaining three developments and among possibilities other than those listed, the second most damaging development cited was individual airline bankruptcies. One very interesting write-in response was offered by the Independent Federation of Flight Attendants. They ranked the following as number three: "[Professional Air Traffic Controller's strike and government reaction to it] made it 'okay' to aggressively replace the general workforce." This response illustrates a climate that is not conducive to labor's trust in management or government.

The unions were then asked to rank the same developments listed in table 10-6 according to how much they positively affected their collective bargaining organization. The responses to this question seem to shed the most light on the unions' feelings toward deregulation. All unions surveyed except one felt that there were no positive affects on their collective bargaining unit due to deregulation. The Association of Flight Attendants, however, felt that management had

learned a valuable lesson in "yield management and rational route systems" as opposed to "cutthroat fare competition."

Table 10-7 shows the respondent's views of the positive and negative effects of airline consolidation (or mergers) on their respective airline unions. The positive effects seem to center around the need for survival. Each union also felt this need for survival during the consolidation phase. The threat of extinction frightened most organizations, and any type of stability in unstable times is usually perceived as "good." The Air Line Pilots Association stated this clearly in their response: "... our members who were working for financially unstable carriers, were merged with strong, viable carriers."

Although the bargaining units may have had difficulty in stating the positive side of consolidation, they were not at a loss for the negative. The unions have been left with an unstable environment in which to maneuver. Consolidation brought with it loss of membership (through layoffs and to other unions), loss of bargaining power, and increased stress in meshing differing workforces.

Table 10-8 presents positive aspects of joining each of the unions surveyed, from the point of view of each organization. The view of the International Association of Machinists seems very global in nature—they are large and powerful, they "set the pace" in airline collective bargain-

Table 10-7
Impact of Airline Consolidation According to Unions

Union	Positive Impact	Negative Impact
IAM	New aircraft, more mechanics and service personnel	Merger and acquisitions made negotiations difficult
ALPA	Merger and acquisitions helped airline stability	Dual scale representation
AFA	Mergers brought larger bargaining units	Merging those workforces
IFFA	New policies on seniority list integration	Loss of bargaining units to other airlines
FEIA	None	None

ing, and they offer many services. The other four unions refer to offering help in making the worker's voice heard by the airline's management.

The Air Line Pilots Association in particular takes an "us against them" perspective with management, the Federal Aviation Administration, and Congress. The Air Line Pilots Association also flexes it financial muscle by bragging about its "budget" and its "war chest." The Association of Flight Attendants takes a support position for their membership. Pay and work rules seem to be paramount in their attraction to flight attendants. The Independent Federation of Flight Attendants also takes a support position for their

perspective members. They sell their organization as a way for their members to find increased satisfaction within their jobs. The strategy of the Flight Engineers International Association revolves around their small size, which they say helps them to represent each member better.

Finally, the respondents were asked to identify the three most important collective bargaining issues facing their organization over the next year (see table 10-9). The most prevalent issue in the responses was the phenomena that has developed out of management's need to decrease labor costs to remain economically viable: the two-tier wage scale, or the B scale. Next in importance, because of the consolidations that have resulted

Table 10-8

Positive Aspects of Union Membership According to Unions

Union	Positive Aspects
IAM	Democratic organization Largest and number-one union in the industry Representatives came up through the ranks Services that are provided to members IAM sets the pace in collective bargaining
ALPA	Working under a contract; guaranteed rights and benefits Forty thousand strong, resources (air safety budget, Political Action Committee Fund, accident investigation) ALPA representation against Federal Aviation Administration's enforcement actions Voice on Capitol Hill Flight time/duty time rules "War chest" of millions of dollars to fight abusive management
AFA	Contract protects against arbitrary management Gives employee a legal voice with management Works to protect employee rights Lobbies for employee interests in Congress and with Federal Aviation Administration Services provided include: Employee Assistance Program, support after accidents, advice on health benefit and retirement issues, and newsletters/magazines to keep employees informed
IFFA	Impossible to have individual voice heard except through the union Career, wage, and ultimate retirement benefits are all enhanced Camaraderie gained from joint action in common cause Provides increased awareness of health, safety, and other job aspects Satisfaction of being a part of a movement that effects constructive changes and social and economic progress
FEIA	Small organization can represent each member better Management respects FEIA

from deregulation, is the need to bargain for labor protective provisions. The unions in general seem to feel that it is time to take a firm stand against further contract concessions. The unions' attitude has become "we've given enough; now it's your turn."

Summary

Airline unions have weathered more than a decade of post-deregulation changes in the industry. As a result of the recent growth in the size of the airline community, some airline unions not only have survived deregulation but have grown and continue to do so. These organizations represent a significant segment of the industry's employees, the number of which appears to be steady and unthreatened.

To maintain this high level of success, airline unions will be forced to follow the trends of the industry. Aviation has begun the movement toward globalization. Worldwide markets will create new stateside opportunities for growth in airline union membership. Whether or not this growth will become a reality depends on the airline union's ability to adapt to new bargaining environments.

Through investigation, this research determined that between 58.2 and 60 percent of all U.S. scheduled airline employees belonged to a union in 1989. With the Federal Aviation Administration forecasting an annual growth rate of 4.2 percent in the domestic airline industry through 2001, what can the future of the union members be? The answer to that question lies in the hands of the unions themselves. The prosperity of their carriers and the perpetuity of their contracts under the Railway Labor Act indicates that they will partake in any growth numberwise. But only through continued struggle and good-faith bargaining can airline unions achieve higher levels of prosperity for their current and future members.

The unions' ability to wrestle nonunion members away from their status quo may rest on their ability to forge a leadership role in the coming years of negotiations. Unlike their counterparts in other industries, their role is assured. Because of the peculiar labor laws affecting this industry, they are an integral part of the operation of any airline with which they are associated, and like it or not, they must assume a quasi-managerial attitude toward their own particular organization and that of the carrier that harbors them.

Despite the clear case that can be made for union stability in the airline industry, times remain stressful for airline employees. Rank-and-file workers need no reminder that they have borne the brunt of the deregulated environment. Expectedly, airline management lays the bulk of the industry's problems at the feet of their unions, citing high wage rates and arcane work rules as the largest obstacles to future growth and profitability. To sidestep these issues, management

Table 10-9
Three Most Important Bargaining Issues According to Unions

Union	First Bargaining Issue	Second Bargaining Issue	Third Bargaining Issue
IAM	Concession free	Two-tier wages	Labor protective provisions
ALPA	Two-tier wages	Industry-wide standard contracts	Labor protective provisions
AFA	Negotiate ten new contracts	Avoid concessions in sound airlines	None
IFFA	Work rules	Retirement benefits	Reinstate wage losses
FEIA	Two-tier wages	Pay decreases (avoid concessions)	Small union

has been using a variety of measures. Most significant have been attempts by airlines flying international routes to use overseas employees, who garner lower wage rates, and efforts by domestic carriers to **contract out** (or farm out) a plethora of services generally provided by existing member unions.

In labor relations, any schooled negotiator will tell you that a quid pro quo exists for every agreement. When one concession is given, there is generally a like gain for the opposing side. It may not be immediate or obvious, but it is nevertheless present.

In the battle for the airlines, labor has been the giver, and management has been an ungrateful benefactor. This one-sidedness has amalgamated the unions' position to seek and receive their quid pro quo for past concessions and for the erosion of their bargaining power. The unions' response is that they are now trading concessions for increased participation in the business. This accomplishment takes the form of ownership, board representation, and direct scrutiny of management's actions and decision-making process. Labor's response to the first four phases of deregulation is characterized not by a refusal to accept change but by a new approach to survival and adaptation— "Buy the suckers out." This approach defines the new and continuing fifth stage of deregulation, union equity.

The phenomena of union representation on a company's board of directors is not a new concept. In 1980, for example, the head of the United Auto Workers gained a seat on the Chrysler Corporation board after the company's near bankruptcy and subsequent government bailout. Although union representation on the board of directors was rather prodigious among the railroads in the 1920s, the representation on Chrysler's board was the first important instance in America since that time. Douglas Fraser, the appointed union official, claimed that his influence helped to sensitize the board to the effects of job loss and increased their willingness to look at alternative strategic options.[4]

The airline industry began its venture into board representation in 1982, when Pan American Airways appointed a pilot to its board and Eastern and Western Airlines followed suit. At Eastern, union representation totaled four members, one for each major union on the property. The Eastern situation, although ultimately ineffective, was a first for the industry, because labor unions formed direct relationships with banks and financial institutions to bring direct pressure on management. In return for concessions, workers received 25 percent of the carrier's common stock. Whether these fledgling partnership arrangements had a foundation in success remains questionable. Of the test cases at Eastern, Western, and Pan American, all have failed to bring the airlines back from the brink of insolvency.

Despite these failures, the fifth wave of deregulation has begun in the industry. Nurtured by lack of profitability, exceedingly unusual circumstances, and long-standing and, according to some, antiquated labor laws, the balance of power in the negotiating process has shifted to the labor side. With labor having more power than usual and the airlines weak, the range of union action is extending to new horizons.

Traditionally, labor and management, though sometimes skeptical of each other's motives, have worked together on substantive issues involving terms and conditions of employment. Occasionally, this cooperation has been taken to such an extent that labor has become involved in supervisory techniques and marketing goals. But it has been uncommon for unions to work on the strategic organizational plans and objectives. Their doing so will create new challenges and opportunities. A paramount question remains. Can such a relationship work to change the fundamental characteristics of a relationship that is adversarial both by its nature and in the scope of labor law?

In the new wave of deregulation, the unions have elected to flex their muscles by becoming steadfastly more and more involved in the managerial aspects of their carriers. Trans World Airlines and Northwest Airlines provide the most tangible examples of labors new influence, having sold 45 percent of their respective equity to employees in exchange for concessions, and having agreed to sell an additional 30 percent. On the heels of these agreements, United Air Lines has sought union concessions to facilitate the development of a new, low-cost carrier (under the so-called U2 agreement), offering in return a significant level of employee ownership arrangements.

A perplexing issue in these employee ownership arrangements is intent. We can be sure that job security and perpetuation of the union is foremost in the minds of those negotiating the union positions. But what is the responsibility of the ownership side to itself and to other shareholders and stakeholders?

In an article written in 1993, the unions at Trans World Airlines and Northwest Airlines insisted that they did not want day-to-day control of the airlines. The Air Line Pilots Association said it is trying to protect its members' interests. The president of the International Association of Machinists and Aerospace Workers, John Peterpaul, who represents the machinists, said, "Deep down we don't want to own any airline, or part of any airline."[5]

In that same article, Bill Compton, the Trans World Airlines pilot now on that airline's board of directors, said that "participatory management is the key to restoring the carrier's health."[6] But of what importance is the health of the carrier to the employees in general, to the stockholders and stakeholders, or simply to the union? Some insight to that question may come from an article published in November 1993 in which Captain Compton discusses the future of Trans World Airlines, the employees' new management, and the changes necessary for the airline to survive. In response to a question addressing the fact that the pay at Trans World Airlines was among the lowest in the industry, Compton stated: "We're about 40 percent lower than the industry.

But we're to get a 5% raise in September 1994." Compton forecasted that if Trans World Airlines made a good recovery, the pilots would get back to top industry wage standards quickly.[7]

Whether this new wave of deregulation is totally self-serving or is designed for the betterment of all remains to be seen. The overall fifth-wave approach was best summed up by Captain Randolph Babbitt, the head of the powerful Air Line Pilots Association, in a February 1994 interview in *Air Line Pilot Magazine.* In response to the question "What response would you give to those who believe unions should not be managing companies, but rather should be looking out only for employee interests?" Babbitt replied:

> They certainly have a point. But a well-run ESOP puts management, other than a union, in place. Remember that in an ESOP a number of unions can be involved; the United Airlines effort, for example, involves several unions. These unions are not going to be the board; they will have seats on the 12 to 15 member board. The unions will have something to say about management decisions, but union members will still be employees. The big difference is that employees accept more risk and more responsibility to be efficient. Employees want to do the best job and work at 100 percent. If you are working at a company that is privately owned and it topples, it's because ballast is lost through poor management decisions. In an ESOP, there is tremendous incentive to work together. Management and employees together make up the ballast. If that kind of thinking troubles some people, then maybe their thinking is antiquated.[8]

Labor-management cooperation at the top levels presents a catch-22 for unions. The labor relations order is structured, by law and tradition, as a contest of power between organizations; cooperation comes from equilibrium in the struggle. Because unions have generally lost power in recent years, there are few opportunities for them to establish cooperation on favorable terms. And—here is the catch—attempts to recoup strength by establishing top-level partnerships only further undermine labor's long-run support, because they make unions appear distant from their members and cut off from outside groups. The more unions pursue power, which is the basis for cooperation in the present order, the more they lose legitimacy and influence.[9]

Successful examples of partnership have paradoxically revealed an underlying weakness of labor relations that are conceived as a balance of power. Such systems have gone beyond their base of legitimacy, and the farther unions go on that road, the weaker they become. If there is a way out of the present crisis, it will have to involve something more different in substance from the strategies of the past.[10] To paraphrase George Santayana, the Spanish-born U.S. philosopher and poet, those who fail to read their history are doomed to repeat it. It is hoped that the people in charge of the recent rounds of concessionary-equity talks remember the past. If history is a guide, airlines who have sought concessions from their employees have fewer chances of survival; Continental is the only survivor of the first wave of concession seekers.

The developments at United Air Lines in the early 1990s are remarkable in several ways and at the same time exhibit much of the same old approach. Though management and unions have traded concessions for equity at Northwest and Trans World Airlines, they did so under the threat of extinction or creditor foreclosure. At United, the unions have been seeking ownership for several years without the immediate threat of impending doom over their heads. Their success quite possibly marks a differential from past employee buyout attempts. But it is not without some of the same old bugaboos.

As secure as United may be, with a reported cash reserve of $1.9 billion, the airline is aware of a predator of a different color, Southwest Airlines. Because of Southwest's recent venture into United's markets and because of United's exposure to Southwest at San Francisco and Los Angeles, a battle looms between the low-cost profitable carrier and the megacarrier highly vulnerable to fare wars. According to most analysts, United cannot win such an encounter, because Southwest's lower costs and labor productivity enable it to charge a minimum of 25 percent less than United and still reap a profit.

In a newspaper article in 1993, Rankesh Gangwal, United's senior vice president of planning, is quoted as saying of their competition with Southwest: "It is like a cancer eating you up. If we cannot fix our domestic business, we will go the way of Pan Am and Eastern."[11] In this context, maybe the United situation is no different from the situations at Pan Am, Eastern, or any of the other airlines in equity talks with their unions. In Margaret Mitchell's classic book *Gone with the Wind*, Scarlett O'Hara took over a devastated business and appropriately named it the Caveat Emporium. The unions of United may want to remember the outcome of Scarlett's venture and the principle of caveat emptor.

Appendix
Notes
Glossary
Name Index
Subject Index

Appendix: The Railway Labor Act

TITLE 45. RAILROADS
CHAPTER 8. RAILWAY LABOR
GENERAL PROVISIONS
45 USCS @ 151 (1993)

@ 151. Definitions; short title

When used in this Act and for the purposes of this Act—

First. The term "carrier" includes any express company, sleeping-car company, carrier by railroad, subject to the Interstate Commerce Act, and any company which is directly or indirectly owned or controlled by or under common control with any carrier by railroad and which operates any equipment or facilities or performs any service (other than trucking service) in connection with the transportation, receipt, delivery, elevation, transfer in transit, refrigeration or icing, storage, and handling of property transported by railroad, and any receiver, trustee, or other individual or body, judicial or otherwise, when in the possession of the business of any such "carrier": Provided, however, That the term "carrier" shall not include any street, interurban, or suburban electric railway, unless such railway is operating as a part of a general steam-railroad system of transportation, but shall not exclude any part of the general steam-railroad system of transportation now or hereafter operated by any other motive power. The Interstate Commerce Commission is hereby authorized and directed upon request of the Mediation Board or upon complaint of any party interested to determine after hearing whether any line operated by electric power falls within the terms of this proviso. The term "carrier" shall not include any company by reason of its being engaged in the mining of coal, the supplying of coal to a carrier where delivery is not beyond the mine tipple, and the operation of equipment or facilities therefor, or in any of such activities.

Second. The term "Adjustment Board" means the National Railroad Adjustment Board created by this Act.

Third. The term "Mediation Board" means the National Mediation Board created by this Act.

Fourth. The term "commerce" means commerce among the several States or between any State, Territory, or the District of Columbia and any foreign nation, or between any Territory or the District of Columbia and any State, or between any Territory and any other Territory, or between any Territory and the District of Columbia, or within any Territory or the District of Columbia, or between points in the same State but through any other State or any Territory or the District of Columbia or any foreign nation.

Fifth. The term "employee" as used herein includes every person in the service of a carrier (subject to its continuing authority to supervise and direct the manner of rendition of his service) who performs any work defined as that of an employee or subordinate official in the orders of the Interstate Commerce Commission now in effect, and as the same may be amended or interpreted by orders hereafter entered by the Commission pursuant to the authority which is hereby conferred upon it to enter orders amending or interpreting such existing orders: Provided, however, That no occupational classification made by order of the Interstate Commerce Commission shall be construed to define the crafts according to which railway employees may be organized by their voluntary action, nor shall the jurisdiction or powers of such employee organizations be regarded as in any way limited or defined by the provisions of this Act or by the orders of the Commission.

The term "employee" shall not include any individual while such individual is engaged in the physical operations consisting of the mining of coal, the preparation of coal, the handling (other than movement by rail with standard railroad locomotives) of coal not beyond the mine tipple, or the loading of coal at the tipple.

Sixth. The term "representative" means any person or persons, labor union, organization, or corporation designated either by a carrier or group of carriers or by its or their employees, to act for it or them.

Seventh. The term "district court" includes the Supreme Court of the District of Columbia [United States District Court for the District of Columbia]; and the term "circuit court of appeals [court of appeals]" includes the Court of Appeals of the District of Columbia [United States Court of Appeals for the District of Columbia].

This Act may be cited as the "Railway Labor Act."

TITLE 45. RAILROADS
CHAPTER 8. RAILWAY LABOR
GENERAL PROVISIONS
45 USCS @ 151a (1993)

@ 151a. General purposes

The purposes of the Act are: (1) To avoid any interruption to commerce or to the operation of any carrier engaged therein; (2) to forbid any limitation upon freedom of association among employees or any denial as a condition of employment or otherwise, of the right of employees to join a labor organization; (3) to provide for the complete independence of carriers and of employees in the matter of self-organization to carry out the purposes of this Act; (4) to provide for the prompt and orderly settlement of all disputes concerning rates of pay, rules, or working conditions; (5) to provide for the prompt and orderly settlement of all disputes growing out of grievances or out of the interpretation or application of agreements covering rates of pay, rules, or working conditions.

TITLE 45. RAILROADS
CHAPTER 8. RAILWAY LABOR
GENERAL PROVISIONS
45 USCS @ 152 (1993)

@ 152. General duties

First. Duty of carriers and employees to settle disputes. It shall be the duty of all carriers, their officers, agents, and employees to exert every reasonable effort to make and maintain agreements concerning rates of pay, rules, and working conditions, and to settle all disputes, whether arising out of the application of such agreements or otherwise, in order to avoid any interruption to commerce or to the operation of any carrier growing out of any dispute between the carrier and the employees thereof.

Second. Consideration of disputes by representatives. All disputes between a carrier or carriers and its or their employees shall be considered, and, if possible, decided, with all expedition, in conference between representatives designated and authorized so to confer, respectively, by the carrier or carriers and by the employees thereof interested in the dispute.

Third. Designation of representatives. Representatives, for the purposes of this Act shall be designated by the respective parties without interference, influence, or coercion by either party over the designation of representatives by the other; and neither party shall in any way interfere with, influence, or coerce the other in its choice of representatives. Representatives of employees for the purposes of this Act need not be persons in the employ of the carrier, and no carrier shall, by interference, influence, or coercion seek in any manner to prevent the designation by its employees as their representatives of those who or which are not employees of the carrier.

Fourth. Organization and collective bargaining; freedom from interference by carrier; assistance in organizing or maintaining organization by carrier forbidden; deduction of dues from wages forbidden. Employees shall have the right to organize and bargain collectively through representatives of their own choosing. The majority of any craft or class of employees shall have the right to determine who shall be the representative of the craft or class for the purposes of this Act. No carrier, its officers or agents, shall deny or in any way question the right of its employees to join, organize, or assist in organizing the labor organization of their choice, and it shall be unlawful for any carrier to interfere in any way with the organization of its employees, or to use the funds of the carrier in maintaining or assisting or contributing to any labor organization, labor representative, or other agency of collective bargaining, or in performing any work therefor, or to influence or coerce employees in an effort to induce them to join or remain or not to join or remain members of any labor organization, or to deduct from the wages of employees any dues, fees, assessments, or other contributions payable to labor organizations, or to collect or to assist in the collection of any such dues, fees, assessments, or other contributions: Provided, That nothing in this Act shall be construed to prohibit a carrier from permitting an employee, individually, or local representatives of employees from conferring with management during working hours without loss of time, or to prohibit a carrier from furnishing free transportation to its employees while engaged in the business of a labor organization.

Fifth. Agreements to join or not to join labor organizations forbidden. No carrier, its officers, or agents shall require any person seeking employment to sign any contract or agreement promising to join or not to join a labor organization; and if any such contract has been enforced prior to the effective date of this Act [enacted May 20, 1926], then such carrier shall notify the employees by an appropriate order that such contract has been discarded and is no longer binding on them in any way.

Sixth. Conference of representatives; time; place; private agreements. In case of a dispute between a carrier or carriers and its or their employees, arising out of grievances or out of the interpretation or application of agreements concerning rates of pay, rules, or working conditions, it shall be the duty of the designated representative or representatives of such carrier or carriers and of such employees, within ten days after the receipt of notice of a desire on the part of either party to confer in respect to such dispute, to specify a time and place at which such conference shall be held: Provided, (1) That the place so specified shall be situated upon the line of the carrier involved or as otherwise mutually agreed upon; and (2) that the time so specified shall allow the designated conferees reasonable opportunity to reach such place of conference, but shall not exceed twenty days from the receipt of such notice: And provided further, That nothing in this Act shall be construed to supersede the provisions of any agreement (as to conferences) then in effect between the parties.

Seventh. Change in pay, rules or working conditions contrary to agreement or to section 156

forbidden. No carrier, its officers or agents shall change the rates of pay, rules, or working conditions of its employees, as a class as embodied in agreements except in the manner prescribed in such agreements or in section 6 of this Act [45 USCS @ 156].

Eighth. Notices of manner of settlement of disputes; posting. Every carrier shall notify its employees by printed notices in such form and posted at such times and places as shall be specified by the Mediation Board that all disputes between the carrier and its employees will be handled in accordance with the requirements of this Act, and in such notices there shall be printed verbatim, in large type, the third, fourth, and fifth paragraphs of this section. The provisions of said paragraphs are hereby made a part of the contract of employment between the carrier and each employee, and shall be held binding upon the parties, regardless of any other express or implied agreements between them.

Ninth. Disputes as to identity of representatives; designation by Mediation Board; secret elections. If any dispute shall arise among a carrier's employees as to who are the representatives of such employees designated and authorized in accordance with the requirements of this Act, it shall be the duty of the Mediation Board, upon request of either party to the dispute, to investigate such dispute and to certify to both parties, in writing, within thirty days after the receipt of the invocation of its services, the name or names of the individuals or organizations that have been designated and authorized to represent the employees involved in the dispute, and certify the same to the carrier. Upon receipt of such certification the carrier shall treat with the representative so certified as the representative of the craft or class for the purposes of this Act. In such an investigation, the Mediation Board shall be authorized to take a secret ballot of the employees involved, or to utilize any other appropriate method of ascertaining the names of their duly designated and authorized representatives in such manner as shall insure the choice of representatives by the employees without interference, influence, or coercion exercised by the carrier. In the conduct of any election for the purposes herein indicated the Board shall designate who may participate in the election and establish the rules to govern the election, or may appoint a committee of three neutral persons who after hearing shall within ten days designate the employees who may participate in the election. The Board shall have access to and have power to make copies of the books and records of the carriers to obtain and utilize such information as may be deemed necessary by it to carry out the purposes and provisions of this paragraph.

Tenth. Violations; prosecutions and penalties. The willful failure or refusal of any carrier, its officers or agents to comply with the terms of the third, fourth, fifth, seventh, or eighth paragraph of this section shall be a misdemeanor, and upon conviction thereof the carrier, officer, or agent offending shall be subject to a fine of not less than $ 1,000 nor more than $ 20,000 or imprisonment for not more than six months, or both fine and imprisonment, for each offense, and each day during which such carrier, officer, or agent shall willfully fail or refuse to comply with the terms of the said paragraphs of this section shall constitute a separate offense. It shall be the duty of any district attorney of the United States [United States attorney] to whom any duly designated representative of a carrier's employees may apply to institute in the proper court and to prosecute under the direction of the Attorney General of the United States, all necessary proceedings for the enforcement of the provisions of this section, and for the punishment of all violations thereof and the costs and expenses of such prosecution shall be paid out of the appropriation for the expenses of the courts of the United States: Provided, That nothing in this Act shall be construed to require an individual employee to render labor or service without his consent, nor shall anything in this Act be construed to make the quitting of his labor by an individual employee an illegal act; nor shall any court issue any process to compel the performance by an individual employee of such labor or service, without his consent.

Eleventh. Union security agreements; check-off. Notwithstanding any other provisions of this Act, or of any other statute or law of the United States, or Territory thereof, or any State, any carrier or carriers as defined in this Act and a labor organization or labor organizations duly designated and authorized to represent employees in accordance with the requirements of this Act shall be permitted—

(a) to make agreements, requiring, as a condition of continued employment, that within sixty days following the beginning of such employment, or the effective date of such agreements, whichever is the later, all employees shall become members of the labor organization representing their craft or class: Provided, That no such agreement shall require such condition of employment with respect to employees to whom membership is not available upon the same terms and conditions as are generally applicable to any other member or with respect to employees to whom membership was denied or terminated for any reason other than the failure of the employee to tender the periodic dues, initiation fees, and assessments (not including fines and penalties) uniformly required as a condition of acquiring or retaining membership,

(b) to make agreements providing for the deduction by such carrier or carriers from the wages of its or their employees in a craft or class and payment to the labor organization representing the craft or class of such employees, of any periodic dues, initiation fees, and assessments (not including fines and penalties), uniformly required as a condition of acquiring or retaining membership, Provided, That no such agreement shall be effective with respect to any individual employee until he shall have furnished the employer with a written assignment to the labor organization of such membership dues, initiation fees, and assessments, which shall be revocable in writing after the expiration of one year or upon the termination date of the applicable collective agreement, whichever occurs sooner.

(c) The requirement of membership in a labor organization in an agreement made pursuant to subparagraph (a) shall be satisfied, as to both a present or future employee in engine, train, yard, or hostling service, that is, an employee engaged in any of the services or capacities covered in section 3, first (h) of this act [45 USCS @ 153, subsec. First, para. (h)] defining the jurisdictional scope of the first division of the National Railroad Adjustment Board, if said employee shall hold or acquire membership in any one of the labor organizations, national in scope, organized in accordance with this act and admitting to membership employees of a craft or class in any of said services; and no agreement made pursuant to subparagraph

(b) shall provide for deductions from his wages for periodic dues, initiation fees, or assessments payable to any labor organization other than that in which he holds membership: Provided, however, That as to an employee in any of said services on a particular carrier at the effective date of any such agreement on a carrier, who is not a member of any one of the labor organizations, national in scope, organized in accordance with this act and admitting to membership employees of a craft or class in any of said services, such employee, as a condition of continuing his employment, may be required to become a member of the organization representing the craft in which he is employed on the effective date of the first agreement applicable to him: Provided, further, That nothing herein or in any such agreement or agreements shall prevent an employee from changing membership from one organization to another organization admitting to membership employees of a craft or class in any of said services.

(d) Any provisions in paragraphs fourth and fifth of section 2 of this act [this section] in conflict herewith are to the extent of such conflict amended.

TITLE 45. RAILROADS
CHAPTER 8. RAILWAY LABOR
GENERAL PROVISIONS
45 USCS @ 153 (1993)

@ 153. National Railroad Adjustment Board

First. Establishment; composition; powers and duties; divisions; hearings and awards; judicial review. There is hereby established a Board, to be known as the "National Railroad Adjustment Board", the members of which shall be selected within thirty days after approval of this Act [enacted June 21, 1934], and it is hereby provided—

(a) That the said Adjustment Board shall consist of thirty-four members, seventeen of whom shall be selected by the carriers and seventeen by such labor organizations of the employees, national in scope, as have been or may be organized in accordance with the provisions of section 2 of this Act [45 USCS @@ 151a, 152].

(b) The carriers, acting each through its boards of directors or its receiver or receivers, trustee or trustees or through an officer or officers designated for that purpose by such board, trustee or trustees

or receiver or receivers, shall prescribe the rules under which its representatives shall be selected and shall select the representatives of the carriers on the Adjustment Board and designate the division on which each such representative shall serve, but no carrier or system of carriers shall have more than one voting representative on any division of the Board.

(c) Except as provided in the second paragraph of subsection (h) of this section, the national labor organizations, as defined in paragraph (a) of this section, acting each through the chief executive or other medium designated by the organization or association thereof, shall prescribe the rules under which the labor members of the Adjustment Board shall be selected and shall select such members and designate the division on which each member shall serve; but no labor organization shall have more than one voting representative on any division of the Board.

(d) In case of a permanent or temporary vacancy on the Adjustment Board, the vacancy shall be filed by selection in the same manner as in the original selection.

(e) If either the carriers or the labor organizations of the employees fails to select and designate representatives to the Adjustment Board, as provided in paragraphs (b) and (c) of this section, respectively, within sixty days after the passage of this Act [enacted June 21, 1934], in case of any original appointment to office of a member of the Adjustment Board, or in case of a vacancy in any such office within thirty days after such vacancy occurs, the Mediation Board shall thereupon directly make the appointment and shall select an individual associated in interest with the carriers or the group of labor organizations of employees, whichever he is to represent.

(f) In the event a dispute arises as to the right of any national labor organization to participate as per paragraph (c) of this section in the selection and designation of the labor members of the Adjustment Board, the Secretary of Labor shall investigate the claim of such labor organization to participate, and if such claim in the judgment of the Secretary of Labor has merit, the Secretary shall notify the Mediation Board accordingly, and within ten days after receipt of such advice the Mediation Board shall request those national labor organizations duly qualified as per paragraph (c) of this section to participate in the selection and designation of the labor members of the Adjustment Board to select a representative. Such representative, together with a representative likewise designated by the claimant, and a third or neutral party designated by the Mediation Board, constituting a board of three, shall within thirty days after the appointment of the neutral member, investigate the claims of the labor organization desiring participation and decide whether or not it was organized in accordance with section 2 hereof [45 USCS @@ 151a, 152] and is otherwise properly qualified to participate in the selection of the labor members of the Adjustment Board, and the findings of such boards of three shall be final and binding.

(g) Each member of the Adjustment Board shall be compensated by the party or parties he is to represent. Each third or neutral party selected under the provisions of (f) of this section shall receive from the Mediation Board such compensation as the Mediation Board may fix, together with his necessary traveling expenses and expenses actually incurred for subsistence, or per diem allowance in lieu thereof, subject to the provisions of law applicable thereto, while serving as such third or neutral party.

(h) The said Adjustment Board shall be composed of four divisions, whose proceedings shall be independent of one another, and the said divisions as well as the number of their members shall be as follows:

First division: To have jurisdiction over disputes involving train- and yard-service employees of carriers, that is, engineers, firemen, hostlers, and outside hostler helpers, conductors, trainmen, and yard-service employees. This division shall consist of eight members, four of whom shall be selected and designated by the carriers and four of whom shall be selected and designated by the labor organizations, national in scope and organized in accordance with section 2 hereof [45 USCS @@ 151a, 152] and which represent employees in engine, train, yard, or hostling service; Provided, however, That each labor organization shall select and designate two members on the First Division and that no labor organization shall have more than one vote in any proceedings of the First Division or in the adoption of any award with respect to any dispute submitted to the First Division: Pro-

vided further, however, That the carrier members of the First Division shall cast no more than two votes in any proceedings of the division or in the adoption of any award with respect to any dispute submitted to the First Division.

Second division: To have jurisdiction over disputes involving machinists, boilermakers, blacksmiths, sheet-metal workers, electrical workers, car men, the helpers and apprentices of all the foregoing, coach cleaners, power-house employees, and railroad-shop laborers. This division shall consist of ten members, five of whom shall be selected by the carriers and five by the national labor organizations of the employees.

Third division: To have jurisdiction over disputes involving station, tower, and telegraph employees, train dispatchers, maintenance-of-way men, clerical employees, freight handlers, express, station, and store employees, signal men, sleeping-car conductors, sleeping-car porters, and maids and dining-car employees. This division shall consist of ten members, five of whom shall be selected by the carriers and five by the national labor organizations of employees.

Fourth division: To have jurisdiction over disputes involving employees of carriers directly or indirectly engaged in transportation of passengers or property by water, and all other employees of carriers over which jurisdiction is not given to the first, second, and third divisions. This division shall consist of six members, three of whom shall be selected by the carriers and three by the national labor organizations of the employees.

(i) The disputes between an employee or group of employees and a carrier or carriers growing out of grievances or out of the interpretation or application of agreements concerning rates of pay, rules, or working conditions, including cases pending and unadjusted on the date of approval of this Act [enacted June 21, 1934], shall be handled in the usual manner up to and including the chief operating officer of the carrier designated to handle such disputes; but, failing to reach an adjustment in this manner, the disputes may be referred by petition of the parties or by either party to the appropriate division of the Adjustment Board with a full statement of the facts and all supporting data bearing upon the disputes.

(j) Parties may be heard either in person, by counsel, or by other representatives, as they may respectively elect, and the several divisions of the Adjustment Board shall give due notice of all hearings to the employee or employees and the carrier or carriers involved in any disputes submitted to them.

(k) Any division of the Adjustment Board shall have authority to empower two or more of its members to conduct hearings and make findings upon disputes, when properly submitted, at any place designated by the division: Provided, however, That except as provided in paragraph (h) of this section, final awards as to any such dispute must be made by the entire division as hereinafter provided.

(l) Upon failure of any division to agree upon an award because of a deadlock or inability to secure a majority vote of the division members, as provided in paragraph (n) of this section, then such division shall forthwith agree upon and select a neutral person, to be known as "referee", to sit with the division as a member thereof and make an award. Should the division fail to agree upon and select a referee within ten days of the date of the deadlock or inability to secure a majority vote, then the division, or any member thereof, or the parties or either party to the dispute may certify that fact to the Mediation Board, which Board shall, within ten days from the date of receiving such certificate, select and name the referee to sit with the division as a member thereof and make an award. The Mediation Board shall be bound by the same provisions in the appointment of these neutral referees as are provided elsewhere in this Act for the appointment of arbitrators and shall fix and pay the compensation of such referees.

(m) The awards of the several divisions of the Adjustment Board shall be stated in writing. A copy of the awards shall be furnished to the respective parties to the controversy, and the awards shall be final and binding upon both parties to the dispute. In case a dispute arises involving an interpretation of the award the division of the Board upon request of either party shall interpret the award in the light of the dispute.

(n) A majority vote of all members of the division of the Adjustment Board eligible to vote shall be competent to make an award with respect to any dispute submitted to it.

(o) In case of an award by any division of the Adjustment Board in favor of petitioner, the division of the Board shall make an order, directed to the carrier, to make the award effective and, if the award includes a requirement for the payment of money, to pay to the employee the sum to which he is entitled under the award on or before a day named. In the event any division determines that an award favorable to the petitioner should not be made in any dispute referred to it, the division shall make an order to the petitioner stating such determination.

(p) If a carrier does not comply with an order of a division of the Adjustment Board within the time limit in such order, the petitioner, or any person for whose benefit such order was made, may file in the District Court of the United States for the district in which he resides or in which is located the principal operating office of the carrier, or through which the carrier operates, a petition setting forth briefly the causes for which he claims relief, and the order of the division of the Adjustment Board in the premises. Such suit in the District Court of the United States shall proceed in all respects as other civil suits, except that on the trial of such suit the findings and order of the division of the Adjustment Board shall be conclusive on the parties, and except that the petitioner shall not be liable for costs in the district court nor for costs at any subsequent stage of the proceedings, unless they accrue upon his appeal, and such costs shall be paid out of the appropriation for the expenses of the courts of the United States. If the petitioner shall finally prevail he shall be allowed a reasonable attorney's fee, to be taxed and collected as a part of the costs of the suit. The district courts are empowered, under the rules of the court governing actions at law, to make such order and enter such judgment, by writ of mandamus or otherwise, as may be appropriate to enforce or set aside the order of the division of the Adjustment Board: Provided, however, That such order may not be set aside except for failure of the division to comply with the requirements of this Act, for failure of the order to conform, or confine itself, to matters within the scope of the division's jurisdiction, or for fraud or corruption by a member of the division making the order.

(q) If any employee or group of employees, or any carrier, is aggrieved by the failure of any division of the Adjustment Board to make an award in a dispute referred to it, or is aggrieved by any of the terms of an award or by the failure of the division to include certain terms in such award, then such employee or group of employees or carrier may file in any United States district court in which a petition under paragraph (p) could be filed, a petition for review of the division's order. A copy of the petition shall be forthwith transmitted by the clerk of the court to the Adjustment Board. The Adjustment Board shall file in the court the record of the proceedings on which it based its action. The court shall have jurisdiction to affirm the order of the division or to set it aside, in whole or in part, or it may remand the proceeding to the division for such further action as it may direct. On such review, the findings and order of the division shall be conclusive on the parties, except that the order of the division may set aside, in whole or in part, or remanded to the division, for failure of the division to comply with the requirements of this Act, for failure of the order to conform, or confine itself, to matters within the scope of the division's jurisdiction, or for fraud or corruption by a member of the division making the order. The judgment of the court shall be subject to review as provided in sections 1291 and 1254 of title 28, United States Code.

(r) All actions at law based upon the provisions of this section shall be begun within two years from the time the cause of action accrues under the award of the division of the Adjustment Board, and not after.

(s) The several divisions of the Adjustment Board shall maintain headquarters in Chicago, Illinois, meet regularly, and continue in session so long as there is pending before the division any matter within its jurisdiction which has been submitted for its consideration and which has not been disposed of.

(t) Whenever practicable, the several divisions or subdivisions of the Adjustment Board shall be supplied with suitable quarters in any Federal building located at its place of meeting.

(u) The Adjustment Board may, subject to the approval of the Mediation Board, employ and fix the compensations of such assistants as it deems necessary in carrying on its proceedings. The compensation of such employees shall be paid by the Mediation Board.

(v) The Adjustment Board shall meet within forty days after the approval of this Act [enacted June 21, 1934] and adopt such rules as it deems necessary to control proceedings before the respective divisions and not in conflict with the provisions of this section. Immediately following the meeting of the entire Board and the adoption of such rules, the respective divisions shall meet and organize by the selection of a chairman, a vice chairman, and a secretary. Thereafter each division shall annually designate one of its members to act as chairman and one of its members to act as vice chairman: Provided, however, That the chairmanship and vice-chairmanship of any division shall alternate as between the groups, so that both the chairmanship and vice-chairmanship shall be held alternately by a representative of the carriers and a representative of the employees. In case of a vacancy, such vacancy shall be filled for the unexpired term by the selection of a successor from the same group.

(w) Each division of the Adjustment Board shall annually prepare and submit a report of its activities to the Mediation Board, and the substance of such report shall be included in the annual report of the Mediation Board to the Congress of the United States. The reports of each division of the Adjustment Board and the annual report of the Mediation Board shall state in detail all cases heard, all actions taken, the names, salaries, and duties of all agencies, employees, and officers receiving compensation from the United States under the authority of this Act, and an account of all moneys appropriated by Congress pursuant to the authority conferred by this Act and disbursed by such agencies, employees, and officers.

(x) Any division of the Adjustment Board shall have authority, in its discretion, to establish regional adjustment boards to act in its place and stead for such limited period as such division may determine to be necessary. Carrier members of such regional boards shall be designated in keeping with rules devised for this purpose by the carrier members of the Adjustment Board and the labor members shall be designated in keeping with rules devised for this purpose by the labor members of the Adjustment Board. Any such regional board shall, during the time for which it is appointed, have the same authority to conduct hearings, make findings upon disputes and adopt the same procedure as the division of the Adjustment Board appointing it, and its decisions shall be enforceable to the same extent and under the same processes. A neutral person, as referee, shall be appointed for service in connection with any such regional adjustment board in the same circumstances and manner as provided in paragraph (1) hereof, with respect to a division of the Adjustment Board.

Second. System, group, or regional boards: establishment by voluntary agreement; special adjustment boards: establishment, composition, designation of representatives by Mediation Board, neutral member, compensation, quorum, finality and enforcement of awards. Nothing in this section shall be construed to prevent any individual carrier, system, or group of carriers and any class or classes of its or their employees, all acting through their representatives, selected in accordance with the provisions of this Act, from mutually agreeing to the establishment of system, group, or regional boards of adjustment for the purpose of adjusting and deciding disputes of the character specified in this section. In the event that either party to such a system, group, or regional board of adjustment is dissatisfied with such arrangement, it may upon ninety days' notice to the other party elect to come under the jurisdiction of the Adjustment Board.

If written request is made upon any individual carrier by the representative of any craft or class of employees of such carrier for the establishment of a special board of adjustment to resolve disputes otherwise referable to the Adjustment Board, or any dispute which has been pending before the Adjustment Board for twelve months from the date the dispute (claim) is received by the Board, or if any carrier makes such a request upon any such representative, the carrier or the representative upon whom such request is made shall join in an agreement establishing such a board within thirty days from the date such request is made. The cases which may be considered by such board shall be defined in the agreement establishing it. Such board shall consist of one person designated by the carrier and one person designated by the representative of the employees. If such carrier or such representative fails to agree upon the establishment of such a board as provided herein, or to exercise its rights to designate a member of the board, the carrier or representative making the request for the establishment of the special board may request the Mediation Board to designate a member of the

special board on behalf of the carrier or representative upon whom such request was made. Upon receipt of a request for such designation the Mediation Board shall promptly make such designation and shall select an individual associated in interest with the carrier or representative he is to represent, who, with the member appointed by the carrier or representative requesting the establishment of the special board, shall constitute the board. Each member of the board shall be compensated by the party he is to represent. The members of the board so designated shall determine all matters not previously agreed upon by the carrier and the representative of the employees with respect to the establishment and jurisdiction of the board. If they are unable to agree such matters shall be determined by a neutral member shall be competent to render an award. Such awards shall be final and binding upon both parties to the dispute and if in favor of the petitioner, shall direct the other party to comply therewith on or before the day, named. Compliance with such awards shall be enforcible by proceedings in the United States district courts in the same manner and subject to the same provisions that apply to proceedings for enforcement of compliance with awards of the Adjustment Board.

TITLE 45. RAILROADS
CHAPTER 8. RAILWAY LABOR
GENERAL PROVISIONS
45 USCS @ 154 (1992)

@ 154. *National Mediation Board*

First. Board of Mediation abolished; National Mediation Board established; composition; term of office; qualifications; salaries; removal. The Board of Mediation is hereby abolished, effective thirty days from the approval of this Act [enacted June 21, 1934] and the members, secretary, officers, assistants, employees, and agents thereof, in office upon the date of the approval of this Act [enacted June 21, 1934], shall continue to function and receive their salaries for a period of thirty days from such date in the same manner as though this Act had not been passed. There is hereby established, as an independent agency in the executive branch of the Government, a board to be known as the "National Mediation Board", to be composed of three members appointed by the President, by and with the advice and consent of the Senate, not more than two of whom shall be of the same political party. Each member of the Mediation Board in office on January 1, 1965, shall be deemed to have been appointed for a term of office which shall expire on July 1 of the year his term would have otherwise expired. The terms of office of all successors shall expire three years after the expiration of the terms for which their predecessors were appointed; but any member appointed to fill a vacancy occurring prior to the expiration of the term for which his predecessor was appointed shall be appointed only for the unexpired term of his predecessor. Vacancies in the Board shall not impair the powers nor affect the duties of the Board nor of the remaining members of the Board. Two of the members in office shall constitute a quorum for the transaction of the business of the Board. Each member of the Board shall receive [a salary at the rate of $ 10,000 per annum, together with] necessary traveling and subsistence expenses, or per diem allowance in lieu thereof, subject to the provisions of law applicable thereto, while away from the principal office of the Board on business required by this Act. No person in the employment of or who is pecuniarily or otherwise interested in any organization of employees or any carrier shall enter upon the duties of or continue to be a member of the Board. Upon the expiration of his term of office a member shall continue to serve until his successor is appointed and shall have qualified.

All cases referred to the Board of Mediation and unsettled on the date of the approval of this Act [enacted June 21, 1934] shall be handled to conclusion by the Mediation Board.

A member of the Board may be removed by the President for inefficiency, neglect of duty, malfeasance in office, or ineligibility, but for no other cause.

Second. Chairman; principal office; delegation of powers; oaths; seal; report. The Mediation Board shall annually designate a member to act as chairman. The Board shall maintain its principal office in the District of Columbia, but it may meet at any other place whenever it deems it necessary so to do. The Board may designate one or more of its members to exercise the functions of the Board in mediation proceedings. Each member of the Board shall have power to administer oaths and affirmations. The Board shall have a seal which

shall be judicially noticed. The Board shall make an annual report to Congress.

Third. Appointment of experts and other employees; salaries of employees; expenditures. The Mediation Board may (1) appoint such experts and assistants to act in a confidential capacity and, subject to the provisions of the civil-service laws, such other officers and employees [subject to the provisions of the civil service laws, appoint such experts and assistants to act in a confidential capacity and such other officers and employees] as are essential to the effective transaction of the work of the Board; (2) in accordance with the Classification Act of 1923, fix the salaries of such experts, assistants, officers, and employees; and (3) make such expenditures (including expenditures for rent and personal services at the seat of government and elsewhere, for law books, periodicals, and books of reference, and for printing and binding, and including expenditures for salaries and compensation, necessary traveling expenses and expenses actually incurred for subsistence, and other necessary expenses of the Mediation Board, Adjustment Board, Regional Adjustment Boards established under paragraph (w) of section 3 [45 USCS @ 153(w)], and boards of arbitration, in accordance with the provisions of this section and sections 3 and 7 [45 USCS @@ 153, 157], respectively), as may be necessary for the execution of the functions vested in the Board, in the Adjustment Board and in the boards of arbitration, and as may be provided for by the Congress from time to time. All expenditures of the Board shall be allowed and paid on the presentation of itemized vouchers therefor approved by the chairman.

Fourth. Delegation of powers and duties. The Mediation Board is hereby authorized by its order to assign, or refer, any portion of its work, business, or functions arising under this or any other Act of Congress, or referred to it by Congress or either branch thereof, to an individual member of the Board or to an employee or employees of the Board to be designated by such order for action thereon, and by its order at any time to amend, modify, supplement, or rescind any such assignment or reference. All such orders shall take effect forthwith and remain in effect until otherwise ordered by the Board. In conformity with and subject to the order or orders of the Mediation Board in the premises, and such individual member of the Board or employee designated shall have power and authority to act as to any of said work, business, or functions so assigned or referred to him for action by the Board.

Fifth. Transfer of officers and employees of Board of Mediation; transfer of appropriation. All officers and employees of the Board of Mediation (except the members thereof, whose offices are hereby abolished) whose services in the judgment of the Mediation Board are necessary to the efficient operation of the Board are hereby transferred to the Board, without change in classification or compensation; except that the Board may provide for the adjustment of such classification or compensation to conform to the duties to which such officers and employees may be assigned.

All unexpended appropriations for the operation of the Board of Mediation that are available at the time of the abolition of the Board of Mediation shall be transferred to the Mediation Board and shall be available for its use for salaries and other authorized expenditures.

TITLE 45. RAILROADS
CHAPTER 8. RAILWAY LABOR
GENERAL PROVISIONS
45 USCS @ 155 (1992)

@ 155. Functions of Mediation Board

First. Disputes within jurisdiction of Mediation Board. The parties, or either party, to a dispute between an employee or group of employees and a carrier may invoke the services of the Mediation Board in any of the following cases:

  (a) A dispute concerning changes in rates of pay, rules, or working conditions not adjusted by the parties in conference.

  (b) Any other dispute not referable to the National Railroad Adjustment Board and not adjusted in conference between the parties or where conferences are refused.

The Mediation Board may proffer its services in case any labor emergency is found by it to exist at any time.

In either event the said Board shall promptly put itself in communication with the parties to such controversy, and shall use its best efforts, by mediation, to bring them to agreement. If such efforts to bring about an amicable settlement through mediation shall be unsuccessful, the said Board shall at once endeavor as its final required action (except as provided in paragraph third of this section and in section 10 of this Act [45 USCS @ 160]) to induce the parties to submit their controversy to arbitration, in accordance with the provisions of this Act.

If arbitration at the request of the Board shall be refused by one or both parties, the Board shall at once notify both parties in writing that its mediatory efforts have failed and for thirty days thereafter, unless in the intervening period the parties agree to arbitration, or an emergency board shall be created under section 10 of this Act [45 USCS @ 160], no change shall be made in the rates of pay, rules, or working conditions or established practices in effect prior to the time the dispute arose.

Second. Interpretation of agreement. In any case in which a controversy arises over the meaning or the application of any agreement reached through mediation under the provisions of this Act, either party to the said agreement, or both, may apply to the Mediation Board for an interpretation of the meaning or application of such agreement. The said Board shall upon receipt of such request notify the parties to the controversy, and after a hearing of both sides give its interpretation within thirty days.

Third. Duties of Board with respect to arbitration of disputes; arbitrators; acknowledgment of agreement; notice to arbitrators; reconvening of arbitrators; filing contracts with Board; custody of records and documents. The Mediation Board shall have the following duties with respect to the arbitration of disputes under section 7 of this Act [45 USCS @ 157]:

  (a) On failure of the arbitrators named by the parties to agree on the remaining arbitrator or arbitrators within the time set by section 7 of this Act [45 USCS @ 157], it shall be the duty of the Mediation Board to name such remaining arbitrator or arbitrators. It shall be the duty of the Board in naming such arbitrator or arbitrators to appoint only those whom the Board shall deem wholly disinterested in the controversy to be arbitrated and impartial and without bias as between the parties to such arbitration. Should, however, the Board name an arbitrator or arbitrators not so disinterested and impartial, then, upon proper investigation and presentation of the facts, the Board shall promptly remove such arbitrator.

If an arbitrator named by the Mediation Board, in accordance with the provisions of this Act, shall be removed by such Board as provided by this Act, or if such an arbitrator refuses or is unable to serve, it shall be the duty of the Mediation Board, promptly, to select another arbitrator, in the same manner as provided in this Act for an original appointment by the Mediation Board.

(b) Any member of the Mediation Board is authorized to take the acknowledgment of an agreement to arbitrate under this Act. When so acknowledged, or when acknowledged by the parties before a notary public or the clerk of a district court or a circuit court of appeals [court of appeals] of the United States, such agreement to arbitrate shall be delivered to a member of said Board or transmitted to said Board, to be filed in its office.

(c) When an agreement to arbitrate has been filed with the Mediation Board, or with one of its members, as provided by this section, and when the said Board has been furnished the names of the arbitrators chosen by the parties to the controversy it shall be the duty of the Board to cause a notice in writing to be served upon said arbitrators, notifying them of their appointment, requesting them to meet promptly to name the remaining arbitrator or arbitrators necessary to complete the Board of Arbitration, and advising them of the period within which, as provided by the agreement to arbitrate, they are empowered to name such arbitrator or arbitrators.

(d) Either party to an arbitration desiring the reconvening of a board of arbitration to pass upon any controversy arising over the meaning or application of an award may so notify the Mediation Board in writing, stating in such notice the question or questions to be submitted to such reconvened Board. The Mediation Board shall thereupon promptly communicate with the members of the Board of Arbitration, or a subcommittee of such Board appointed for such purpose pursuant to a provision in the agreement to arbitrate, and arrange for the reconvening of said Board of Arbitration or subcommittee, and shall notify the respective parties to the controversy of the time and place at which the Board, or the subcommit-

tee, will meet for hearings upon the matters in controversy to be submitted to it. No evidence other than that contained in the record filed with the original award shall be received or considered by such reconvened Board or subcommittee, except such evidence as may be necessary to illustrate the interpretations suggested by the parties. If any member of the original Board is unable or unwilling to serve on such reconvened Board or subcommittee thereof, another arbitrator shall be named in the same manner and with the same powers and duties as such original arbitrator.

(e) Within sixty days after the approval of this Act [enacted June 21, 1934] every carrier shall file with the Mediation Board a copy of each contract with its employees in effect on the 1st day of April 1934, covering rates of pay, rules, and working conditions. If no contract with any craft or class of its employees has been entered into, the carrier shall file with the Mediation Board a statement of that fact including also a statement of the rates of pay, rules, and working conditions applicable in dealing with such craft or class. When any new contract is executed or change is made in an existing contract with any class or craft of its employees covering rates of pay, rules, or working conditions, or in those rates of pay, rules, and working conditions of employees not covered by contract, the carrier shall file the same with the Mediation Board within thirty days after such new contract or change in existing contract has been executed or rates of pay, rules, and working conditions have been made effective.

(f) The Mediation Board shall be the custodian of all papers and documents heretofore filed with or transferred to the Board of Mediation bearing upon the settlement, adjustment, or determination of disputes between carriers and their employees or upon mediation or arbitration proceedings held under or pursuant to the provisions of any Act of Congress in respect thereto; and the President is authorized to designate a custodian of the records and property of the Board of Mediation until the transfer and delivery of such records to the Mediation Board and to require the transfer and delivery to the Mediation Board of any and all such papers and documents filed with it or in its possession.

TITLE 45. RAILROADS
CHAPTER 8. RAILWAY LABOR
GENERAL PROVISIONS
45 USCS @ 156 (1993)

@ 156. Procedure in changing rates of pay, rules, or working conditions

Carriers and representatives of the employees shall give at least thirty days' written notice of an intended change in agreements affecting rates of pay, rules, or working conditions, and the time and place for the beginning of conference between the representatives of the parties interested in such intended changes shall be agreed upon within ten days after the receipt of said notice, and said time shall be within the thirty days provided in the notice. In every case where such notice of intended change has been given, or conferences are being held with reference thereto, or the services of the mediation Board have been requested by either party, or said Board has proffered its services, rates of pay, rules, or working conditions shall not be altered by the carrier until the controversy has been finally acted upon as required by section 5 of this Act [45 USCS @ 155], by the Mediation Board, unless a period of ten days has elapsed after termination of conferences without request for or proffer of the services of the Mediation Board.

TITLE 45. RAILROADS
CHAPTER 8. RAILWAY LABOR
GENERAL PROVISIONS
45 USCS @ 157 (1993)

@ 157. Arbitration

First. Submission of controversy to arbitration. Whenever a controversy shall arise between a carrier or carriers and its or their employees which is not settled either in conference between representatives of the parties or by the appropriate adjustment board or through mediation, in the manner provided in the preceding sections, such controversy may, by agreement of the parties to such controversy, be submitted to the arbitration of a board of three (or, if the parties to the con-troversy so stipulate, of six) persons: Provided, however, That the failure or refusal of either party to submit a controversy to arbitration shall not be construed as a violation of any legal obligation imposed upon such party by the terms of this Act or otherwise.

Second. Manner of selecting board of arbitration. Such board of arbitration shall be chosen in the following manner:

(a) In the case of a board of three the carrier or carriers and the representatives of the employees, parties respectively to the agreement to arbitrate, shall each name one arbitrator; the two arbitrators thus chosen shall select a third arbitrator. If the arbitrators chosen by the parties shall fail to name the third arbitrator within five days after their first meeting, such third arbitrator shall be named by the Mediation Board.

(b) In the case of a board of six the carrier or carriers and the representatives of the employees, parties respectively to the agreement to arbitrate, shall each name two arbitrators; the four arbitrators thus chosen shall, by a majority vote, select the remaining two arbitrators. If the arbitrators chosen by the parties shall fail to name the two arbitrators within fifteen days after their first meeting, the said two arbitrators, or as many of them as have not been named, shall be named by the Mediation Board.

Third. Board of arbitration; organization; compensation; procedure.

(a) Notice of selection or failure to select arbitrators. When the arbitrators selected by the respective parties have agreed upon the remaining arbitrator or arbitrators, they shall notify the Mediation Board; and, in the event of their failure to agree upon any or upon all of the necessary arbitrators within the period fixed by this Act, they shall, at the expiration of such period, notify the Mediation Board of the arbitrators selected, if any, or of their failure to make or to complete such selection.

(b) Organization of board; procedure. The board of arbitration shall organize and select its own chairman and make all necessary rules for conducting its hearings: Provided, however, That the board of arbitration shall be bound to give the parties to the controversy a full and fair hearing, which shall include an opportunity to present evidence in support of their claims, and an opportunity to present their case in person, by counsel, or by other representative as they may respectively elect.

(c) Duty to reconvene; questions considered. Upon notice from the Mediation Board that the parties, or either party, to an arbitration desire the reconvening of the board of arbitration (or a subcommittee of such board of arbitration appointed for such purpose pursuant to the agreement to arbitrate) to pass upon any controversy over the meaning or application of their award, the board, or its subcommittee, shall at once reconvene. No question other than, or in addition to, the questions relating to the meaning or application of the award, submitted by the party or parties in writing, shall be considered by the reconvened board of arbitration or its subcommittee.

Such rulings shall be acknowledged by such board or subcommittee thereof in the same manner, and filed in the same district court clerk's office, as the original award and become a part thereof.

(d) Competency of arbitrators. No arbitrator, except those chosen by the Mediation Board, shall be incompetent to act as an arbitrator because of his interest in the controversy to be arbitrated, or because of his connection with or partiality to either of the parties to the arbitration.

(e) Compensation and expenses. Each member of any board of arbitration created under the provisions of this Act named by either party to the arbitration shall be compensated by the party naming him. Each arbitrator selected by the arbitrators or named by the Mediation Board shall receive from the Mediation Board such compensation as the Mediation Board may fix, together with his necessary traveling expenses and expenses actually incurred for subsistence, while serving as an arbitrator.

(f) Award; disposition of original and copies. The board of arbitration shall furnish a certified copy of its award to the respective parties to the controversy, and shall transmit the original, together with the papers and proceedings and a transcript of the evidence taken at the hearings, certified under the hands of at least a majority of the arbitrators, to the clerk of the district court of the United States for the district wherein the controversy arose or the arbitration is entered into, to be filed in said clerk's office as hereinafter pro-

vided. The said board shall also furnish a certified copy of its award, and the papers and proceedings, including testimony relating thereto, to the Mediation Board, to be filed in its office; and in addition a certified copy of its award shall be filed in the office of the Interstate Commerce Commission: Provided, however, That such award shall not be construed to diminish or extinguish any of the powers or duties of the Interstate Commerce Commission, under the Interstate Commerce Act as amended.

(g) Compensation of assistants to board of arbitration; expenses; quarters. A board of arbitration may, subject to the approval of the Mediation Board, employ and fix the compensation of such assistants as it deems necessary in carrying on the arbitration proceedings. The compensation of such employees, together with their necessary traveling expenses and expenses actually incurred for subsistence, while so employed, and the necessary expenses of boards of arbitration, shall be paid by the Mediation Board.

Whenever practicable, the board shall be supplied with suitable quarters in any Federal building located at its place of meeting or at any place where the board may conduct its proceedings or deliberations.

(h) Testimony before board; oaths; attendance of witnesses; production of documents; subpoenas; fees. All testimony before said board shall be given under oath or affirmation, and any member of the board shall have the power to administer oaths or affirmations. The board of arbitration, or any member thereof, shall have the power to require the attendance of witnesses and the production of such books, papers, contracts, agreements, and documents as may be deemed by the board of arbitration material to a just determination of the matters submitted to its arbitration, and may for that purpose request the clerk of the district court of the United States for the district wherein said arbitration is being conducted to issue the necessary subpoenas, and upon such request the said clerk or his duly authorized deputy shall be, and he hereby is, authorized, and it shall be his duty, to issue such subpoenas.

Any witness appearing before a board of arbitration shall receive the same fees and mileage as witnesses in courts of the United States, to be paid by the party securing the subpoena.

TITLE 45. RAILROADS
CHAPTER 8. RAILWAY LABOR
GENERAL PROVISIONS
45 USCS @ 158 (1992)

@ 158. Agreement to arbitrate; form and contents; signatures and acknowledgment; revocation

The agreement to arbitrate—

(a) Shall be in writing;

(b) Shall stipulate that the arbitration is had under the provisions of this Act;

(c) Shall state whether the board of arbitration is to consist of three or of six members;

(d) Shall be signed by the duly accredited representatives of the carrier or carriers and the employees, parties respectively to the agreement to arbitrate, and shall be acknowledged by said parties before a notary public, the clerk of a district court or circuit court of appeals [court of appeals] of the United States, or before a member of the Mediation Board, and, when so acknowledged, shall be filed in the office of the Mediation Board;

(e) Shall state specifically the questions to be submitted to the said board for decision; and that, in its award or awards, the said board shall confine itself strictly to decisions as to the questions so specifically submitted to it;

(f) Shall provide that the questions, or any one or more of them, submitted by the parties to the board of arbitration may be withdrawn from arbitration on notice to that effect signed by the duly accredited representatives of all the parties and served on the board of arbitration;

(g) Shall stipulate that the signatures of a majority of said board of arbitration affixed to their award shall be competent to constitute a valid and binding award;

(h) Shall fix a period from the date of the appointment of the arbitrator or arbitrators necessary to complete the board (as provided for in the agreement) within which the said board shall commence its hearings;

(i) Shall fix a period from the beginning of the hearings within which the said board shall make and file its award: Provided, That the parties may agree at any time upon an extension of this period;

(j) Shall provide for the date from which the award shall become effective and shall fix the period during which the award shall continue in force;

(k) Shall provide that the award of the board of arbitration and the evidence of the proceedings before the board relating thereto, when certified under the hands of at least a majority of the arbitrators, shall be filed in the clerk's office of the district court of the United States for the district wherein the controversy arose or the arbitration was entered into, which district shall be designated in the agreement; and, when so filed, such award and proceedings shall constitute the full and complete record of the arbitration;

(l) Shall provide that the award, when so filed, shall be final and conclusive upon the parties as to the facts determined by said award and as to the merits of the controversy decided;

(m) Shall provide that any difference arising as to the meaning, or the application of the provisions, of an award made by a board of arbitration shall be referred back for a ruling to the same board, or, by agreement, to a subcommittee of such board; and that such ruling, when acknowledged in the same manner, and filed in the same district court clerk's office, as the original award, shall be a part of and shall have the same force and effect as such original award; and

(n) Shall provide that the respective parties to the award will each faithfully execute the same.

The said agreement to arbitrate, when properly signed and acknowledged as herein provided, shall not be revoked by a party to such agreement: Provided, however, That such agreement to arbitrate may at any time be revoked and canceled by the written agreement of both parties, signed by their duly accredited representatives, and (if no board or arbitration has yet been constituted under the agreement) delivered to the Mediation Board or any member thereof; or, if the Board of arbitration has been constituted as provided by this Act, delivered to such board of arbitration.

TITLE 45. RAILROADS
CHAPTER 8. RAILWAY LABOR
GENERAL PROVISIONS
45 USCS @ 159 (1993)

@159. Award and judgment thereon; effect on individual employee

First. Filing of award. The award of a board of arbitration, having been acknowledged as herein provided, shall be filed in the clerk's office of the district court designated in the agreement to arbitrate.

Second. Conclusiveness of award; judgment. An award acknowledged and filed as herein provided shall be conclusive on the parties as to the merits and facts of the controversy submitted to arbitration, and unless, within ten days after the filing of the award, a petition to impeach the award, on the grounds hereinafter set forth, shall be filed in the clerk's office of the court in which the award has been filed, the court shall enter judgment on the award, which judgment shall be final and conclusive on the parties.

Third. Impeachment of award; grounds. Such petition for the impeachment or contesting of any award so filed shall be entertained by the court only on one or more of the following grounds:

(a) That the award plainly does not conform to the substantive requirements laid down by this Act for such awards, or that the proceedings were not substantially in conformity with this Act;

(b) That the award does not conform, nor confine itself, to the stipulations of the agreement to arbitrate; or

(c) That a member of the board of arbitration rendering the award was guilty of fraud or corruption; or that a party to the arbitration practiced fraud or corruption which fraud or corruption affected the result of the arbitration: Provided, however, That no court shall entertain any such petition on the ground that an award is invalid for uncertainty; in such case the proper remedy shall be a submission of such award to a reconvened board, or subcommittee thereof, for interpretation, as provided by this Act: Provided further, That an award contested as herein provided shall be construed liberally by the court, with a view to favoring its validity, and that no award shall be set aside for trivial irregularity or clerical error, going only to form and not to substance.

Fourth. Effect of partial invalidity of award. If the court shall determine that a part of the award is invalid on some ground or grounds designated in this section as a ground of invalidity, but shall determine that a part of the award is valid, the court shall set aside the entire award: Provided, however, That, if the parties shall agree thereto, and if such valid and invalid parts are separable, the court shall set aside the invalid part, and order judgment to stand as to the valid part.

Fifth. Appeal; record. At the expiration of ten days from the decision of the district court upon the petition filed as aforesaid, final judgment shall be entered in accordance with said decision, unless during said ten days either party shall appeal therefrom to the circuit court of appeals [court of appeals]. In such case only such portion of the record shall be transmitted to the appellate court as is necessary to the proper understanding and consideration of the questions of law presented by said petition and to be decided.

Sixth. Finality of decision of circuit court of appeals [court of appeals]. The determination of said circuit court of appeals [court of appeals] upon said questions shall be final, and, being certified by the clerk thereof to said district court, judgment pursuant thereto shall thereupon be entered by said district court.

Seventh. Judgment where petitioner's contentions are sustained. If the petitioner's contentions are finally sustained, judgment shall be entered setting aside the award in whole or, if the parties so agree, in part; but in such case the parties may agree upon a judgment to be entered disposing of the subject matter of the controversy, which judgment when entered shall have the same force and effect as judgment entered upon an award.

Eighth. Duty of employee to render service without consent; right to quit. Nothing in this Act shall be construed to require an individual employee to render labor or service without his consent, nor shall anything in this Act be construed to make the quitting of his labor or service by an individual employee an illegal act; nor shall any court issue any process to compel the performance by an individual employee of such labor or service, without his consent.

TITLE 45. RAILROADS
CHAPTER 8. RAILWAY LABOR
GENERAL PROVISIONS
45 USCS @ 159a (1992)

@ 159a. Special procedure for commuter service

(a) Applicability of provisions. Except as provided in section 510(h) of the Rail Passenger Service Act [45 USCS @ 590(h)], the provisions of this section shall apply to any dispute subject to this Act between a publicly funded and publicly operated carrier providing rail commuter service (including the Amtrak Commuter Services Corporation) and its employees.

(b) Request for establishment of emergency board. If a dispute between the parties described in subsection (a) is not adjusted under the foregoing provisions of this Act and the President does not, under section 10 of this Act [45 USCS @ 160], create an emergency board to investigate and report on such dispute, then any party to the dispute or the Governor of any State through which the service that is the subject of the dispute is operated may request the President to establish such an emergency board.

(c) Establishment of emergency board.

(1) Upon the request of a party or a Governor under subsection (b), the President shall create an emergency board to investigate and report on the dispute in accordance with section 10 of this Act [45 USCS @ 160]. For purposes of this subsection, the period during which no change, except by agreement, shall be made by the parties in the conditions out of which the dispute arose shall be 120 days from the date of the creation of such emergency board.

(2) If the President, in his discretion, creates a board to investigate and report on a dispute between the parties described in subsection (a), the provisions of this section shall apply to the same extent as if such board had been created pursuant to paragraph (1) of this subsection.

(d) Public hearing by National Mediation Board upon failure of emergency board to effectuate settlement of dispute. Within 60 days after the creation of an emergency board under this section, if there has been no settlement between the parties, the National Mediation Board shall conduct a public hearing on the dispute at which each party shall appear and provide testimony setting forth the reasons it has not accepted the recommendations of the emergency board for settlement of the dispute.

(e) Establishment of second emergency board. If no settlement in the dispute is reached at the end of the 120-day period beginning on the date of the creation of the emergency board, any party to the dispute or the Governor of any State through which the service that is the subject of the dispute is operated may request the President to establish another emergency board, in which case the President shall establish such emergency board.

(f) Submission of final offers to second emergency board by parties. Within 30 days after creation of a board under subsection (e), the parties to the dispute shall submit to the board final offers for settlement of the dispute.

(g) Report of second emergency board. Within 30 days after the submission of final offers under subsection (f), the emergency board shall submit a report to the President setting forth its selection of the most reasonable offer.

(h) Maintenance of status quo during dispute period. From the time a request to establish a board is made under subsection (e) until 60 days after such board makes its report under subsection (g), no change, except by agreement, shall be made by the parties in the conditions out of which the dispute arose.

(i) Work stoppages by employees subsequent to carrier offer selected; eligibility of employees for benefits. If the emergency board selects the final offer submitted by the carrier and, after the expiration of the 60-day period described in subsection (h), the employees of such carrier engage in any work stoppage arising out of the dispute, such employees shall not be eligible during the period of such work stoppage for benefits under the Railroad Unemployment Insurance Act [45 USCS @@ 351 et seq.].

(j) Work stoppages by employees subsequent to employees offer selected; eligibility of employer for benefits. If the emergency board selects the final offer submitted by the employees and, after the expiration of the 60-day period described in subsection (h), the carrier refuses to accept the final offer submitted by the employees and the employees of such carrier engage in any work stoppage arising out of the dispute, the carrier shall not participate in any benefits of any agreement between carriers which is designed to provide benefits to such carriers during a work stoppage.

TITLE 45. RAILROADS
CHAPTER 8. RAILWAY LABOR
GENERAL PROVISIONS
45 USCS @ 160 (1992)

@ 160. Emergency board

If a dispute between a carrier and its employees be not adjusted under the foregoing provisions of this Act and should, in the judgment of the Mediation Board, threaten substantially to interrupt interstate commerce to a degree such as to deprive any section of the country of essential transportation service, the Mediation Board shall notify the President, who may thereupon, in his discretion, create a board to investigate and report respecting such dispute. Such board shall be composed of such number of persons as to the President may seem desirable: Provided, however, That no member appointed shall be pecuniarily or otherwise interested in any organization of employees or any carrier. The compensation of the members of any such board shall be fixed by the President. Such board shall be created separately in each instance and it shall investigate promptly the facts as to the dispute and make a report thereon to the President within thirty days from the date of its creation.

There is hereby authorized to be appropriated such sums as may be necessary for the expenses of such board, including the compensation and the necessary traveling expenses and expenses actually incurred for subsistence, of the members of the board. All expenditures of the board shall be allowed and paid on the presentation of itemized vouchers therefor approved by the chairman.

After the creation of such board and for thirty days after such board has made its report to the President, no change, except by agreement, shall be made by the parties to the controversy in the conditions out of which the dispute arose.

TITLE 45. RAILROADS
CHAPTER 8. RAILWAY LABOR
GENERAL PROVISIONS
45 USCS @ 161 (1992)

@ 161. Effect of partial invalidity of Act

If any section, subsection, sentence, clause, or phrase of this Act is for any reason held to be unconstitutional, such decision shall not affect the validity of the remaining portions of this Act. All Acts or parts of Acts inconsistent with the provisions of this Act are hereby repealed.

TITLE 45. RAILROADS
CHAPTER 8. RAILWAY LABOR
GENERAL PROVISIONS
45 USCS @ 162 (1992)

@ 162. Authorization of appropriations

There is hereby authorized to be appropriated such sums as may be necessary for expenditure by the Mediation Board in carrying out the provisions of this Act.

TITLE 45. RAILROADS
CHAPTER 8. RAILWAY LABOR
GENERAL PROVISIONS
45 USCS @ 163 (1992)

@ 163. Repeal of prior legislation; exception

Title III of the Transportation Act, 1920, and the Act approved July 15, 1913 providing for mediation, conciliation, and arbitration, and all Acts and parts of Acts in conflict with the provisions of this Act are hereby repealed, except that the members, secretary, officers, employees, and agents of the Railroad Labor Board, in office upon the date of the passage of this Act [enacted May 20, 1926], shall receive their salaries for a period of 30 days from such date, in the same manner as though this Act had not been passed.

TITLE 45. RAILROADS
CHAPTER 8. RAILWAY LABOR
GENERAL PROVISIONS
45 USCS @ 164 (1992)

@ 164. [Repealed]

TITLE 45. RAILROADS
CHAPTER 8. RAILWAY LABOR
CARRIERS BY AIR
45 USCS @ 181 (1993)

@ 181. Application of 45 USCS @ 151, 152, 154–163 to carriers by air

All of the provisions of Title I of this Act [45 USCS @@ 151–163], except the provisions of section 3 thereof [45 USCS @ 153], are extended to and shall cover every common carrier by air engaged in interstate or foreign commerce, and every carrier by air transporting mail for or under contract with the United States Government, and every air pilot or other person who performs any work as an employee or subordinate official of such carrier or carriers, subject to its or their continuing authority to supervise and direct the manner of rendition of his service.

TITLE 45. RAILROADS
CHAPTER 8. RAILWAY LABOR
CARRIERS BY AIR
45 USCS @ 182 (1992)

@ 182. Duties, penalties, benefits, and privileges

The duties, requirements, penalties, benefits, and privileges prescribed and established by the provisions of Title I of this Act [45 USCS @@ 151–163], except section 3 thereof [45 USCS @ 153], shall apply to said carriers by air and their employees in the same manner and to the same extent as though such carriers and their employees were specifically included within the de-

finition of "carrier" and "employee", respectively, in section 1 thereof [45 USCS @ 151].

TITLE 45. RAILROADS
CHAPTER 8. RAILWAY LABOR
CARRIERS BY AIR
45 USCS @ 183 (1992)

@ 183. Disputes within jurisdiction of Mediation Board

The parties or either party to a dispute between an employee or a group of employees and a carrier or carriers by air may invoke the services of the National Mediation Board and the jurisdiction of said Mediation Board is extended to any of the following cases:

(a) A dispute concerning changes in rates of pay, rules, or working conditions not adjusted by the parties in conference.

(b) Any other dispute not referable to an adjustment board, as hereinafter provided, and not adjusted in conference between the parties, or where conferences are refused.

The National Mediation Board may proffer its services in case any labor emergency is found by it to exist at any time.

The services of the Mediation Board may be invoked in a case under this title [45 USCS @@ 181 et seq.] in the same manner and to the same extent as are the disputes covered by section 5 of Title I of this Act [45 USCS @ 155].

TITLE 45. RAILROADS
CHAPTER 8. RAILWAY LABOR
CARRIERS BY AIR
45 USCS @ 184 (1993)

@ 184. System, group, or regional boards of adjustment

The disputes between an employee or group of employees and a carrier or carriers by air growing out of grievances, or out of the interpretation or application of agreements concerning rates of pay, rules, or working conditions, including cases pending and unadjusted on the date of approval of this Act [enacted April 10, 1936] before the National Labor Relations Board, shall be handled in the usual manner up to and including the chief operating officer of the carrier designated to handle such disputes; but, failing to reach an adjustment in this manner, the disputes may be referred by petition of the parties or by either party to an appropriate adjustment board, as hereinafter provided, with a full statement of the facts and supporting data bearing upon the disputes.

It shall be the duty of every carrier and of its employees, acting through their representatives, selected in accordance with the provisions of this title [45 USCS @@ 181 et seq.] to establish a board of adjustment of jurisdiction not exceeding the jurisdiction which may be lawfully exercised by system, group, or regional boards of adjustment, under the authority of section 3, Title I, of this Act [45 USCS @ 153].

Such boards of adjustment may be established by agreement between employees and carriers either on any individual carrier, or system, or group of carriers by air and any class or classes of its or their employees; or pending the establishment of a permanent National Board of Adjustment as hereinafter provided. Nothing in this Act shall prevent said carriers by air, or any class or classes of their employees, both acting through their representatives selected in accordance with provisions of this title [45 USCS @@ 181 et seq.], from mutually agreeing to the establishment of a National Board of Adjustment of temporary duration and of similar limited jurisdiction.

TITLE 45. RAILROADS
CHAPTER 8. RAILWAY LABOR
CARRIERS BY AIR
45 USCS @ 185 (1992)

@ 185. National Air Transport Adjustment Board

When, in the judgment of the National Mediation Board, it shall be necessary to have a permanent national board of adjustment in order to provide for the prompt and orderly settlement of disputes between said carriers by air, or any of

them, and its or their employees, growing out of grievances or out of the interpretation or application of agreements between said carriers by air or any of them, and any class or classes of its or their employees, covering rates of pay, rules, or working conditions, the National Mediation Board is hereby empowered and directed, by its order duly made, published, and served, to direct the said carriers by air and such labor organizations of their employees, national in scope, as have been or may be recognized in accordance with the provisions of this Act, to select and designate four representatives who shall constitute a board which shall be known as the "National Air Transport Adjustment Board." Two members of said National Air Transport Board shall be selected by said carriers by air and two members by the said labor organizations of the employees, within thirty days after the date of the order of the National Mediation Board, in the manner and by the procedure prescribed by Title I of this Act [45 USCS @@ 151 et seq.] for the selection and designation of members of the National Railroad Adjustment Board. The National Air Transport Adjustment Board shall meet within forty days after the date of the order of the National Mediation Board directing the selection and designation of its members and shall organize and adopt rules for conducting its proceedings, in the manner prescribed in section 3 of Title I of this Act [45 USCS @ 153]. Vacancies in membership or office shall be filled, members shall be appointed in case of failure of the carriers or of labor organizations of the employees to select and designate representatives, members of the National Air Transport Adjustment Board shall be compensated, hearings shall be held, findings and awards made, stated, serve, and enforced, and the number and compensation of any necessary assistants shall be determined and the compensation of such employees shall be paid, all in the same manner and to the same extent as provided with reference to the National Railroad Adjustment Board by section 3 of Title I of this Act [45 USCS @ 153]. The powers and duties prescribed and established by the provisions of section 3 of Title I of this Act [45 USCS @ 153] with reference to the National Railroad Adjustment Board and the several divisions thereof are hereby conferred upon and shall be exercised and performed in like manner and to the same extent by the said National Air Transport Adjustment Board, not exceeding, however, the jurisdiction conferred upon said National Air Transport Adjustment Board by the provisions of this title [45 USCS @@ 181 et seq.]. From and after the organization of the National Air Transport Adjustment Board, if any system, group, or regional board of adjustment established by any carrier or carriers by air and any class or classes of its or their employees is not satisfactory to either party thereto, the said party, upon ninety days' notice to the other party, may elect to come under the jurisdiction of the National Air Transport Adjustment Board.

TITLE 45. RAILROADS
CHAPTER 8. RAILWAY LABOR
CARRIERS BY AIR
45 USCS @ 186 (1992)

@ 186. [Omitted]

TITLE 45. RAILROADS
CHAPTER 8. RAILWAY LABOR
CARRIERS BY AIR
45 USCS @ 187 (1992)

@ 187. Separability of provisions

If any provision of this title [45 USCS @@ 181 et seq.] or application thereof to any person or circumstance is held invalid, the remainder of the Act and the application of such provision to other persons or circumstances shall not be affected thereby.

TITLE 45. RAILROADS
CHAPTER 8. RAILWAY LABOR
CARRIERS BY AIR
45 USCS @ 188 (1992)

@ 188. Authorization of appropriations

There is hereby authorized to be appropriated such sums as may be necessary for expenditure by the Mediation Board in carrying out the provisions of this Act.

Notes

1. Labor Law and Public Policy

1. James Berkeley, John Rouse, and Ray Begovich, *The Craft of Public Administration* (Dubuque, Iowa: William C. Brown, 1984), 99.

2. *Webster's Encyclopedia Unabridged Dictionary of the English Language*, 10th ed., s.v. "policy."

3. Thomas R. Dye, *Understanding Public Policy*, 3d ed. (Englewood Cliffs, N.J.: Prentice Hall, 1978), 3.

4. Clarke E. Cochren, Lawrence C. Mayer, T. R. Carr, and N. Joseph Cayer, *American Public Policy*, 3d ed. (New York: St. Martin's Press, 1990), 2.

5. Albert P. Melone, *Researching Constitutional Law* (New York: Harper Collins, 1990), 137–38.

6. Samuel H. Beer, "The Modernization of American Federalism," *Publius: The Journal of Federalism*, fall 1973, 65.

7. Glenn W. Miller, *Problems of Labor* (New York: Macmillan, 1951), 493.

8. Alexander T. Wells, *Air Transportation: A Management Perspective*, 2d. ed. (Belmont, Calif.: Wadsworth, 1989), 164–65.

9. Regional Airline Association, *Annual Report*, Washington, D.C., 1991, 10.

10. Ibid., 12.

11. Ibid.

12. U.S. Department of Transportation, Federal Aviation Administration, *FAA Aviation Forecasts: Fiscal Years 1991–2002* (Washington, D.C.: U.S. Government Printing Office, 1991), 101.

13. Ibid., 99.

14. Wells, *Air Transportation*, 126.

15. Based on estimates from the General Aviation Manufacturers Association, *The General Aviation Story* (Washington, D.C., 1979).

16. Wells, *Air Transportation*, 146–47.

17. Harry P. Wolfe and David A. NewMyer, *Aviation Industry Regulation* (Carbondale: Southern Illinois University Press, 1985), 10.

18. Transportation Research Board, "Future Aviation Activities: Sixth Annual Workshop," *Transportation Research Circular* 352 (Feb. 1990): 42–43.

19. Berkeley, Rouse, and Begovich, *The Craft of Public Administration*, 111.

20. Ibid., 112.

21. David H. Rosenbloom, *Public Administration: Understanding Management, Politics, and Law in the Public Sector*, 2d ed. (New York: Random House, 1989), 232.

22. Berkeley, Rouse, and Begovich, *The Craft of Public Administration*, 148.

23. Meany as quoted by Chester A. Newland, in "Collective Bargaining Concepts: Applications in Government," *Public Administration Review* 28, no. 2 (Mar.–Apr. 1968): 135.

2. Early Collective Bargaining Legislation

1. Selig Perlman, *A History of Trade Unionism in the United States* (New York: Macmillan, 1922), 3–18.

2. Fred Knee, "The Revolt of Labor," *Social Democrat*, Nov. 1910, 144.

3. Arthur Sloane, *Labor Relations*, 3d ed. (Englewood Cliffs, N.J.: Prentice Hall, 1977), 59–60.

4. Richard Rosecrance, "Why England Slipped," *Wilson Quarterly*, fall 1987, 101.

5. Jerre S. Williams, *Labor Relations and the Law*, 3d ed. (Boston: Little, Brown, 1965), 20.

6. Daniel Quinn Mills, *Labor-Management Problems*, 1st ed. (New York: McGraw-Hill, 1980), 31.

7. Charles M. Rhemus, "Evolution of Legislation Affecting Collective Bargaining in the Railroad and Airline Industries," in *The Railway Labor Act at Fifty*, National Mediation Board (Washington, D.C.: U.S. Government Printing Office, 1976), 1.

8. Sloane, *Labor Relations*, 58.

9. Frank N. Wilner, *The Railway Labor Act and the Dilemma of Labor Relations* (Omaha: Simmons-Boardman), 25.

10. Sloane, *Labor Relations,* 58–59.

11. Mills, *Labor-Management Problems,* 1st ed., 33.

12. Sanford Cohen, *Labor in the United States* (Columbus, Ohio: Charles E. Merrill, 1960), 59.

13. Foster Rhea Dulles, *Labor in America* (New York: Crowell, 1966), 140.

14. Perlman, *Trade Unionism in the United States,* 123–24.

15. Ibid., 154–55.

16. Ibid., 93.

17. David Wallechinsky, "On the Way to the 8-Hour Day—The Haymarket Affair," in *The Peoples Almanac,* ed. David Wallechinsky and Irving Wallace (Garden City, N.Y.: Doubleday, 1975), 41.

18. David Wallechinsky and Irving Wallace, eds., *The Peoples Almanac* (Garden City, N.Y.: Doubleday, 1975), 206.

19. Florence Peterson, *Strikes in the U.S.* (Washington, D.C.: U.S. Government Printing Office, 1938), 30.

20. Wilner, *The Railway Labor Act,* 28.

21. Gerald G. Eggert, *Railroad Labor Disputes* (Ann Arbor: University of Michigan Press, 1967), 59.

22. Rhemus, "Legislation Affecting Collective Bargaining," 4.

23. 25 Stat. 209 (1890) 15 U.S.C. 1–7.

24. *Plant v Woods,* 57 N.E. 1011 (Mass. 1900).

25. Ibid.

26. Wilner, *The Railway Labor Act,* 13.

27. Edwin E. White, *The Government in Labor Disputes,* (New York: McGraw-Hill, 1931), 234.

28. *Loewe v Lawler,* 208 U.S. 274 (1908).

29. *Hitchman Coat Company v Mitchell,* 245 U.S. 229.

30. Mills, *Labor-Management Problems,* 1st ed., 35–36.

31. *Adair v United States,* 208 U.S. 161 (1908).

32. Wilner, *The Railway Labor Act,* 34.

33. John F. Stover, *The Life and Decline of the American Railroad* (New York: Oxford University Press, 1970), 120.

34. *Wilson v New,* 243 U.S. 382 (1917).

35. *Loechner v United States,* 198 U.S. 45 (1905).

36. Edwin Witte, *The Government in Labor Disputes* (New York: McGraw-Hill, 1932), 68–69.

37. Clayton Act, 38 Stat. 730 (1914).

38. *Duplex Printing v Deering,* 254 U.S. 443 (1921).

39. *Bedford Cut Stone Co. v Journeymen Stone Cutters Association of North America,* 274 U.S. 37 (1927).

40. Army Appropriation Act, 39 Stat. 619 (1916).

41. Stover, *Life and Decline of the American Railroad,* 166.

42. Rhemus, "Legislation Affecting Collective Bargaining," 6.

43. Harry D. Wolf, *The Railroad Labor Board* (New York: Columbia University Press, 1971), 58.

44. Leonard Lecht, *Experience under Railway Labor Legislation* (New York: Columbia University Press, 1955), 36.

45. These railroad unionization statistics are drawn from information in Wolf, *The Railroad Labor Board,* 58.

46. Austin K. Kerr, *American Railroad Politics* (Pittsburgh: University of Pittsburgh Press, 1968), 204.

47. *Pennsylvania R.R. v United States Railway Labor Board,* 261 U.S. 72.

48. *Pennsylvania Railroad System v Pennsylvania Railroad Company,* 267 U.S. 203; 45 SCt 307; 69 LEd 574.

49. Jacob J. Kaufman, *Collective Bargaining in the Railroad Industry* (New York: Kings Crown, 1954), 65.

50. Wilner, *The Railway Labor Act,* 46.

51. Ibid.

3. Major Collective Bargaining Legislation

1. K. Austin Kerr, American Railroad Politics (Pittsburgh: University of Pittsburgh Press, 1968), 41.

2. Irving Bernstein, *The New Deal Collective Bargaining Policy* (Los Angeles: University of California Press, 1950), 41

3. Irving Bernstein, *The Lean Years* (Boston: Houghton Mifflin, 1960), 216.

4. Charles M. Rhemus, "Evolution of Legislation Affecting Collective Bargaining in the Railroad and Airline Industries," in *The Railway Labor Act at Fifty,* National Mediation Board (Washington, D.C.: U.S. Government Printing Office, 1976), 8.

5. *Texas and New Orleans Railroad v The Brotherhood of Railway and Steamship Clerks,* 281 U.S. 548 (1930).

6. *Adair v United States,* 208 U.S. 161 (1908).

7. Charles O. Gregory, *Labor Laws and Legislation* (New York: Norton, 1958), 253.

8. Beatrice Burgoon, "Mediation under the Railway Labor Act," *The Railway Labor Act at Fifty*, National Mediation Board (Washington, D.C.: U.S. Government Printing Office), 73.

9. Charles M. Rhemus, "The First Fifty Years—And Then?" in *The Railway Labor Act at Fifty*, National Mediation Board (Washington, D.C.: U.S. Government Printing Office, 1976), 243.

10. National Mediation Board, *Fifty-Third and Fifty-Fourth Report*, (Washington, D.C.: U.S. Government Printing Office, 1989), 15.

11. John W. Gohmann, *Air and Rail Labor Relations* (Dubuque, Iowa: Kendal Hunt, 1979), 4.

12. Ibid., 5.

13. Bernstein, *The Lean Years*, 43.

14. Leonard Lecht, *Experience under Railway Labor Legislation* (New York: Columbia University Press, 1955), 79.

15. Decision 83 of the National Labor Relations Board established a maximum flying time for pilots of eighty-five hours per month. Hourly and mileage pay increments were also provided.

16. John M. Baitsell, *Airline Industrial Relations: Pilots and Flight Engineers* (Cambridge, Mass.: Harvard University Press, 1966), 32.

17. Lindley H. Clark, "Airlines and Railroads: A Weird Marriage," *Wall Street Journal*, Mar. 15, 1988.

18. *Railway Employees' Department v Hanson*, 351 U.S. 225 (1956).

19. Norris-La Guardia Act, 47 Stat. 70 (1932).

20. Edward I. Barrett, *Constitutional Law* (Westbury, N.Y.: Foundation Press, 1989), 213.

21. National Industrial Recovery Act, 48 Stat. 198 (1933).

22. *Schechter Poultry Corp. v United States*, 295 U.S. 495 (1935).

23. John Stern, "Collective Bargaining Legislation or Negotiation," *Harvard Law Review* 59 (June–July 1955), 657–63.

24. Barrett, *Constitutional Law*, 222.

25. 295 U.S. 495 (1935).

26. *NLRB v Jones and Laughlin Steel Corp.*, 301 U.S. 1 (1937). In addition to the *Jones & Laughlin* decision, four companion cases involving the constitutionality of the Wagner Act were decided by the Supreme Court: *NLRB v Fruehauf Trailer Co.*, *NLRB v Friedman-Harry Marks Clothing Co.*, *Washington,* *Virginia & Maryland Coach Co. v. NLRB*, and *Associated Press v NLRB*.

27. Reed C. Richardson, *Collective Bargaining Objectives* (Englewood Cliffs, N.J.: Prentice Hall, 1971), 37.

28. Ibid., 64.

29. Daniel Quinn Mills, *Labor-Management Relations*, 3d ed. (New York: McGraw-Hill, 1986), 41.

30. *Retail Clerks, Local 1625 v Schermerhorn*, 375 U.S. 96.

31. R. Alton Lee, *Truman and Taft-Hartley* (Garden City, N.Y.: Doubleday, 1966; reprint, 1980).

32. Northcote C. Parkinson, *Internal Disruption* (London: Leviathan House, 1981), 131.

33. Landrum Griffin Act, 73 Stat. 519 (1959), Sec. 2(b).

34. Mark I. Kahn, ed., *Cleared for Takeoff: Airline Labor Relations since Deregulation* (Ithaca, N.Y.: ILR Press, 1988), 2.

35. Alfred Kahn, "In Defense of Deregulation," in *Cleared for Takeoff: Airline Labor Relations since Deregulation*, ed. Mark I. Kahn (Ithaca, N.Y.: ILR Press, 1988), 344.

36. *NLRB v Bildisco and Bildisco*, 104 U.S. 118 (1984).

Additional Study Material: Detailed Examination of the Events Leading to Rule #83 Decision

1. Smith, *Airways*, p. 224; Knowlton, *Air Transportation in the United States*, p. 9; Fruedenthal, *The Aviation Business*, p. 311. [For complete references, see George Hopkins, *The Airline Pilots: A Study in Elite Unionization* (Cambridge, Mass.: Harvard University Press, 1971).]

2. "What's What Among Pilots!" *Aviation*, 32 (Mar. 1933), 91.

3. *New York Times*, Feb. 11, 1933, Sec. 7, p. 10.

4. *The Air Line Pilot* (Jan. 1933), p. 1.

5. James M. Mead to Behncke, Jan. 10, 1933.

6. *The Air Line Pilot* (Feb. 1933), p. 8.

7. Milton Derber, "Growth and Expansion," *Labor and the New Deal*, ed. Milton Derber and Edwin Young (Madison: University of Wisconsin Press, 1957), pp. 3–8.

8. ALPA, *Proceedings of the 1932 Convention*, pp. 50, 127–129.

9. Behncke to All Local Chairmen, Sept. 2, 1932.

10. ALPA, *Proceedings of the 1932 Convention*, pp. 84–94.

11. Charles Frederick Roos, *N.R.A. Economic Planning*, Cowles Commission for Research in Economics, No. 2 (Bloomington, Ind,: Principia Press, 1937), pp. 28–32.

12. ALPA, *Proceedings of the 1932 Convention*, pp. 168–190.

13. Frederick C. Warnshuis, Chairman, Aeromedical Association, to Behncke, Sept. 22, 1932.

14. ALPA, *Proceedings of the 1932 Convention*, pp. 168–190.

15. *The Air Line Pilot* (Feb. 1933), p. 1.

16. ALPA, *Proceedings of the 1932 Convention*, pp. 27–28.

17. *New York Times*, Feb. 26, 1933, p. 23.

18. *The Air Line Pilot* (Feb. 1933), p. 6.

19. Charles A. Madison, *American Labor Leaders: Personalities and Forces in the Labor Movement* (New York: Frederick Ungar, 1950), pp. 108–135.

20. Green to Behncke, Mar. 2, 1933.

21. *The Air Line Pilot* (March 1933), p. 1.

22. Arthur M. Schlesinger, Jr., *The Coming of the New Deal*, Vol. 2: *The Age of Roosevelt* (Boston: Houghton Mifflin, 1958), pp. 87–102.

23. Roos, *N.R.A. Economic Planning*, Appendix II, p. 537.

24. ALPA, *Proceedings of the 1934 Convention*, pp. 21–27.

25. Schlesinger, *The Coming of the New Deal*, Vol. 2, pp. 108–109; Roos, *N.R.A. Economic Planning*, pp. 55–82.

26. Schlesinger, *The Coming of the New Deal*, Vol. 2, pp. 107–108.

27. Minutes of the meeting of June 15, 1933, Central Executive Council, ALPA.

28. Minutes of the meeting of July 6, 1933, Central Executive Council, ALPA.

29. *The Air Line Pilot* (July 1933), p. 1.

30. Wallace S. Dawson to Behncke, Sept. 4, 1933.

31. *The Air Line Pilot* (July 1933), p. 1.

32. *Ibid.* (Aug. 1933), p. 6.

33. Minutes of the meeting of Aug. 3, 1933, Central Executive Council, ALPA; Schlesinger, *The Coming of the New Deal*, Vol. II, p. 126; Behncke to Hugh S. Johnson, Aug. 1, 1933.

34. Green to Behncke, Aug. 15, 1933.

35. ALPA, *Proceedings of the 1934 Convention*, pp. 61–64.

36. Minutes of the meeting of Aug. 15, 1933, Central Executive Council, ALPA.

37. Minutes of the meeting of Aug. 23, 1933, Central Executive Council, ALPA: *The Air Line Pilot* (Sept. 1933), p. 1.

38. ALPA, *Proceedings of the 1932 Convention*, pp. 21–22; *The Air Line Pilot* (Sept. 1933), p. 1. The pilot committee which attended the code hearings was composed of E. Hamilton Lee (United), Howard E. Hall (T&WA), Walter J. Hunter (American), Eugene Brown (Eastern), Sam Carson (Kohler), John H. Neale (Pacific), Mal B. Freeburg (Northwest), and John H. Tilton and C. M. Drayton (Pan American).

39. "Code for the Air Transport Industry," *Aviation*, 32 (Sept. 1933), 290–291.

40. "Coding Air Transport," *Aviation*, 32 (Oct. 1933), 311–312.

41. *New York Times*, Aug. 28, 1933, p. 12.

42. *Ibid.*, Aug. 29, 1933, p. 16.

43. "Coding Air Transport," *Aviation*, 32 (Oct. 1933), 311–312; minutes of the meeting of Oct. 10, 1933, Central Executive Council, ALPA.

44. ALPA, *Proceedings of the 1934 Convention*, pp. 24–26; "Blue Eagle Takes Wing," *Aviation*, 32 (Sept. 1933), 369–370; *New York Times*, Sept. 12, 1933, p. 15. Muir signed the code on Sept. 11 and passed it on to the White House for presidential approval, which finally came on Nov. 20, 1933.

45. William Randolph Hearst to M. A. Roddy, Editor, *The Air Line Pilot*, Dec. 8, 1933. In a letter to the nominal editor of the union newspaper, Hearst expressed his admiration for the airline pilots. He considered them a kind of ready reserve for the defense of the country, since they would, in his opinion, need little or no training before they started manning bombers. "The next war . . . which God forbid, will be decided in the air," he said, "and some of the brave men to whom this letter comes will determine the decision. The nation owes them much now and may in the future owe them many times more."

46. ALPA, *Proceedings of the 1942 Convention*, pp. 70–80; ALPA, *Proceedings of the 1934 Convention*, p. 24.

47. ALPA, *Proceedings of the 1934 Convention*, pp. 27–28; *New York Times*, Sept. 22, 1933, p. 19. On

Sept. 21, the "Big Five" finally issued a public statement declaring their intention to impose the new hourly pay system. Behncke knew about it early in September, however.

48. *New York Times*, Sept. 3, 1933, p. 7; minutes of the meeting of Oct. 10, 1933, Central Executive Council, ALPA.

49. *New York Times*, Sept. 22, 1933, p. 19; *The Air Line Pilot* (Jan. 1934), p. 1; ALPA, *Proceedings of the 1934 Convention*, p. 76.

50. Behncke to W. M. Leiserson, Secretary, N.L.B., Sept. 20, 1933; "Truce," *Aviation*, 32 (Sept. 1933), 297.

51. Schlesinger, *Coming of the New Deal*, Vol. 2, pp. 146–147.

52. ALPA, *Proceedings of the 1934 Convention*, pp. 28–30.

53. *The Air Line Pilot* (Oct. 1933), p. 1; minutes of the meeting of Oct. 10, 1933, Central Executive Council, ALPA.

54. *New York Times*, Sept. 3, 1933, Sec. 8, p. 7.

55. Roos, *N.R.A. Economic Planning*, pp. 33, 56–57, 221.

56. ALPA, *Proceedings of the 1934 Convention*, pp. 30–35.

57. *New York Times*, Sept. 27, 1933, p. 9; *ibid.*, Oct. 1, 1933, p. 27.

58. National Recovery Administration, National Labor Board, *In the Matter of the Hearing Between Representatives of the Air Line Pilots Association and Representatives of United Air Lines, American Airways, and North American Aviation Corporation* (abridged transcript in the ALPA archives).

59. *Ibid.*

60. *Ibid.*

61. *Ibid.*; ALPA, *Proceedings of the 1934 Convention*, pp. 37–40; *New York Times*, Oct. 3, 1933, p. 15; *ibid.*, Oct. 5, 1933, p. 1; *ibid.*, Oct. 6, 1933, p. 9; "Pilots' Debate," *Aviation*, 32 (Nov. 1933), 354.

62. *New York Times*, Oct. 28, 1933, p. 18; *ibid.*, Oct. 29, 1933, p. 25.

63. ALPA, *Pilots' Final Brief Before a Fact Finding Committee Held by Judge Shientag, Chairman of the Committee Studying the Air Line Pilot Wage and Hour Question*, p. 1.

64. Reginald M. Cleveland, "Pilots' Pay Is Debated," *New York Times*, Nov. 5, 1933, Sec. 8, p. 7.

65. ALPA, *Proceedings of the 1934 Convention*, pp. 40–41.

66. *Ibid.*, pp. 41–43.

67. "Wages of Pilots," *Aviation*, 32 (Dec.1933), 382.

68. *Ibid.*; *New York Times*, Nov. 7, 1933, p. 24.

69. ALPA, *Proceedings of the 1934 Convention*, pp. 45–48; "Wages of Pilots," *Aviation*, 32 (Dec.1933), 382.

70. "Wage Scale Arbitration," *Aviation*, 33 (Jan. 1934), 26–27; ALPA, *Pilots' Report of a Conference Held at the Mayflower Hotel, December 15, 1933, Between the Pilots' Subcommittee and the Operators in Compliance with a Suggestion of the National Labor Board at the Hearing of December 14, 1933*. The Pilots present at the meeting were Behncke and Jack O'Brien for United, Eugene Brown for Eastern, Alexis Klotz for Western Air Express, and Clyde Holbrook for American. The officials representing the operators were W. A. Patterson for United, Harris M. "Pop" Hanshue for North American Aviation (which by this time controlled Eastern, T&WA, and Western), and Lester D. "Bing" Seymour for American.

71. "No Quarter in Wage War," *Aviation*, 33 (Feb. 1934), 54–55; *The Air Line Pilot* (Jan. 1934), p. 1; minutes of the meeting of Jan. 16, 1934, Central Executive Council, ALPA.

72. John M. Baitsell, *Airline Industrial Relations; Pilots and Flight Engineers* (Cambridge, Mass.: Harvard University Press, 1966), p. 32.

73. Mark L. Kahn, *Pay Practices for Flight Employees on U.S. Airlines* (University of Michigan—Wayne State University, Institute of Labor and Industrial Relations, No. 23, 1961), p. 12. Reprinted from U.S., President's Railroad Commission, *Report of the Presidential Railroad Commission*, Appendix, Vol. 4 (Washington: U.S. Government Printing Office, 1962), pp. 1–38.

4. Elections, Certifications, and Procedures

1. *Gibbons v Ogden*, 22 U.S. 1 (1824).

2. *Champion v Ames*, 188 U.S. 100 (1902); *Schechter Corp. v U.S.*, 295 U.S. 495 (1935); *NLRB v Jones and Laughlin Steel Corp.*, 301 U.S. 1 (1937); *U.S. v Darby*, 312 U.S. 100 (1941).

3. *Northwest Airlines Inc.*, 2 NMB 19 (1948); *Northwest Airlines Inc.*, 2 NMB 25 (1948).

4. *Braniff Airways*, 5 NMB 6 (1968); *Frontier Airlines Inc.*, 5 NMB 88 (1970).

5. *International Brotherhood of Teamsters & Midway Airlines, Inc.*, 18 NMB 42, NMB R-6021 (1991).

6. 45 U.S.C. 152, Ninth (1982).

7. 45 U.S.C. 151, Sixth (1988).

8. 45 U.S.C. 151a, Ninth (1988).

9. *Brotherhood of Railway & Steamship Clerks, Freight Handlers, Express & Station Employees v Association for the Benefit of Non-Contract Employees*, 380 U.S. 650 (1965).

10. 29 CFR 101.4 (1991).

11. 29 CFR 1203.2 (1991).

12. Ibid.

13. Ibid.

14. National Mediation Board, *Administration of the Railway Labor Act* (Washington, D.C.: U.S. Government Printing Office, 1970), 66.

15. *Erie Railroad Company*, 3 NMB 187 (1955).

16. 29 CFR 1206.4 (1991).

17. 45 U.S.C. 152, Ninth (1988).

18. *National Federation of Railroad Workers v NMB*, 110 2d 529 (1940).

19. *International In-Flight Catering Co. v NMB*, 121 DLR A-6 (9th Cir., 1977).

20. Ibid.

21. *Virginian Railroad v Federation*, 300 U.S. 515 (1937).

22. 29 CFR 1202.5 (1991).

23. 29 CFR 1202.7 (1991).

24. 45 U.S.C. 152, Ninth (1988).

25. 45 U.S.C. 152, Fourth (1988).

26. 1 NMB 167 (1940).

27. *Switchman's Union v NMB*, 320 U.S. 297 (1943).

28. Ibid.

29. 29 CFR 1202.8 (1991).

30. 45 U.S.C. 151a, Ninth (1988).

31. *American Airlines, Inc.*, 1 *NMB* 394, 399 (1945).

32. 6 NMB 180 (1977).

33. *American Airlines, Inc.*, 1 NMB 371 (1944).

34. *United Airlines, Inc.*, 3 NMB 56 (1961).

35. *American Airlines*, 1 NMB 394 (1945).

36. Ibid.

37. *Continental Airlines*, NMB R-2714 (1953); *Pan American World Airways*, NMB R-2777 (1953).

38. 45 U.S.C. 152, Fourth (1988).

39. *Virginian Railroad Company v System Federation No. 40*, 300 U.S. 515, 547 (1937).

40. 380 U.S. 650 (1965).

41. James Ott, "Board Decisions Muddle Rules on Unions' Role after Mergers," *Aviation Week and Space Technology*, Aug. 28, 1989.

42. "Current Labor Statistics," *Monthly Labor Review*, Apr. 1990, 49–100.

43. *Ohio Power Co. & Utility Workers Union of America*, 23 LRRM 1242, 80 NLRB 205 (1948).

44. Ibid.

45. *NLRB v Textron Inc.*, 85 LRRM 2945 (1974).

46. *B.F. Goodrich & Co. and Local No. 281*, 37 LRRM 1383, 115 NLRB 103 (1956).

47. National Labor Relations Board, *A Guide to Basic Law and Procedures under the National Labor Relations Act* (Washington, D.C.: U.S. Government Printing Office, 1990), 43.

48. *Advance Pattern Co. & Printing Specialists and Paper Converters Union No. 363*, 23 LRRM 1022, 80 NLRB 10 (1948).

49. *Kennecott Copper Corp.*, 29 LRRM 1300, 98 NLRB 14 (1952).

50. *J.C. Penney & Retail Clerks Intl.*, 25 LRRM 1039, 86 NLRB 109 (1949).

51. Daniel Quinn Mills, *Labor-Management Relations*, 4th ed. (New York: McGraw-Hill, 1989), 118.

52. *NLRB v Metropolitan Life Ins. Co.*, 58 LRRM 2721, 380 U.S. 438 (1965).

53. *B.F. Goodrich & Co. and Local No. 281*, 37 LRRM 1383, 115 NLRB 103 (1956).

54. *National Torch Tip Co.*, 33 LRRM 1369, 107 NLRB 269 (1954).

55. *Booth Broadcasting Co.*, 49 LRRM 1278, 134 NLRB 80 (1961).

56. *Sportswear Industries Inc.*, 56 LRRM 1307, 147 NLRB 79 (1964).

57. Mills, *Labor-Management Relations*, 4th ed., 117.

58. *National Tube Co.*, 21 LRRM 1292, 76 NLRB 169 (1948).

59. *American Potash & Chemical Corp.*, 33 LRRM 1380, 107 NLRB 290 (1954).

60. *Mallinckrodt Chemical Works*, 64 LRRM 1011 (1966).

61. Michael Ballot, *Labor Management Relations in a Changing Environment* (New York: John Wiley and Sons, 1992), 170.

62. *Brooks v NLRB*, 348 U.S. 96 (1954).

Additional Study Material: Examination of the Events Surrounding the Strike by Trans World Airline Flight Attendants

1. Carol J. Loomis, "The Comeuppance of Carl Icahn," *Fortune Magazine*, Feb. 17, 1986.

2. Ibid.

3. Ibid.

4. Ibid.

5. Aaron Bernstein and Chuck Hawkins, "Icahn Ponders Dismembering His New Airline," *Business Week Magazine*, Mar. 17, 1986.

6. Ibid.

7. Paul Wagman, "TWA Flying at Half-Strength," *St. Louis Post-Dispatch*, Mar. 8, 1986.

8. Ibid.

9. Paul Wagman, "Talks Between Company, Attendants to Resume," *St. Louis Post-Dispatch*, Mar. 11, 1986.

10. Ibid.

11. Ibid.

12. Paul Wagman, "More Than Pay at Stake for TWA Strikers," *St. Louis Post-Dispatch*, Mar. 26, 1986.

13. Paul Wagman, "Talks Between Company, Attendants to Resume," *St. Louis Post-Dispatch*, Mar. 11, 1986.

14. Paul Wagman, "TWA, Attendants Halt Talks," *St. Louis Post-Dispatch*, Mar. 13, 1986.

15. Ibid.

16. Paul Wagman, "TWA Strikers Swimming Against Tide," *St. Louis Post-Dispatch*, Apr. 13, 1986.

17. Dave Hage and Conrad de Fiebre, "Replacing Strikers Is Growing Industry Trend," *Minneapolis Star Tribune*, Jan. 12, 1986.

18. Nancy Peacock, "Flight Attendants Bailing Out of Not-So-Elite Corps," *Akron Beacon Journal*, July 27, 1986.

19. Jim Davis, and John Dauner, "TWA Says It's Quit Hiring Attendants," *Kansas City Times*, Apr.29, 1986.

20. John Dauner, "TWA Loses Fight over Union Dues," *Kansas City Times*, Aug. 2, 1986.

21. Ibid.

22. Ibid.

23. John Dauner, "TWA Appeals Due for Flight Attendants," *Kansas City Times*, Aug. 8, 1986.

24. Jeff Taylor, "TWA Strikers Fail in Bid to Get Their Old Jobs Back," *Kansas City Times*, Aug. 26, 1986.

25. Dave Hage and Conrad de Fiebre, "Replacing Strikers Is Growing Industry Trend," *Minneapolis Star Tribune*, Jan. 12, 1986.

26. Carolyn Friday and David Pauly, "A Fatal Flight Takes Its Toll," *Newsweek Magazine*, Sept. 8, 1986.

27. Ibid.

28. Daniel Seligman, "Keeping Up: A Soviet Election," *Fortune Magazine*, July 3, 1989.

29. "Railway Labor Act Isn't Excess Baggage," letters to the editor, *Wall Street Journal*, June 5, 1987.

5. Contractual Negotiations

1. Robert N. Corley, *The Legal Environment of Business* (New York: McGraw-Hill, 1977).

2. Ibid.

3. Leonard R. Saleys and George Strauss, *Managing Human Resources* (Englewood Cliffs, N.J.: Prentice Hall, Inc., 1981).

4. Daniel Quinn Mills, *Labor-Management Relations*, 3d ed. (New York: McGraw-Hill, 1986).

5. 18 NMB 89, R-6040 (1991).

6. Personal discussion between the author and Delle-Femine, August 1985.

7. 73 LRRM 2278, (1970)

8. William E. Simkin, *Mediation and the Dynamics of Collective Bargaining* (Washington, D.C.: Bureau of National Affairs, 1971), 77–106.

9. 45 U.S.C. 160 (1988).

10. Alexander Wells, *Air Transportation: A Management Perspective*, (Belmont, Calif.: Wadsworth, 1984).

11. Rollo Foster, *Aviation Law: An Introduction* (Lanham, Md.: Maryland Historical Press, 1985), 11.

12. Howard J. Anderson, *The Labor Board and The Collective Bargaining Process* (Washington, D.C.: U.S. Government Printing Office, 1971).

13. Reed C. Richardson, *Collective Bargaining Objectives* (Englewood Cliffs, N.J.: Prentice Hall, 1971), 113.

14. Anderson, *The Labor Board*.

15. 29 U.S.C. 158 (1988).

16. 29 U.S.C. 176 (1988).

17. 29 U.S.C. 173 (1988).

18. Ibid.

19. Mills, *Labor-Management Relations*, 3d ed.

20. Ibid.

21. *Ottawa Silica Co. v NLRB*, 482 F.2d 945 (1972).

22. Mills, *Labor-Management Relations*, 3d ed.

23. Edmund Pinto, "Intelligence," *Aviation Daily*, Apr. 11, 1991, 75.

24. Tom Bethel, "Labor Pains (Filibuster Stymies Enactment of Worker Replacement Bill)," *National Review*, July 11, 1994.

25. *NLRB v Mackay Radio & Telegraph Co.*, 304 U.S. 333 (1938).

26. Aaron Bernstein, "You Can't Bargain with a Worker Whose Job Is No More," *Business Week*, Aug. 5, 1991.

6. Grievance Procedures

1. J. W. Friedman, "Individual Rights in Grievance Arbitration," *Arbitration Journal* 27, no. 4 (1972): 252–73.

2. A. B. Smith Jr., "The Impact on Collective Bargaining of Equal Employment Remedies," *Industrial & Labor Relations Review* 28, no. 3 (1975): 376–94.

3. A. H. Levy, "The Collective Bargaining Agreement as a Limitation on Union Control of Employees' Grievances," *Industrial Relations Law Digest* 13, no. 4 (1971): 27–54.

4. J. A. Lapp, *How to Handle Labor Grievances* (Deep Haven, Conn.: National Foreman's Institute, 1946).

5. H. W. Davey, *Contemporary Collective Bargaining* (Englewood Cliffs, N.J.: Prentice Hall, 1972).

6. 16 NLRB 744.

7. Gerald Somers, *Grievance Settlement in Coal Mining* (Morgantown, Va: Bureau of Business Research, College of Commerce, West Virginia University, 1956).

8. *International Association of Machinists, AFL-CIO, v Central Airlines, Inc.*, 372 U.S. 682 (1963).

9. *Brotherhood of Railroad Trainmen v Chicago River & Indiana Railroad Co.*, 353 U.S. 30 (1915).

10. *United Steelworkers v Enterprise Wheel & Car Corp.*, 363 U.S. 593 (1960).

11. *Brotherhood of Railroad Trainmen v Central of Georgia Railway Co.*, 415 F.2d 403 (1969).

12. "Arbitration Provisions in Collective Agreements," *Monthly Labor Review*, Mar. 1993, 262–66.

13. *United Steelworkers v Warrior & Gulf Navigation Co.*, 363 U.S. 574 (1960).

14. *United Steelworkers v Enterprise Wheel & Car Corp.*, 363 U.S. 593 (1960).

7. Unfair Labor Practices

1. Railway Labor Act, U.S. Code, Title 45, CH8 Tenth, 45 U.S.C. 152 (1993).

2. *Texas & N.O.R. Co. v Brotherhood of Railway & Steamship Clerks*, 281 U.S. 548 (1930).

3. *Virginia Railroad Co. V. System Federation No. 40*, 300 U.S. 515 (1937).

4. *Allegheny Airlines, Inc.*, NMB R-3470 (1962).

5. *Linea Aeropostal Venezolana*, NMB R-2938 (1955).

6. *Teamsters v Braniff Airways, Inc.*, 70 LRRM 3333 (1969).

7. *Association of Flight Attendants v Horizon Air, Industries*, U.S. Fed. District Ct. 017-5308, Oregon (1989).

8. *United States v TACA Airways Agency, Inc.*, Indictment 24270 E.D. LA (1952).

9. *United States v Jerry Winston & Broome County Aviation, Inc. d/b/a Commuter Airlines, Inc.*, Indictment 75-CR-83, Northern District, NY (1976).

10. George E. Hopkins, *Flying the Line: The First Half-Century of the Air Line Pilots Association* (Washington, D.C.: Air Line Pilots Association, Intl., 1982), 175.

11. National Labor Relations Act, 49 Stat. 449 (1935), amended P.L. No. 101, 80th Congress (1947), and P.L. 257, 86th Congress (1959); 29 U.S.C. 159–161.

12. Reed C. Richardson, *Collective Bargaining by Objectives* (Englewood Cliffs, N.J.: Prentice Hall, 1947), 47.

13. *NLRB v Dale Industries, Inc.*, 355 F.2d 851, (6th Cir., 1966).

14. *Master Touch Dental Laboratories*, 65 LRRM 1368, 165 NLRB 73 (1967).

15. *Darlington Manufacturing v Amalgamated Clothing and Textile Workers Union*, 58 LRRM 2657, USS Ct. (1965).

16. *Medo Photo Supply Corp. v NLRB*, 14 LRRM 581, USS Ct. (1941); *Standard Coil Products, Inc.*, 30 LRRM 581, 99 NLRB 131 (1952); *NLRB v Exchange Part Co.*, 55 LRRM 2098, 375 U.S. 405 (1965).

17. *Pacific Southwest Airlines*, 201 NLRB 647 (1973).

18. *Raleys, Inc. v NLRB*, 703 F.2d 410 (9th Cir., 1983).

19. *NLRB v Collins & Aikman Corp.*, 15 LRRM 826, 146 F.2d 454 (1944); *NLRB v Swan Fastener Corp.*, 31 LRRM 2082, 199 F.2d 935 (1952).

20. *Excelsior Laundry Co.*, 186 NLRB 914 (1970).

21. *General Engineering, Inc.*, 131 NLRB 901 (1961).

22. *Montgomery Ward & Co. v NLRB*, 385 F.2d 769 (8th Cir., 1967).

23. *NLRB v Somerville Buick, Inc.*, 29 LRRM 2379, 194 F.2d 935, 952 (1952); *NLRB v Swan Fastener Corp.*, 31 LRRM 2082, 199 F.2d 935 (1952).

24. *Phelps Dodge Corp. v NLRB*, 313 U.S. 177 (1941).

25. *Smith v NLRB*, 132 NLRB 1493 (1961).

26. *Hoisting and Portable Engineers, Local 302*, 144 NLRB 1449 (1963).

27. *NLRB v Hershey Foods Corp.*, 513 F.2d 1083 (9th Cir., 1975).

28. *Stoddard-Quirk Manufacturing Co.*, 51 LRRM 1110, 138 NLRB 75 (1962).

29. *J. P. Stevens & Company v NLRB*, 623 F.2d 322 (1981).

30. *NLRB v Gissel Packing Company*, 395 U.S. 575.

31. *Pan American World Airways v IBT*, 275 F.Supp 986 (S.D.N.Y. 1967).

Additional Study Material: National Mediation Board Rulings in Laker, Key, and America West Certification Elections

16 NMB No. 88 (Key Airlines)

1. The *Laker* ballot is a modified ballot procedure designed to correct the effects of carrier interference. It was first used by the Board in *Laker Airways, Ltd.*, 8 NMB 236 (1981). The ballot provides "Do you desire to be represented by the [name of applicable organization]?" with boxes marked "yes" and "no". No space for write-in votes is provided and the majority of valid ballots actually cast determines the outcome of the election.

2. The pay raise for pilots and flight engineers was announced the day before the IBT filed a representation application on December 22, 1988 for these employees.

17 NMB No. 63 (American West Airlines)

1. A "Laker" election involves a "yes" or "no" ballot. The majority of votes cast determines the outcome of the election.

2. In a "Key" election the majority of the eligible voters must vote against representation in order to prevent certification.

3. In *Laker Airways, Ltd.*, 8 NMB 236 (1981), the Board, stated,

> . . . it is a *per se* violation of the [Act] for any carrier or its officials to solicit employees to turn their ballots in to the carrier. It is, furthermore, a *per se* violation to provide mailing envelopes for this purpose. . . . It is a *per se* violation to poll employees during a representation election conducted by the Board. . . .

See, also Key Airlines, 16 NMB 358 and 296 (1989), and 13 NMB 153 (1986), where the Board found "egregious" such carrier actions as discharge and transfer of known union supporters.

4. Among the revised language proposed by the carrier are statements such as:

> "While the union's allegations of coercive threats and reprisals were not supported by the evidence . . ."
>
> . . .
>
> . . . "the carrier is free under the First Amendment to express its opinion regarding the union".

8. The Labor Relations Environment

1. John R. Meyer et al., *Airline Deregulation: The Early Experience* (Boston, Mass.: Auburn House, 1981).

2. Nawal K. Taneja, *The Commercial Airline Industry* (Lexington, Mass.: D. C. Heath, 1976), 124.

3. U.S. Civil Aeronautics Board, *Report No. 33*, 33 CAB 307 (1961).

4. Taneja, *The Commercial Airline Industry*, 126.

5. Ibid.

6. Meyer et al., *Airline Deregulation*, 8.

7. John Dunlop, "Trends and Issues in Labor Relations," (speech before the Employee-Management Relations Committee of the National Academy of Sciences, Harvard University, Jan. 14, 1985).

8. Ibid.

9. Robert J. Joedicke, *The Goose That Laid Golden Eggs* (Lehman Brothers, Inc., New York, Feb. 1981, photocopy). Courtesy of the author.

10. United States Senate, *Report No. 631*, 95th Cong., 2d sess. (1978): 2.

11. John T. Dunlop, "Trends and Issues in Labor Relations: Working Towards Consensus," *Challenge* 25 (July–Aug. 1985): 26–34.

12. Frank Borman, untitled presentation at the Lehman Brothers—Kuhn Loeb—Airline Industry Seminar, New York, Feb. 11–13, 1982.

13. A. Brown, *The Politics of Airline Deregulation* (Knoxville: University of Tennessee Press, 1987), 2.

14. United States Senate, *Report No. 631*, 95th Cong., 2d sess. (1978): 12.

15. Brown, *The Politics of Airline Deregulation.*

16. For a more detailed description of the regulatory impact of deregulation, see Harry P. Wolfe and David A. NewMyer, *Aviation Industry Regulation*, (Carbondale: Southern Illinois University Press, 1985).

17 Meyer et al, *Airline Deregulation*, 211.

18. Alexander T. Wells, *Air Transportation: A Management Perspective* (Los Angeles: Wadsworth, 1984), 435.

19. Frank H. Cassell and Frank A. Spencer, *Airline Labor Relations under Deregulation: From Oligopoly to Competition and Return?* (Evanston, Ill.: Northwestern University, Transportation Center, n.d.).

9. Annual Activity

1. Airline Deregulation Act, 49 U.S.C. 1302 (1978).

2. William Curtain, "Airline Labor Relations under Deregulation," *Monthly Labor Review*, June 1986, 30.

3. Reginald Stuart, "Competition Thins out at 30,000 Feet," *New York Times*, June 29, 1986.

4. Harold Seneker, "Fare Wars," *Forbes Magazine*, Sept. 1, 1980, 37.

5. Thomas S. Robertson and Scott Ward, "Management Lessons from Airline Deregulation," *Harvard Business Review*, Jan.–Feb. 1983, 41.

6. Frank H. Cassell and Frank A. Spencer, *Airline Labor Relations under Deregulation: From Oligopoly to Competition and Return?* (Evanston, Ill., Northwestern University, Transportation Center, n.d.).

7. George Rubin, "Collective Bargaining in 1982," *Monthly Labor Review*, Jan. 1983, 33.

8. Seth D. Rosen, *Airline Collective Bargaining*

since Deregulation: Some Perspectives (Washington, D.C.: Air Line Pilots Association, Intl., 1987).

9. Argument made by Delle-Femine during concessionary negotiations between Ozark Air Lines, Inc. and the Aircraft Mechanics Fraternal Association; contained in Robert W. Kaps's minutes of negotiation, Sept. 1983.

10. *NLRB v Bildisco and Bildisco*, 104 U.S. 118 (1984).

11. *Wheeling-Pittsburgh Steel Corp. v United Steelworkers of America*, 791 F.2d 1074, 14 C.B.C. 2d 955 (3d Cir., 1986).

12. George Rubin, "Modest Settlements in 1984," *Monthly Labor Review*, Jan. 1985, 6–7.

13. *International Brotherhood of Teamsters v Texas International Airlines, Inc.*, 8 NMB 217 (1981).

14. George Rubin, "Labor and Management Continue to Combat Mutual Problems in 1985," *Monthly Labor Review*, Jan. 1986, 7.

15. Ibid., 6.

16. Rosen, *Airline Collective Bargaining since Deregulation*, 35.

17. George Rubin, "Review of Collective Bargaining in 1987," *Monthly Labor Review*, Jan. 1988, 26–27.

18. Ibid., 28.

19. George Rubin, "Labor Management Relations in 1988," *Monthly Labor Review*, Jan. 1989, 26.

20. Michael Cimini, "Collective Bargaining in 1990," *Monthly Labor Review*, Jan. 1991, 29.

21. Michael Cimini and Susan L. Behrmann, "Collective Bargaining, 1991," *Monthly Labor Review*, Jan. 1992, 28.

10. The View of the Unions

1. P. Gaudin, "Striking Attitudes", *Airline Business Magazine*, Feb. 1987, 22–26.

2. J. Nammack, "Labor vs. Management," *Airline Executive Magazine*, Feb. 1984, 21–25.

3. R. K. Ellingsworth, J. Baumgarner, and L. Townsend, "Status of Airline Labor Contracts as of July 25, 1989," *Aviation Daily*, July 17, 1989, 297.

4. Douglas A. Fraser, "Labor on Corporate Boards: An Interview with Douglas A. Fraser" *Challenge*, July–Aug. 1981, 30–33.

5. Mean Jennings, "Labor Bites Back! Sharing Your Troubles," *Airline Business*, July 1993.

6. Ibid.

7. William Flannery, "TWA's Fight Chance," *Career Pilot*, Nov. 1993.

8. Esperison Martinez Jr., "ALPA's Presidential Scorecard," *Air Line Pilot Magazine*, Feb. 1994.

9. Charles C. Heckscher, *The New Unionism: Employee Involvement in the Changing Corporation* (New York: Basic Books, 1988), 127.

10. Jeremy Rifkin and Randy Barber, *The North Will Rise Again: Pensions, Politics, and Power in the 1980's,* (Boston: Beacon Press, 1978).

11. Adam Bryant, "United Fights for Its Health as Unions Fight for United," *New York Times*, Aug. 22, 1993.

Glossary

The language of labor relations, in many instances, is closely associated with the language of the law. The definitions of many of the terms used to discuss labor relations are derived from the general usage of the terms in the field of law. This glossary defines terms as they are used in this book. Each of these terms appears in **boldface** where it first occurs in text.

Affirmative action programs. Programs that provide goals and timetables by which employers will target specific groups for hiring, promotion, and so on.

Agency shop. A provision requiring nonmembers of a certified union to pay a sum equal to union dues. A company has an agency shop when the union serves as the agent for and receives dues and assessments from all employees in the bargaining unit whether or not they are union members.

Airline Deregulation Act of 1978. Act relinquishing all governmental controls regulating the operation of airlines, except for safety requirements.

Amendable date. Date at which the provisions of a contract are open to renegotiation. More generally a part of the terminology of the RLA, under which contracts are amendable. Under the NLRA, contracts are terminable; therefore, the *contract termination date* is more a part of that terminology.

American Arbitration Association. Organization of professional arbitrators commonly used as third-party mediators and/or arbitrators in labor disputes and grievance hearings.

American Federation of Labor. Labor organization formed in 1886 by Samuel Gompers, who became known as the father of the American labor movement. The AFL was the forerunner of the AFL-CIO.

American Federation of Labor and Congress of Industrial Organizations. Commonly called the AFL-CIO. Organization formed in 1955 by the merger of the AFL and the CIO to stave the effects of the Taft-Hartley Act and bond labor to a cohesive front. Membership includes the majority of labor unions in the country. Notable exceptions are the Teamsters and the United Auto Workers.

Arbitration. Method of determining a final solution to a dispute between parties to a labor agreement. The final decision from an outside disinterested party is usually binding on the parties.

Arbitrator. Third party neutral to a dispute. Employed jointly by union and management officials to make binding decisions on employee grievances.

Authorization card. A statement signed by an employee designating a union to act on his or her behalf in collective bargaining or in requesting either the National Mediation Board or the National Labor Relations Board to hold a certification election.

Award. Final decision rendered in various types of disputes. For example, an award of an arbitrator in a grievance decision.

Back pay. Wages required to be paid to a worker who has been discharged and reinstated with full rights or wages required to be paid to a worker or workers because a contract is signed with a retroactive effective date.

Bargaining unit. The defined area eligible to be represented by a particular union. Defined as "craft" or "class" under the Railway Labor Act.

Benefits. Portion of compensation other than direct wages, such as vacation time, hospitalizations, and so on. Basically came into existence during World War II, when the federal government froze all wage increases.

Binding arbitration. Agreement by both parties to a dispute to agree to the final decision of a disinterested third party, after both sides have had the opportunity to present arguments in favor of their particular position.

Boycott. Refusal to deal with or purchase goods or services of a business, in an attempt to exert pressure in a labor dispute.

Cease and desist order. A command issued by a labor board requiring either the employer or the union to refrain from an unfair labor practice.

Certification. Official designation by either the National Labor Relations Board or National Mediation Board that a particular union is the exclusive bargaining representative of employees in a particular unit or class and craft.

Checkoff. Arrangement between an employer and a union in which the employer agrees to deduct union dues directly from employees' pay checks and forward the dues to the union.

Check rides. Pilot performance evaluations made by supervisory personnel during scheduled airline flights.

Civil Aeronautics Board. An independent federal agency that regulated carrier operations, including rates, routes, operating rights, and mergers, prior to the Deregulation Act of 1978.

Clayton Act. Federal legislation passed in 1914 declaring that human labor is not an article of commerce.

Closed shop. Arrangement between an employer and a union that only members of the union may be hired. Illegal under the Taft-Hartley Act, except in the construction industry. Not illegal under the Railway Labor Act.

Coalition. A group of unions that makes a joint or cooperative effort for their common good in negotiation of contracts or methods of operation. Became pronounced in the airline industry during the late 1970s, when wage concessions were being requested from all unions.

Collective bargaining. Attempt between union and management to resolve conflicting interests in a manner suitable to both parties.

Commonwealth v Hunt. A landmark decision rendered in 1842 in the State of Massachusetts that declared that the criminal conspiracy doctrine was not applicable in that state. The first decision rendered declaring that unions had a right to exist.

Company union. Union organization that receives financial help and support from the company whose employees it represents. This type of arrangement is illegal.

Concessionary bargaining. Negotiation process wherein the company is generally seeking a reduction of wage and/or benefits or a change in work rules. The negotiation of pay freeze, pay cuts, rollbacks, and other work rule changes occurred frequently in the 1980s.

Conciliation. Efforts by a third party to resolve opposing points of view and accommodate a voluntary settlement.

Congress of Industrial Organizations. Labor organization formed in 1938 to unionize employees on an industrial basis rather than a craft or trade basis. Merged with the American Federation of Labor in 1955 to become the AFL-CIO.

Contract bar rule. Period of time and rules, applied by both the National Labor Relations Board and the National Mediation Board, determining when an existing contract between an employer and a union will stop a representation election by a rival or raiding union.

Contract out. Same as subcontracting. An action in which an employer, with or without agreement of the union, has work performed outside the traditional workforce.

Cooling-off period. Period of time during which employees are forbidden to strike and the employer is forbidden to lock out. Cooling-off periods literally mean time for the parties to rethink their positions before they are permitted to utilize self-help methods.

Craft and class determinations. Decisions rendered by the National Mediation Board as to workers following a particular craft or class in which they work.

Craft union. Labor organization that seeks to include all workers who have a common skill, such as carpenters or plumbers.

Craft unit. Bargaining unit consisting of workers following a particular craft (e.g., carpenters) or using a particular type of skill.

Decertification election. Election held by the National Labor Relations Board to determine employee desire to maintain union status.

Deregulation. Process of lifting artificial barriers or governmental control of an industry.

Direct negotiations. The period of time when both the company and the union representatives are engaged in bargaining without the presence of a mediator.

Double-breasting. The existence of separate union and nonunion divisions or companies in a single firm.

Duty of fair representation. The responsibility of unions to represent fair and impartially all union and nonunion members of a bargaining unit.

Emergency board. Board appointed by the president of the United States to investigate the effect potential strikes might have on commerce. Cooling-off periods are implemented while the board considers the situations abetting the potential strikes. Such a board may be convened under both the Railway Labor Act and the National Labor Relations Act.

Employee ownership. A form of worker ownership in which employees of a firm also own and direct a sizable share of the company.

Employee Retirement Income and Security Act. Federal statute passed by Congress to ensure that employer pension plans meet minimum participation, vesting, and funding requirements.

Employee Stock Ownership Plan. Program in which employer gives employees the opportunity to become shareholders in the company by matching employees' payment toward stock purchase or by providing matching stock for wages forgone in concessionary bargaining.

Fact finding. Process used to determine facts and make recommendations in major disputes.

Featherbedding. Contractual requirements that employees be hired into positions for which their services are not required. This practice was made illegal under the National Labor Relations Act by

the Taft-Hartley Act. No such proscription exists under the Railway Labor Act.

Furlough. As used in the airline industry, synonymous with **layoff**.

Good-faith bargaining. Obligation of negotiators to demonstrate a sincere and honest intent to enter into a labor agreement. The National Labor Relations Act sets forth specific regulations concerning good-faith bargaining. The Railway Labor Act does not specifically establish good-faith bargaining issues.

Grievance. An employee complaint alleging that a contract violation has occurred. May also be used by a union or an employer to voice their allegations of a violation by the opposite party.

Haymarket Riot of 1886. Protest over the establishment of an eight-hour workday. Violence characterized its outcome, leading to the tide of public opinion against labor.

Impasse. Time in negotiations when no movement is either evident or obtainable. The parties are unable to resolve issues among themselves. Third-party intervention is usually required at this juncture.

Injunction. Mandatory order by the court to perform or discontinue a specific activity. Willful failure to comply can lead to fines, penalties, and/or jail terms for the party violating the terms of the injunction.

Intent. What the negotiators had in mind when they entered into some specific language. Usually, minutes of negotiation are maintained by the parties to indicate intent should a dispute arise over the contractual language.

Labor agreement. Also called a labor contract. A legal document negotiated between the union and the employer that states the terms and conditions of employment.

Laboratory conditions. The notion under both the Railway Labor Act and the National Labor Relations Act that workers should be free to judge whether they want union representation in an environment free of coercion and misinformation.

Labor-Management Relations Act. More commonly known as the Taft-Hartley Act of 1947.

Basic law regulating labor relations of firms whose business affects interstate commerce. Incorporated into the National Labor Relations Act.

Labor-Management Reporting and Disclosure Act. More commonly known as the Landrum-Griffin Act. Established a code of conduct for unions and required union constitutions and by-laws for the benefit of union members. Incorporated into the National Labor Relations Act.

Labor union. An organization of workers formed to bargain collectively with employers over wages and working conditions.

Lockout. An employer's closing down of a business to put economic pressure on the employees to accept the employer's contract proposals. The opposite of an economic strike.

Management rights clause. Contractual provision setting forth the rights of management under the terms of the working agreement. Such rights may include the right to hire, fire, control the workforce, make assignments, and so on.

Mediation. Usage of a third party to attempt to find common ground for the settlement of a dispute. A mediator acts on behalf of both parties, making proposals for settlement. Decisions and/or proposals are not binding on the parties.

Mediator. Third party to a dispute who attempts to cajole the parties to come to terms. Has no binding authority, as does an arbitrator.

National Industrial Recovery Act. Federal legislation passed in 1933 by the Roosevelt administration that included language giving employees the right to organize into unions.

National Labor Relations Act. Commonly known as the Wagner Act. Amended in 1947 by the Taft-Hartley Act and in 1959 by the Landrum-Griffin Act. All three acts have been incorporated to make up the National Labor Relations Act.

National Labor Relations Board. Five-member board appointed by the president of the United States and confirmed by the Senate to oversee representation and election questions, investigate unfair labor practice charges, and issue complaints over such charges.

National Mediation Board. Agency set up under the Railway Labor Act to mediate labor disputes in the railroad and air transportation industries and to conduct elections for choice of bargaining agents. The makeup of the board consists of three members appointed by the president of the United States and confirmed by the Senate.

National unions. The parent bodies that help organize, charter, guide, and assist affiliated local unions.

Norris-La Guardia Act. Popular name for the Federal Anti-Injunction Act of 1932. Eliminated yellow-dog contracts and made injunctions in labor matters more difficult to obtain.

No-strike clause. Portion of a contract in which a union agrees to not strike during the term of the contract for any reason. Usually, a company condition to prohibit the company from engaging a lockout is also present.

Opener. Formal proposal to begin negotiations. Details items to be considered during the process.

Pattern bargaining. Occurs when the same or essentially the same contract is used as a guidepost for subsequent agreements for several companies, often in the same industry.

Picketing. The establishment by union members of lines around the employer's premises for the purpose of achieving specific bargaining objectives.

Proffer of arbitration. A formal offer by the National Mediation Board to arbitrate a negotiation dispute. Both parties to the agreement must be willing to accept the offer or it fails.

Railway Labor Act. Legislation passed in 1926 that laid the foundation for the Wagner Act of 1935. Established administrative procedures for the prompt and orderly settlement of labor disputes between railroad unions and carriers. Guaranteed to unions the rights to self-organization and collective bargaining. Amended in 1936 to bring airlines under its jurisdiction.

Rank-and-file employees. The members of a union, excluding the officers.

Ratification. Approval required by the rank-and-file membership to implement a tentative contract agreed to by the negotiating committee of the union.

Representation election. A vote taken by employees in an election unit to determine whether a union is desired.

Right-to-work laws. Laws that ban union security agreements by forbidding contracts that make employment conditional on union membership or nonmembership. Passed as a result of the Taft-Hartley Act, these laws are not applicable to the Railway Labor Act or the employees of the railroads or airlines.

Run-off election. A second employee election, held when the first election fails to show more than half the votes recorded for any one choice presented under the terms of the National Labor Relations Act or to receive a majority of the votes cast under the Railway Labor Act.

Scab. Term applied to a nonstriking employee or to an employee hired during a strike.

Secondary boycott. Refusal to deal with or buy goods from a customer or supplier of an employer with whom strikers have a dispute. Can take the form of direct pressure by the establishment of picket lines against the supplier, which endeavors to stop the boycotted establishment's employees from working or to stop others from doing business with the boycotted employer.

Section 401 certification. Civil Aeronautics Board authorization permitting a carrier to engage in air transportation. Derived from Section 401 of the Federal Aviation Act of 1958.

Section 6 notice. The formal notification from either party to a dispute under the Railway Labor Act that begins the process of negotiations.

Self-help. A strike, a lockout, or any legal maneuvering designed to promote or force agreement with an opposition party.

Seniority. Length of service with an employer.

Steward. A union steward is usually an elected worker whose position in the union is to help covered employees present their problems to management.

Strike. Cessation of work by employees to gain economic benefit or changes in work rules. Generally is organized and occurs after contract termination or after termination of the cooling-off period.

Strikebreakers. Employees who continue to work after the union has called a strike and who are willing to cross the union's picket lines. Also applied to employees hired specifically to work during a strike.

Strike deadline. The date at which a collective bargaining contract expires (under the National Labor Relations Act) or thirty days after the beginning of the cooling-off period (under the Railway Labor Act), at which time a strike can start if a settlement is not reached.

Subcontracting. The action by an employer to give to other than union employees work that falls under the union's scope clause (portion of a contract outlining the rights and portions of work highlighted as belonging to the exclusive jurisdiction of the union). The rationale is usually that subcontracting is less costly or that the union does not have the proficiency to perform the work.

Superseniority. Seniority granted to certain individuals in excess of that afforded by normal length of service. It is generally granted, for example, to union stewards to protect them from layoff or to obtain working hours and days off that allow them to perform union duties.

Supervisor. An individual with the authority to hire and fire, bind an employer to a contract, authorize payment of bills, and so on. Under the National Labor Relations Act, supervisors enjoy no protection of bargaining rights. Such is not necessarily the case under the Railway Labor Act.

Sympathy strike. Strike called to influence the outcome of a dispute in another company or industry.

System board of adjustment. The airline counterpart to the Railway Labor Act's National Railroad Adjustment Board. Usually consists of at least one member from the company and one from the union; a third neutral is impaneled to make independent tie-breaking decisions in grievance matters.

Taft-Hartley Act. Popular term applied to the Labor-Management Relations Act of 1947.

Thirty-day cooling-off period. After a proffer of arbitration is refused by either party to a dispute, the National Mediation Board releases the case.

This begins a thirty-day period during which no strike or lockout may take place.

Two-tier wage agreement. Wage settlement that decreases the pay rates of future hires while maintaining or increasing the pay rates of existing employees. A two-tier pay structure occurs when one group of employees (usually new hires) receives a different wage rate than other employees and may remain at a reduced rate for the life of their employment tenure or until some merge date. The employer achieves lower labor costs by paying new workers less than existing workers.

Unfair labor practices. Actions employed by unions, management, or both that are prohibited by section 8 of the Taft-Hartley Act.

Union security clause. A contractual provision recognizing a union as the bargaining representative for a company. Such a provision makes it easier for unions to enroll and retain members.

Union shop. Arrangement with a union where the employer may hire anyone desired, but a newly hired employee is required within a specified period of time to join the union certified on the property.

Wagner Act. The National Labor Relations Act, passed in 1935 and named after its sponsor Robert F. Wagner, a senator from New York. Recognized unions in industries other than the railroads and provided requirement for employers in dealing with unions.

Walkout. Strike or other concerted effort where employees leave the work area.

Wildcat strike. Spontaneous work stoppage that takes place without the sanction of the union leadership and in violation of the labor contract.

Work rules. Rules directly related to the terms and conditions negotiated between management and labor. Work rules consist of all employment issues of a nonwage nature.

Yellow-dog contract. Agreement in which an employee, in turn for the opportunity to work, guarantees that he or she will not join or become involved with union activity. Declared illegal by the Norris-La Guardia Act and provisions of the Railway Labor Act.

Name Index

Babbitt, Randolph, 247
Bailey, F. Lee, 96
Barnes, Charles R., 160
Beauvais, Edward, 172
Benning, Ray, 160
Bianchi-Sand, Susan, 166
Black, Hugo, L., 42
Borman, Frank, 205
Breech, Ernest R., 53
Brittin, L. H., 42
Brown, Walter Folger, 42
Buel, Meridith, 92
Burns, Thomas, 172
Bush, George, 55

Calder, Alex, 151
Checci, William, 228
Cleary, Patrick, 56
Cleveland, Grover, 51
Coburn, Frederick W., 48
Cohen, David M., 140
Compton, William, 247
Conway, Michael J., 166, 171
Cook, Mary, 156
Cord, E. L., 42

Dawson, Wallace S., 47
Debs, Eugene V., 17
Delle-Femine, O. V., 100, 220
Dodd, Jedd, 57
Doe, Thomas, 42
Douglas, William O., 94
DuBose, Thomas, 57
Dunlop, John T., 205
Duscoe, Rudolph, 135
Dye, Thomas R., 3

Easton, Joseph B., 27

Farnham, Clifford E., 160
Ford, Gerald, 205

Foster, Barbara, 166
Frankovich, Victoria, 89
Freeburg, Mal B., 48
Friedman, Bruce, 160

Gangwal, Rankesh, 248
Genoese, William, 151, 160
Gill, William A., 185
Gilmartin, Edward J., 166
Golien, W. A., 50
Gompers, Samuel, 20, 30
Green, Ralph, 48
Green, Ronald M., 151
Green, Walter, 48
Green, William, 43, 45, 55
Greene, Norman, 151
Greenfield, Deborah, 166
Griswold, Marvin L., 160

Hamilton, David J., 166
Hamilton, Eddie, 54
Hammer, Mark, 142
Harper, Edwin, 58
Hawks, Frank M., 54
Hearst, William Randolph, 49
Hogan, Henry M., 52
Holbrook, Clyde, 51
Holmes, Oliver Wendell, 17
Hopkins, Charles, 58
Hopkins, George, 42
Huber, John, 44

Icahn, Carl, 70, 224
Irvin, Robert J., 57

Jackson, Andrew, 10
Joedicke, Robert J., 200
Johnson, Hugh, 46
Johnson, Lyndon, 11
Johnson, Lynn, 58
Jolley, William, 89

Jones, Martha, 166

Kahn, Alfred E., 199
Kelly, Edward J., 55
Kolfenbach, Thomas, 155, 160
Komoroff, Michael I., 113
Kremer, J. Bruce, 53

La Follette, Robert M., 23
La Guardia, Fiorello H., 30, 48
Laker, Sir Freddie, 142, 151
Lalli, Dennis A., 151
Lauren, Lyman D., 42
Lee, E. Hamilton, 48
Leiserson, W. M., 50
Liebman, Wilma B., 151
Lorenzo, Frank, 38, 39, 56, 214, 220, 229
Loretz, Mitzi, 166

Marcellino, Thomas, 174
Marshall, John, 65
Maxwell, Charles, 151
McKersie, Robert B., 59
Mead, James M., 42
Meany, George, 12
Moody, G. R., 135
Muir, Malcolm, 48, 49

Nammack, James, 239
Norris, George, W., 30
Northrup, Herbert R., 58

O'Connor, Sandra Day, 226
O'Donnell, John, 206
Olander, Victor, 47, 51, 52, 55
Olney, Richard, 51

Patterson, William A., 47, 50
Paulson, Valerie, 166
Perkins, Frances, 50

Peterpaul, John, 247
Post, Wiley, 54
Powderly, Terrence, 14

Quinn, Rowland K., 151

Reagan, Ronald, 12
Reynolds, Morgan, 61
Rivera, Theresa, 167
Robson, John, 199
Russell, Tony, 156

Sachs, Howard, 91
Schlesinger, Arthur M., 50
Schmiege, Robert, 58
Seymour, Lester D., 48
Shaw, Lemuel, 13
Shientag, Bernard L., 53, 54
Shugrue, Martin, 229
Somers, Gerald G., 113
Summers, Linda, 166

Taneja, Nawal K., 197
Trump, Donald, 228

Vidal, Eugene, 53

Wagner, Robert F., 54
Waite, Morrison, 3
Walsh, Michael, 58
Warnshuis, Frederick C., 44
Watkins, Roland, 140
Whalen, Martin J., 166, 173
Williams, Wayne, 52, 53
Willits, John B., 166
Wilson, Gary, 228
Wilson, Woodrow, 19
Wolman, Leo, 51

Subject Index

Adair v United States, 25

Adamson Act (1916), 19–20

Aeromedical Association, 48

Aeronautical Chamber of Commerce, 47

Age Discrimination in Employment Act (1967, 1984, 1986), 39

agency shop, 35

Airborne Express, 164

Air California, 240

Air Canada, 164

Air Conference, 58

Aircraft Mechanics Fraternal Association (AMFA), 7, 74, 100, 220

Aircraft Mechanics Fraternal Assoc. v United Airlines, 145

Air Florida, 240

Air India, 7

Airline Deregulation Act (1978), 4, 38, 78, 97, 199, 201, 205, 211–12, 231. *See also* deregulation

Air Line Labor Executives Association, 47

Air Line Pilots Association (ALPA), 5, 7, 28, 42–55, 79, 89, 135–36, 201, 202, 215, 224, 225, 226, 227, 228, 230, 231, 232, 233, 243, 244, 247

airlines: commuter, 5, 6, 7; major, 5, 6, 7; national, 5, 6, 7; regional, 5, 6, 7, 8. *See also under specific names*

Air Mail Act (1934), 55

Air Mail Pilot Medal of Honor, 48

Air One, 218

Air Transport Code, 52

Air Transport Employees Union, 226

Alaska Airlines, 215

Alitalia, 7

Allegheny Airlines, 131

Allen v United Transportation Union, 234

Allied Pilots Association, 7

Amalgamated Association of Iron, Steel, and Tin Workers, 16

American Airlines, 7, 215, 222, 224, 226, 227, 228, 230, 232

American Airways, 48, 49

American Arbitration Association, 118

American Federation of Labor (AFL), 15, 43, 48, 49

American Federation of Labor and Congress of Industrial Organizations (AFL-CIO), 12, 35, 109

American labor movement, 13

American Pilots Association, 226

American Potash decision, 85

American Railway Union, 14, 17

Americans with Disabilities Act (1990), 40

American Train Dispatchers Association, 57

America West Airlines, 78, 230; dispute with AFA, 161–85

Amtrak, 3

Arbitration Act (1888), 16, 17, 18

Army Appropriation Act (1916), 21

Association of Flight Attendants (AFA), 7, 133, 134, 226, 228, 243, 244; dispute with America West Airlines, 161–85

Association of Professional Flight Attendants, 75, 226, 227

authorization card, 68, 84

aviation industry, 5

aviation manufacturing, 5

award, 18

Bakri v Continental Air Lines, Inc., 234

Bankruptcy Act (1984), 38

Bankruptcy Reform Act (1978), 39

bargaining unit, 11, 65

Bates v Baltimore & Ohio Railroad, 235

Bedford Cut Stone Co. v Journeymen Stone Cutters Assoc. of North America, 20

Board of Mediation and Conciliation, 19

Boeing Aircraft, 6, 232

BRAC v Assn. for the Benefit of Non-Contract Employees, 149

Braniff Airways, 210, 214, 217, 218; bankruptcy, 216

British Airways, 164

Brotherhood of Locomotive Engineers, 14

Brotherhood of Locomotive Firemen and Enginemen, 14, 22

Brotherhood of Railroad Trainmen, 14

Brotherhood of Railroad Trainmen v Chicago River & Indiana Railroad Co., 116

Bureau of Air Commerce, 53

Burlington Northern Railroad, 58

Byrnes Act (1936), 38

Capital Airlines, 198

Caribbean Airline Services decision, 235

Carnegie Steel, 16

Caterpillar strike, 109

cease and desist order, 33

Century Airline strike, 42

certification, 26

Cesar Chavez Workplace Fairness Act, 109

Chicago, Burlington and Quincy Railroad, 16

Civil Aeronautics Act (1938), 8, 197

Civil Aeronautics Board (CAB), 4, 93, 197–99, 203, 205–7, 208, 223

Civil Rights Act (1964), 39

Civil Service Reform Act (1978), 10

Clayton Act (1914), 20, 30

closed shop, 13, 36

code-sharing, 8

collective bargaining, 5, 11, 27, 32, 66

Command Airways, 75

Commonwealth v Hunt, 13, 17

Communication Workers of America, 127

company unions, 27

concessionary bargaining, 216

conciliation, 25

conspiracy doctrine, 13

Continental Air Lines, 7, 39, 89, 97, 214, 215, 218, 222, 224, 227, 230, 231, 239; bankruptcy, 220–21

contract ratification, 112

cooling-off period, 5, 26, 90, 102, 202

Cordwainers decision, 13

corporate aviation, 5

craft and class determinations, 70, 72–74

craft union, 7

Crum v American Airlines, Inc., 237

CSX Corp., 58

Danbury Hatters case. *See Loewe v Lawler*

Davies v American Airlines, Inc., 235

decertification election, 70

Decision 83. *See under* National Labor Board

Delta Airlines, 79, 202–3, 218, 219, 225, 226, 227–28, 230

Department of Transportation, 10

deregulation, 8, 103–4, 199–205, 206, 211, 241. *See also* Airline Deregulation Act

destructive competition, 4

developmental subsidy, 4

Disabilities Act (1991), 39

double-breasting, 215

Duplex Printing v Deering, 20

duty of fair representations, 114

Eastern Air Lines, 42, 45, 55, 97, 215, 218, 219, 225, 227, 228, 229, 230, 246

Egypt Air, 7

eight-hour workday, 19

El Al Airlines, 7

emergency board, 26

employee ownership, 223

Employee Retirement Income and Security Act (1974), 40

Employee Stock Ownership Plan (ESOP), 89, 217, 219, 225, 230, 247

employment at will, 9

enabling legislation, 10

English common law, 13

Equal Employment Opportunity Act (1972), 39

Equal Pay Act (1963), 39

Erdman Act (1898), 18–19

essential public good, 4

Executive Order 11246 (1965), 39

Fair Labor Standards Act (1938), 21, 24, 38

featherbedding, 35, 135

Federal Aviation Administration (FAA), 5, 7, 227, 245

Federal Emergency Railroad Transportation Act (1933), 25

federal employees, 9

Federal Express, 80, 232

federal injunctions, 30

Federal Labor Relations Authority, 9, 11

Federal Mediation and Conciliation Service (FMCS), 35, 36, 100, 105, 118

Federal Society of Cordwainers, 13

fixed-base operators, 5, 9

Flight Engineers Beneficial Association, 227

Flight Engineers International Association, 244

Florida East Coast Railway Strike, 109
Flying Tiger Airlines, 80, 240
Fourteenth Amendment, 19, 20
Frontier Airlines, 209, 215, 219, 223, 231, 240
fuel cost reductions, 207

general aviation, 8–9
General Aviation Manufacturers Association
    (GAMA), 9
General Dynamics, 6
General Electric, 6
Gibbons v Ogden, 98
Gould Railway System, 16
government aviation, 5, 9
Great Depression of 1929, 25
grievance, 21, 111–12
grievance arbitration, 113–15
grievance procedure, 111, 113
Griffin v ALPA, 236

Hat Finishers Union, 14
Haymarket Riot of 1886, 16
Hirras v National Railroad Passenger Corp., 236
Homestead Strike of 1892, 16
Horizon Airlines, 134
Howell-Barkley Bill, 23
Hughes v Transkentucky Transportation Railroad,
    Inc., 184

Illinois State Federation of Labor, 47
Immigration Act (1924), 23
impasse, 11
Independent Association of Continental Pilots, 231
independent contractors, 9
Independent Federation of Flight Attendants
    (IFFA), 7, 225, 243, 244; strike against TWA,
    88–96
industry concentration, 8
injunctions, 17
International Association of Machinists, 220, 225,
    230, 232, 233, 242, 243
International Association of Machinists and Aero-
    space Workers (IAMAW), 6, 55, 88, 91, 119,
    228, 231, 247
International Brotherhood of Teamsters (IBT, or
    Teamsters), 6, 139, 222, 226, 227, 232; dispute
    with Key Airlines, 152–61; dispute with Laker
    Airways, 140–52
International In-Flight Catering, 71

interstate commerce, 65
Interstate Commerce Act, 67
Interstate Commerce Commission, 19
Interstate Transportation of Strikebreakers Act.
    See Byrnes Act
Iron Molders Union, 14

Japan Airlines, 71
Johns-Manville Products Corp., 108

Key Airlines, dispute with IBT, 155–61
Key ballot, 76, 78
Knights of Labor, 14–15
Kulavic v Chicago & Illinois Midland Ry. Co., 236

Labor-Management Relations Act. *See* Taft-Hart-
    ley Act
Labor-Management Reporting and Disclosure
    Act. *See* Landrum-Griffin Act
Laker Airways, 140; dispute with IBT, 140–52
Laker ballot, 76–78
Landrum-Griffin Act (1959), 24, 33, 36–38
liberty of contract, 20
Linea Aeropostal Venexolana, 133
Lockheed, 233
lockout, 5
Loewe v Lawler, 18, 20

Machinists v Alaska Airlines, Inc., 237
Machinists v NMB, 101
Mallinckrodt Chemical case, 85
management rights clauses, 12
Martin Marietta, 233
McClellan Committee, 36
McDonnell Douglas, 6, 232, 233
mediation, 11, 18, 26
mediator, 18
mergers, 8
Merit System Protection Board, 10
Mexicana Air, 7
Midway Airlines, 165, 174, 229
Miles's Law, 3
Military Selection Act (1967), 40
Miller v ALPA, 234
Munn v Illinois, 3
Mutual Aid Pact, 92, 103, 197

National Air Transport Adjustment Board
    (NATAB), 26, 114–15, 116

National Basis of Pay Committee, 43

National Commission to Ensure a Competitive Air Line Industry, 232

National Emergency Boards, 36

National Industrial Recovery Act (NIRA), 21, 27, 28, 31–32, 46

National Labor Board, 28; and Decision 83, 42–55

National Labor Relations Act (NLRA, 1935), 5, 24, 31–33, 55; arbitration, 108; bargaining topics, 104–6; bargaining unit determination, 83–85; certification election, 85–87; collective bargaining process (chart), 107; contract bar rule, 87; decertification election, 70; differences from RLA, 27, 41, 87, 98, 100, 109, 118, 135; employees, 80; employer requests, 81; employers, 81; grievance procedure (chart), 117; interference, 138; investigation, 81–83; jurisdictional standards, 66; mediation, 107–8; negotiation process, 105; notice of election, 86; representation petition, 82; representation process (chart), 83; self-help, 105; supervisory personnel, 80; unfair labor practices, 136–39; union authorization card, 84; union organization campaigns, 137; union petition, 81. *See also* Wagner Act

National Labor Relations Board (NLRB), 10, 65

National Mediation Board (NMB), 10, 26, 27, 65, 67–80, 131–33, 202, 225, 230

National Railroad Adjustment Board (NRAB), 26, 114, 116

National Recovery Administration, 46

National Right to Work Committee, 35

National Transportation Safety Board, 10

National Tube decision, 85

National Typographers Union, 14

national unions, 14

nationwide strike, 19

New Deal, 31

new entrant airlines, 207

Newlands Act (1913), 19

New York Air, 214, 215, 224

NLRB v Bildisco and Bildisco, 39, 221

NLRB v Crown Can Co., 148

NLRB v Exchange Parts Co., 147, 159

NLRB v Gissel Packing Co., 139

NLRB v Jones & Laughlin Steel Corp., 33

NLRB v Makay Radio & Telegraph, 110

NLRB v Standard Lime & Stone Co., 149

Norris-La Guardia Act (1932), 18, 24, 28, 30–31, 40

Northwest Airlines, 42, 223, 226, 227, 228, 230, 231, 232, 239, 247, 249

Occupational Safety and Health Act (1970), 39

Office of Personnel Management, 10

Ohio Power Co. v Utilities Workers Union of America, 80

Order of Railway Conductors, 14

Ozark Air Lines, 100, 207, 215, 218, 224, 240

Pacific Southwest Airlines, 209, 219, 222, 226, 227, 240

Pan American World Airways, 89, 214, 215, 218, 219, 227, 229, 230, 246

pattern bargaining, 100

Pendleton Act (1883), 10

Pennsylvania Federation of the Brotherhood of Maintenance of Way Employees, 57

Peoples Express, 89, 215, 224

Piedmont Airlines, 80, 185, 215, 223, 226, 228, 240

Pinkerton Detective Agency, 16, 18

Plant v Wood, 17

policy initiatives, 4

political appointment, 10

Pratt and Whitney, 233

presidential emergency board, 58

proffer of arbitration, 27

Professional Air Traffic Controllers (PATCO), 12, 92, 97, 209, 216–17, 243

Public Law 93–36 (1974), 33

public policy, 3, 26

public subsidization, 4

public union, 10

Pullman Palace Car Co., 17

Pullman Strike, 16, 17

Racketeering Influenced and Corrupt Organizations Act (RICO, 1970), 40

Radio Officers Union v NMB, 149

Railroad Labor Board, 22, 23

railroad labor disputes, 15

Railway Labor Act (RLA, 1926), 5, 23–30, 55; airline grievance procedure (chart), 115; amendable dates, 98; amendment of 1934, 24, 27–28; amendment of 1936, 24, 28; amendment of 1940, 24, 28; amendment of 1951, 24, 28, 30; authorization card, 7, 68; bar rules, 70; class and craft determination, 72; collective bargaining process (chart), 99; differences from NLRA, 27, 41, 65, 67, 76, 87, 98, 100, 109, 118, 135; disputes, 26, 68; eligibility of employees, 68; emergency board, 56, 102; employees, 65; flight attendant class, 74; flight personnel class, 74; impasse, 100; interested party, 68; interference in elections penalties, 133–35; laboratory conditions, 78; mediation process, 100–2; negotiation time frame, 98; openers, 95; proffer of arbitration, 27, 101; provisions, 29; representation election, 74–75; representation process, 68; representative, 67; Section 6 notice, 95; showing of interest, 72; subordinate official, 65; super mediation, 102; system board of adjustment, 26, 115; union security clause, 93; union shop, 28

Railway Labor Executives' Association v Interstate Commerce Commission, 235

Railway Labor Executives' Association, 57

rank-and-file employees, 6

regulatory policy initiatives, 4

representation election, 36, 74–75

Republic Airlines, 207, 217, 219, 223, 224, 226, 227, 240

restraint of trade, 17

right to strike, 57

right-to-work laws, 30, 35

Ruck v Atchison, Topeka and Santa Fe R.R., 236

Schechter v U.S., 31–32

scope of bargaining, 11

Seaboard Air Line Railroad decision, 72

secondary action, 18

secondary boycott, 18, 36

secondary picketing, 55

Section 401 certification, 8, 212, 213

self-help, 5, 57, 103

self-organization, 32

seniority, 44

Sherman Antitrust Act (1890), 17–18, 20

Simmon Airlines, 164

Social Security Act (1935), 40

Southern Airlines, 198

Southwest Airline Pilots Association, 222

Southwest Airlines, 209, 248

Southwestern Bell Telephone, 127

statutory law, 13

Stone Cutters Union, 14

strike, 5

strikebreaker, 15

supervisor, 36

Switchmen's Union of North America, 14

Switchmen's Union of North America v NMB, 145

sympathy strike, 17

system board of adjustment, 26, 115

Taft-Hartley Act (1947), 5, 18, 24, 33–36, 80–81, 105, 136; major provisions, 37

T&WA, 42, 45, 50, 53

Teamsters v Braniff Airways, Inc., 133–34

Texas Air, 38, 56, 214, 227

Texas and New Orleans Railroad v Brotherhood of Railway and Steamship Clerks, 25, 131, 132, 144, 176–77

Texas International, 199, 214, 215

Textron, 233

Transportation Act (1920), 22

transportation policy, 3

Transportation Research Board, 9

Transport Workers Union (TWU), 7, 75, 228, 229

Trans World Airlines (TWA), 70, 119, 215, 218, 219, 224, 225, 230, 231, 239, 247, 249; dispute with IFFA, 88–96

"Truth About Pilot Pay, The" (Behncke), 45

two-tier wage agreement, 220

unfair labor practices, 11, 32, 130

union-free agreement, 18

Union of Professional Airmen v Alaska Aeronautical Industries, 147

union security agreements, 35

union shop, 28

United Air Lines, 50, 74, 198, 213, 217, 222, 224, 225, 229, 230, 231, 232, 233, 247, 248

United Auto Workers, 6, 246

United Cigarmakers Union, 14

United States v Jerry Winston, 135, 148

United States v Taca Airways Agency, Inc., 92, 135

United Technologies, 6, 233

United Transportation Union, 57

United Transportation Union v Consolidated Rail Corp., 234

USAir, 80, 215, 226, 227, 228, 230

Vietnam Era Veteran Readjustment Assistance Act (1974), 40

Virgin Atlantic Airways, Ltd. v National Mediation Board, 235

Virginia Railroad Co. v System Federation No. 40, 75, 131, 132

Vocational Rehabilitation Act (1973), 39

Wabash Railroad, 15

wage formula, 54

Wagner Act (1935), 5, 21, 32, 33, 34, 111, 136. *See also* National Labor Relations Act

Washington Post Pressman Strike, 109

Watson-Parker Bill, 23

welfare capitalism, 43

Westair Commuter Airlines, 165

Western Air Express, 45

Western Airlines, 79, 217, 219, 223, 226, 228, 240, 246

Wheeling-Pittsburgh Steel Corp. v United Steelworkers, 222

wildcat strike, 47

Worker Adjustment and Retraining Notification (WARN, 1988), 40

Workplace Fairness Act, 109

work rules, 20

World Airways, 155

yellow-dog contract, 18, 21, 30

Zantop International Airlines, 145, 175–76

Robert W. Kaps is an associate professor of aviation management in the Department of Aviation Management and Flight at Southern Illinois University at Carbondale. His background in the aviation industry consists of positions in labor relations with both Trans World Airlines and Ozark Air Lines, where he held a variety of labor relations positions, including staff vice president, chief contractual negotiator, director of personnel, manager of labor relations, and ramp and operations supervisor. Apart from aviation, he represents both labor and management in negotiations.